The Precious Raft of History

The Precious Raft of History

THE PAST, THE WEST, AND THE WOMAN QUESTION IN CHINA

Joan Judge

STANFORD UNIVERSITY PRESS

STANFORD, CALIFORNIA

Stanford University Press
Stanford, California

Library of Congress Cataloging-in-Publication Data

Judge, Joan, 1958-
  The precious raft of history : the past, the West, and the woman question in China / Joan Judge.
    p. cm.
  Includes bibliographical references and index.
ISBN 978-0-8047-5589-4 (cloth : alk. paper) ISBN: 978-0-8047-7326-3
  1. Women—China—Social conditions—History. I. Title.
HQ1767.J834 2008
305.40951—dc22

                              2007037656

Typeset by Bruce Lundquist in 10.5/14 Adobe Garamond

For Josh, Antigone, and Avital,
my own precious raft

Contents

Illustrations

Acknowledgments

This book has been a long time in the making and the debts accrued in the process are weighty.

I am most grateful to colleagues in East Asia who have helped me find rare texts without which this book could not have been written. They include Xia Xiaohong, of Beijing University; Zhou Yichuan, formerly of Ochanomizu University in Tokyo; Ishikawa Yoshihiro and Hazama Naoki, of Kyoto University; Yu Chien-ming, of the Academia Sinica in Taipei; Zhu Zongzhen, of the Institute of Modern History at the Chinese Academy of Social Sciences; Xiong Yuezhi, of the Shanghai Academy of Social Sciences; Lu Da, of the People's Education Press; and Wang Min, of the Shanghai Academy of Social Sciences. Special thanks also to Cai Rong, of Emory University, for helping locate sources in Nanjing; and Paula Harrell, who generously shared her personal archive of Sanetō bunko materials.

I am indebted to librarians and colleagues in the United States and Europe who directed me to important sources, most notably, Martin Heijdra, of the Gest Library, Princeton University; Greg Pflugfelder, of Columbia University; and Jianye He, of the U.C. Berkeley East Asian Library. I also greatly benefited from the energetic assistance of Rudolf Wagner and Barbara Mittler in using the excellent periodicals collection held at the Institute for Chinese Studies, Heidelberg University.

Friends and colleagues who read entire drafts of the book deserve exemplar status. Hu Ying read the very first draft in its entirety, and helped me parse difficult texts and think through conceptual issues. Henrietta Harrison gently gave incisive criticism that has greatly increased the book's readability. David Fogel offered wholehearted support while demanding much needed clarity. Gail Hershatter and a second anonymous reader for the press were ideal critics: attuned to my objectives yet acutely aware of how far I had fallen short of achieving them. Their comments were crucial to the manuscript's revision.

Others have offered invaluable advice on drafts of various chapters, given important feedback at conferences and in the process of publishing volumes, and brought sources to my attention. Sincere thanks to Paul Cohen, Benjamin Elman, John Fitzgerald, James Hevia, Rebecca Karl, Dorothy Ko, Joachim Kurtz, Susan Mann, Meng Yue, Qian Nanxiu, Ellen Widmer, Xu Huiqi, and Peter Zarrow. Qian Nanxiu also generously helped with a number of translation questions.

I have benefited from numerous grants in researching and writing the book. They include an ACLS/SSRC International Postdoctoral Fellowship; a Regents' Junior Faculty Fellowship at the University of California, Santa Barbara; a Frederick Burkhardt Residential Fellowship for Recently Tenured Scholars; and a Chiang Ching-kuo Foundation for International Exchange Post-doctoral Research Grant. The luxury of spending two years as a Visitor at the School of Historical Studies, Institute for Advanced Study, on the last two of these grants made it possible to add unanticipated dimensions to the study. I learned a tremendous amount from colleagues at the institute both in the China field—Henrietta Harrison, Hsiung Ping-chen, Hu Ying, Martin Kern, Joachim Kurtz, Hugh Shapiro—and outside of it, including Carolyn Bynum, Catherine Gallagher, Jan Goldstein, Martin Jay, and William Sewell, Jr. Dagmar Herzog's engagement with the project and uncategorical support, and Joan Scott's always non-normative insights have been sustaining beyond my time in Princeton.

Muriel Bell has maintained her strong interest in the manuscript through the long process of preparation and the protracted period of revisions. I am extremely grateful for her confidence and encouragement. Sincere thanks also to Kirsten Oster, Joa Suorez, and especially Carolyn Brown for their responsiveness and enthusiasm.

My greatest debt is, ultimately, to my husband, Josh, my closest colleague and meticulous in-house editor who has provided unlimited scholarly advice and support. He has also selflessly taken over the breakfast shift for more years than I care to admit, giving me what all writing mothers most desperately need—time.

Chronology

1049–221 BCE	Zhou dynasty
	Warring States period (479–221 BCE)
221–207 BCE	Qin dynasty
206 BCE–220 CE	Han dynasty
	Former Han dynasty (206 BCE–9 CE)
	Latter Han dynasty (25–220)
220–589	Six Dynasties period
	Wei dynasty (220–65)
	Jin dynasty (280–420)
	Chen dynasty (557–89)
589–618	Sui dynasty
618–907	Tang dynasty
907–60	Five Dynasties
960–1126	Northern Song dynasty
1127–1279	Southern Song dynasty
1260–1368	Yuan dynasty
1368–1644	Ming dynasty
1644–1911	Qing dynasty
1912–	Republic of China
1949–	People's Republic of China

The Precious Raft of History

Introduction

Women and Temporality

> In the fall of 1898 a woman by the name of Li Run
> was informed that her husband, Tan Sitong, had been
> executed in the coup that ended the Hundred Days'
> Reforms. Li had worked with Tan to promote women's
> education and end the practice of footbinding. At the
> news of his death, she traveled to the capital of their
> native Hunan Province and protested the execution
> by slitting her neck with a dagger in the presence of
> the governor. She did not die until the next morning,
> however, when she reopened her wound, calling out
> with venom the name of the official who had overseen
> her husband's execution. She was buried with her teeth
> broken, her hands clenched, and the character for
> dagger formed in blood on her chest.
>
> *"Tan liefu zhuan"*
> *(Biography of the Heroic Woman Tan), 1899*

The author of this account, published in an influential reform journal, pro-
ceeds to invest Li Run's dramatic story with profound historical resonances.
Noting that Li had herself compiled a collection of biographies of past
women martyrs, he uses one of the entries from this collection to illuminate
his biography of her.[1] It is the story of Lady Zhang (fl. 1550) of the Ming dynasty, who had protested the wrongful death of her husband, the famous re-
monstrating official Yang Jisheng (Zhongmin, 1516–55), by slitting her throat
with a dagger in front of the imperial palace.[2] Li's martyrdom, which so
closely echoed Zhang's, also became legendary. Her biography was included

in major compendia of primary sources in the early twentieth century and repeated in later secondary materials.[3] These include the most comprehensive history of modern Chinese women to date, Ono Kazuko's *Chinese Women in a Century of Revolution,* which appeared in English translation in 1989.[4]

What is most fascinating about Li's biography, however, is that it is completely apocryphal. Li Run did not die in 1898 but in 1925. Rather than sacrifice her life for her husband, she devoted it to female education, directing a school she founded in eastern Hunan Province from shortly after Tan's execution until her own death twenty-seven years later.

This bifurcated story of Li Run's life highlights one of this book's pivotal themes: the authority of history and the weight of politics in signifying Chinese women's lives. Li's biographer vindicated Tan Sitong and the 1898 reformers by situating Li within a genealogy of righteous female martyrs. He confirmed Tan's political loyalty by asserting Li's marital fidelity, invoking the age-old homology between minister and state, wife and husband: Tan had died for his country just as Li had died for Tan. Li Run's doubled story thus offers insights into the politically driven process of transforming women in historical time into exemplars in paradigmatic time. It also exposes disjunctions between metatemporal categories of women—such as the righteous female martyr—and the temporal lives these categories allegedly contain.

The account is rife with the gender paradoxes, strategic historical appropriations, and competing national meanings that marked the turn of the twentieth century, a key moment in the unfolding of Chinese modernity. Both the "woman question" and the question of history are central to understanding the politics of this moment. This book maps the gender categories and historical imaginaries that underpinned these politics. It examines the ways ideas of woman, history, and nation are imbricated with one another, and probes the impact of these imaginings on women's everyday lives.[5] Its aim is not to reassert but to elucidate the complexity of the era by tracing patterns and seeking meanings in the intricate weave of Chinese modernity.

Chinese Modernity

Modernity is an amorphous concept. It slides across chronologies, absorbs a range of contents, and is qualified with a plethora of adjectives. Modernities can be repressed, contested, colonial, competing, hygienic, lost—to give a few examples from the recent field of East Asian studies alone. Inundated by such coinages and saturated with the often obfuscating theoretical literature on the topic, I was committed to never using the word in this book. I maintained this conviction throughout the first but not the final draft. This is partly for reasons of communicability. It is mostly, however, because the term—perhaps due to its amorphousness—best encompasses the specific processes that are central to understanding China at the turn of the twentieth century.

I use modernity to refer to the interaction among three processes: secularization, globalization, and temporalization. Although these labels resonate within broader discourses on modernity, they denote processes with distinctive meanings both in late imperial China and in the context of this book. First and foremost, they were not unidirectional. Confucian and "progressive" values, local and Western ideas, conceptions of past, present, and future, were mutually determining. Existing epistemologies were not fixed entities replaced or overwritten by alternatives. Rather they were fluid points of departure that were transformed and often revitalized in interaction with these alternatives.

On the highest level of abstraction, secularization refers to changes instigated by the mid- to late-nineteenth-century encounter between Confucian ritual teachings (lijiao) and "advanced," foreign-inspired (wenming) ideas.[6] While not the doctrine of a deocentric, churchlike organization, Confucian ritual teachings did have certain quasi-religious elements. They were a source of ultimate value based on ancient texts and notions of correlative cosmology that guided human behavior and proper social relations.[7] These teachings were, however, this-worldly rather than other-worldly, their truths immanent rather than transcendent.[8] This social embedment is manifest in an important locus of late imperial ritual teachings—and a crucial nexus of analysis in this book—the "regime of feminine virtue."[9] A woman who adhered to this regime followed Ming and Qing dynasty interpretations of ancient principles of gender propriety such as the strict separation of the sexes and a rigid division of the inner (nei) and outer (wai) spheres. In upholding these principles, she allegedly contributed to the preservation of not only familial and social but also cosmological order.

These gender principles were variously upheld, reinterpreted, or summarily dismissed at the turn of the twentieth century. Western missionizing, the Opium (1839–42, 1856) and Sino-Japanese (1894–95) Wars, and intensified diplomatic and intellectual exchanges had disrupted the Confucian view of a self-contained and correlative cosmos, and demanded a more secular recontextualization of notions of polity, society, and womanhood.[10] In the words of a 1906 women's textbook, the "absurd" notion that China represented "all under Heaven" (*tianxia*) now had to be refuted: the terminal political community had shifted, in Joseph Levenson's famous formulation, from "all under Heaven" to the nation-state (see Figure 1).[11] The great Qing dynasty (1644–1911) had become in the eyes of many of its subjects, a nation among nations; the Han people, one race among many; the clan one of a number of possible modes of social organization. At the same time, individuals—both male and female—were increasingly disembedded from the nested worlds they once inhabited. The family no longer served as the singular context for female self-definition as women—once idealized as the cloistered guarantors of a concordant cosmos—were interpellated as national subjects and assumed unprecedented public roles.

The secular idea that had most profoundly disembedded Chinese women at the turn of the twentieth century was public education.[12] It was the public rather than the education component that posed the greatest threat to the regime of feminine virtue. According to the ancient principles underpinning the regime, gender differentiation was reinforced by distinct male and female educational trajectories. The "Domestic Regulations" (Nei ze) section of the *Record of Rites* (*Li ji*) stipulated that boys would leave home

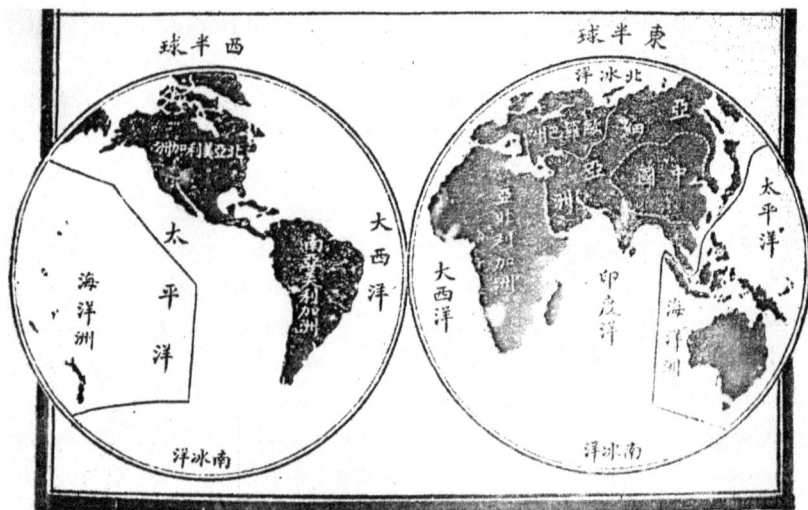

Figure 1 Textbook image used to help female students reject the "absurd" notion that China represented "all under Heaven"
SOURCE: Xie Chongxie, 48b

to attend school at age ten while girls would remain in the household and receive instruction from female tutors.[13] Although the content of household instruction expanded considerably over the next two millennia, it was not until the turn of the twentieth century that the movement for formal female education directly challenged the institutional model put forward in the *Record of Rites*.[14]

Reluctant supporters and passionate promoters of this movement held widely varying views of women's education. For some, its purpose was to reproduce ritual principles, for others to train mothers of citizens, and for still others to instill revolutionary ideas. Even the more secular of these educational visions did not necessarily nullify the regime of virtue's principles, however. The notion of female service to the cosmos via the family as righteous mothers and steadfast wives was, for example, transformed into the notion of female service to the nation as patriotic mothers and loyal citizens. This blurring of epistemes was further apparent in the ways novel secular and ancient ritual pedagogies were enabling or constraining for female students. While nationalism created new conditions of possibility that many women willingly embraced, those conditions were limited within well-defined national rubrics. In contrast, adherence to rigid Confucian principles could earn them the moral capital necessary to constitute themselves as individual historical subjects.

Similar fusions are evident in the translation of new global models, the second process central to Chinese modernity. The foreign ideas that inspired secular change in China at the turn of the twentieth century did not supplant an existing conceptual universe. Rather, forward- and outward-looking Chinese of the period translated these ideas into the historical lexicon of that universe. This "host" language of Chinese history is more difficult for us to learn than the "guest" language of the modern West, which is, after all, a "dialect" of our own. Knowledge of the vernacular languages the Chinese used to decode and interpret new secular ideas is, however, crucial to understanding how those ideas were appropriated and assimilated. Similarly, a grasp of the concrete micro-processes through which Western ideas were mediated is essential to our understanding of the more abstract macro-processes of ideational translation.

Meiji Japan (1868–1912) played a critical role in the mediation of Western ideas and in the unfolding of Chinese modernity. Western political, social, and gender theory reached China primarily through Japanese translations of European and American works. Sixty percent of the estimated 533 books translated into Chinese between 1902 and 1904 were from Japanese, for example, while only 16 percent were from English and 3 percent from French.[15] The translators of these works were usually Chinese living in the highly politicized overseas community in Tokyo and Yokohama. Among them were exiles from the Qing government (including Tan Sitong's surviving co-reformers), publicists, and, over the course of the first decade of the twentieth century, thousands of male and hundreds of female students. Japan offered the members of this community more than a translated repertoire of Western ideas, however. It also provided its own East Asian models of nationhood and womanhood that highlighted relative deficiencies in Chinese political and social practices. Ultimately, Japan stood as a crucial temporal benchmark. Chinese men and women who learned from, traveled to, and compared their nation with the Meiji state often mapped the historical distinction between an evolved present and an archaic past onto the cultural and spatial distinction between China and Japan.[16]

As this mapping of China's relations with Japan suggests, globalization and secularization in late Qing China (1890–1911) were closely linked to new modes of temporalization. These disrupted times—ravaged not only by imperialist wars, but by the Taiping (1851–64) and Boxer (1899–1901) Rebellions—disrupted conventional notions of time, jolting China into national consciousness and provoking shifts in time consciousness.[17] Individuals who held widely divergent visions of China's national future attempted to initiate change in the present by reappropriating elements of "the past" in politically significant ways.[18] This past, which was never entirely cohesive or homogenous, became an increasingly fractured and heterogeneous cultural resource that often opened up, rather than foreclosed, new possibilities for both nation and women.

Chinese modernity was, thus, the outcome neither of a sharp rupture with "tradition" nor of a zero-sum game between East and West—reductive binaries that have been widely discredited if not fully overcome in the literature on this period.[19] Instead, it was the product of an intricate triangulation among myriad visions of the Chinese past, a plethora of imagined futures, and current global forces generally reified as "the West" and largely mediated by Japan. Forward-looking turn-of-the-twentieth-century Chinese men and women promoted new ideas by translating them into local historical knowledge. They advanced novel Western-inspired agendas by seeking new meanings in their own history. Linking cognitive innovation to historical restitution, they produced the new by creatively (re)producing the old.[20]

The hermeneutics of historical change developed in this book eluci-dates this complex experience of temporality. It examines what promoters of modernity both trumpeted and suppressed by reading self-consciously "progressive" texts and practices alongside those not readily recognizable as "new."[21] Brushing artifacts from the era "against the grain," it highlights a web of discourses that complicate existing historical narratives and follows the disparate traces of oblique life stories.[22] We find that new schools did not necessarily produce new women; that didactic texts condemned as ob-solete continued to serve even their harshest critics as crucial sites of mean-ing production. We discover that an antiquarian collection of exemplary women's biographies contains a discourse on emotion resonant with, while historically and ideologically distinct from, later iconoclastic discussions of human feeling. And we come to understand the early-twentieth-century drive for national heroism in light of the late imperial politics of female chastity martyrdom.

Women and Modernity

As these examples suggest, the "woman question" (*nüzi wenti* or *funü wenti*)—how, or whether, to redefine female virtue, talent, and heroism within the modern world order—epitomizes the tensions between past and present, Chinese principles and Western practices, Confucian ritual teach-ings and new ideas.[23]

Scholars of various regions are increasingly recognizing the importance of this connection among women, history, and modernity. Rita Felski has urged (Western) feminist theorists to go beyond the examination of spatial distinctions of private versus public in order to consider different represen-tations of temporality and history.[24] Deniz Kandiyoti has asked to what extent "discourses on modernity in the Middle East [are] conditioned not only by colonial encounters with the West but by societies' changing and troubled relations to their varied ancien régimes."[25] And Kumkum Sangari and Sudesh Vaid have asked scholars of India to become more attentive to how "the past enters differently into the [gendered] consciousness of other historical periods."[26]

These broad global resonances underscore the centrality of women to modernity. The Chinese woman question can best be understood not as part of some vaguely universal phenomenon of epochal change, however, but as the product of China's own distinct history. Through the early twentieth century, Chinese girls and women who abided by the regime of feminine virtue as faithful wives, devoted mothers, and custodians of the ritual order represented society's sacred core. Their physical bodies further bore the imprint of Han civilizational values; their bound feet were a cultural marker that even the Manchu Qing emperors had been powerless to eliminate; their sexual purity was the alleged source of lineage, social, and cosmic stability. When the Chinese political and ritual order was challenged by the "great powers" from the mid- to late-nineteenth century, the feminine norms that embodied that order came under intensive scrutiny. Those engaged in what was deemed to be the struggle for China's national survival tied the woman question to the pressing political and cultural questions of the era, keeping women at the increasingly secularized core of Chinese society as the objects and subjects of national reforms.

This convergent treatment of gender and national issues marks the distinctiveness of the Chinese woman question. In Western nations, the influence of new egalitarian ideas gradually extended from the political to the social spheres, confronting political power often centuries before it confronted patriarchal power.[27] In China, however, the entire corpus of Western rights thinking—from the Enlightenment through the late nineteenth century, from conceptions of natural rights to notions of political and women's rights—was imported at once and at a time of national crisis.[28] While the French, English, and Americans began to address issues of sexual equality and female education almost a full century after modern ideas of nationhood were put forward, Chinese reformers simultaneously took on the problems of national rejuvenation and female liberation.[29]

As a direct or indirect result of this imbrication of female and national reform, elite women were arguably more deeply affected by late Qing modernizing trends than any other segment of the population. Injunctions against footbinding—which had rapidly been transformed from a marker of Han civilization to an emblem of national backwardness—altered women's relationships to their own bodies (see Figure 2). Unprecedented opportunities to study, either abroad—mostly in Japan—or in private schools in China, and to found their own journals modified the gendered mapping of the inner and outer realms (see Figure 3). And calls to emulate foreign social practices challenged existing notions of feminine normativity. The imperial government belatedly acknowledged and attempted to regulate these developments by authorizing formal schooling for girls and women in 1907. This historic initiative vitiated the ritual principles of female seclusion and

Figure 2 A bound-footed woman watching young girls with unbound or natural feet exercise with barbells in a physical education
class
SOURCE: Xu Jiaxing, 3b

Figure 3 One of the first classes of Chinese female overseas students in Tokyo
SOURCE: *XNJZZ* 1 (February 5, 1907)

gender separation by officially sanctioning women's entry into public space and public culture (see Figure 4).

The magnitude of these changes and the passions they aroused are reflected in the instability, proliferation, and contestedness of the categories used to designate women in this period.[30] These include long-standing rubrics whose normative power was sustained if increasingly diminished at the turn of the twentieth century: "exemplary women" (*lienü*), "chaste women" (*jiefu*), "faithful maidens" (*zhennü*), "heroically chaste girls or women" (*lienü* or *liefu*), and "talented women" (*cainü*). Prominent at the turn of the twentieth century as well were vigorously promoted—if not uniformly revered—new categories including "female students" (*nü xuesheng*),

Figure 4 A temporally marked visual summation of changes for late Qing women: footbinding denotes the past, reading in public the present, and armed militancy, the future

SOURCE: *THRB*, 12:9 [1:141]

"mothers of citizens" (*guomin zhi mu*), and variously signified "heroines" (*nü yingxiong, nü haojie, nüjie*). These novel and time-worn terms were not purely discursive constructions superimposed onto the material reality of late Qing society. Rather they both shaped and were shaped by the subjectivities of individual women who selectively embraced or rejected them in constituting themselves as new historical subjects. Some turn-of-the-twentieth-century women upheld the legacy of righteous exemplars (*lienü*) by devoting their scholarly abilities to reproducing exemplary lore. Others staked out their own positions as new-style public women writers by condemning talented women (*cainü*) of the past. Still others promoted female political engagement by dramatically assuming new heroic identities (*nü yingxiong*).

These various categories were imbued with historical meaning and moral force through the two-millennia-long tradition of female "biography."[31] Biography—both female and male—functioned in the Confucian cultural tradition not only as a means of commemoration but, more important, as a technology of the self.[32] Individuals were enjoined to seek moral improvement not by following the rites but by following the example of former paragons.[33] The first collection of such paragons for women was the *Arrayed Traditions of Women's Lives* (*Lienü zhuan*) compiled by Liu Xiang (79–8 BCE) in 34 BCE. As this collection was repeatedly redacted and expanded over the subsequent two thousand years, biography continued to be a powerful tool of female ethical transformation.

Ancient biographical accounts had never been static artifacts. Even if the integrity of a canonical tale from the *Records of the Grand Historian* (*Shi ji*) by Sima Qian (145–ca. 86 BCE), Liu Xiang's *Arrayed Traditions*, or the dynastic histories was preserved in later editions, its meaning was often transformed through the introduction of new "parabiographical" elements. These included changes in textual form, new accompanying illustrations or, most important, appended commentaries.[34] Like palimpsests—documents that were "written upon several times with remnants of erased writing often still visible"—historical life narratives acquired new layers of significance as subsequent generations repeatedly grafted new "hypertexts" onto existing biographical "hypotexts."[35] Later readers, thus, encountered a Han dynasty paragon or a heroine of the Northern and Southern Dynasties through levels of sedimented meanings and centuries of textual transformations.

While long-standing, this practice of overwriting was greatly intensified at the turn of the twentieth century. Authors and compilers of the period broadened the moral purpose of women's life stories, making them tools of national transformation and the new women's education. Responding to new global imperatives that trumped the sanctity of the past, they aggressively reinterpreted historical stories to reflect their own political purposes. Altering once authoritative meanings and stripping away later semantic accretions, they promoted their own visions of gender and historical change through the biographical narrative form.

The shifting geopolitical realities that inspired these radical rewritings compelled certain authors not only to resignify biographies in the existing Chinese repertoire but to expand that repertoire to include new Western models. As they absorbed the dramatic tales of European and American women—including Joan of Arc (1412–31), Madame Roland (1754–93), and Harriet Beecher Stowe (1811–96)—into the Chinese canon, they simultaneously altered biography's basic function and temporal thrust. Using it as a technology of self-creation and no longer exclusively of emulation, they shifted the emphasis in the reader/biography encounter from the self-sacrificing model of the past to the self-constituting subject of the future. One author used the evocative language of Buddhist salvation to describe this enabling function of foreign biographies. In his introduction to a Chinese collection of the lives of Western women, he encouraged young Chinese women to cling to these accounts as to a "precious raft" (*baofa*) that would gently ferry them through the turbulent waters of their uncertain times.[36]

The image of a precious raft is this book's ruling metaphor. In the chapters that follow, I analyze the ways turn-of-the-twentieth-century individuals—from male officials to female activists—used the precious raft of history and historical biography to mediate their own experience of epochal change and national crisis. While all clung to this singular vehicle in negotiating the temporal tides, the courses they charted through the once calm waters of the distant past and the vortex of more recent history were multiple.

A New Hermeneutics of Historical Change

These various approaches to historical time were not random responses to the turn-of-the-twentieth-century global crisis, but strategic "chronotypes" through which individuals reappropriated paradigmatic moments in the past in the political service of the present and future.[37] I have isolated four prominent chronotypes that reflect the range of historical, political, and gender views in this period. On one end of the spectrum the past represents the golden standard while on the other the future is normative. At one pole, the past is used to criticize the present (*jiegu foujin*), while at the other, visions of the future reshape consciousness of the past.

Adherents of the first, "eternalist" chronotype believed in the normativity of the ancient past. They attempted to place women beyond the flow of historical time as bearers of the cosmic order and custodians of hearth and home. Their feminine constructions were, in actuality, however, a direct response to their historical moment. Opposed to newly imported values and troubled by the heightened sense of cultural crisis, they engaged in a defensive "labor of eternalization," promoting classical feminine norms as timeless, inviolable, and immutable.[38]

Proponents of the second, "meliorist," chronotype shared certain characteristics with the eternalists: they remained committed to fundamental Confucian ritual principles, generally valorized the past over the present, and held a continuous view of history that allowed them to celebrate female paragons of Confucian virtue from the ancient period through the late nineteenth century.[39] Meliorists were also distinct from eternalists in that they willingly embraced important turn-of-the-twentieth-century changes for women including public schooling. What most distinguished them, however, was their immanent critique of the late imperial cult of female chastity, a subject ignored by eternalists and not explicitly addressed by more radical writers for at least another decade. This meliorist critique was itself part of a historical continuum, the extension of a three-hundred-year-old debate on the compatibility of ritual principles with human feeling (*renqing*).

Exponents of the third, "archeomodern," chronotype extolled the same ancient Chinese exemplars that meliorists and eternalists celebrated. They departed significantly from their counterparts, however, in their attitude toward the recent past and their invocation of Western exemplars. Meliorists remained fully engaged with this immediate past, not only decrying the excesses of the chastity cult but celebrating virtuous and talented women of the Ming and Qing dynasties. Archeomodernists, in contrast, dismissed recent history as irrelevant and vilified the Ming-Qing woman of talent as a metonym for China's cultural degradation. While this strategy was similar to that of previous Confucian reformers who used the authority of the "Ancients" to condemn the inheritance of the recent past, archeomodernists differed from their predecessors in appealing not only to ancient Chinese glories but to modern Western achievements in seeking to remedy past deficiencies.[40] In their newly reconstituted female biographical repertoire, archeomodernists, thus, filled the historical gap left by unworthy late imperial Chinese women with courageous Western heroines from precisely the same historical period. The term archeomodern signifies this spatio-temporal approach: "archeo" refers to the continued appropriation of archaic Chinese paragons, and "modern" to the concomitant break with recent history and the embrace of global models.[41]

Proponents of the final, "presentist," approach, like the archeomodernists, valorized the new, were generally disdainful of the recent past, and simultaneously appealed to Chinese and Western exemplars. Unlike the archeomodernists, however, they radically rewrote women's life narratives in the light of their own preoccupations, infusing them with "now-time" to an unparalleled degree.[42] Their primary concern was to promote a new, heroic national ethos and new "feminine-heroic" possibilities. To this end, they drew exclusively on the life stories of courageous exemplars, whether Chinese women warriors or Western female revolutionaries and anarchists. In reappropriating Chinese life stories, they explicitly privileged prowess over propriety, challenging the Chinese practice of only including women—even women warriors—in the historical record by reason of their exceptional virtue. Liberating historical Chinese heroines from the regime of virtue's cyclical feminine time, they encouraged their female compatriots to follow Western women into linear, national, masculine time.[43]

Each of these four chronotypes was defined by its stance on the linked woman and national questions. For eternalists, ritual principles of female virtue had to be sustained for the nation to be strengthened. Meliorists concurred, while insisting that human emotion could not be sacrificed on the altar of ritual purity. Archeomodernists and presentists both trumped the age-old emphasis on female virtue with new values. Archeomodernists emphasized talent over virtue, promoting patriotic women's education as the basis of utilitarian national knowledge. Presentists overrode what they described as the crippling morality of the past with a new mode of female heroism that would release China's latent political power. In brief, the priority for eternalists was ritual purity, for meliorists measured ritualism, for archeomodernists nation-minded female talent, and for presentists radical heroism.

These chronotypes are theoretical constructs, not tangible elements of early-twentieth-century social reality. Historical individuals, texts, and events may embody aspects of archeomodernism or meliorism, but they never completely disappear into them.[44] Rather than ignore this problem

I highlight it by concluding each chapter with a counterpoint. The historical figures or texts introduced in these concluding sections keep my own narrative off balance and remind the reader that my carefully delineated rubrics can neither contain the rich heterogeneity of time nor stabilize the categories of women. Just as the individuals featured in this book often defied imposed pedagogies in their own day, they continue to resist neat theorization in ours.[45]

The chronotypes, nonetheless, are of heuristic value. Purposefully defamiliarizing, they highlight the as yet unacknowledged centrality of both history and gender to the late Qing political landscape. Vaguely analogous to the more familiar conservative, reformist, and revolutionary rubrics, they, nonetheless, signify cultural and historical tendencies that do not precisely correlate with what we now recognize as coherent political factions—factions that were decidedly lacking in coherence at the turn of the century.

Most important, the terms liberate the cultural and historical tendencies they represent from an implicitly progressive, conservative-to-radical continuum. Within the complex weave of Chinese modernity, the four approaches often lined up in unexpected ways. Meliorists and presentists expressed the most concern for female subjectivity, while eternalists and archeomodernists objectified women as instruments of patriarchy and the new nationalist patriarchy, respectively. Both meliorists and archeomodernists advocated an indirect political role for women as mothers but it was meliorists who invoked the more empowering image of sagely counselors of adult sons, while archeomodernists heralded moral instructresses of young sons. Archeomodernists embraced new global models that eternalists and meliorists ignored, but often used these models to confirm Chinese ritual principles rather than promote new values. While meliorists alone offered a reflective critique of the late imperial chastity cult, archeomodernists and presentists, who scorned the notion of chastity, were not immune to the cult's enduring power. This is evident in the publication of Li Run's false tale of martyrdom in a journal that was an emblem of archeomodernism.

Juxtaposing these four modes of temporalization also highlights what their adherents attempted to banish or repress. Archeomodernists and presentists penned vitriolic condemnations of the late imperial woman of talent while refusing to engage the complex of issues raised by the late imperial faithful maiden. Eternalists and meliorists only obliquely addressed the Western challenge that was, nonetheless, the latent source of their appeals for ritual purity. These omissions and occlusions reveal as much about the turn-of-the-twentieth-century cultural field as do the cacophony of public proclamations on the woman question.

Sources

These often highly revealing silences only become apparent through the examination of a broad range of turn-of-the-twentieth-century texts. Certain genres illuminate facets of the woman question that others obscure; omissions in one set of materials are prominent themes in another. No single genre, therefore, can be an authoritative index to this period.[46] Rather than privilege sources marked both at the time and in later scholarship as either "new" or "old," I examine a range of the often hybrid materials *simultaneously available to a single turn-of-the-twentieth-century reader.* I focus on the migration of one specific narrative form, women's biography, among texts that were ideologically diverse but uniformly concerned with promoting feminine pedagogies. These include official documents, didactic materials, new-style textbooks, polemical essays, women's journals, and various collections of Chinese and/or Western women's life stories.

These different textual genres generally correspond to different chronotypes. While some texts contain material representative of a number of different chronotypes and others straddle both chronotypes and genres, we can draw a rough typology of sources, with exceptions often illuminating the norms. In outlining this typology here, I briefly introduce the texture of the various sources that will be more closely examined in the following chapters.

Eternalist materials confirm the importance of Confucian ritual principles and condemn new foreign values. They include Education Board (Xue bu) documents on female education, such as the 1907 regulations for female elementary and normal schools. The regulations explain that the government reluctantly approved the new education policy only after trusted authorities had unequivocally demonstrated its compatibility with ancient principles.[47] They further declare that new schools could impart new knowledge only if it was consistent with the ritual codes followed by virtuous women (*yimei zhi lijiao*).[48] Together with earlier memorials on female education, they recommend that Confucian female didactic texts published over the last two millennia, including Liu Xiang's *Arrayed Traditions* and the

Precepts for Women (*Nü jie*) by Ban Zhao (ca. 48–ca. 120), serve as textbooks in the new schools.[49]

A contemporary text that did meet the standards of the Education Board in 1908 was the *Elementary Learning for Girls and Women* (*Nü xiaoxue*).[50] The author, Dai Li (fl. 1905), a gentry woman from Yuhuan in Zhejiang Province, situated her text within an ancient lineage of female didactic books and ritual classics. She claimed her method was similar to, but more ambitious than, Ban Zhao's in the *Precepts for Women*, the earliest and most influential female instruction book. Whereas Ban had explicated the meaning and relevance of passages related to women in the *Record of Rites* and the *Rites of Zhou* (*Zhou li*), Dai had gathered material from various early sources, including the classics, biographies, and histories.[51]

Meliorist authors also wrote didactic books for women that were less strictly doctrinaire about ritual principle and less averse to Western knowledge. Zeng Yi (1857–1917), a gentry woman from Huayang in Sichuan Province, published one such text, *Exhortation to Women's Learning* (*Nüxue pian*), in 1907.[52] An accomplished poet and a respected theorist and practitioner of Chinese medicine, Zeng Yi adopted a self-consciously moderate position in the *Exhortation*. She concluded her preface by stating that staunch conservatives would detest her treatise, reformists would ridicule it, and still others would sneer at its neutrality. This last charge, she claimed, would particularly please her.[53]

The most characteristic meliorist materials were, however, expansions of Liu Xiang's *Arrayed Traditions of Women's Lives*.[54] They consisted of a number of biographies from the original *Arrayed Traditions* together with life story narratives drawn from such later materials as local gazetteers, dynastic histories, and literati writings. Mirroring the meliorists' commitment to change within historical continuity, these texts added new women to the two-millennia-old exemplar repertoire and new commentaries to canonical stories in the existing repertoire.

One of the few extant turn-of-the-twentieth-century expansions of the *Arrayed Traditions* is the *Illustrated Biographies of Resourceful Women, Past and Present* (*Xiuxiang gujin xiannü zhuan*).[55] Compiled by Wei Xiyuan (Chengbo, *zi* Lianshang, fl. 1908), a poet and legal reformer with apparent connections to the Qing court, the text includes 106 entries from the pre-Qin period to the Qing dynasty chronologically arranged in nine thematic sections.[56] As in other texts in this genre, each section opens with one or more biographies from Liu Xiang's *Arrayed Traditions*, followed by selections from successive dynastic or local histories. The biographies include standard parabiographical elements: each ends with a commentary and features an illustration of the celebrated woman. While illustrations in the expansion genre were generally in the active narrative style, Wei Xiyuan chose to have his subjects presented in the static beauty (*meiren* or *baimei* [hundred beauties]) mode. Focused on a woman's adornments and pose, this style developed in conjunction with late imperial hundred beauties collections, one of which Wei directly drew upon for his illustrations (Figures 5 and 6).[57]

While this style of illustration together with other aesthetic elements unique to the *Illustrated Biographies* seems to mark the collection as a mere artifact in the connoisseurship of women, such a view is strongly countered by the profound sense of moral purpose that animates Wei's text.[58] The lengthiest final section of his collection, entitled "Virtue" (Zhenjie, 25 biographies), presents weighty reflections on female righteousness and the excesses of the female chastity cult. It is preceded by sections on, for

Figure 5 Hua Mulan in *New Poems and Pictures for One Hundred Beauties*
SOURCE: Yan Xiyuan, 66

Figure 6 Hua Mulan in *Illustrated Biographies of Resourceful Women, Past and Present*
SOURCE: WXY, I.3

example, "Education of Sons" (Jiaozi) and "Service to In-laws" (Shi jiugu) with similar ethical gravity.[59] In his prefaces to each of these nine sections, his general introduction, and his commentaries on individual biographies, Wei conveys his vision of a coherent moral universe in which women played a crucial and active role. Their kindness was the source of life, their virtue a manifestation of the moral justice of Heaven and earth, their sagely instruction the foundation of a stable political order.[60]

Convinced of the importance of women to society and the cosmos, Wei was an avid promoter of female education. He seems to have compiled the *Illustrated Biographies* for use as a textbook in the new schools: it was published the year after the government announced its regulations for elementary and normal girls' schools by a book company that specialized in pedagogical materials.[61] At various points in the compilation, Wei extols the value of girls' schools, praises women who founded educational institutions, and underscores the need to educate mothers so that they could successfully instruct their children.[62] An advertisement heralding what appears to be Wei's text as an "unrivaled textbook for girls' schools" appeared in a 1910 issue of the Shanghai daily newspaper *"The Eastern Times"* (*Shibao*), one of the primary forums for the promotion of new-style textbooks. The ad further suggests, however, that expansions of the *Arrayed Traditions* had been increasingly eclipsed in the new-style print world. The collection could be most effectively used as a copybook for classes on calligraphy or drawing, the advertisement further announces. And it was currently being sold at half price.[63]

Texts in the genre of the *Arrayed Traditions*, were, however, published in new-style organs of the late Qing periodical press. A remarkable example is a column entitled "New Chinese and Foreign Arrayed Traditions of Women's Lives" (Zhong-wai xin lienü zhuan), which appeared in the popular newspaper *Daily Pictorial* (*Tuhua ribao*) in 1909.[64] The eminent scholar of Shanghai history Xiong Yuezhi has argued that the importance of this pictorial lies in the tangible evidence it provides of a world that has largely disappeared from the historical record, from buildings that were not preserved to details of the lives of petty urbanites and commoners.[65] Similarly, the "New Chinese and Foreign Arrayed Traditions" provides us with vestiges of a strain of gender ideology that has been muted or silenced in many other sources from the period. The editors of the pictorial, who were as obsessed with the nation's survival and as seduced by "the new" as the publishers of any other journal of the period, nonetheless, chose to air the meliorist conviction that the recent past was redeemable and that it could serve Chinese women as a bridge to the new.[66]

While the reference to Chinese *and* foreign women in the title of the series may have reflected the editors' original aspirations, no foreign women were ultimately featured.[67] Instead, the column exclusively celebrates Chinese women of the late Ming through the Qing dynasties. They include the wives, mothers, and daughters of famous scholars and officials, together with women who were direct or, more often, indirect actors in events that marked the era, from the fall of the Ming dynasty to the Taiping Rebellion (see Figure 7). Following Liu Xiang's practice of reappropriating existing biographies rather than writing new ones, *Daily Pictorial* journalists did not compose these late imperial life stories themselves.[68] Most can be traced to a slightly earlier text, the informal jottings (*suibi*) of a late-nineteenth-century official, scholar, and master of the historical anecdote (*zhanggu*), Chen Kangqi (1840–90).[69]

The invocation of "arrayed traditions" in the title of the column together with the principles that informed a number of the individual biographies, places the series in the lineage of Liu Xiang's original collection. At the same time, however, the "New Chinese and Foreign Arrayed Traditions" marks a semantic and formal departure from that tradition. The compilers granted the celebrated women a modicum of personal autonomy and subjectivity, and condemned adherence to "barbaric" principles of chaste self-denial. While the series had formal narrative integrity, each consecutive entry appeared in separate issues of the vibrantly cacophonous popular pictorial. The decorum exuded by the "New Chinese" exemplars on one page is, thus, juxtaposed on the next with the new cultural cachet of women (most often courtesans) who zoom through the streets on bicycles, smoke in public, and sport dark glasses (see Figure 8).

This accelerated cultural tempo is a defining feature of archeomodern materials, which include new-style women's textbooks, various organs of the periodical press, and Western women's biographies. These materials defined the cultural field of the new female education, a field that extended far outside the physical classroom and well beyond strictly pedagogical texts. The authors of these materials enthusiastically embrace foreign-inspired ideas, harshly criticize the recent past, and often simultaneously honor ancient Chinese and Western exemplars.

New-style textbooks for girls and women are the quintessential archeomodern source. Published from 1904, they differ from previous didactic

Figure 7 Mother Li, an exemplar from the *Daily Pictorial*'s "New Chinese and Foreign Arrayed Traditions" renowned for her fetal education
SOURCE: "Li taifuren"

Figure 8 Women on bicycles in the *Daily Pictorial*
SOURCE: "Funü yi"

books for women in their production, dissemination, form, and content. While earlier texts were generally produced by private presses and locally distributed, turn-of-the-century textbooks were published by recently founded commercial publishing houses such as the Commercial Press (Shangwu yinshuguan) and the Progressive Press (Wenming shuju), and were disseminated by numerous agencies in various parts of the country.[70] Editors of these textbooks were highly conscious of the newness of the genre. Their titles often included the term for new or newest (*xin, zuixin*) and/or the new character compound for textbook, *jiaokeshu*, that had been introduced into the Chinese lexicon from Japan in the first years of the twentieth century.[71]

Progressive structure was the formal feature that most sharply distinguished these new textbooks from materials in the earlier didactic style. While the latter—from Ban Zhao's *Precepts for Women* to Dai Li's *Elementary Learning*—present ideas at one, often elevated, level of instruction, the new textbooks target specific educational levels, generally either lower or upper elementary. Within these graded volumes, successive lessons become increasingly difficult and cumulatively introduce new vocabulary.[72]

Other features of the textbooks, including their content and illustrations, are an amalgam of innovation and continuity, revealing that even self-consciously modern genres produced the new by creatively recycling the old. While the textbooks engage and propagate new nationalist and gender ideas, they were not the first pedagogical materials in Chinese history with an ideological purpose. Just as old-style primers like the *Trimetrical Classic* (*Sanzi jing*) had reproduced Confucian orthodoxy while imparting basic literacy skills, new-style textbooks introduced new global ideas while instructing students in the fundamentals of reading and writing.[73] Neither do the new textbooks exclusively present new content. They generally combine lessons on such topics as citizenship, superstition, and free marriage, with lessons on serving in-laws, submission (*shuncong*), and historical Chinese paragons. The ratio of new to familiar content varies from textbook to textbook, but all present a mix of values weighted toward the new. The author of one of the more hybrid textbooks announced that the lessons in his *Newest Ethics Textbook for Girls and Women* (*Zuixin nüzi xiushen jiaokeshu*) were based on selections from two ancient didactic books for women, Ban Zhao's *Precepts* and *Women's Instructions* (*Nü xun*) by Cai Yong (133–82), together with excerpts from "ethics books for women from all countries, East and West."[74] Although more chapters (ten in all) were devoted to chastity (*jiecao*) than to any other theme, the textbook also includes lessons on such current topics as "Patriotism" (*Aiguo*), "Martial Spirit" (*Shangwu*), and "Physical Education" (*Tiyu*).[75]

Textbook illustrations were the product of similar fusions. Unlike Ban Zhao's *Precepts* but similar to extant editions of Liu Xiang's *Arrayed Traditions*, the new textbooks generally include images that underscore the point of a particular lesson. Artists commissioned to illustrate textbooks—or pictorial journals—used the relatively new lithographic medium to portray often startling new content such as the women on bicycles in the figure above.[76] At the same time, these artists continued to use the methods of previous woodblock illustrators, assembling images from a pool of stock elements to represent familiar subject matter.[77] This is evident in an almost identical image used to represent Ban Zhao in an ethics textbook and the Qing dynasty woman of talent Kong Luhua (Jinglou, fl. 1800) in the "New Chinese and Foreign Arrayed Traditions of Women's Lives." The most immediate shared source for these images was the rendering of Ban Zhao in the "One Hundred Beauties, Past and Present" (Gujin baimei tu) by Wu Youru (1846?–96?).[78] While the details in the textbook and the pictorial were cruder than in Wu's original, the placement of the figures, the main props, and the solemn aura of a learned woman's study were nearly identical (see Figures 9, 10, and 11).

Figure 9 Cao Dagu
(Ban Zhao)
SOURCE: Xie Chongxie, 46a

Figure 10 Kong Luhua
SOURCE: "Ruan"

Figure 11 Cao Dagu
SOURCE: Wu Youru, 2: 1, 18

In addition to illustrated, hybrid textbooks, archeomodern materials include various organs of the periodical press. The relationship between the new education and these new print products—from reformist and daily newspapers to overseas student and women's journals—was intimate and mutually supporting.

The woman question and the question of women's education were first theorized in reform journals of the late 1890s. The seminal essay on this topic was "On Female Education" (Lun nüxue) by Liang Qichao (1873–1929), a subsection of his influential "General Discussion of Reform" (Bianfa tongyi, 1896–97). In this treatise, Liang put forward four separate justifications for women's education as a key component of national strengthening.[79]

This link between the woman and national questions was upheld through the symbiotic relationship between new-style textbooks—whose contents were directly inspired by Liang's essay—and the periodical press. The Commercial Press not only published the most influential textbooks of the era but journals such as *The Eastern Miscellany* (*Dongfang zazhi*) and the *Educational Review* (*Jiaoyu zazhi*) that offered detailed advertisements for and introductions to those textbooks. Commercial Press also had a contract to advertise its textbooks on the first page of the widely read Shanghai daily newspaper, "*The Eastern Times.*"[80] A supplement to the newspaper, the *Women's Eastern Times* (*Funü shibao*), featured advertisements for women's textbooks.

Just as the periodical press promoted textbooks, textbooks encouraged young women to acquire "knowledge of the times" (*yueshi*) by reading newspapers.[81] A lesson in an elementary ethics primer urged young students to read newspapers in order to overcome their isolation and increase their awareness of the outside world (see Figure 12).[82] A chapter in a reader

Figure 12 "Exhortation to Read Newspapers"
SOURCE: Xie Chongxie, 43

for older women—whose title, "The Benefit of Reading Newspapers" (Lun yuebao zhi yi) echoed a famous essay by Liang Qichao, "The Beneficial Effect of Newspapers on National Affairs" (Lun baoguan youyi yu guoshi)—elaborates on this theme.[83]

The new periodicals that were most integral to the field of women's education were, however, specialized women's journals. Journal editors who assumed that female students would be among their most avid readers published essays urging the development of female education in China, reports on international advances in women's learning, and practical information about schools in both China and Japan. (Figure 3 is from such a journal.) Some even reproduced parts of female textbooks. The *Women's World* (*Nüzi shijie*), for example, published the introduction to Yang Qianli's influential *New Reader for Girls and Women* (*Nüzi xin duben*).[84] At the same time, there was significant overlap between journalists for the women's press, textbook authors, and educators. Jiang Weiqiao (1873–1958) wrote for *Women's World*, penned one of the Commercial Press's earliest textbooks for women, and taught at one of the first private girls' schools in Shanghai, the Patriotic Girls' School (Aiguo nüxuexiao).[85] A female overseas student in Japan, Sun Qingru (fl. 1907), compiled a women's normal school textbook approved by the Education Board in 1909 and wrote for the influential *Magazine of the New Chinese Woman* (*Zhongguo xin nüjie zazhi*).[86]

While many journals were platforms for archeomodern views on women's education, the periodical press was not uniformly archeomodern. Just as the *Daily Pictorial* included the meliorist "New Chinese and Foreign Arrayed Traditions of Women's Lives" column alongside news of the latest trends in Shanghai, other new media were richly varied in content. Daily newspapers including *"The Eastern Times," Beijing-Tianjin Times* (*Shuntian shibao*), *L'Impartiel* (*Dagong bao*), and *Shanghai News* (*Shenbao*) printed advertisements for the latest textbooks, polemical essays on the woman question, *and* records of official rewards granted to chastity martyrs, for example.

Among women's journals, a few were meliorist. They included the earliest Chinese-run women's journal, founded in 1898, *Chinese Girls' Progress* (*Nüxue bao*), in which the journal's editor, the female scholar-poet Xue Shaohui (1866–1911), rebutted the archeomodern critique of traditional forms of female talent.[87] They also included the *Beijing Women's Journal* (*Beijing nübao*), which had close ties to the Manchu court.[88] Other journals that vigorously promoted women's education were more presentist than archeomodern. These include the *Journal of Women's Learning*, published by Chen Xiefen (1883–1923), which became increasingly radicalized after Xiefen and her father, *Jiangsu Journal* (*Subao*) editor Chen Fan (1860–1913), sought refuge from Qing government persecution in Japan in 1903.[89] They also include *Women's World*, which published radical essays and presentist biographies of women warriors.[90]

Collections of Western women's biographies were, again, characteristically but not exclusively archeomodern. An isolated meliorist example is the *Arrayed Traditions of Foreign Women's Lives* (*Waiguo lienü zhuan*), which was published in 1906. Translated and compiled by Xue Shaohui and her husband, Chen Shoupeng (1857–?), the collection is erudite and broad. It does not, however appear to have been a source, or even a point of reference, for other materials on Western women produced in this period.[91]

This is in sharp contrast to the widely influential *Twelve World Heroines* (*Shijie shier nüjie*). This collection, like the majority of biographies of

Western women that appeared in Chinese in this period—including Liang Qichao's influential "Biography of Madame Roland, the Foremost Heroine of Modern Times" (Jinshi diyi nüjie Luolan furen zhuan)—was translated from Japanese.[92] Its source was Iwasaki Sodō and Mikami Kifū's text of the same name (*Sekai jūni joketsu*), which was published in Tokyo in February 1902 and translated into Chinese by Zhao Bizhen (fl. 1903) almost exactly a year later.[93]

Zhao's *Twelve World Heroines* was the basis for representations of Western women in a number of influential late Qing pedagogical materials. It was the principle source for eight of the ten Western women's biographies featured in Yang Qianli's *New Reader for Girls and Women*, a textbook first published in the summer of 1904 and already in its fifth printing by the end of the next year.[94] The first of the reader's two volumes featured eighteen historical Chinese exemplars, while the second introduced truncated versions of biographies from Zhao's *Twelve World Heroines*. These biographies in Yang's text in turn were the source for three of five chapters on Western women in the *Newest Chinese Reader for Women* (*Zuixin funü guowen duben*), published in Fuzhou in 1908.[95] Zhao's translation was also the acknowledged source for a song with exactly the same title—"Twelve World Heroines"—included in a popular songbook published by the Commercial Press in 1907.[96] A single Japanese text was thus the point of origin for a number of the most widely circulating tales of heroic foreign women in the late Qing cultural imaginary, and a key impetus for the archeomodern questioning of Chinese women's customary roles.

Presentists interrogated these normative female roles even more thoroughly. Condemning feminine morality as a national handicap, they encouraged dramatic and often violent acts of female heroism. They established their position in presentist-minded articles in women's journals, including the already-mentioned *Journal of Women's Learning* and *Women's World*, together with the *Magazine of the New Chinese Woman*. The last, a monthly published in Tokyo in 1907, was run almost single-handedly by a female medical student at Waseda University, Yan Bin (b. 1870). The journal espoused a radical political vision—the magazine was forced to close after urging women to become assassins—and a proto-feminist agenda.[97] A writer who called herself a fellow townswoman of the legendary woman warrior Hua Mulan (ca. 500) warned her readers against letting political concerns overwhelm "the imposing woman question" (*zhongda de nüzi wenti*)—one of the first Chinese uses of the term.[98]

All presentist women's journals included biographies of historical Chinese women—generally women warriors like Hua Mulan—together with accounts of recent Western women usually translated from the Japanese. Seven biographies of European and North American women published in the *Magazine of the New Chinese Woman* were direct translations—often with illuminating Chinese commentaries—from *Famous Women* (*Ō-Bei joshi risshin den*) by Nemoto Shō (Tadashi).

Presentists also compiled book-length collections of the tales of both Chinese and Western heroines. Xu Dingyi (ca. 1888–ca. 1909), an overseas student in Japan, radically resignified the accounts of thirty-nine historical Chinese women noted for their learning, martial competence, and patriotism in *Biographies of Great Women of Our Country* (*Zuguo nüjie weiren zhuan*).[99] Compilers of Western women's biographies emphasized similar qualities. The most prominent of these is the *Ten World Heroines* (*Shijie shi nüjie*), whose anonymous author claimed he had been directly inspired by Zhao Bizhen's translation of the *Twelve World Heroines*.[100] The tone and content of the *Ten* diverged significantly from the *Twelve*, however, highlighting differences between the presentist and archeomodernist positions. While the *Twelve* celebrated self-determination and national commitment as extensions of domestic roles, the *Ten* extolled a passion for liberty, and often bloody political engagement unmediated by familial ties.

Structure

This book is divided into three parts, reflecting the fundamental preoccupations of adherents of the four chronotypes: virtue for eternalists and meliorists, talent for archeomodernists, and heroism for presentists. Each part takes into account all four approaches to the central issues under consideration whether they be chastity, motherhood, or political violence. Because the distinctiveness of each chronotype is often most salient in tension with one other chronotype, however, individual parts and chapters generally highlight the most revealing tension between two historical approaches. The first part highlights tensions between the eternalist and meliorist, and the eternalist and archeomodern approaches to history; the second, between the archeomodernist and meliorist approaches; and the third, between the archeomodernist and presentist. Part One is primarily concerned with feminine virtue, Part Two with female talent, and Part Three with heroism.

These neat divisions are largely for heuristic purposes, however. The three parts are closely imbricated. The regime of feminine virtue is integral to each of them. The first examines tensions between private feminine virtues and new public female roles *within* the regime. The second and third trace tensions *between* the regime and notions of female talent and female heroism, respectively. Feminine talent is an issue in all three parts, which are variously concerned with the new women's education. Conceptions of female heroism—from chaste to national to revolutionary martyrdom—are invoked throughout the book. This thematic overlap reminds us that the incidents, individuals, and temporal reflections discussed in the various parts coexisted within the same historical moment—a moment remarkable for both its cultural productivity and its political and ideational instability.

The following chapters identify patterns in this complex moment. They offer readers—if not a precious—at least a serviceable raft to ferry them through the historical byways, cultural labyrinths, and tangled politics of China's woman question at the turn of the twentieth century.

PART ONE

The Regime of Feminine Virtue

In 1909, a betrothed female student from a good family took part in the mid-autumn festival with a girlfriend. Her actions were in no way unusual, as it was common practice in her native Fujian Province for men and women to circulate freely on the two nights of the festivities. When a friend of the student's future husband saw her on the street, however, he wrote her fiancé and described her public behavior as "obscene" (*huixie*). The fiancé was incensed and immediately broke off the engagement. Entrapped, angry, and defensive, the young woman composed three suicide poems and hanged herself that evening.

In the first two poems she wrote:

Jade is inherently flawless.
Who could guess that there would be transgressions in the inner chambers?
Yes, people were jostling freely in the streets,
but wasn't I in a rickshaw holding my girlfriend's hand?
At the time, I was even praising my future husband for his understanding of statecraft.
Who would have thought that because of this my body would be condemned to wither like a dead flower.
I send [a warning] to my sisters,
bury your heads and close your windows!

I have just turned seventeen and hesitate to hang myself.
My mother—clever, wise, and good—bore me for nothing.
My husband—less than kind in throwing me off.

> Today I sacrifice my body as if it was that of a worthless ant.
> This very year we were to begin looking forward together as
>   husband and wife.
> In death I will become a tragic, homeless ghost.
> I must send my husband a letter.
>
> *"Nü xuesheng touhuan"*
> *(A Female Student Hangs Herself)*   ˙

This tragedy reveals the enduring power of the "regime of feminine virtue" at the turn of the twentieth century: women who blurred the lines between appropriate and inappropriate womanly conduct, between the inner and outer spheres, continued to die by its codes. The incident also highlights the threat the figure of the female student posed to the regime as the emblem of the new public woman.

Two specific modes of female behavior the Fujianese student allegedly transgressed defined the regime of feminine virtue: service to marital family, and modesty in dress, speech, and demeanor. In late imperial society as in ancient Chinese gender principles, marriage constituted female personhood and the marital family represented the sole legitimate sphere for female self-definition. Women were included in only one of Confucianism's five human relationships, the relationship between husband and wife. Their place in the ritual order was determined by their marital status and their ritual obligations were heaviest as wives.[1] The most extreme expression of marital devotion was the suicide of widows or betrothed young women, a late imperial phenomenon, uncommon until the sixteenth century and still highly contentious at the turn of the twentieth. Less controversial was the demeanor of a proper woman, the second of the regime's core creeds. Whether a chaste widow, a devoted spouse, or a faithful fiancée, she was expected to conduct herself with modesty and a sense of gender propriety. The pinnacle of this ideal—physical seclusion in the inner chambers—had been enforced with difficulty throughout Chinese history. It, nonetheless, remained a powerful norm in the late Qing, as the Fujianese student's story demonstrates.

Based on these two pillars of modesty and fidelity, the late dynastic regime of virtue had both objective and subjective dimensions. It was the source of orthodox prescriptions for female behavior. These prescriptions were not upheld by official regulations—the student was not guilty of transgressing a codified law—but by informal, historically and socially generated principles of female behavior to which the student felt hopelessly bound.[2] At the same time, the regime defined virtue as the single acceptable mode of female self-expression: the young woman could only attempt to redeem herself by verbally and physically defending her honor. This conjuncture of internalized values and external norms produced the regime's continuing power.

The late Qing marked a decisive stage in the regime's history, however, as the sanctity of ritual principles was challenged by the introduction of new, "progressive" values. The woman poet Xu Zihua (1873–1925) lamented the suicide of two female students under circumstances similar to the Fujianese student's, and expressed astonishment that in a period of enlightened progress (*wenming jinbu zhi shi*) "barbaric" slander could force young women to take their own lives.[3] It was precisely because of this "enlightened progress," however, that "barbaric" tactics were deemed increasingly necessary. For eternalist defenders of the regime of virtue, public female education threatened to weaken the marital bond and undermine feminine decorum. Juxtaposing women's timeless virtue to the pernicious new women's education, they considered the new schools attended by the Fujianese student and the young women Xu mourned to be among the prime sources of an encroaching moral disorder.

The new public phenomenon of female education and the time-honored practice of female chastity—the obverse and the pinnacle of the regime's principles, respectively—were key issues through which adherents of the four chronotypes defined their positions. Eternalists, who reviled the new education and insisted on the strictest form of gender separation, considered widow chastity to be the singular act that could earn women public recognition. Meliorists, who strongly endorsed the principles of the regime, openly criticized widows who followed their husbands in death and tentatively embraced public roles for women in education. Archeomodernists generally elided the issue of chastity but continued to uphold, while shifting the endpoint of, the regime's core principles of service and modesty. No longer tying the notion of service exclusively to the marital family, they linked it to the nation via the marital family. Presentists most forcefully distanced themselves from the regime. Dismissing chaste practices as archaic nonsense, they called for a new female pedagogy that would promote heroic service to the nation unmediated by familial obligations and unfettered by gender norms.

The two chapters in Part One examine these various interpretations of the regime of feminine virtue by focusing on two controversial figures who stood at its opposite poles: chaste women and public women. The first chapter probes reactions to widow chastity and faithful maidenhood, the epitome of female devotion to marital family. The second examines responses to public women—the new cultural category of the Western heroine and the new social category of the Chinese female student—who challenged the regime's physical and moral bounds.

ONE

Chaste Women

Sacred, Praiseworthy, or Misguided

> All love life and hate death, so why doesn't anyone pay
> attention when chaste women mutilate themselves and
> slit their own throats? All thrive on human contact and
> shun isolation, so why do the chaste sever themselves
> from society? Those who follow the precepts on chastity
> and purity abandon right principles in order to follow
> elevated norms.
>
> *"Shouzhen shuo" (On Preserving Chastity), 1903*

Female chastity, which the author of the epigraph so passionately criticizes, was one of many feminine qualities honored in early Chinese texts. The imperative of lifelong devotion to one husband (*congyi er zhong*) was first articulated in the *Record of Rites* and further developed in Ban Zhao's *Precepts for Women*. Both chaste widows (*jiefu*) and faithful maidens (*zhennü*) were among the women honored in Liu Xiang's *Arrayed Traditions of Women's Lives*.[1] Not until the Ming and Qing dynasties, however, did the chastity ideal became the basis of a veritable cult.[2] From the sixteenth century, sexual purity became the sine qua non of the regime of feminine virtue, self-mutilation a sign of chaste intent, and suicide a bulwark against personal disgrace and cultural pollution.

Female marital fidelity also had profound social, political, and religious ramifications in the late empire. Faithful wives marked the fundamental distinction between mankind and beasts, keeping patriarchal bloodlines clear and maintaining domestic order. They were honored as exemplars of righteousness and Ming-Qing values by elaborate systems of government rewards that attempted to co-opt and control their dramatic acts of self-denial. Finally, as the term *cult* suggests, sexually pure women had supernatural and quasi-religious attributes. They could allegedly divert or provoke natural disasters, and were objects of worship and sacrifice in local or imperial shrines.[3]

Recent scholarship has greatly enriched our knowledge of the chastity cult, particularly in the seventeenth and eighteenth centuries.[4] Our understanding of the meanings of chastity from the late nineteenth century remains, however, incomplete. Scholars of the Qing dynasty have generally argued that the cult lost its vigor from the mid-nineteenth century as it became bureaucratically routinized, ideologically diluted, and increasingly democratized. This assessment is almost exclusively based on an analysis of state policy and of retrospective evaluations of the cult, however.[5] A close reading of sources from the late Qing inevitably yields a more complex view of chastity as both a cultural phenomenon and a social value.

These sources indicate that female sexual purity constituted one of the more sacrosanct cultural elements that had to be accommodated, defended, or abandoned in the face of new global challenges at the turn of the twentieth century.[6] Representatives of the four chronotypes who held competing views of the past and visions of the future all engaged the figure of the chaste woman, whether to celebrate or malign her. The full range of their views only becomes apparent when we read across materials. This requires examining biographical genres that had served as forums for discussions of female chastity since the Ming dynasty together with new print genres such as women's textbooks, mainstream newspapers, and more popular journals. It also entails comparing representations of historical and contemporary chaste paragons, and examining how exemplars from the past were invoked—or disparaged—as models for women of the present.

Eternalists considered chastity a hallowed value. They attempted to mitigate the threat of public female schooling and maintain chastity's social relevance by making it the basis of the new women's education. Meliorists also upheld the sanctity of wifely fidelity. They alone critically engaged the chastity cult from within, however, continuing a three-hundred-year-long debate on the ritual and social appropriateness of its more extreme manifestations. Archeomodernists either ignored chaste practices altogether or elided their complexity. The few textbook authors who celebrated chaste paragons alongside Western notions of free marriage failed to confront the disjunctions such juxtapositions produced. Presentists took this trend toward secularization one step further. They pointedly announced the exclusion of all "worthless" chaste exemplars from their biographical collections and satirically exposed the futility of the female martyr's sacrifices.

This broad spectrum of views confirms that the chastity ideal continued to be invested with layers of social meaning in the late Qing dynasty. Seeming disjunctures in moral logic across sources reflect the inherent complexity of all cultural processes, a complexity that tends to be occluded once a retrospective view of the "rise" or "decline" of a particular practice is formulated. At the turn of the twentieth century, chaste widowhood was neither a universally scorned vestige of the past nor an unambiguously desired future value. It was an element of the present.

Chastity: The Singular Source of Female Social Capital

Eternalists were powerless to stop what they considered to be the socially and morally destabilizing trend toward public female schooling. They, nonetheless, attempted to shore up the regime of feminine virtue by tying the new education to cosmological notions of women's virtue and to the practice of female chastity. Their didactic materials, educational regulations, and commemoration of a heroic female educator illuminate this position.

Dai Li's *Elementary Learning for Girls and Women* (*Nü xiaoxue*), a text based on selections from ritual classics, underscored the eternalist view that female virtue ensured the harmonious alignment of heaven and earth. In the opening chapter, Dai quoted from the *Book of Changes* (*Yi jing*): "gender propriety is a great cosmic principle" (*nannü zheng tiandi zhi dayi ye*).[7] She further cited Lan Dingyuan, whose influential early-eighteenth-century female instruction book was a model for her own, in asserting that women's virtue was the source of stability under heaven (*tianxia zhi zheng*). While women's virtue was the foundation of well-regulated families, well-regulated families were the basis of correct social customs, and correct social customs were the fount of earthly stability.[8]

Eternalists considered female chastity the highest form of this cosmically embedded female virtue and the singular source of female social capital. According to the high officials Rongqing (1854–1912), Zhang Boxi (1847–1907), and Zhang Zhidong (1837–1909), only women who upheld the two fundamental principles of the regime of virtue—chastity and modesty—could be trusted with a public education. In a 1904 memorial that was one of the earliest official Qing documents on schooling for girls and women, Zhang, Zhang, and Rongqing followed the *Record of Rites* in stipulating that female education had to be subsumed under education in the family (*jiating jiaoyu*).[9] Any instruction of young women outside of the household would be limited to training primary caregivers (*baomu*) who, in accordance with the general educational reforms of 1904, were needed to instruct pre-school-aged boys.[10] Rather than advocate the establishment of new educational institutions to train preschool teachers, Zhang, Zhang, and Rongqing proposed that proto-schools be grafted onto preexisting social organizations at the provincial, prefectural, and county levels. They specifically advocated using one of the institutional mainstays of the late imperial regime of virtue, halls for revering chastity (*jingjie tang* or *xuli tang*), as a site for these early training schools.[11] Chaste widows living in seclusion in these halls, the officials believed, would remain uncorrupted by their teacher training.[12]

Although this proposal was not broadly implemented, some chaste widow homes did become training centers for primary caregivers both before and after the memorial's publication. Zhang Zhidong himself established a School for Revering Chastity (Jingjie xuetang) in Wuchang in 1904, where some one hundred chaste widows enrolled as students.[13]

Eternalists further insisted that women who made significant contributions to female education could only be honored for their chaste virtue, not for their devotion to teaching. This was evident in the famous case of Huixing, a Manchu banner woman who sacrificed her life for female education but whom the government would only recognize as a faithful widow.[14]

Huixing had established the Women's School of Purity and Progress (Zhenwen nüxuexiao) in Hangzhou in October of 1904. She explained that the term "zhen" in the school's name signified chasteness and purity, and "wen" the hope for enlightened progress. The day the school opened she delivered a speech from the podium in which she declared that the development of education was crucial to China's national strengthening. She then took a knife and cut a piece of flesh out of her upper arm (*gegu*). The audience was shocked, but Huixing, bleeding profusely from her wound, remained composed. "This piece of flesh," she said, "commemorates the opening of the Women's School of Purity and Progress. If from today the school continues to grow, my arm will heal. If, however, the school is forced to close before having reached its full potential, I will take my own life." When the school lost its financial support a year later, Huixing ingested poison. She died on December 21, 1905, at the age of thirty-six.[15]

Local officials immediately sought to commemorate Huixing. General Ruixing of the Hangzhou Garrison was deeply moved by what he described as a sense of conviction "rarely seen among women, Manchu or Han." Nine days after Huixing's death, he petitioned the Ministry of Rites for a four-character tablet that would read "exemplary righteous virtue" (*yilie kefeng*).[16] A few months later, in April of 1906, Ruixing, together with the governor of Zhejiang Province and the lieutenant general of Hangzhou, petitioned that Huixing be awarded an imperial testimonial of merit (*jingbiao*).[17]

This moderate request was threatening to eternalist high officials, however. At the moment Ruixing's petition was forwarded, the Qing court remained reluctant to endorse public female education and was unwilling to lionize a woman who had martyred herself for that cause. Education Board officials who responded to the petition announced that because the Women's School of Purity and Progress had recently been reopened as the Huixing Girls' School (Huixing nü xuexiao), the institution itself would serve to commemorate its founder.[18]

Unwilling to completely ignore the public sympathy that drove Ruixing's request for official honors, however, the officials went on to explain that in investigating the case, they had learned that Huixing's life was not only a testament to progressive new ideals but to chastity and purity (*zhenjie*). Before taking her own life, she had lived as a chaste widow for fifteen years following the death of her husband, a garrison official.[19] Ministry of Rites officials concluded that she had earned a testimonial of merit on this basis and the emperor readily concurred.[20]

Authors of the entry on Huixing in the *Draft History of the Qing Dynasty* (*Qing shi gao*) followed the Qing court in foregrounding Huixing's womanly virtues. They emphasized her early widowhood and praised her for serving flesh from her own forearm to her ailing mother-in-law.[21] This remarkable banner woman whom admirers in Hangzhou, Shanghai, Beijing, Tianjin, and Tokyo had hailed as "the greatest woman in China in the last six thousand years" for her devotion to female education, could only enter the official record as a chaste widow and dutiful daughter-in-law.[22]

An Immanent Critique

Meliorists, who were preoccupied with the contemporary fate of long-standing practices, addressed the issue of female chastity more thoroughly than any other group at the turn of the twentieth century. Whereas eternalists deemed chastity an unqualified good, presentists condemned it as a debilitating evil, and archeomodernists elided its complexity, meliorists most thoughtfully confronted the many facets of this issue in a range of sources. These include biographical collections, which, together with funerary inscriptions, dynastic histories, and local gazetteers, had conventionally celebrated chaste acts. They also included new print forms, most notably organs of the popular, pictorial, and women's press.

In these various materials, meliorists advanced an immanent critique of the cult of female sexual purity. Rather then categorically condemn or condone chaste acts in principle, they examined the complexities of both historical and current practice. And rather than view the question of female martyrdom through an exclusively contemporary lens, they joined a historical debate that had unfolded over the last three hundred years in conjunction with the cult itself.

THE CHASTITY IDEAL

While critical of the excesses of the cult of chastity, meliorists did not dispute the value of chastity itself. This was evident in Wei Xiyuan's *Illustrated Biographies of Resourceful Women, Past and Present*, the text that offers the most sustained reflection on the theme among the various materials examined here. In his commentaries, Wei expounds on the cosmic ramifications and civilizational value of female chastity. He also laments its contemporary erosion.

Wei opens the preface to the section of his collection on "Virtue" with a quotation from the *Record of Rites*. Chaste virtue is, the quotation declares, one of the human manifestations of the "snell and icy wind" that embodies "righteous justice" and "blows between heaven and earth."[23] The righteous virtue of the twenty-five women presented in this section, Wei explains, had sustained the link between the human and cosmic realms from ancient through recent times.[24]

One of these virtuous exemplars is Heroic Lady Qi (Qi liefu), who remained faithful to her betrothed after he had fallen ill. Even as her prospective mother-in-law urged her to break off the engagement, Lady Qi steadfastly clung to the conviction that a woman could only serve one heaven (*congyi er zhong*). After her fiancé died, she assumed the role of a dutiful daughter-in-law, supporting her in-laws with her handiwork. Upon their deaths, she killed herself.[25]

Consistent with the lore on the supernatural powers of chaste women, Lady Qi's martyrdom gave rise to two miracles.[26] The first occurred when the Qianlong emperor (r. 1736–96) allegedly saw an apparition of her in her native place of Baoying, Jiangsu Province, when he was on one of his southern tours. Deeply moved by her spirit, Qianlong had a shrine erected in her honor. Some one hundred years later, hoodlums desecrated the shrine by carousing in it with prostitutes. In the midst of their revelry, a violent wind came up and killed the men: heaven's revenge against those who did not show chaste martyrs proper reverence.[27]

Wei asserts that sexual purity not only links chaste women to cosmic processes but distinguishes humankind from beasts. He celebrates Tao Ying, a chaste widow first celebrated in the *Arrayed Traditions of Women's Lives*, for embracing lifelong fidelity and carefully raising her children after her husband had died. Unlike "finches which lose a mate in the morning and have a new one by evening," he declares, Tao Ying is an exemplar of the elevated principles of humanity.[28]

In his account of another extraordinary figure from the *Arrayed Traditions*, the wife of Qi Liang, Wei laments that contemporary women lack the conviction of previous exemplars.[29] When Qi Liang is killed in battle, his wife mourns him with both ritual propriety and heartfelt emotion. She refuses public condolences from the powerful Duke Zhuang and grieves so passionately by her husband's corpse that her tears dissolve the city wall behind him. Because she has no family either to support or depend on, she then commits suicide.[30]

Wei complains in his commentary on the biography that, while many widows in Chinese history had kept their virtue (*shoujie*) or followed their husbands in death for the sake of propriety (*siyi*), their displays of fidelity had been largely perfunctory and did little to improve society. Only genuine devotion like that of Qi Liang's wife had the power to affect social mores. Wei underlines this point by concluding with a quotation from the poet Yu Kaifu (Xin, 513–81). In the poem, Yu celebrates the grief of the mythic consorts of the legendary Emperor Shun who drowned themselves in the Xiang River after his death. Just as the tears of Qi Liang's wife had dissolved a city wall, the consorts' teardrops remain forever as speckles on the bamboo at the river's edge.[31]

Wei held not only his contemporaries but historical exemplars to the high standard set by the ancient paragons. The wife of Li Zhongyi, Lady Liu, of the Yuan dynasty, is widely praised in late imperial accounts for offering to die in Li Zhongyi's place when starving Mongol soldiers wanted to cook and eat him during a great famine in 1353. In the version of the story Wei records, however, Liu offers the starving soldiers her family's reserve of rice before sacrificing herself. According to Wei, this gesture vitiated her martyrdom. The honorable death of a loyal official, righteous scholar, or chaste wife could not, he insists, be the product of negotiation.[32]

WIDOW SUICIDE AND SELF-MUTILATION

Despite Wei's rigorous standards for chaste exemplars, he and other meliorists refused to celebrate women who "followed their husbands in death." (Wei glorified the wife of Qi Liang for the purity of her grief, not for her suicide.) They tread a fine line between commending wifely fidelity and condemning widow suicide, a line the Qing emperors repeatedly transgressed as they struggled to establish a morally sound and socially constructive policy on female chastity.[33] Meliorists generally followed the Kangxi emperor's dictum that women who took their own lives after their husbands died "treated life lightly" by shirking the difficulties and responsibilities of widowhood.[34] Wei Xiyuan, thus, celebrates Tao Ying for embracing the difficult task of living on. The *Beijing Women's Journal* honors contemporary widows who did the same.[35]

Meliorists who denounced widow suicide also decried women who mutilated themselves in order to deflect pressure to remarry. This practice, which made women both unattractive and ritually "unwhole," was featured in the *Arrayed Traditions of Women's Lives*.[36] It only became widespread in the Ming dynasty, however, when it reached its gory apogee. Although dramatic acts of self-destruction were often replaced by more prosaic expressions of self-denial in the Qing dynasty, turn-of-the-twentieth-century texts suggest that they had not altogether disappeared.[37]

Wei was opposed to any form of bodily mutilation, whether through judicial torture, extreme expressions of filiality—slicing off one's own flesh (*gegu*) or scooping out one's heart (*wanxin*)—or chaste self-disfigurement.[38] He condemns chaste widows who mutilated themselves in his entries on the Han dynasty paragons, Lady Huan, the wife of Liu Zhangqing, and Lady Xiahou, the wife of Cao Wenshu.

The original *Later Han History* biography of Lady Huan reprinted in Wei's compilation describes how her community honored her for cutting off her ear to preserve her chastity. Wei condemns her action, however, quoting Mencius's criticism of overzealous acts of virtue: "[there are cases of reproach when] one seeks to be perfect" (*you qiuguan zhi hui*).[39] Wei's aversion to self-inflicted violence is further evident in the image he chose to accompany the text. Unlike the compiler of the late Ming *Illustrated Arrayed Traditions of Women's Lives*, who graphically depicted Lady Huan's ear bleeding on the table, Wei chose to portray the moment preceding the violent act, with Lady Huan gracefully raising the knife (see Figure 13).[40] When Lady Xiahou's husband died and family members repeatedly tried to force her to remarry, she first cut off her hair, then both her ears, and finally her nose. Although she had been praised at the height of the chastity cult for exemplifying civilizational values, Wei Xiyuan claims such a view only perpetuated the worst kind of deception.[41]

In his entry on Lady Wang, wife of Wei Jingyu, of the Tang dynasty, Wei most directly condemns families like Lady Xiahou's who tried to force women into a second marriage.[42] When Lady Wang's parents and in-laws

Figure 13 Lady Huan gracefully raising the knife before cutting off her ear
SOURCE: WXY, IX.5

insist she remarry after Wei Jingyu dies, she cuts off her ear in defiance. She then plants a tree at her husband's grave to avow her continued steadfastness. A pair of birds build a nest in the tree and when one of the two dies, the other returns alone the next spring. These "lovebirds"—symbols of genuine romantic feeling in Chinese literature—operate on a higher moral plane, Wei suggests, than those who would force a young women to find a second mate.[43]

Wei considers self-mutilation—whether a filial daughter-in-law's serving of her own flesh or a chaste widow's severing of her ear or nose—a transgression of the middle way. He, nonetheless, condones the virtuous impulse that drives such acts, and lauds more moderate channels for their expression. These include giving blood rather than flesh or organs to a sickly parent or neglecting rather than permanently disfiguring one's appearance to avoid remarriage.[44] He praises Lady Wang, the young widow of Zhao Ziyi, for "perfecting her virtue" (*quanzhen*) by disheveling her hair and dirtying her face (*penggou*). Women fortunate enough to be attractive, but unfortunate enough to be widowed, he explains, have to find—nonviolent—ways to hide their beauty.[45]

FAITHFUL MAIDENHOOD

The meliorists' most virulent critique of chastity was reserved for faithful maidens (*zhennü*), betrothed young women who swore lifelong fidelity to their dead, deranged, or ill fiancés. These women, who had few ancient predecessors, emerged as a distinct social category—and became a troubling social issue—in the Ming dynasty.[46] The noblest exemplars of the late imperial regime of virtue's principles, they were also the most poignant symbols of its potential excesses. From the Ming through the early Republican eras, they remained at the pinnacle of the chastity hierarchy as the women who most fully embodied honor-bound duty (*yi*) and personal sacrifice. Whereas chaste widows remained faithful to a single husband with whom they had shared emotional and physical love, faithful maidens submitted to the sexual monopoly of a single husband before having experienced romance or engaged in conjugal relations. If the chaste widow's role was parallel to that of a loyal minister who resolutely served his ruler, the faithful maiden's was homologous to the subject who sacrificed his life for a master he had not yet served.[47]

Because of their controversial role, faithful maidens were the subject of Confucian scholarly debate from the sixteenth through the early twentieth centuries. The terms of the debate evolved over time, and there were two notable shifts in both its context and content in the late Qing dynasty. Discussions were no longer exclusively aired in conventional forums such as scholarly essays, literati jottings, and biographical collections, but in the new organs of the popular and pictorial press (*xiaobao, huabao*). And while the three-hundred-year controversy had been over ritual practice with some reference to human emotion, the turn-of-the-twentieth-century discussion was most focused on human emotion with some reference to ritual practice. This emphasis on human feeling foreshadowed the categorical repudiation of the chastity cult in the following decades. Significantly, however, it neither referenced Western values nor served as a direct antecedent to the May Fourth anti-chastity discourse.

In the earlier debate, defenders of the cult of chastity generally de-emphasized human feeling and centered their argument on a technical ritual question: at which precise stage in the engagement and marriage rites did a betrothed maiden become a full-fledged wife? They frequently based their position on the "Zengzi Asked" (Zengzi wen) section of the *Record of Rites* on mourning rituals. Knowing at what level a maiden mourned her betrothed, they argued, would make it possible to determine at what stage she was deemed fully married.[48]

The cult's critics, in contrast, tended to foreground the emotional rather than the ritual ramifications of faithful maiden practice.[49] Ma Zhide of the early seventeenth century wrote, for example, that faithful maidens violated not only the rites but human feelings by sacrificing their lives for men with whom their love had not had a chance to fully develop.[50] Yu Zhengxie (1775–1840) of the High Qing, an outspoken critic of both the chastity cult and footbinding, similarly argued that true fidelity resulted from sentiments that arose only *after* a couple had married. And Li Shenchuan of the nineteenth century claimed a faithful maiden's actions were not only ritually but emotionally inappropriate.[51] Turn-of-the-twentieth-century authors followed this line of critical argument, highlighting the question of emotion in the faithful maiden controversy rather than parsing the ritual conundrums it raised.

A report on an incident involving a faithful maiden published in the popular newspaper *Forest of Laughter* (*Xiaolin bao*) appeals to human sentiment. The incident involves the niece of He Qixun, a Cantonese official. The young woman had been engaged to a man named Chen Pu of Lü. When Chen died before the two could be married, she declared her intention to preserve her chastity. Her uncle then petitioned to have her intention recorded in the Lü residential register. An assistant commandant in the Han Martial Banner sees the entry and takes public issue not only with honoring He's niece but with the faithful maiden cult itself.[52]

The commandant first marshals scholarly evidence to criticize the cult. He states that the Ming scholar Gui Youguang (1506–71) had effectively invoked the "Zengzi Asked" in declaring the ritual impropriety of faithful maiden practice. Wang Zhong (1744–94) of the High Qing and Zhang Wenhu (1808–85) of more recent times had developed Gui's position.[53] The commandant then presents his own arguments (excerpted in the epigraph to this chapter). The first was based on the notion of sexual equality. Significantly, he makes no reference to the already circulating Western discourse on this theme, arguing from within Chinese paradigms instead. He declares that men and woman constitute a composite whole (*nannü yiti*) and should be treated equally. If a woman is expected to preserve chastity for her husband, a man must do the same for his wife. Both exemplary literature and popular customs contributed to the perpetuation of disparities in normative gender behavior, however. While a widower could immediately take a second wife or concubine, a widow could not even contemplate relations with a handsome suitor.[54]

The commandant appeals to human emotion in his second argument. Foreshadowing the diatribe of Lu Xun (1881–1936) against chastity in 1918, he declares that all people love life and hate death, so why, he asks, do women mutilate their bodies? All thrive on human contact and shun solitude, so why do faithful maidens willfully isolate themselves? He concludes that the discourse on female sexual purity defies correct principles. Gender inequality and self-denial, which had become normative, are unnatural, he contends, while sexual equality and self-fulfillment are not only natural but ethical.[55]

The debate was also aired in the biography of a faithful maiden published in the *Daily Pictorial*'s "New Chinese and Foreign Arrayed Traditions of Women's Lives." At the age of fifteen, a young woman of Jiangxi Province who became known as Chaste Mother Wang (Wang jiemu) was determined to follow her deceased fiancé "below the earth." When her parents deterred her, she insisted on marrying into the Wang household. For the next forty-two years (at the time of writing), she lived in seclusion on the upper floor of a two-story separate building within the Wang family compound. The illustration accompanying the biography portrays Lady Wang reading at the window under a plaque engraved with the characters "The Chaste Mother's Building" (Jiemu lou).[56] (See Figure 14.)

The *Daily Pictorial* account was derived from an essay by the scholar-official and critic of the chastity cult Chen Kangqi.[57] In his commentary on the story of Lady Wang, Chen invokes the views of the late Ming/early Qing literatus Gui Zhuang (Zhenchuan, 1613–73), who had opposed the faithful maiden cult on both ritual and emotional grounds.[58] Gui had declared the conduct of unmarried women who sacrificed themselves for their fiancés "excessively emotional" (*guoqing*) and not in accordance with the rites (*fei li zhi zheng*). Such women were, he insisted, more pitiable than admirable.[59] Chen Kangqi passionately concurs.[60]

Gui Zhuang's plea to curb the excesses of the chastity cult was increasingly relevant in the last half of the nineteenth century when the number of chastity awards was rising so rapidly that women had to be honored with communal arches, one for all widows from a particular province in a specific year.[61] Chen bemoans this trend, which escalated from the 1850s to

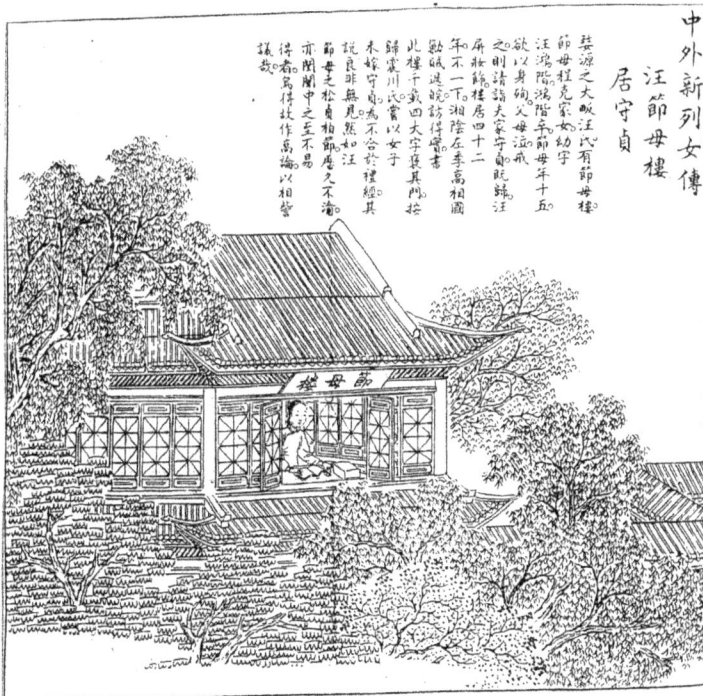

Figure 14 Lady Wang reading at the window of "The Chaste Mother's Building"
SOURCE: "Wang jiemu"

the time of his writing in the early 1880s (and would continue through the reprinting of his text in the 1909 *Daily Pictorial*). He—and we can assume the editors of the "New Chinese and Foreign Arrayed Traditions of Women's Lives"—was not only concerned with the widespread expansion of the cult, however, but with its impact on the lives of individual women. Chen represents faithful maidens as prisoners of barbaric ideological practices. Using a trenchant historical analogy, he relates the biography of Lady Wang to the story of Su Ziqing (Su Wu, d. 60 BCE), a Leader of Court Gentlemen in the Han dynasty, who had been captured and held in captivity by the northern Xiongnu for nineteen years.[62]

Chen explains that he had written the essay on Lady Wang to warn future generations against "barbaric" notions of exemplary womanhood. His commentary ends with a call—resonant with the Han Martial commandant's in the previous example—for the abandonment of what had become normative views of chastity.[63] The *Daily Pictorial* editors reproduced the spirit if not every detail of Chen's argument.[64] They conclude the new print biography with a defense of the judiciousness of Gui Zhuang's views and a repudiation of contemporary scholars who criticize them.[65]

In contrast to these new-style forums for views on faithful maidenhood, Wei Xiyuan's *Illustrated Biographies of Resourceful Women, Past and Present* was precisely in the genre scholars had conventionally used to voice their opinions on female chastity. Wei's contribution, while consistent with his own views on chaste widowhood, was not, however, directly aligned with either position in the earlier faithful maiden debate. He includes three biographies of chaste maidens in the *Illustrated Biographies* and offers different evaluations of each. He praises the first woman, who lived on after the death of her betrothed, he remains neutral in recording the story of the second, who died of grief but not of suicide, and he decries the fate of the third, who took her own life. His text thus reveals the complexity of both the chastity issue and the meliorist position in the early twentieth century.

The first of the three biographies is of a Lady Jin of the Qing dynasty. When her betrothed, Zhang Wenbao, dies before their marriage could take place, Lady Jin not only takes care of the funeral arrangements but of a concubine Zhang had impregnated while formally engaged. The concubine soon gives birth to a son, and Lady Jin takes over as the boy's "social mother." She instructs her adopted son so effectively that he becomes a palace graduate degree holder.[66] The biography contains one of the dominant tropes in faithful maiden lore: a young woman dedicates her life to a "husband" she had never known by raising a son she had not borne to bring honor to her "marital" lineage. A widely performed drama that popularized this theme from the late fifteenth through the early twentieth centuries may have been the source of inspiration for Lady Jin's actions and/or her biography.[67]

In his commentary, Wei Xiyuan praises Lady Jin for ensuring the continuation of her husband's descent line and successfully raising his son. Wei also applauds her emotional investment in preserving her husband's memory. Unlike some critics of faithful maidens, such as Yu Zhengxie, who claimed a young woman bore neither an affective nor a material debt to her dead fiancé, Wei describes Lady Jin's actions as a proper expression of the gratitude she owed her "husband."[68] His encomium is ultimately more a reaffirmation of the importance of patrilineal continuity than an endorsement of the faithful maiden cult, however. Lady Jin's renunciation of sexual and emotional fulfillment was honorable in Wei's eyes because it secured the future of the Zhang line, not as an end in itself.

The second account of a faithful maiden in Wei's compilation is the well-known story of Yuan Ji (Suwen, fl. 1730), the third younger sister of the poet, scholar, and promoter of women writers Yuan Mei (1716–98). As recorded in the *Illustrated Biographies*, Yuan Ji is betrothed at a young age to the son of a man named Gao. As the time of the marriage approaches, the Gao family tries to annul the engagement, claiming that the young man is ill. Yuan Ji refuses with the classic declaration: "Women follow only one man in life. If he is sick I will care for him, if he dies I will remain faithful to him." The marriage rites are thus completed as Yuan Ji alone wished. She soon learns, however, that her husband is not physically but mentally ill. Irritable and cruel, he abuses her and spends the money from her dowry in brothels. When he makes plans to sell her, she finally returns to her natal family heartbroken. Gao dies shortly thereafter. Yuan Ji lives in great sorrow for another year before dying herself.[69]

Wei's commentary on the biography expresses sympathy for Yuan Ji without explicitly criticizing the faithful maiden cult. It also conveys respect for her choice without defending faithful maiden practice. Wei faults Gao's violence rather than Yuan Ji's conviction for the tragedy, representing the incident as a misfortune for the Yuan family that had otherwise known happiness and longevity. He neither acknowledges nor echoes the views of critics like Wang Zhong who saw Yuan Ji's fate as the outcome of her own "stupidity." Neither does he follow Yuan Mei himself in blaming Yuan Ji's desire to sacrifice herself on her knowledge of historical exemplars and feminine norms.[70]

While the account in his collection does mention the three volumes of the *Arrayed Traditions of Women's Lives* and one of the *Book of Odes* that Yuan Ji carried with her—and the illustration depicts her with book in hand—Wei draws no link between her learning and her tragedy (see Figure 15).[71]

In sharp contrast to Wei's commentary on Yuan Ji's life, his response to the third faithful maiden selection, the story of Wei Jingqing of the late nineteenth century, is not neutral. The preceding poem and the biographical narrative itself fail to foreshadow Wei's criticism of the young woman's actions in his concluding commentary. The poem ends with the pronouncement that Jingqing's "virtue was complete, her chastity preserved." The account itself expresses admiration for Jingqing's classical education and poetic gifts. These gifts had been recognized by her fiancé, a lower-level degree holder named Zeng Shufan. When Zeng suddenly dies before the wedding, Jingqing prepares to rush to the funeral but her parents deter her. She then locks herself in her room and hangs herself. She was twenty-six years old.[72]

Figure 15 The faithful maiden Yuan Ji holding a book
SOURCE: WXY, IX.21

Wei begins his commentary by stating that Jingqing was only engaged, not married, and that it would have been appropriate for her to wed after Zeng's death. He uses an historical analogy to support his argument, comparing Jingqing to Boyi and Shuqi, Shang loyalists who in 1200 BCE chose to starve to death in the mountains rather than serve the Zhou conquerors. Although it would not have been against propriety for Boyi and Shuqi to "eat the grain of the Zhou" (or for Jingqing to marry another), these two men were (like Jingqing) steadfast in their loyalty until death. As Wei must have been aware, Wang Wan (fl. 1700), a participant in the early Qing debate on the faithful maiden cult, had used this same allusion to defend rather than denounce self-sacrificing maidens. He declared that Confucius had not condemned Boyi and Shuqi because they had served as exemplars of loyalty at a time of social disarray. By analogy Wang argued that the extreme behavior of faithful maidens should be praised as a source of inspiration for those of lesser moral mettle.[73]

Wei, who had expressed his disapproval of female suicide elsewhere in the *Illustrated Biographies*, would have been disturbed by Jingqing's death. In the conclusion to his commentary he discloses a second reason for his strong reaction to her tragedy, however. He had familial ties to Jingqing's native Hengyang in Hunan Province, and her father, Wei Zhaoting, was one of his paternal uncles. This bond not only deepened Wei's sense of connection to Jingqing, but most probably provided him with access to private sources on her life. This access freed him from reliance on a biography of her published in an 1872 Hengyang County gazetteer. In contrast to the typically laconic entry in the gazetteer, the tone of the biography in Wei's compilation is more personal and sentimental. It waxes eloquent on the perfect match between Jingqing and Zeng, and on the young maiden's literary skills. Where the gazetteer formulaically states that Jingqing demonstrated cleverness from a young age and was poetically gifted, Wei's account describes in detail how she had studied with her mother, ultimately mastering the *Classic of Filial Piety* (*Xiao jing*), the *Book of Odes* (*Shi jing*), and the *Analects* (*Lun yu*).[74] The author of the *Illustrated Biography*'s version—whether Wei or someone else—also had access to Jingqing's poems, from one of which he quotes a line.[75]

Given his personal relationship to Jingqing, Wei reacts to her death like the "scholarly fathers" of the Qing dynasty whose intellectual position either as defenders or opponents of the faithful maiden cult was often determined by their subjective experience as brothers, fathers, or uncles of chastity martyrs.[76]

Wei sanctions the practice of faithful maidens who lived on to raise adopted sons in his commentary on the story of Lady Jin. He is pained by Yuan Ji's misfortune without questioning her devotion to Gao. It is only when confronted with the meaningless death of his own poetically gifted cousin that he articulates a forceful critique of faithful maiden practice.

Occlusion and Dispassion

Sustained and complex reflections on the issue of female chastity like Wei Xiyuan's were absent from the archeomodern discourse. This lack does not signal the cultural irrelevance, but rather the deep social embeddedness, of the chastity problem. While women of talent (*cainü*) became metonyms for China's past failings and women of valor (*nü haojie*) symbols of its projected virility in archeomodern and presentist discourses, chastity martyrs were awkward markers of its conflicted present. Often mentioned only to be dismissed, they were too entrenched in family histories, cultural practices, and moral registers to constitute an objective social category.

Immanent meliorist critiques of chastity continued to appear through the late Qing and into the early Republic.[77] The first critique voiced from *outside* the regime of virtue did not appear, however, until May 1918. Its author was, significantly, not Chinese or male but the great Japanese feminist poet Yosano Akiko (1878–1942).[78] Published in the New Culture journal *New Youth* (*Xin qingnian*), Yosano's essay was closely followed by two Chinese-penned articles: Hu Shi's "The Problem of Chastity" (Zhencao wenti), which was written in response to Yosano's piece, and Lu Xun's "My Views on Chastity" (Wo zhi jielie guan).[79]

Largely absent from late turn-of-the-century archeomodern polemics, the issue of chastity was not completely ignored in new-style textbooks. While faithful maidens—the most contested symbol of female virtue—were excluded from all such materials, chaste widows were not.[80]

Xie Chongxie's widely distributed *Lower-Level Elementary Female Ethics Textbook*, a typical example of this hybrid genre, combines lessons on ethics, historical Chinese exemplars, and foreign customs. While it introduces new ideas, such as Western women's education and patriotism, it also includes a lesson on "Chastity" (Shuo jie), with an accompanying illustration of a memorial arch to the chaste and filial (see Figure 16). The text explains that chastity is a woman's greatest virtue and that faithful wives are honored by the state, respected by their local communities, and admired by their de-

Figure 16 A memorial arch to the chaste and filial
SOURCE: Xie Chongxie, 58a

scendants. Although Xie concedes that such paragons of fidelity are rare, he encourages his young readers to emulate them.[81]

Most textbook authors who featured specific historical Chinese exemplars excluded chastity martyrs altogether. An important exception was Xu Jiaxing, the compiler of the *Newest Ethics Textbook for Girls and Women*, arguably one of the most blended texts in this highly blended genre. Xu uncritically celebrates chaste women, using conventional tropes and dramatic illustrations. His examples of the most extreme acts of female self-sacrifice share textual space with such progressive themes as Western honeymoons and militarism. Figures 17 and 18 capture the fused character of Xu's text.[82]

Most remarkably, Xu uses foreign values not to criticize but to sanction the Chinese cult of fidelity. He notes in his preface that the principle of chastity was honored in Europe and America as it was in China, but that Westerners were more concerned with forging lasting marital bonds than with gender separation. While he admits that the strength of European and

Figure 17 The modern spirit conquers
nature
SOURCE: Xu Jiaxing, 83b

Figure 18 The "righteous and courageous martyr Jiang" drowns herself in
a basin for her husband
SOURCE: Xu Jiaxing, 78b

American marriages could be attributed, in part, to the lack of a Western
system of concubinage, he, nonetheless, holds Chinese women responsible
for building stronger Chinese marriages. By including "a particularly high
number of stories concerning chastity" in his textbook, he hopes that the
"brilliance of China's women [sages]" (*nüzhe zhi guang*)—a euphemism for
chaste widows—would inspire emulation among his readers.[83] Xu's unwill-
ingness to acknowledge—or his inability to perceive—the incongruities in a
text that introduces Western women who freely married in one chapter and
Chinese women who died to preserve the honor of their arranged marriages
in the next, reflects the unresolved contradictions underlying the archeomodern discourse.

Xu uncritically records stories of past chastity martyrs. These include Lady
Liu, whom Wei Xiyuan disparages for offering rice to starving Mongol soldiers
before volunteering to sacrifice herself in the place of her husband. In Xu's
account, Lady Liu deserves praise for convincing the soldiers that her body
contained more fat than her husband's and ultimately dying in his place.[84]

Xu introduces the relatively restrained story of the chaste widow Tao
Ying, which Wei Xiyuan had also featured in the *Illustrated Biographies*,
together with more extreme examples of chaste devotion. These included

tales of self-mutilation that Wei abhorred. The wife of Fang Yuanling of the Tang dynasty, for example, assures her dying husband that she will remain faithful by cutting out one of her eyes.[85] Xu also glorifies widow suicide by presenting both ancient and Ming-period examples of women who followed their husbands in death. One was the wife of Jiao Zhongqing of the Han dynasty, whose story was the source for the romantic poem "A Peacock Southeast Flew" (Kongquan dongnan fei). Jiao's wife has been forced out of the household by her mother-in-law and is resolved not to remarry. When her natal family insists on finding a new husband for her, she (in Xu's version) slits her throat. Upon hearing the news of her death, her husband kills himself as well.[86] In the "Righteous Heroism" (Yilie) section of his text, Xu retells the story of a learned woman of the Ming dynasty, Heroic Madame Jiang (Jiang liefu). The widow of Jiang Shijin, Lady Jiang drowns herself in a water basin—as illustrated in Figure 18—in order to preserve her fidelity and escape the advances of one of her deceased husband's uncles.[87]

Derision

While the few archeomodernists who included chaste women in their texts left the moral and ideological status of these virtuous exemplars unresolved, presentists either dismissed or ridiculed them. In the introduction to his collection *Biographies of Great Women of Our Country*, Xu Dingyi asserts that the only laudable female quality was heroism disassociated from servile feminine virtue. He announces that the women featured in his compilation had all made significant public contributions "to the nation or the race." At the same time, he explicitly excluded much heralded faithful maidens and chaste widows because they only display "private virtues."[88] The anonymous author of *Ten World Heroines* makes precisely the same argument. Among typically revered exemplary and gentry women (*lienü* and *guixiu*), he complains, one only finds "those who martyr themselves for their husbands, those who martyr themselves for their mothers-in-law, those who martyr themselves for their parents, and those who martyr themselves for their lovers (*suohuan*)." Although "those for whom they martyr themselves, and the means they use to martyr themselves differ," he continues, they share an essential flaw. All "sacrifice themselves for one person. None sacrifices herself for the entire country."[89]

Other authors writing in this iconoclastic spirit declare the irrelevance of chaste women by subtly or sarcastically exposing the futility of their actions.

They include a Japanese writer, Takano Hiromu, who published a Chinese account of "The Virtuous Lady Ma" (Ji jiefu Ma shi shi) in Tokyo in 1905. As this was the height of the Chinese overseas student movement in Japan, Takano's targeted audience was most probably Chinese students. His account is openly derisive, the mark—and privilege—of a cultural outsider. The virtuous Lady Ma is the wife of Ma Engui (Yinzhi) from Shanhaiguan, a city at the eastern end of the Great Wall. In the winter of 1900, as the foreign Joint Expeditionary Forces (Lianjun) draw near the pass, Ma is responsible for local security. Before he leaves to undertake his duties, he tells his wife that he does not expect to come back alive and that if he has not returned by a specified time, she would have to assume that he was dead. Ma survives but is delayed and returns late. By the time he reaches home, his wife has already killed herself. "What forbidding virtue and courage!" Takano exclaims. This story "should be transmitted for ten thousand generations."[90]

Counterpoint: The Contemporary Chaste Woman

Turn-of-the-twentieth-century sources highlight widely divergent assessments of female chastity, one of the cornerstones of the late imperial regime of feminine virtue. Eternalists attempted to temper the threat women's education posed to the regime by linking it to marital fidelity. They recommended that residents of chaste widow homes be the only women educated outside the household, and they honored a school founder who sacrificed her life for education as a chastity martyr. Archeomodernists generally ignored the question of female sexual purity in their polemics. In their rare textbook discussions of the subject, they treated it with a superficial neutrality, evading the hard questions it raised. Presentists were the most explicitly dismissive of the notion of chastity, which they declared not only irrelevant but harmful to China's national struggle.

These representations of female chastity as detrimental to the nation, unworthy of serious consideration, or crucial to social stability, fail to do justice not only to the historical but the contemporary complexity of the issue. This complexity is apparent in late Qing press reports that record recent incidents involving chaste widows and faithful maidens. Unlike polemical essays, literati jottings, or women's biographies that use the question of female sexual purity to make larger historical and ideological statements, these *faits divers* provide relatively underdetermined glimpses into current practices. Rather than celebrate legendary exemplars who could dissolve city walls with their tears, they present everyday heroines faced with quotidian social and economic pressures. Making little reference to past norms and no allusions to correlative cosmology, they present their chaste subjects in secular terms as honorable women deserving at most imperial and at least legal recognition for their trials.

These anecdotal press reports thus reveal that practices once tied to Confucian ritual teachings and imbued with cosmological significance were not eviscerated of all social meaning even as the ritual and cosmological order was increasingly questioned. While reports on chaste women were recorded under the rubric of local news in the periodical press, they were still considered newsworthy. And while they were often presented as sensational human interest stories, these stories reflected and carried current moral values. Less imposing than the memorial arches to the chaste and filial that dotted the countryside, they, nonetheless, brought news of local cases to the attention of a national readership and reaffirmed the importance of wifely fidelity. Featuring women from a range of social classes and geographical regions, the reports variously functioned as exemplar texts, petitions for government recognition, and appeals for justice.

The exemplar reports present contemporary models "to be followed" (*kefeng*). They generally adopt the conventions of dynastic and local histories, situating the woman under discussion genealogically and geographically before describing the particular incident that defines her exceptional virtue. They also function like government gazette (*jingbao*) notices of imperial testimonials of merit that announced honors granted to exceptional women.[91] A February 1906 article in the "Tianjin News" section of the *Beijing-Tianjin Times* states, for example, that an imperial testimonial of merit had been granted to a faithful maiden named Wang. She had taken care of her deceased fiancé's mother for twenty years before committing suicide herself.[92] The wife of a certain Bai Guowen of Zhili was another "paragon of the inner chambers" awarded an imperial testimonial of merit in 1896 after remaining chaste for over fifty years. According to the press report, this simple, uneducated widow understood the way of women, the instructions for the inner chambers, and the proper relationship between the generations.[93] The daughter of a Fengtian official, a Lady Xin of Jilin, dutifully served her fiancé's family after he died. She was hailed as a model of virtue in a report that ran for several days in the *Beijing-Tianjin Times*.[94]

Newspapers also publicized petitions generated at various social and bureaucratic levels demanding government recognition of chaste women. As recorded in the *Daily Pictorial*, local gentry, merchants, and scholars appealed to higher authorities in 1909 to bestow honors on a woman surnamed Zhu of Tongli Village in Wujiang County, Jiangsu Province. Lady Zhu, whose example, her petitioners assert, would improve popular customs, had mourned at her deceased husband's altar for the ritually required forty-nine days before suddenly dying herself.[95] In February 1907, the *Beijing-Tianjin Times* printed a petition that had been presented to the Ministry of Rites by Anhui's governor, Enming (1846–1907). Enming had requested that 30,000 unnamed martyrs be honored in shrines to chaste and virtuous women.[96] Turn-of-the-twentieth-century scholars also initiated petitions on behalf of chaste martyrs they did not personally know, continuing a Qing literati practice.[97] In a case from Kaifeng, a noodle merchant married his daughter Chen Huizhen (fl. 1900) to the son of a prostitute in a local brothel. When Huizhen refused to entertain guests, she was whipped by both her husband and his mother, and eventually expired from the abuse. A graduate of a nearby academy heard the tragic story and encouraged Huizhen's father to request that a plaque be placed for her in the local government-financed Shrine for the Chaste and Filial (Jiexiao si).[98]

Late Qing press reports further present chaste widows as plaintiffs. These women faced the same social pressures and adopted the same self-protective measures as historical exemplars. After the death of her husband some ten years earlier, a Lady Chang Shi from Xian County devotes herself to educating her sons and expanding the family assets. When she learns that her husband's older brother covets her property and hopes to marry her off, she cuts her hair—both a means of making herself less attractive and of asserting her pledge not to remarry—and appeals to the county office for justice.[99] Another story bizarrely conflates conventional elements of a chaste widow's trials, including self-mutilation and aggressive relatives. A certain Mr. Liu of Xinyang County in Suzhou wants to seduce his younger brother's widow and claim her property for himself. One day as the widow is about to set off for a trip to her native village in Hunan, Liu goes by her house and cuts off her hand (usually a chaste woman would sever her own hands after inappropriate physical contact with a man). When the story went to print, the widow's wound was still being treated as her case was being heard in local courts (see Figure 19).[100] In a report published in "*The Eastern Times*," Wang Zhu of Huzhou resists her uncle's pressure to remarry by ending her own life. When he arrives at her house with a band of men to coerce her, she immediately slits her throat. The story ends with the assertion that local officials and gentry would see to it that this wrongdoing was properly punished.[101]

Although the women featured in these press reports worked within the secular sphere of legal justice rather than the sacred realm of correlative cosmology, they used the same strategies as past paragons to assert and protect their chastity—suicide and self-mutilation. Among the various late Qing social commentators, from newspaper reporters, to polemical essayists and textbook authors, meliorists alone reflected critically on the cultural and personal questions this self-sacrifice raised.

While meliorists believed marital fidelity represented the apogee of human civilization, they considered self-inflicted violence to be its nadir. Their condemnation of the social and ideological pressures that led chaste widows to mutilate or kill themselves followed a morally driven intellectual tendency associated with such figures as Lü Kun (1536–1618), Gui Youguang, Mao Qiling (1623–1716), Qian Daxin (1728–1804), and Wang Zhong over

Figure 19 The severing of a chaste woman's hand
SOURCE: "Zhenfu"

the course of the Ming and Qing dynasties. These individuals argued that ritual propriety had to express rather than distort authentic human feelings, that the rites must be compatible with the emotions.[102] Wei Xiyuan directly echoes these sentiments in the *Illustrated Biographies* when he states "the teachings of the sages did not include practices difficult for the human emotions to bear."[103]

There are both clear resonances and important differences between late Qing and May Fourth writings on the inhumanness of the practice of female chastity. While Wei Xiyuan and other meliorists argued that the rites had to be consistent with human emotions, they did not question the value of properly executed rites. Over the course of the first decade of the Republican period, archeomodern vagueness on and presentist derision of female chastity evolved into a coherent position that declared ritual teachings inherently antithetical to human feeling. In his 1918 essay "My Views on Chastity," Lu Xun declares the chastity ideal anathema to human flourishing. "All human beings have their ideals and hopes," he writes. "Their [lives] must have meaning. . . . To be chaste is difficult and painful, of profit neither to others nor to oneself."[104] Hu Shi also criticizes the practice of chastity for not being in accordance with human feelings.[105]

Despite this shared attention to the question of emotion—a question archeomodernists and presentists ignored—the late Qing meliorist critique was not a lineal antecedent to New Culture views. Lu Xun, Hu Shi, and others made no reference to the Ming-Qing chastity debate within which the meliorist trend was firmly grounded. This may have been due to ignorance, to the dismissal of a trend that May Fourth writers considered too entrenched in obsolete ritualism to be of any use to them, or to the willful amnesia necessary to the New Culture project of positing a rupture with "tradition." The two critiques of chastity just a little over a decade apart from one another, thus, represent two distinct historical processes, the first, predicated on an immanent engagement with, and the second, an iconoclastic rejection of, the past. What made the late Qing meliorist trend historically significant was its heretofore unacknowledged challenge to the worst excesses of the late imperial regime of virtue—excesses that continued to be apparent in the pages of the turn-of-the-twentieth-century press—in the name of human feeling and feminine subjectivity.

Chaste women were figures of public controversy because of their intensely private actions: taking up residence in their dead fiancé's homes; cutting off hair, ears, and noses in the inner chambers; or hanging themselves from the rafters of the women's quarters. At the opposite pole of the regime of feminine virtue were women who provoked debate not because of their private devotion to the principles of female virtue but because of their alleged public flaunting of those very principles.

Public Women

Licentious or Evolved

> Recently in Shanghai a kind of debauched woman
> (*dangfu*) who is like a prostitute while not being a true
> prostitute has appeared. These women assume the dress
> of female students and incite licentiousness through-
> out the city. . . . This is most harmful to the future of
> women's education.
>
> *"Maochong nüxuesheng zhi huangdan"*
> *(The Ridiculous Practice of Pretending to be Female*
> *Students), 1909*

Female chastity was an ancient principle that took on unprecedented prominence in the late imperial regime of feminine virtue. Female publicness, in
contrast, was a new phenomenon that extended and, in the eyes of many,
exceeded the regime's bounds. While chaste paragons were honored for
their profoundly *private* feminine acts, the few Chinese heroines who inter-
vened directly in the public realm did so either disguised as, or as stand-ins
for, men.[1]

Publicness was, in contrast, the defining quality of Western heroines who
were renowned in Chinese sources for directly leaving their mark in national and world history. The new cultural category of the public Western
woman, thus, became an emblem of global engagement in the late Qing
imaginary while divergent reactions to this category reflect divergent views
of Chinese integration into the international community. Eternalists, who
most vigorously defended a model of cultural isolation, disparaged generic
"Western women" as a threat to Chinese notions of propriety. Meliorists,
who tentatively acknowledged China's current international situation, also
tentatively acknowledged foreign exemplars. Archeomodernists, whose pri-

mary concern was to enhance China's global stature, lauded the Western woman's courageous exploits while often overwriting them with familiar notions of feminine virtue. Presentists most unequivocally embraced heroic foreign women as vanguards of global revolution.

The cultural category of the Western woman had its local corollary in the new—and similarly contentious—social category of the female student (*nü xuesheng*), the native incarnation of Western ways. A novel presence in the urban landscape, these students were carriers of progressive values such as free marriage and female autonomy. Symbols of both the promise of Chinese social evolution and the danger of impending social breakdown, they provoked the alarm of social critics like the author of the epigraph above. The figure of the female student—and actual late Qing students like the young Fujianese woman introduced in the epigraph to Part One—thus became the prime bearers of turn-of-the-century tensions between the principles of the regime of feminine virtue and new *wenming* values.

A New Cultural Category: The Western Heroine

Western heroines and Western gender practices were the inverse of Chinese women and Chinese ritual principles in late Qing polemics. The foreign heroine was more than a mere feminine foil, however; she also functioned as China's national foil. Politically engaged and historically prominent, she was the antithesis of the secluded woman of the inner chambers who symbolized China's international isolation. Perceptions of the Western woman were, thus, not exclusively tied to notions of gender propriety but to attitudes toward the world beyond China's border.

THE WEST AS A SOURCE OF SOCIAL DEGRADATION

Eternalists, the group most opposed to public female education and most committed to maintaining the Confucian social order, believed the adoption of Western ways would undermine the Chinese regime of feminine virtue. Officials and authors of female didactic texts posited a sharp dichotomy between sacred Chinese values and subversive Western ways, between demure and retiring Chinese women and debauched and assertive Western women. While they made few references to specific foreign figures, they warned that Western gender practices—specifically free marriage and sexual equality—would destabilize Chinese society. Their apprehension about public education for Chinese women was thus driven by their trepidation about Western values and the modern world order.

The high officials who published the first memorial on female education in 1904 were extremely wary of outside influences. Female schooling was dangerous, they contended, because it would enable young women to read Western books.[2] Two years later, as the question of formal female education was heatedly debated in the Qing court, Liu Xun, an official in the Ministry of Public Works, warned against "Europeanized" approaches to schooling Chinese girls and women. Such approaches were, he contended, based on "wild talk" of gender equality and free marriage (*ziyou jiehun*) recently imported from the West and currently "filling Chinese newspapers." Misdirected individuals who would apply such ideas in China betrayed a reckless ignorance of the differences between Chinese and foreign customs. Their efforts would "poison hearts and destroy customs."[3] The Education Board echoed Liu's views in the 1907 school regulations. The document on normal schools warns against exposing students to Western-inspired wayward talk of free marriage that blurs the distinction between the sexes.[4]

Dai Li, the female author of the cosmologically grounded and government approved *Elementary Learning for Girls and Women*, expressed the same fear of Western-inspired cultural corruption. Dai explains that she had written her didactic text to reinforce the eternal value of Chinese ritual teachings and stem the infiltration of foreign ideas of sexual equality and freedom of marriage. She equates the breakdown of Chinese principles of gender differentiation with the end of Chinese civilization. If the proper distinctions are not maintained and young people begin to choose their own marriage partners, she declares, their "behavior would be no different from that of the birds and the beasts."[5] In a preface to Dai's text, the Hanlin scholar Zhang Qin specifically warns against the corrosive influence of foreign textbooks. Echoing Liu Xun's view, he announces that the "customs of China and the outside world [are] different," particularly when it comes to women's education.[6]

The Qing government attempted to ban the kinds of texts Zhang Qin warned against. Education Board authorities announced in 1907 that a songbook promoting free marriage, *Improved and Reprinted Girls' School Songs* (*Gailiang zaiban nüxue changge*), contravened both the newly published regulations for girls' schools (the censure of the songbook came one month after the school regulations were announced) and established ritual teachings. They requested that local educational bureaus bar any books of this kind from schools and bookshops.[7] Such measures were clearly ineffective as officials continued to call for the prohibition of foreign textbooks through the end of the Qing. In 1909, two years after the official sanction of female education, Zhang Xiangguo (fl. 1909) of the Education Board forbid the sale or reading of a newly imported women's textbook. He declared that the book was "filled with words that would damage public morality, agitate the populace, and ultimately hinder [the development of] women's education."[8]

THE WEST AS TENTATIVE MODEL

Meliorists, like eternalists, rarely discussed specific Western women. The editors of the *Daily Pictorial's* column "New Chinese and Foreign Arrayed Traditions of Women's Lives" promised tales of foreign exemplars, but never delivered. Wei Xiyuan's *Illustrated Biographies* kept within generic bounds and discussed only historical Chinese paragons. An exception is Xue Shaohui and Chen Shoupeng's *Arrayed Traditions of Foreign Women's Lives*, which exclusively featured Western women. Although Xue and Chen made every effort to present these women's stories free of moralizing, they still had to negotiate the tension between new social roles and the Chinese regime of feminine virtue. Chen, whose view ultimately prevailed, insisted they structure the text according to the subjects' public occupations. Xue, however, had wanted to organize the biographies according to private feminine virtues.[9]

Meliorists like Xue and Chen were more measured than eternalists in their assessment of Western influences. This is further apparent in the writings of Zeng Yi, author of the *Exhortation to Women's Learning* (*Nüxue pian*). Like Dai Li and Zhang Qin, Zeng Yi emphasized the differences between Western ways and Chinese teachings. She was, however, receptive to the new, Western-derived rhetoric on gender relations that eternalists condemned. Whereas Western notions of free marriage and equal rights became metonyms for barbarity and social collapse in the writings of Dai, Zhang, and government officials, Zeng Yi approvingly cites the view of the British Social Darwinist Herbert Spencer (1820–1903) that "love and respect" are the wellsprings of a harmonious marriage. She also advocates "equal rights" (*pingquan*) based on equal educational opportunities for boys and girls.[10]

Zeng was ultimately critical of the misguided appropriation of Western ideas rather than of the ideas themselves—a view parallel to the meliorist critique of excessive expressions of the chastity ideal rather than the ideal itself. She criticizes reformists who base their proposals on a superficial understanding of Western ideas, for example. She also derides individuals who blindly imitate Western ways of eating and dressing but lack a deeper understanding of Western principles.[11]

THE CELEBRATED WESTERN SOCIAL
REFORMER AND SOCIAL MOTHER

Unlike their meliorist and eternalist counterparts, archeomodernists and presentists promoted the new value of publicness and embraced Western principles, practices, and heroines. In the *Newest Ethics Textbook for Girls and Women*, Xu Jiaxing declares Chinese women inferior to their foreign counterparts because of their insularity. Confined to the inner quarters, they are weak, conformist, and timorous. As a result, China could claim no more than one or two heroines throughout its long history. In contrast, Xu continues hyperbolically, Western women are all heroic.[12] He underlines this point with the illustration of a Western woman shooting a tiger in the midst of a forest—a distant physical and psychological remove from the boudoir (Figure 20).

In addition to praising generic Western heroines as Xu did, archeomodernists and presentists celebrated specific historical foreign women. Both the content and the structure of their biographies of these bold and worldly Western exemplars highlight the social isolation of Chinese women and the international isolation of the Chinese nation. While from the time of Liu Xiang, accounts of Chinese paragons ended with citations from the ancients that drew the reader deeper into the world of Confucian values, the codas to these tales of foreign heroines underscored China's inferior international status and exhorted Chinese women to join the national struggle.

Archeomodernists and presentists shared a fundamental commitment to this struggle. They, nonetheless, held different national aspirations that were reflected in their respective appropriations of Western women. Archeomodernists tended to honor the Western social heroines discussed in this chapter, women devoted to such causes as public health reform, temperance, and racial equality. Presentists, in contrast, most admired more radical political heroines, including revolutionaries, assassins, and anarchists who are the subject of Chapter 5. When the two groups celebrated the same women—Florence Nightingale, Mary Lyon, and Madame Roland appear in both sets of materials, for example—they framed their narratives differently. While archeomodernists infused the tales of foreign social paragons with

Figure 20 An intrepid female explorer shoots a tiger
SOURCE: Xu Jiaxing, 87b

familiar tropes of love, nurturing, and service, presentists excised almost all relational references and privileged the heroine's dramatic entrée into world history.

An array of Western female social reformers were featured in turn-of-the-twentieth-century textbooks and journals. Most prominent were the British nurse Florence Nightingale (1820–1910) and three American women: the social reformer Frances Willard (1839–98), the abolitionist Harriet Beecher Stowe, and the educator Mary Lyon (1797–1849).

Nightingale was one of the most renowned Western heroines in China at the turn of the twentieth century. A hospital nurse who eased the suffering of British soldiers in the Crimean War in the early 1850s, she had spearheaded public health reform in Britain thereafter. Authors used her story to enlighten young Chinese women about global humanitarian issues, inform them of the workings of international organizations, and encourage them to serve as politically engaged nurses in China.

Nightingale's name became synonymous in late Qing materials with the International Red Cross, an organization reform-minded Chinese lamented their country had yet to join.[13] The *Magazine of the New Chinese Woman* celebrated her as the founder of an International Red Cross nurses' team, for example.[14] Her story was further used to criticize Chinese ignorance of international protocols. A certain Gan Hui announced in the commentary to his freely translated biography of Nightingale that Westerners had been forced to reprimand members of a Beijing relief society (*jiuji shanhui*) for misappropriating the Red Cross banner at the time of the Boxer Uprising.[15]

Authors also used Nightingale's story to mobilize Chinese women to serve as nurses in battles for China's national survival. Yang Qianli wrote his *New Reader for Girls and Women* at one of the critical moments in the national struggle, the year 1903 when young patriots agitated to restore their country's sovereignty in Manchuria, where Russians had been amassing troops since the Boxer Rebellion.[16] Yang dramatically concludes the biography of Nightingale in his reader with an exhortation to Chinese women to serve as nurses in the northeast. "Alas, Florence died some five years ago," he declares.

> The people of Western Europe have benefited from her kindness, and Japanese women are continuing her work [in Asia]. At this time, mighty and crafty Russia is again extending its claws into the east, ensuring that the north of China will be a bloody battlefield in the future. The women of China who have risen up on hearing the news have embraced Florence's ambition.[17]

Textbook authors and journalists also used the example of Frances Willard, founder of the National Women's Temperance Union, to rouse Chinese women to patriotic action and expose China's international seclusion. The Temperance Union, which Willard established in the early 1870s, had a broad social mandate that included the promotion of anti-drinking policies and the provision of aid to recently released prisoners. From 1883 the organization was internationalized as branches were established in Europe and union leaders disseminated its message in various corners of Asia.[18]

A biography that appears in both Yang Qianli's *New Reader for Girls and Women* and Guang Zhanyun, Guang Yiyun, and Chen Yuxin's *Newest Chinese Reader for Women* highlights the global dimensions of Willard's work and criticizes Chinese insularity. Of all the nations Temperance Union delegates had visited from Australia to Japan and India, the biography laments,

China alone had been reluctant to follow Willard's program. The "hands of women in countries all over the world" are working to transform customs and hearts in accordance with Willard's principles, it continues. Only in China did the people remain "lost in a deep, long night."[19] This refusal to join the global community not only diminished China's international stature but Chinese women's social stature. While "the new civilization of the Americas" esteems women, a journalist wrote, "the old civilization of Asia" continues to disdain them.[20]

This same journalist used Willard's story to urge Chinese women to collective action. In a short biography appended to his article, he describes how the young Frances, who had had no interest in sewing, loyally stitched flags for the July Fourth parade in her hometown every year.[21] The textbook author Wu Tao similarly heralds Willard as a model of patriotism in a lesson on cooperation as the basis of national strength. Through Willard's example, Wu demonstrates what Chinese women could achieve if they would work together toward social ends.[22]

Harriet Beecher Stowe, the American abolitionist and author of the renowned antislavery novel *Uncle Tom's Cabin*, became a model of a different kind of social action in the late Qing social imaginary. While Chinese authors used Willard's and Nightingale's achievements to raise awareness of specific humanitarian organizations, they invoked Stowe's example to underline the principle of global equality. Whether their priority was to liberate their country from its dual "slavery" to the ruling Manchus and foreign imperialists, or to improve its international stature by alleviating domestic social inequities, they appropriated Stowe's abolitionist message.

The writer and poet Jiang Zhiyou (1865–1929), who freely translated the most influential biography of Stowe in this period, declared the abolitionist greater than either the celebrated Chinese woman warrior Hua Mulan or the renowned French patriot Joan of Arc. While Mulan was merely an exemplar of familism (*shenjia zhuyi*), and Joan a paragon of nationalism (*guojia zhuyi*), Stowe was a symbol of cosmopolitanism (*shijie zhuyi*).[23]

The source of Stowe's cosmopolitan power was her abolitionist writing. Jiang's biography and derivative versions of it published in Yang Qianli's *New Reader for Girls and Women* and Guang, Guang, and Chen's *Newest Chinese Reader for Women* state that her famous antislavery work circulated in over one million copies, was translated into nine languages, and published in twenty-one editions.[24] While these claims are largely true, Jiang—and by extension the textbook compilers—identifies this famous novel not as *Uncle*

Tom's Cabin but as *The Mayflower*—a series of vignettes Stowe wrote on New England life—rendered as *Flower of May* (Wuyue hua) in Chinese.[25] Yang further credits *Flower of May* with bringing an end to slavery "in less than a year."[26]

Stowe's message of human dignity and equality—however attributed—was resonant in turn-of-the-twentieth-century China when anxieties about China's international stature ran high and social disparities were increasingly viewed as one of the causes of China's global inferiority. In a speech recorded in the press in late 1902, the woman Du Qingchi (fl. 1902) stated that the widespread mistreatment of domestic servants by their mistresses signified China's underdevelopment. If the Chinese were to overcome the current "barbarian stage" of social evolution as Americans had when they abolished slavery, they would have to follow the example of *Flower of May*.[27] Similarly, the authors of a code of conduct for students at the Xiangshan Girls' School in Guangzhou in 1904 used Stowe's example to admonish against the abuse of female servants.[28]

As the Xiangshan school example suggests, archeomodernists and presentists believed female education would both broaden Chinese women's consciousness and enhance China's international standing. While they rarely translated the many accounts of Western women novelists, painters, or poets available to them in Japanese sources, they widely appropriated the life story of Mary Lyon—the doyenne of Western women's education in turn-of-the-twentieth-century East Asian materials.[29]

A biography published in the *Magazine of the New Chinese Woman* in 1907 offers details about Lyon's background, her character, and her accomplishments (see Figure 21). It describes how she helped her widowed mother during her childhood in Massachusetts while always remaining focused on her studies. Having taught in local schools from the age of seventeen, she founded Mount Holyoke Female Seminary in 1834. Her teachings were transformative not only for her students, but for American womanhood and for the American nation.[30]

Both archeomodernists and presentists drew on accounts of Western women like Lyon to advance their agendas, while differently framing those accounts in accordance with their respective agendas. While archeomodernists used the principles of the regime of virtue to translate foreign lives into a local moral register, presentists adopted a new language of universalism and female autonomy.

In archeomodern biographies, the foreign women's *public* achievements

Figure 21 "The Great American Educator, Mary Lyon"
SOURCE: *XNJZZ* 2 (March 5, 1907)

were tied to *private* feminine impulses to mother and nurture. Although they never presented Westerners as exemplary *biological* mothers—a sacrosanct status reserved for Chinese models—they did represent them as *social* mothers whose maternal qualities were metaphorically, rather than biologically inscribed.[31] Presentists used maternal metaphors rarely and differently. Whereas biological Chinese mothers nurtured descendants of the patriline, and archeomodern social mothers treated patients and students with maternal love, presentist mothers redeemed the universe.[32]

Archeomodernists imbued the imposing figure of Florence Nightingale with reassuringly maternal qualities. Yang Qianli records how injured soldiers in the Crimea regarded her as a "loving mother" (*cimu*) and includes an image of her ministering to the wounded that exudes maternal love (Figure 22).[33] This same term for loving mother is repeated in versions of biographies of both Nightingale and Mary Lyon published in the *Magazine of the New Chinese Woman*.[34]

Figure 22 Nightingale ministering to soldiers in the Crimea
SOURCE: Yang Qianli, *Nüzi xin duben,* frontispiece to vol 2

Presentists, in contrast, presented Western heroines more as universal saviors (*pujiu zhu*) than as loving mothers.[35] Gan Hui claims Nightingale's oath not to marry (*shiyuan bu jiaren*) reflects her commitment to a higher form of universal love.[36] The author of the *Ten World Heroines* declares the British nurse a female bodhisattva who, like the all-merciful Guanyin, is committed to saving all living beings (*pujiu zhongsheng*). She embodies the rare flowering of love in a desolate world.[37] An early-twentieth-century ballad honoring Harriet Beecher Stowe employs similar language. She is rendered as a transcendent figure, a universal philanthropist or Western bodhisattva, whose love extends to all of humanity and can relieve any kind of distress.[38] A journalist depicts Willard's motherliness in equally grandiose terms. She is the mother of civilization, the mother of the mothers of great heroes, and honored by all wise mothers.[39]

Whereas presentists emphasized a transcendent female heroism, archeo-modernists kept their exemplars lodged in webs of worldly relations. They insisted the bold extra-domestic initiatives undertaken by women like Stowe, Nightingale, and Lyon were dependent on the assistance of men. In both Jiang's account of Stowe's life and the textbook versions of it, the visionary abolitionist feels compelled to seek the assistance of her husband

and former teacher, Calvin Ellis Stowe (1802–86), in formulating her antislavery message. On their wedding night she discloses her ambition to write a book to save the black slaves and enlists Calvin's support, modestly claiming she lacks the necessary knowledge to undertake the task. Although she does ultimately write the book herself, this initial self-deprecating assessment of her own abilities was deemed a necessary private preface to her book's resounding public impact.[40]

Presentists de-emphasized real and metaphorical familial ties and foregrounded heroic independence. This is evident in the account of Lyon's life in the *Magazine of the New Chinese Woman*. The translator of the account, Lingxi, faithfully renders the biography from her Japanese source—Nemoto Shō's *Famous Women*—including his description of Lyon as a loving mother. The lesson she ultimately encourages her audience to derive from Lyon's life story in her own concluding commentary diverges radically from Nemoto's, however. In Nemoto's excised Japanese conclusion, he makes Lyon's accomplishments compatible with East Asian familial norms, lauding her for nurturing good wives and wise mothers (*ryōsai kenbo*) through her educational work.[41] Lingxi, in contrast, uses Lyon's story to underline the importance of social activism. She claims that the great educator had sacrificed her life so that other American citizens could seek happiness and become enlightened. In Lingxi's retelling, Mary Lyon is revered not as a maternal figure but as a "beloved hero" (*jing'ai yingxiong*) and immortalized as a "hero" (*renjie*).[42]

The source of Lyon's public heroism in presentist accounts is her strong sense of autonomy. The pseudonymous Shoujuan declares that she had been inspired to translate an account of Lyon's life in the *Women's Eastern Times* because of the famous American's determination to remain single (*shou dushen zhuyi*) and develop women's education.[43] The author of the *Ten World Heroines* extends the ramifications of this theme of self-determination. He claims that, unlike most revolutionaries, diplomats, politicians, and scholars, Lyon had not relied on family connections or social position to achieve her goals. Her self-sufficiency was unparalleled.[44] While he sees this sense of independence reflected in Lyon's decision not to marry, as Shoujuan does, he interprets this decision in political terms. Lyon was not opposed to the happiness of family life, he explains, but she knew private passion and romantic attachment would weaken her love of nation and hinder her broader educational objectives.[45] In this presentist formulation, the regime of feminine virtue no longer serves as an analogue of social activism. Familial ties have become a direct impediment to female political engagement.

A New Social Category: The Female Student

It is difficult to map the influence these accounts of Western exemplars had on young Chinese at the turn of the twentieth century. A number of women discussed in Chapter 6 did assume increasingly public roles in this period, however.[46] Many followed Mary Lyon and became educators in newly established girls' schools. Others were inspired by Florence Nightingale to join a Chinese wing of the Japanese Association of Dedicated Nurses (Tokushi kangofu kai) or the Women's Red Cross Army (Nüzi hongshizi jun).[47] Still others took on relief work like Frances Willard through such organizations as the Chinese Women's Association (Zhongguo furenhui) or national fundraising efforts through such associations as the Female Citizen's Fund (Nü guomin juan).[48]

The range of new public female roles that emerged in this period provoked often harsh reactions. Even the progressive writer Lu Xun suggested that the most visible of these increasingly visible women—the dramatic orator and revolutionary martyr Qiu Jin—was the victim of her own publicness. Qiu had been, in Lu's famous statement, clapped to death.[49]

While it is not surprising that women like Qiu Jin who engaged in radical politics were targets of social criticism, it is remarkable that female students who were included in relatively moderate programs for national renewal became objects of disparagement. Both before and after the Qing government officially approved schooling for girls and women, female students were perceived as the local incarnation of progressive (wenming) values and the Chinese corollary of the Western women discussed above. Although their actual numbers were small, they aroused incommensurate anxieties over the erosion of Chinese gender principles and the emergence of a new form of unconstrained female sexuality.[50] This reaction was expressed particularly by eternalists but also by meliorists and archeomodernists. Broadly publicized in the popular press, it reflects the acute cultural sensitivity to even the least menacing of new public roles for women in this period.

PROGRESS INCARNATE

The first official document on women's education, drafted in 1904, was written in alarmed response to the increasing presence of young girls in public as private female schools began to open at the turn of the twentieth century.[51] The memorial attempted to reverse this trend by proclaiming that young girls should not be allowed to attend schools or walk freely on the streets. Instead they should be educated *in the home* and *for the home*. Their curriculum would mirror the basic instruction young women had received since the ancient Three Dynasties period on the proper roles of wives and mothers.[52]

Mounting social pressure ultimately forced the Qing government to ignore the recommendations of the 1904 memorial and establish a system of public education for girls and women in 1907. Official school regulations attempted to limit the female students' activities in public, however, by forbidding young women from joining political associations, attending public lectures, or becoming social activists. While the regulations conceded that sexual discrimination was wrong, and that girls and women deserved to be properly treated and educated, they, nonetheless, insisted that it was a man's duty—not a woman's right—to initiate social change.[53]

The students who officials wanted to deter from demanding expanded rights were often referred to as *wenming nü xuesheng*, "enlightened" or "progressive female students."[54] These young women engaged in new practices also labeled *wenming*. They included new-style marriage (*wenming jiehun*), foot unbinding, and wearing modish dress.

Enlightened marriage was the Chinese correlate of Western "free marriage"—the prime source of consternation in the eternalist critique of foreign social practices.[55] The most prominent difference between new and traditional Chinese nuptials was that new brides and grooms freely chose their own partners. The wedding ceremony that formalized their union also followed foreign-inspired protocols such as exchanging jewelry, and the couple often wore Western clothing and shoes.[56] These new-style marriages were closely associated with the new women's education: both, according to advocates, were crucial to national strengthening.[57] The bride was usually a student and the ceremony was often held at a women's school or at the home of a women's school principal or educator. In 1905, for example, Miss Gu, a student at the Chengzhi Girls' School (Chengzhi nü xuetang) in Nanjing, and a certain Wu Jin were married in the garden of the home of Chengzhi school principal, Cao Jialin.[58]

Miss Gu's wedding attire would most likely have included leather shoes designed for natural feet—the marker of the female student. Unlike the bound foot, whose aura derived from its concealment under perfumed layers of bindings, socks, and ornately embroidered slippers, the student's unbound foot was exposed and pedestrian, unadorned and unimpeded.[59] Eternalist critics decried this unabashed display of the female foot for violating a distinctively Han Chinese form of feminine modesty. While women had privately made their own shoes and covered their bound feet in the past, one complained, they now purchase shoes in public and brazenly bare their unbound feet.[60]

As critics of the natural foot movement mourned the passing of a world of female concealment, anti-footbinding advocates celebrated unbinding as women's entrée into the world of public education. From footbinding's inception in the mid-imperial period, it had reinforced the spatialized and gendered differences in education first articulated in the *Record of Rites*. Whereas for boys, enrolling in school marked the beginning of a life of learning and public service, for girls, footbinding initiated a retreat into the inner sphere and a limited domestic education. Late-nineteenth-century reformers including Song Shu (1862–1910) and Zheng Guanying (1842–1922) highlighted the link between footbinding and restricted female education.[61] From 1883, when Kang Youwei established the first Chinese-initiated anti-footbinding association, the movements for natural feet and women's public schooling were intimately connected. Kang's disciple, Liang Qichao, who was active in an anti-footbinding society founded in 1897, associated unbound feet with both women's learning and national strengthening in his influential essay "On Female Education."[62]

The earliest schools for Chinese girls and women in both China and Japan followed Liang and Kang's lead and made natural or unbound feet a prerequisite for enrollment. They included the Chinese Women's School (Zhongguo nü xuetang), established in Shanghai in 1898 by Liang among others, and Shimoda Utako's Jissen Women's School (Jissen jogakkō) in Tokyo, which accepted Chinese students from 1901.[63] Wu Ruoan (fl. 1902), a student at another early school founded in 1902, the Shanghai School of Fundamental Women's Learning (Wuben nüshu), recounted that its anti-footbinding policy attracted many students.[64] The Manchu Qing government, which had attempted to ban the practice as early as 1636 and as late as 1902, explicitly forbade it in the Education Board's 1907 regulations for government schools.[65]

Late Qing textbooks reinforced these developments by pronouncing bound feet incompatible with the new female education. The promotional introduction to one of the earliest elementary primers declared that because one of its aims was to include girls in formal education, all illustrations depicted young women with natural feet.[66] Textbooks written explicitly for girls and women almost universally contained lessons criticizing footbinding.[67] The *Chinese Reader for Girls* even included a supplement with detailed instructions on how to unbind feet over the course of a month.[68]

Older female students who were also new-style women writers, not only unbound their own feet but publicly denounced the practice. An overseas student in Japan, Chen Yan'an (Maoxie, b. ca. 1883), laments that while it is the norm for "young boys to be educated even if they are poor," young girls of all social classes are expected to "pierce their ears, bind their feet, and make up their faces to look like playthings."[69] Another overseas student, Wang Lian, claims that bound feet and pierced ears are forms of physical mutilation that had kept women secluded and ignorant. Like "torture meted out to criminals," these practices so debilitated women that they lacked the energy and the will to study.[70]

Students like Wang and Chen, whose feet had been bound when they were young, faced the daunting prospect of reversing what Dorothy Ko describes as "an irrevocable bodily process."[71] Wang Lian provides a public account of her experience of unbinding—and the sense of empowerment that resulted—while a student in Tokyo in her late twenties. She describes the doctor at the Japanese school she attended using carbolic acid and warm water to wash the unbearably tender and swollen feet three times every day before wrapping them in cotton. She claims that after undergoing this treatment for several days, her toes gradually relaxed and she was able to regain control of her body. Wearing Western socks and leather shoes, she was now able to walk "the twelve or thirteen *li* [about four miles] to and from school a day with no trouble at all."[72]

Han eternalists opposed natural feet for precisely the reasons Wang Lian and Chen Yan'an celebrated them: they allowed women to assume new public roles.[73] As late as 1907, fierce opposition to what some viewed as the potent mix of unbound feet and female education resulted in the coerced suicide of a young woman from Haizhou Prefecture in Jiangsu Province named Hu Fanglan (d. 1907). Hu's in-laws condemned her for defying tradition by unbinding her feet and encouraging her close female relatives to do the same. Her actions were an ill omen for the family, they charged, and would provoke both social ridicule and ancestral wrath.[74] When the Jiangsu General Educational Association (Jiangsu jiaoyu zonghui) investigated Hu's death, however, they found that her greatest "crime" against tradition had not been unbinding her feet per se—she had unbound them two years before her in-laws forced her to take her own life—but her educational aspirations that unbinding enabled.[75] The full force of her in-laws abuse was only unleashed when the act of unbinding was linked to Fanglan's intention to enter a "Western-style school" (*yang xuetang*), the local Liangjiang Girls' Normal School (Liangjiang nüzi shifan xuexiao).[76]

New female students—whose ranks Hu Fanglan had tragically hoped to join—were physically defined not only by their unbound feet but by their often controversial attire. The most public mark of social status, this attire was subject to the strict codes of "sartorial correctness" that had regulated female demeanor (*rong*) from ancient times.[77] Women had to dress appropriately if the upright were to be distinguished from the fallen, wives from courtesans, and students from whores.

From the opening of the first private schools for women at the turn of the twentieth century, principals, government officials, and social critics sought to attenuate the potentially sensational spectacle of female students in public by imposing dress codes that emphasized modesty and simplicity. The regulations for the School of Fundamental Women's Learning state, for example, that hats, shoes, clothing, and pants have to be plain and refined. Natural-colored cotton is preferred and only white or light blue cotton is acceptable for unlined clothing. Face powder, rouge, and jewelry—trademarks of the prostitute when used to excess—are strictly forbidden.[78]

The Education Board's 1907 school regulations include similar stipulations. Students and instructors are required to dress modestly in long cotton jackets free of ornamentation. White silk, make-up, and Western-style clothing are prohibited.[79] Two years later, the board reiterates that students are required to dress in Chinese rather than Japanese or Western style. It proposes that each school provide a uniform for teachers, administrators, and students of the upper level (younger and, presumably, less socially threatening lower-level elementary students would continue to wear their own clothing), consisting of long garments of a specified length and color, and appropriate footwear and head dress.[80]

These and subsequent regulations appear to have had little impact in the late Qing or the early Republic. A 1908 article in *L'Impartiel* (*Dagong bao*) apparently written by the editor, Ying Liangzhi (1867–1926), criticizes the "weird" and "seductive" appearance of teachers in Tianjin.[81] Five years later, a journalist for the *Women's Eastern Times* disparages the nation's fashion trendsetters, female students in Shanghai. These "progressive" students wear outlandish and "eye-catching" (*qili*) clothing characteristic of prostitutes, he complains. Who but the most sophisticated can distinguish between the two?[82]

SEXUAL MORES AND THE STUDENT BODY

These images of young women in eye-catching dress highlight the most threatening aspect of the new female students: their social, gender, and sexual liminality. The students destabilized the normative nexus of private and public women where the former were coded as reputable and the latter as disreputable. Anxieties about the female students' sexuality underlay discussions of their dress, feet, and social practices. These fears were most explicit, however, in the indictment of school girls as near prostitutes, would-be men, or same-sex lovers.

By sanctioning the presence of nubile women in public, the new education eroded long-standing strictures of gender separation. It also allowed for the confusion of two social worlds that the regime of feminine virtue had long sought to separate: the world of illicit sexual pleasure and the world of respectable femininity. The article from which the epigraph to this chapter is taken highlights this confusion in describing "a kind of debauched woman" who dresses like a female student but is actually a prostitute. The author intones one of the most often repeated arguments against the new women's education from the late Qing through the Republican period: it opened a social space in which prostitutes posing as students could shamelessly carry on their trade (see Figure 23).[83] While this new space facilitated the streetwalkers' vocation, it complicated the policemen's. Those responsible for enforcing social order often mistook students for prostitutes and vice versa. In early Republican-era Anhui, for example, students whose normal school was located near a brothel were arrested on the assumption that they were whores.[84]

Students were often charged with less than innocently contributing to such confusion themselves. In 1910 the *The Eastern Times* recorded a complaint that young women at the Gracious and Refined Girls' School (Huixiu nü xuetang) in Shanghai had invited prostitutes to play the leading roles in a public fund-raising play for the school. Most egregiously, some twenty students joined the prostitutes in singing on stage near the end of the performance.[85] At the same time, efforts to universalize education made it possible for prostitutes to not only pose as, but to become students. The principal of a Shanghai girls' school complained in June 1906 that prostitutes were enrolling in half-day classes. He feared that their participation would subvert the aim of these classes, which was to improve social customs. By simultaneously raising the status of prostitutes and lowering the status of female students, the half-day programs would weaken rather than strengthen morality and undermine rather than advance female education.[86]

Figure 23 A group of prostitutes pretending to be female students
SOURCE: "Maochong"

The perceived slippage between the social worlds of students and prostitutes extended to the blurring of lines between girls' schools and dens of
iniquity. The charge that schools were the sites of disreputable activities was
often ideologically driven. When the first private girls' schools opened at the
turn of the twentieth century, eternalists immediately condemned them as
fronts for gambling halls or brothels (*shuchang*) (see Figure 24). In 1903, two
county officials from Changzhou, Jiangsu Province, called for the prohibition of women's education on the grounds that local girls' schools were in
actuality gambling dens that "harmed mores and destroyed social customs"
(*shangfeng baisu*).[87] After 1907, when the government had allegedly taken
control of the development of female education, grievances of this kind
multiplied rather than diminished. A *Daily Pictorial* article reports in 1909,
for example, that a higher-level school set up by officials in a temple in
Songjiang has become the site for the illicit mixing of the sexes.[88]

Critics blamed female education for not only producing social ambiguities between reputable and disreputable women, but for creating gender

Figure 24 School or Brothel?
SOURCE: "Shuchang"

and sexual ambiguities. They disparaged the masculine appearance of many female students. A member of the Hanlin Academy complains in a 1906 memorial on reforming student dress that all female students wore unfeminine short jackets and narrow pants.[89] Other critics fault women for following the long-standing cross-dressing practices of courtesans by cutting their hair and sporting trousers or long gowns.[90] The author of a *Beijing Women's Journal* article laments that "women [imitate] men in everything today," not simply in their trousers but in their "hats, shoes, hairstyles, spectacles, and cigarette-smoking."[91] Some blamed this cross-dressing trend on progressive theories of a great unity, which included unity of the sexes and inspired educated women to pose as males.[92] (See Figure 25.)

Opponents of female education also believed the new schools promoted perverse intimate relations between women. Female same-sex love was first identified as a social issue at precisely the time formal female education became a controversial political issue. It remained intricately linked to the figure of the female student and the milieu of women's schools from the

Figure 25 "Males and Females in a World of Great Unity"
SOURCE: "Datong"

turn of the twentieth century through the Republican period.[93] The ostensible site of "unorthodox" erotic practices between various permutations of female students and teachers, girls' schools were identified as a threat not only to the long-standing gender order but to the existing economic and reproductive order.

The first article to address the subject of female same-sex love appears in the *Women's Eastern Times* shortly after the founding of the Republic. Written by a certain Shan Zai, the article presents female homoeroticism as abhorrent, foreshadowing a more extensive discussion of the relationship between education and same-sex love less than a decade later. Shan Zai attacks the phenomenon as the product of both nature and nurture. Some women are not physically attracted to men, he explains, while others lack opportunities to meet men, and still others have a salacious interest in women. He traces the history of female same-sex love from ancient Greece and Rome through its later emergence in various European and "barbarian" lands.[94]

The context that most urgently concerns Shan Zai, however, is the contemporary Chinese female student community in Japan. Although my own research on this community has found no other references to this, albeit, rarely discussed topic, Shan Zai asserts that female same-sex love had become a pressing concern in Tokyo. He offers a number of tentative solutions to this "problem" including abolishing dormitories for female students, placing close friends in separate rooms, and educating young women about their desires. Ultimately, however, he advocates the age-old solution to unseemly feminine behavior: moral edification.[95] The newly perceived threat posed by women who refused to be enclosed and dependent in conformity with the age-old sexual order, or to embrace "republican motherhood" as exacted by the new national order, was met with a familiar appeal to the principles of the regime of feminine virtue.

Unlike Shan Zai and other eternalists, who were resistant to female education in China and abroad, meliorists embraced the new schooling without painting frightening scenarios of moral turpitude, social collapse, and the contamination of Western values. Like eternalists, however, they considered it the mandate of this new education to consolidate, rather than challenge, the authority of ancient models; to mold young female minds in accordance with ancient principles rather than an alternative system of values.[96]

Archeomodernists, who founded many of the first private girls' schools and championed Western heroines as models for Chinese women, dismissed the more extreme criticism of female students as anti-*wenming* propaganda. They were not immune, however, from the concern that new female students were too quickly abandoning social mores and familial obligations. Although they did not attempt to contain educated young women within the sphere of Confucian ritual practice, they did establish new normative parameters for "good wives and wise mothers" (*liangqi xianmu*) and "mothers of citizens" (*guomin zhi mu*)—categories examined in detail in Part Two.[97] These new parameters significantly broadened the scope of the regime of feminine virtue. No longer exclusively encompassing the familial sphere, it was extended to include the social, national, and global arenas within which Florence Nightingale, Frances Willard, Harriet Beecher Stowe, and Mary Lyon operated. This new realm of female action continued, nonetheless, to be grounded in the basic principles of Chinese gender ideology. A woman's purpose in life was to nurture and serve—whether her biological, social, or national family.

Counterpoint: Female Virtue as Social Capital

In concluding Part One, we return to the story of a particular female student, the young woman from Fujian featured in the Part's opening epigraph. Her tale of betrayal and suicide, following what she insisted was an innocent foray into the public realm, highlights the ideological, institutional, and social instability young women faced at the turn of the twentieth century. They were exposed to public models in their schoolbooks and in the press, but they could be denounced for taking the most tentative of public actions themselves. The new schools they attended were heralded as progressive institutions and condemned as licentious lairs. Their painfully unbound feet were pronounced both the source of national strength and omens of a wayward modernity. At the same time, the unprecedented quantity and new genres of reading materials available to these young women presented dramatically changing and wildly uneven notions of feminine normativity. Meliorist texts like the *Illustrated Biographies of Resourceful Women, Past and Present* and the "New Chinese and Foreign Arrayed Traditions of Women's Lives" question the human cost of the chaste martyrs' sacrifices, while a new-style textbook praises suicide and self-mutilation as the epitome of female devotion. Archeomodernists celebrated Western heroines that eternalists disparaged, but continued to frame their accounts with familiar tropes of motherhood and service.

While the Fujianese student, the aspiring student Hu Fanglan, and countless other late Qing women fell victim to this instability, a certain Du Chengshu (fl. 1907) successfully negotiated it. Her story, a counterpoint to the prologue in Part One, complicates our understanding of the relationship between the new women's education and the regime of feminine virtue, and challenges notions of private modesty and public expediency.

Like the young woman from Fujian, Du was a student. She attended the Sichuan Girls' School (Sichuan nü xuetang), which her father and uncle had founded in Beijing. The school's meliorist mandate was to "plant the seeds of female intellectual empowerment" while emphasizing the overriding importance of moral self-cultivation. Du was aware of new global trends but was not pro-Western. In her own words, she followed Confucius, not Rousseau.[98] She was, nonetheless, something of a Western-style social activist. She was the secretary of the Chinese Women's Association (Zhongguo furenhui), an organization inspired by the work of Frances Willard and similar to the Red Cross.[99] Despite her public roles as Women's Association member and student, however, Du shared the eternalist and meliorist sense of gender propriety. She was committed to following the rites and upholding righteousness (*xunli shouyi*), and she derisively dismissed the new "discourse on freedom" (*ziyou zhi shuo*).[100]

In December 1906 Du received a letter from an admirer named Qu Jiang, an employee of the Translation Study Bureau (Yixue guan).[101] She was shocked and offended by what she interpreted as an inappropriate romantic proposal. Rather than suffer this perceived insult in silence or take her own life as chaste recipients of unwelcome advances often did in the past, however, she transferred the shame aroused by Qu's "affront" from her private body to the public body. She sent her response to Qu's letter to "all newspapers"—including *L'Impartiel* and the *Beijing-Tianjin Times*—to the Education Board, and to Qu's supervisor at the Translation Study Bureau. In the letter she wrote, "you privately approached me, I publicly denounce you" (*jun yi silai shu yi gongbu*), a bold gesture that reverses the gendering of humiliation in the story of the Fujianese student.[102]

The incident reveals the extent to which the principles of the regime of virtue could be a source of female social capital at the turn of the twentieth century. Du's sanctimonious denunciation of Qu suggests her tactical sense of moral expediency as much as her reverence for immutable moral values. She understood that women's virtue had to be strategically deployed if new turn-of-the-twentieth-century institutions were to develop. Progressive establishments like female schools and women's associations would flourish only if their students, teachers, and members continued to uphold the principles eternalists had declared inviolable. Female virtue, thus, functioned as more than a constraining set of norms in this period. It also served, as it had in the past, as a powerful source of female moral authority.

Virtue was no longer the sole source of female capital in the early twentieth century, however. Its authority was increasingly challenged by both its long-standing counterpart, female talent, and by a newly valorized female heroism.

PART TWO

History, Nation, and Female Talent

A lower-level degree holder, Zhang Zhongshan,
returned from studying in Japan to Wenren Village,
Zhili Province in 1905. He was shocked to find how
undeveloped women's education was in the Chinese
hinterland and decided to establish a village school.
The principle aims of the school would be to cultivate
women's virtue (*kaitong fude*) and educate mothers of
citizens. This would require eliminating old habits and
imitating Japan and the West. It would also require
excluding from the school's curriculum the study of
poetry (*shi*), prose-poems set to music (*ci*), songs (*ge*),
and descriptive prose interspersed with verse (*fu*).

"Chang li nüxue"
(Initiative for the Establishment of Women's Education), 1905

Zhang Zhongshan's archeomodern blueprint for the Wenren village school
is premised on an expanded vision of the regime of feminine virtue and
a new notion of female talent. While he emphasizes the development of
female morality, he privileges Japanese and Western ways over "old habits."
Among these old habits that would have to be abandoned in order to promote new skills is the study of what had been coded as distinctively feminine Chinese poetic forms.

Two female figures are invoked in Zhang's proposal. The first—and the
subject of the first chapter in Part Two—is the woman of talent (*cainü*), the
prime practitioner of the verse forms Zhang would exclude from his curriculum. The second—and the subject of the second chapter—is the nation-
minded and globally aware mother of citizens whom he is determined to
educate. The obverse of the woman of talent in both Zhang's proposal for

the Wenren school and in the broader archeomodern discourse, this patriotic figure also stood in opposition to the overindulgent mother (*cimu*). Both this indulgent mother and the woman of talent were signifiers of the degraded recent history archeomodernists were determined to overcome. The mother of citizens was, in contrast, the centerpiece of their new political vision.

In both chapters in Part Two, meliorism serves as archeomodernism's historical and heuristic foil. Advocates of these two chronotypes had widely differing understandings of the parameters of female talent and the purpose of female education. Their divergent views were based on deep ideological fissures and profoundly dissimilar conceptions of the relationship among China's past, its present, and its future. Tensions between the two groups thus provide insights into a question that would continue to vex officials and cultural critics through the twentieth century: whether China's identity should be based on the celebration, suppression, or selective reappropriation of its own history.

THREE

Women of Talent

Valorized and Repudiated

> So-called women of talent (*cainü*) have only the slight-
> est grasp of the principles of language, yet they delight
> in poetic raptures to the wind and ecstatic ditties to the
> moon. . . . Smug in their accomplishments, they know
> no shame. This is the source of the saying that only a
> woman without talent is virtuous.
>
> W U   T A O , Nüzi shifan xiushenxue
> *(Ethics for Female Normal School Students), 1907*

Wu Tao's textbook critique of the woman of talent signals the partiality for sound morality over flashy talent in Chinese culture. It also reflects the early gendering of the talent/virtue dichotomy and the strong bias against the free expression of female talent.[1] From ancient times, normative masculinity was based on the mutually reinforcing unity of virtue and talent, both of which were channeled toward public service. Normative femininity, in contrast, rested on an uneasy tension between female talent, which lacked a sanctioned public function and was, thus, inherently suspect; and female virtue, which ordered the private realm and was, therefore, universally valued. Two trends in the late Ming dynasty's vibrant commercial print culture threatened the delicate virtue/talent balance: the rise of female literacy and the emergence of the urbane courtesan as the model woman of talent.[2] It was at precisely this time that the saying Wu Tao and other early-twentieth-century authors used to disparage women writers was first popularized: "a man with virtue is a man of talent; a woman without talent is a woman of virtue" (*nanzi you de bian shi cai, nüzi wu cai bian shi de*).[3]

The meaning of the virtue/talent binary continued to shift from the late sixteenth through the early twentieth centuries. While opponents of women's learning initially asserted that female talent was incompatible with feminine virtue, by the eighteenth century the key question was no longer whether women should develop their talents but to what end. The High Qing classical revivalist Zhang Xuecheng (1738–1801) declared that true feminine talent could only emanate from understanding of the rites. He disparaged the female disciples of his rival, Yuan Mei (1716–98), who wrote what Zhang deemed trivial poetry that destroyed the rites (*shi er baili*).⁴ The gentry woman writer and anthologist Wanyan Yun Zhu (1771–1833) similarly valued female talent exclusively as a mode of moral reflection.⁵

These various late imperial notions of talent and virtue figured prominently in turn-of-the-twentieth-century debates over the new women's education. Eternalists confirmed the classical revivalists' conviction that ritual knowledge was the basis of female talent. They featured Zhang Xuecheng's essay on "Women's Learning" (Fuxue) among their recommended course materials in the 1907 girls' school regulations, for example.⁶ Meliorists also followed their High Qing predecessors in celebrating women of talent as moral paragons. At the same time, however, they emphasized the cultivation of nationally relevant female literary abilities and the expression of female subjectivity. Archeomodernists, whose nationalist polemics focused on the promotion of female education, most overtly condemned the figure of the woman of talent—the subject of Wu Tao's vitriol. Radically reconfiguring—*and* reinforcing—the talent/virtue dichotomy, they juxtaposed what they described as obsolete female poetic talent with new patriotic virtue. Presentists expended the least ink debating the moral merits or demerits of talented women.

Archeomodernists and meliorists not only validated and repudiated the abstract figure of the woman of talent but appropriated biographies of specific talented women of the past. Archeomodernists advanced their cultural vision by invoking ancient Chinese literary exemplars together with modern Western women writers. In contrast, meliorists exclusively celebrated Chinese paragons of both the early and late imperial periods, valorizing recent talented women whom archeomodernists maligned. The two groups' resignifications of historical and recent, local and global women's accomplishments highlight late Qing views not only of female talent but of the political and moral uses of knowledge.

The Figure of the Woman of Talent

By the time Wu Tao wrote his turn-of-the-twentieth-century textbook, the woman of talent had long been controversial in Chinese history. Although often criticized, she was differently perceived at various historical junctures as conceptions of talent and virtue, and the desirable relationship between them, shifted. Over a millennia and a half before the popularization of the saying that "only a woman without talent is virtuous," Ban Zhao had already proclaimed that women's virtue must not be tainted by "exceptional talent or perspicacity" (*bubi caiming jue yi*).[7] In the ethos of the Six Dynasties (220–589) only a few centuries later, however, female virtue's primacy was eclipsed as exceptionally talented but morally transgressive women were openly celebrated.[8] At the turn of the twentieth century, as debates raged over the relative value of Chinese and Western learning, and the need for women's education, divergent notions of female talent emerged and merged with increasingly unstable notions of female virtue.

FEMALE TALENT AND FEMININE VIRTUE

Eternalists, for whom the principles of the regime of feminine virtue were sacrosanct, followed High Qing classical revivalists in asserting that female talent had to be in full accord with ritual teachings. In her *Elementary Learning for Girls and Women*, Dai Li follows Zhang Xuecheng in attempting to channel women's education away from "worthless" poetry and toward ritual principles.[9] She condemns female authors of song lyrics—as Zhang had condemned Yuan Mei's disciples—for composing "nothing but dissolute vanities." Her text would properly instruct female students by introducing and explicating ritual material from a range of classical and historical materials relevant to women.[10]

The principles of the regime of feminine virtue guided the meliorists' position on female talent as well. In the *Illustrated Biographies of Resourceful Women, Past and Present*, Wei Xiyuan celebrates only women whose talents are supported by the requisite virtues. At the same time, meliorists attempted to make this morally grounded female talent more responsive to China's current national crisis. Zeng Yi, author of the *Exhortation to Women's Learning*, was a noted woman of talent herself, gifted in poetry, painting, and calligraphy. As the high official Zhang Boxi explains in a preface to her didactic text, however, Zeng had abandoned her "idle" literary and artistic pursuits after realizing they could not resolve China's current crisis.[11] Although Zeng followed Dai Li and Zhang Xuecheng in criticizing women who wrote meaningless poetry, her proposed antidote to this superficiality was not a return to ritual learning but a new, more practical form of women's education. Informed by her knowledge of Chinese medicine, the *Exhortation to Women's Learning* would help strengthen the nation by better preparing women to raise their children, care for elders, and maintain household hygiene.[12]

Female meliorists like Zeng Yi thus linked women's education to national strengthening as did archeomodernists. They, nonetheless, disputed the archeomodernists' wholesale condemnation of past traditions of women's learning. Zeng was unperturbed that more avid reformists would find the *Exhortation's* moderate stance on female education objectionable.[13] The scholar-poet Xue Shaohui challenged the archeomodernists more directly. She rejected Liang Qichao's proposals for women's education as "illusory and extravagant," and systematically disputed his criticism of the woman of talent. The nation could only be strengthened, Xue insisted, if women continued to study the literary forms that had long nurtured their moral strength and subjectivity.[14]

FEMALE TALENT AND NATIONAL VIRTUE

In the critique Xue rejected, the woman of talent served as a metonym for the failings of Chinese culture and the weakness of the Chinese nation.[15] Archeomodernists denounced her for immersing herself in sentimental poetic forms and antiquated scholarly traditions while remaining ignorant of national exigencies and global politics. In formulating their critique, they distanced themselves from all vestiges of what they considered an obsolete past. They, nonetheless, continued to follow the binary logic of their historical predecessors in subordinating talent to higher principles of virtue. Recasting the age-old dichotomy in a new nationalist idiom, they replaced the maxim that "only a woman without talent is virtuous" with the unspoken dictum that only a woman whose talents served the public was patriotic. They thus shifted the context for women's loyalty and service from ritualism to nationalism, from husband and family to the polity (via husband and family). No longer romanticizing the private sphere of women's writing as a haven from the vainglorious world of masculine politics, they insisted that female literacy be mobilized to serve a new politics.

This critique of the woman of talent was driven by the political need to posit a categorical break with the past in order to promote radical change in the present. Characterizing *all* women's poetry as "boudoir poetry" and condemning *all* women writers of the recent past for their political ignorance and frivolity, the archeomodernists condemned the culture these women represented as trite and perilously apolitical. This reductive view occluded elements within the Chinese female literary heritage that would have been potentially recuperable for the turn-of-the-twentieth-century nationalist program. They include the figure of the loyalist woman writer and a centuries-old tradition of women poets who had reflected on politics.[16]

This tradition can be traced at least to Cai Yan (Wenji, fl. 170), a controversial figure of the Later Han dynasty. Cai had married and bore two sons to a Xiongnu prince after the death of her first husband, and before being ransomed and married off again. In her "Poem of Lament and Indignation" (Beifen shi), she wrote not only of her own tragic fate but of the broader political trauma at the end of the Han dynasty.[17] In the succeeding centuries, women—including Li Qingzhao (1084–ca. 1151) of the turbulent Southern Song dynasty—continued to write politically engaged poetry.[18]

This mode of lyrical testimony reached its apogee, however, in the period archeomodernists most specifically condemned for its political vacuity: the seventeenth through the late nineteenth centuries, their own immediate past. Late Ming dynasty poets, including Bi Zhu (Taowen) (fl. 1643) and Wang Duanshu (1621–after 1701), wrote poignantly of the destruction and social disarray at the time of the Manchu conquest. Late Qing women writers such as Huang Shuhua (ca. 1850–67), Zhang Qieying (1792–after 1841), Zuo Xixuan (fl. 1850), Li Changxia (fl. 1860), and Wang Caipin (d. 1893) produced a second wave of poetic witnessing in response to the social upheaval and personal loss during the Opium Wars and the Taiping Rebellion.[19] Several of these women were celebrated in early-twentieth-century texts—Huang Shuhua in Wei Xiyuan's *Illustrated Biographies*, and Zhang Qieying in Xu Dingyi's *Guide to Great Women Writers of Our Country* (*Zuguo nüjie wenhao pu*), for example. This suggests that archeomodernists self-consciously ignored rather than were genuinely ignorant of this poetic legacy.

This erasure of recent woman of talent as a mode of cultural critique was unique neither to the archeomodernists nor to Chinese history.[20] In the High Qing, classical revivalists intent on promoting a new, genteel feminine culture elided the accomplishments of Ming dynasty women whose writings were, in their view, tainted with a courtesan aesthetic.[21] In the Republican period, May Fourth polemicists asserted their own proto-feminist position by effacing Qing dynasty women writers.[22] In these instances, as at the turn of the twentieth century, the recent past was first flattened and then dismissed in order to facilitate change in the present.

Archeomodernists believed political change in the present had to include a radically new form of women's education. In their struggle to understand the reasons for China's degraded status in the international arena, they were persuaded by the relatively simple proposition that Western societies were strong because their women were educated. Convinced Chinese women were as intelligent and educable as their Western counterparts, they blamed Confucian ritual teachings for restricting female access to learning and consigning women to idle and cloistered lives.[23] Unable—or unwilling—to immediately dismantle the ideological and structural forces that led to the social reproduction of these teachings, however, they focused their invective on the small percentage of women privileged enough to have been educated in the past. Claiming these women had squandered their abilities on poetic indulgences and worthless pedantry, archeomodernists made the "woman of talent" a stand-in for the unfulfilled promise of Chinese culture.

The late Qing critique of the woman of talent unfolded in three stages. It was first launched by reformists at the end of the nineteenth century. Female overseas students in Japan developed it further in the early twentieth century, and textbook authors—like Wu Tao—who were often returned overseas students integrated it into national pedagogy shortly thereafter. The radical nationalist aspirations that drove the critique became increasingly explicit in its later incarnations.

Liang Qichao sets the critique's language and tone in his 1896 essay "On Female Education," one installment in a serial essay that would establish him as a leader of the reform movement.[24] In the second of the four justifications for women's education outlined in the essay, Liang refutes the long-standing view that only women who lacked talent are virtuous. It was not female talent per se that was problematic, he argues, but the uses to which it had conventionally been put. "Those who were called talented women in the past," he writes, "were capable of doing nothing more than accumulating volumes of poems on the sadness of spring and the pain of parting, chanting about the sun and the moon, and toying with images of flowers and grass."[25] Two years later, Yan Fu also writes disapprovingly of women's talents. He claims that of the 10 to 20 percent of Chinese women who are literate, only 1 or 2 percent are truly cultured (*zhishu*). Their abilities are wasted, however, on crude exegesis of literary works.[26]

Kang Tongwei, daughter of Liang's mentor, the famous reformer Kang Youwei, was one of the first women to publicly embrace the critique of the woman of talent. In an essay entitled "The Advantages and Disadvantages of Education for Girls and Women" (Nüxue libi shuo), which appeared in both *Know the New News* (*Zhixin bao*) in May 1898 and in Xue Shaohui's *Chinese Girls' Progress* (*Nüxue bao*) four months later, Kang sets her argument in a nationalist register.[27] She complains that the Qing government had so ignored the education of girls and women that China had become the object of foreign ridicule. Following other reformist critics, however, Kang ultimately blames the underdevelopment of Chinese women's education and the perception that only untalented women were virtuous on the moral failings of the woman of talent herself. These women lack propriety, she claims, because they privilege intellectual achievements and "brilliance of mind" (*caihua*) over virtuous conduct. Their arrogant flaunting of their own abilities instilled in men the fear that even slightly literate women would dominate the household and become unnatural creatures, like "hens announcing the dawn." To allay this fear, men limit their wives' and daughters' access to learning and deem the preparation of food and wine to be the only appropriate female activities.[28]

Having criticized the woman of talent for her lack of virtue, Kang goes on to condemn the substance of her writings. The most sophisticated of these women, she writes, "wallow in their own compositions of prose-poems set to music (*ci*) and descriptive prose interspersed with verse (*fu*)." While the sound of lamentation fills the inner chambers, their poems on the spring flowers and the fall moon yield nothing but confusion. Women with less refined talents immerse themselves not in poetry but in novels and rhymed stories chanted to music (*tanci*). Men who worry that these prosaic and poetic indulgences would divert women from following the Way prohibit their daughters and wives from engaging in any kind of literary activity. Kang considers such restrictions excessive, equivalent to gouging out the eyes of the shortsighted or cutting off the feet of the lame. She is, nonetheless, as contemptuous as men had become of women's literary practices.[29]

Kang's essay, which echoes both the moral tenor of Zhang Xuecheng's "Women's Learning" and the nationalist zeal of Liang Qichao's "On Female Education," had profound reverberations itself, particularly in the writings of Chinese female overseas students in Tokyo. As this community became increasingly radicalized in the early years of the twentieth century, overseas female students devalued the feminine literary heritage in language that was more sharply politicized than that of their reformist predecessors. Rather than claim cultural capital by identifying with accomplished women writers of the past, they established a new subject position for themselves by deriding their literary forebears as selfish traitors to the collective good.

He Xiangning (1878–1972), one of the first women both to study in Japan and to join one of China's earliest revolutionary organizations, the Revolutionary Alliance (Tongmeng hui), considered existing forms of women's writing anathema to the project of national strengthening. Literate women of the past only indulged their emotions, she wrote disparagingly, and did nothing to serve the nation. Her disdain was not only resonant with earlier reformist writings, it was directly derivative of them: some thirty-two characters of her approximately 600-character essay were taken directly from Kang's description of upper-class women wallowing in prose-poems and prose interspersed with verse. He Xiangning ultimately pushed her argument further than Kang had, however, by not only criticizing the woman of talent's emotional verbiage but directly attacking her lack of patriotism.[30]

Female overseas students who were members of the Humanitarian Association (Gongai hui), a nationalist women's organization founded in Tokyo in the spring of 1903, expressed views consonant with He Xiangning's. In a collective essay published in the overseas student *Jiangsu Journal* (*Jiangsu*), they declare that women who write poetry are as good as illiterate. Chinese women in the past were either unlettered and "stupid as beans," they claim, or literate and capable of nothing more than "discoursing on the spring flowers and the autumn moon, chanting poems in a sing-song voice, and writing ditties in order to express and seek comfort in their own feelings."[31]

These overseas female critics considered women who delighted in prose to be as irresponsible as those who reveled in poetry. Wang Lian, whose account of the liberating process of unbinding her feet was discussed in Chapter 2, writes that learned women of the past are deemed exceptional because they "read the classics when they were young and perused novels or Tang poetry when they were older." But such learning lacks all relevance, Wang exclaims. "In these Chinese classics and novels, besides the depiction of loyal subjects, filial sons, hated husbands, and spurned wives, where is there any discussion of patriotism?" she asks. What is the value of a literary tradition that only offers rejected and tragic figures as models, like the character Cui Yingying from *The Story of the Western Wing* (*Xixiang ji*) or Lin Daiyu of *Dream of the Red Chamber* (*Honglou meng*)? If these are literate women, how can China claim it has ever had any kind of female education? In the end, Wang joins the anti-*cainü* chorus in reiterating "our literate sisters are the same or even worse than illiterate ones." It is this situation that has given rise to the saying that "only a woman without talent is blessed."[32]

This critique became more entrenched in early-twentieth-century discourse as new-style textbook authors—avid readers of the reformist press and frequently returned overseas students themselves—integrated it into nationalist pedagogy. In tandem with historical and contemporary critics—classical revivalists, eternalists, and other archeomodernists—these authors condemned the talented woman's lack of modesty and virtue. Wu Tao, who wrote the ethics textbook cited in the epigraph of this chapter, accuses those who had "a reputation for talent and brilliance in the composition of verse, calligraphy," and other feminine literary arts of being "smug, complacent, and shameless." Their arrogance created the perception that only untalented women were virtuous.[33] Xie Chongxie makes a similar claim in his elementary-level textbook. Female poets debase the literate tradition and provoke the "conservative" claim that virtue can only be found in women lacking in talent.[34]

These authors not only continued but deepened the critique of the woman of talent by merging it with a broader cultural critique that had only been implicit in earlier essays. Writing after the abrogation of the civil service examination system in 1904–5, which sounded the death knell for Confucian orthodoxy, they were emboldened to merge their disparagement of talent (*cai*) with an indictment of scholarly learning (*xue*). Conflating "desiccated" scholarly practices with "sentimental" women's writings, they reviled both.

In a chapter on self-respect in the *Ethics for Female Normal School Students*, Wu Tao claims that the "slightly literate" women of talent's practice of "commenting on the wind and the moon" was no better than "the poison" of the eight-legged essay (*baguwen*) and the poetry men had been required to write in order to pass the civil service examinations.[35] Yang Qianli also couples women's learning with male literati traditions in his introduction to the *New Reader for Girls and Women*. While there are women with refined literary talents in both the Chinese historical record and in contemporary society, he states, they have been corrupted by "the poisonous influence of male Han and Song studies." He argues that uneducated women, whose minds had not yet been corrupted by male or female literary legacies, represent Chinese culture's only hope.[36]

Biographies of Women of Talent

ANCIENT CHINESE AND MODERN WESTERN EXEMPLARS

According to Yang Qianli and other archeomodernists, the only Chinese literary exemplars who could speak to the current national crisis were those of the ancient past. They used these canonical paragons, who had been widely featured in classical revivalist texts, to new, political ends. Unconcerned with restoring ancient ways, they strove to establish a new global way, to demonstrate that, despite the frivolity of recent women of talent—and the corresponding infirmity of recent Chinese culture—there were recuperable elements in the Chinese past that could serve as the foundation of a new polity as viable as nations of the modern West.

Kang Tongwei's discussion of talented exemplars was based on this national utilitarian approach. "Women [of the ancient period], more so than men," she writes, "understood that there was no advantage to studying what one would not be able to apply, or to applying what one had not studied."[37] Ancient exemplars used their literary talents to serve the highest possible collective purpose: to enrich, transmit, and preserve the wisdom contained in the classical Confucian canon. "Wise women of the past could quote the classics and rely on moral principles *in order to resolve difficult situations*," Kang writes. "If they were not literate how could they have done this?" She links this ancient wisdom to modern Western women's education, the standard spatio-temporal move in the archeomodern discourse. Westerners understand "the principles of the past," Kang argues, and thus "promote female education."[38]

Kang gives three specific examples of ancient learned women, all of whom appear in eighteenth-century classical revivalist texts. The first is Ban Zhao, a central figure in women's learning from the first through the twentieth centuries. Ban Zhao's life story was initially recorded in a *Later Han History* account entitled "The Wife of Cao Shishu," which celebrates both her talents and her virtues. It records that she finished the work of her brother Ban Gu (32–92) on the *Han History* when he died, and that she had served the Han court as an instructress and an advisor to Empress Deng. It also praises Ban for being a faithful wife, devoted sister, and the author of the famous didactic text, *Precepts for Women*.[39]

Representations of Ban in the following centuries drew selectively on this official biography. From the early through the late imperial period, these narratives emphasize her virtues—her chaste widowhood and her treatise on female morality, for example—over her talents. It was not until the eighteenth century that her literary achievements were again fully acknowledged.[40] Kang Tongwei builds on this High Qing legacy. She highlights Ban's role in compiling the *Han History* and contributing to the cultural canon.[41] Textbook authors similarly herald Ban's learning in tandem with—rather than in subordination to—her contribution to the feminine domestic arts.[42]

A second handmaiden to the classical tradition featured in both High Qing texts and Kang's essay is the daughter of the classical scholar Fu Sheng (b. 260 BCE).[43] When the ruling emperor of the Former Han dynasty (202 BCE–9 CE), Emperor Wen (r. 180–57 BCE), sought instruction on the *Book of Documents* (*Shang shu*), he learned that Fu Sheng, the only living authority on this text, was too old to be summoned to court. The emperor thus sent an emissary to the Fu home. It was only through the aid of Fu's daughter that the aged scholar's barely intelligible words could be transmitted to the imperial envoy.[44]

A third, parallel story featured Lady Song, "Master of Illustrious Culture."[45] Rulers of the Former Qin dynasty (351–94) were intent on establishing an educational system but realized that a crucial ritual text, the *Rites of Zhou*, had been lost. When scholars submitted a memorial stating that Lady Song, mother of Chamberlain of Ceremonials Wei Cheng (fl. 380), came from a family that had transmitted the ritual classic from generation to generation, the emperor declared her home a lecture hall. Lady Song maintained her modesty by instructing scholars and officials on the ritual text from behind a curtain. She both exhibited female decorum and commanded useful knowledge—qualities recent women of talent allegedly lacked.[46]

When archeomodernists featured Chinese women who wrote rather than completed or transmitted texts, they again chose women revered by High Qing scholars and focused on these women's instrumental contributions to Chinese culture. A number of these female authors had written didactic books. Together with Ban Zhao, they include two ostensible authors of the Tang-era female instruction texts the *Analects for Women* (*Nü lunyu*) and the *Classic of Filiality for Women* (*Nü xiaojing*): Song Ruohua (fl. 820) and Lady Zheng (Zheng shi, fl. 750).[47] Archeomodernists also celebrated the calligrapher Wei Furen (272–349) of the Eastern Jin dynasty. Wei contributed to the cultural patrimony by instructing the male progenitor of calligraphy as an art, Wang Xizhi (ca. 303–61).[48]

The archeomodernists' advocacy of politically useful female talents and their aversion to "frivolous" literature for literature's sake are apparent in their presentation of Western women writers. They portray these women as the antithesis of the late imperial woman of talent. Neither sentimental nor solipsistic, they are committed to the greater social good. Not smug or flighty, they are characterized by moral seriousness.

A *Magazine of the New Chinese Woman* biography of the British writer George Eliot (1819–80)—like accounts of Harriet Beecher Stowe examined in Chapter 2—emphasizes the novelist's devotion to social service rather than her literary abilities. It focuses on her benevolence and chivalry, and describes her generously donating her earnings to the poor, to struggling scholars, and to women's schools.[49]

The Chinese translator of the account, a certain Qizhan, reinforces this emphasis in her appended commentary. Continuing to ignore Eliot's literary contribution, she underscores the novelist's "ethical conduct and righteousness" (*xingyi*) in daily life. She simultaneously uses Eliot's example to highlight the deficiencies of her own female compatriots as did translators and compilers of Western biographies examined in Chapter 2. Qizhan laments that her countrywomen are superstitious and idle "insense-burning and idol-worshipping" parasites who are ignorant of foreign women like Eliot. She hopes this biography will guide them in more effectively using their own talents.[50]

Lingxi, who translated the *Magazine of the New Chinese Woman*'s biography of Mary Lyon, offers young Chinese women another foreign writer as a guide: the transcendentalist Margaret Fuller Ossoli (1810–50).[51] In this instance, Lingxi, does not add her own commentary to the original Japanese account of Fuller's life—letting the highly moralistic portrait that first appeared in Nemoto Shō's collection stand on its own.[52]

A feminist and a learned woman, Fuller had made a career for herself in journalism (see Figure 26). Lingxi's translated biography presents her, however, as a paragon of Confucian intellectual modesty. The narrative emphasizes Fuller's classical training, in particular, her knowledge of Latin and Greek. It describes her rigorous daily study schedule and her scholarly devotion in terms that resonate with depictions of upright Confucian scholars. She studies so hard that she would forget to eat and drink, just as Confucius was a "man who in his eager pursuit [of knowledge] forgets his food."[53] She shuns a public role, following both the Confucian teaching that "the superior man is not distressed by men's not knowing him" and Zhang Xuecheng's later admonition that "the woman who is stirred by reputation

Figure 26 Illustration accompanying the biography of
Margaret Fuller Ossoli
SOURCE: *XNJZZ* 1 (February 5, 1907)

or fame is not acting according to her kind."[54] Fuller realizes, as did good
Confucians, that personal difficulties were a source of knowledge, and she
was deeply filial.[55]

LATE IMPERIAL EXEMPLARS

Meliorists made no mention of the Western women writers archeomodernists celebrated, and they honored the late imperial women of talent archeomodernists derided. Unlike Wu Tao and others who claimed that all female
poets were shamelessly lacking in virtue, meliorists celebrated women renowned for both their talent and their virtue.

   In compiling the *Illustrated Biographies of Resourceful Women, Past and
Present*, Wei Xiyuan used the same selection strategy as Qing anthologists
of women's poetry: a writer had to be eminently virtuous in order to be
included.[56] This privileging of virtue over talent is further evident in Wei's

categorization of literary women. Most are included in the "Virtue" (Zhenjie) section of his compilation, and he presents them—with two intriguing exceptions—as devoted family members rather than as women of talent.

One woman of talent whom Wei does not include in his section on virtue is the poet and scholar Cai Wan (Jiyu, 1695–1755). Cai's father was the late Ming general Cai Yurong (1633–99) and her mother was, reputedly, a former concubine of the rebel Wu Sangui (1612–78), against whom Cai Yurong had fought. Wei praises Cai Wan's exceptional talent and beauty, and the nobility and wisdom of her poems. He highlights her gift as a writer in the subtitle to the entry, "Ji Yu's Poems and Memorials" (Jiyu shi jian), and in the accompanying image, one of the few in his compilation of a woman holding a writing brush (see Figure 27). Wei's ultimate focus is on Cai's wifely virtue rather than her poetic talent, however. He places her story in the section of his text devoted to supportive wives ("Xiangfu"), and ad-

Figure 27 The late imperial woman of talent, Cai Wan, holding a writing brush
SOURCE: WXY III.1

dresses her in the biography's title as "Gao's wife." In Wei's estimation, Cai's literary abilities are not intrinsically noteworthy. They are of instrumental value in advancing the career of her husband, the official Gao Qizhuo (1676–1738).[57]

Other women of talent whom Wei does put in the "Virtue" section of the *Illustrated Biographies* include a courtesan, a faithful maiden, and a heroic chastity martyr. He commends the Tang courtesan Guan Panpan (fl. 800) for her moral delicacy—she delayed her suicide after the death of her lover so as not to sully his name—rather than for her renowned talents. Guan exhibited less debauchery, he declares, than women in the powerful families he saw around him.[58] He decries—and highlights—the excessive virtue of his niece, the faithful maiden Wei Jingqing discussed in Chapter 1, who was also an accomplished poet.[59] He celebrates another chastity martyr, Huang Shuhua of the Taiping era, for avenging her family and for relaying her story of murder and revenge to posterity in verses that were so artful they "would move all women."[60]

In some instances Wei holds women of talent to even higher moral standards than had classical revivalists. He refuses, for example, to include in his collection Xie Daoyun (fl. 350), the exceptionally gifted Eastern Jin poet whom both Zhang Xuecheng and Wanyan Yun Zhu had both praised.[61] Wei invokes Xie only as a negative example in conjunction with another biography, that of the wife of the charioteer Yanzi of the Minister of Qi.

This biography, which first appeared in the *Arrayed Traditions of Women's Lives*, recounts how the charioteer's wife rebuked Yanzi after observing how arrogantly he acted in preparing his master's chariot. Her reprimand precipitates such a profound change in Yanzi's behavior that the minister rewards him with an official post and his wife with an imperial title. In his commentary, Wei distinguishes women who effectively reproach their husbands, as the charioteer's wife had, from women who were inappropriately scornful of their husbands, as he claims Xie Daoyun had been. Describing Xie's sense of superiority to her husband as poisonous, Wei criticizes those who lament that she had not been able to marry her literary match, the talented Liu-Song poet Bao Canjun (414–66, who actually lived a half-century after her). Wei declares Xie's example so potentially harmful to the two hundred million women of China that it could throw the institution of marriage and the cosmos itself into disarray.[62]

The image of the exemplary woman of talent that emerges from Wei's negative portrayal of Xie Daoyun and his celebration of principled women

of talent is complicated by the last two entries of the "Virtue" section. The
first features a Daoist nun of the Yuan dynasty, the younger sister of the
poet Yuan Yishan (1190–1257) and a poet herself.[63] The second celebrates
Ye Xiaoluan (1616–32) of the late Ming dynasty, who wrote brilliantly, died
young, and exemplified the era's cult of feeling (*qing*).[64] These two narratives
are anomalous within the contours of Wei's collection in a number of ways.
They disrupt the chronological sequence followed in the previous eight sections, skipping from the late Qing in the immediately preceding entries
back to the Yuan and the Ming dynasties. More important, neither of the
two young women they honor had undergone the trials other exemplars in
this section of Wei's text—and virtuous Confucian paragons in general—
endured: a fiancé's death, early widowhood, or near rape. Nor were their
talents used in the service of their families: they did not write memorials for
their husbands or poems to avenge their family's honor. Yuan even resisted
marriage in order to fulfill her religious aspirations.[65]

In these remarkable entries, Wei ties female talent not to conventional
notions of feminine virtue, but to the subjectivity and otherworldly power
of sexually pure, religiously inclined young women. He disagrees with those
who claimed that Daoist nuns defied "the teachings of the sages," declaring instead that such women were among "the most refined members of
humankind."[66] He records that Ye had prophesied her own death, and suggests, as had Ye's own mother, that she ultimately transcended the lowly
world of fleshly women as an immortal.[67] Departing from the moralistic
familism that underpinned his other biographies of women of talent, Wei
thus concludes not only this section but his entire compilation with the in-
timation that female talent need not be unequivocally bound to the regime
of feminine virtue.

The "New Chinese and Foreign Arrayed Traditions of Women's Lives" includes another meliorist representation of a woman of talent, Kong Luhua
(Jinglou, fl. 1800), who is not solely defined by her familial role. The editors of this column foreground the importance of female talent by placing
Kong's entry first in the series. Although their biography of Kong notes her
distinguished cultural pedigree as "the eldest member of the seventy-third
generation of Confucius' descendants," it highlights her own abilities as a
learned woman and a poet. Her renown as the author of the *[Drafts] of
Poems from the Jiujing Pavilion of the Tang and Song Eras* (*Tang Song jiujing
loushi [gao]*) had earned her the title of Lady of Jinglou. She is also known

as Lady Ruan (Ruan furen), the second wife of the distinguished statesman and scholar Ruan Yuan (1764–1849).[68]

The "New Chinese and Foreign" biography of Kong, like the biography of the faithful maiden Wang discussed in Chapter 1, was drawn from an essay by the late-nineteenth-century scholar Chen Kangqi. The difference in the titles of Chen's essay and the later adaptation reflects their different emphases. Chen's essay, "The Gentlemen Bi and Ruan Are United in Wedlock Via Lady Kong" (Bi Ruan er gong diyin Kongshi), focuses on the importance of Ruan Yuan's marriage to his career.[69] The "New Chinese and Foreign" biography entitled "Lady Ruan's Profound Knowledge of the Classics and Histories" (Ruan furen zhanshen jingshi) shifts the emphasis to Kong's literary accomplishments. She is not portrayed kneeling submissively before the emperor with her grandmother at her side as she is in Chen's essay. Nor are her talents represented as constituents of her husband's cultural capital. The illustration that accompanies the account (see Figure 10) shows her in a canonical pose used to depict the literatus Ban Zhao. Kong sits alone with a female maid-servant in her well-stocked study, one volume open on her lap, another by her side, and her maid reaching to bring her yet another set of tomes.[70]

Counterpoint: Talent without Virtue

While Confucian virtue was not all-determining in the accounts of Kong Luhua, Ye Xiaoluan, and the sister of Yuan Yishan, it was the stuff of the universe in which these narratives operated. Presentist writers stripped that moralizing firmament away and depicted talent as completely divorced from virtue. Xu Dingyi, who refused to include chaste widows or faithful maidens in his *Biographies of Great Women of Our Country*, was equally adamant about leaving virtue out of his *Guide to Great Women Writers of Our Country*.

Xu's *Guide* straddles a number of genres, including histories of women's writing, hundred-beauties albums, and biographical collections.[71] Its ideology is, however, clear-cut. The compilation's front matter states that women writers are not necessarily gentry women (*guixiu*), and that questionable virtue does not disqualify a talented woman from inclusion in the volume.[72] This is apparent not only in the text's extensive table of contents—365 women are included—but in the beauties-style images of the thirty-six women Xu deems the most prominent writers in the Chinese tradition.[73] These thirty-six include Cai Yan (Wenji), the twice-remarried Han dynasty

widow of remarkable talent but questionable virtue (see Figure 28); Xie
Daoyun, whom Wei Xiyuan so reviled; and the courtesan Guan Panpan.[74]
Xu justifies his celebration of Guan and other less upright courtesans by
declaring that neither occupation nor social status determines one's abilities
or respectability. Talent, he claims, is in and of itself evidence of the presence of heaven.[75]

As this declaration suggests and as the content of this chapter demonstrates, Chinese views of female talent shifted in tandem with definitions
of female virtue, and definitions of female virtue were linked to broader
cultural and political trends. In the late Qing, as social critics reassessed the
primacy of Confucian morality in the face of the Western challenge and
revisited the issue of female talent in the context of formalizing women's
education, the long-standing dance between talent and virtue took on both
familiar and surprisingly new configurations.

Figure 28 The twice-remarried Han dynasty
widow, Cai Wenji
SOURCE: Xu Dingyi, *Zuguo nüjie wenhao*, n.p.

Eternalists did not move far beyond the legacy of High Qing classical revivalists in upholding ritual appropriateness as the single criterion for assessing female talent. The meliorists' position was less rigid. Although virtue continued to hold the high ground, they granted female talent some autonomy and their conception of virtue reflected new nationalist concerns.

The archeomodernists' rhetoric on the woman of talent was the most strident and the most influential. Reformist essays were reprised in overseas student publications and refracted in early-twentieth-century textbooks. The deepening of the critique of the talented woman over this short period—from Liang Qichao's 1896 "On Female Education" through essays written in Tokyo in the first years of the twentieth century and women's textbooks published from 1904—gives a sense of the pace of cultural change. Although reformers like Liang Qichao and Kang Tongwei resisted aspects of their Confucian heritage, they had been trained in its values and remained bound by its referents. Female overseas students, who were among the first Chinese women to study abroad, were less culturally constrained, more radically politicized, and more contemptuous of their female literary forebearers. Textbook authors who were often returned overseas students themselves and who wrote after the abrogation of the civil service examination expanded the literary critique of the woman of talent to include criticism of Confucian learning. Well beyond the late Qing dynasty, Leftist commentators continued to use the figure of the talented woman as the vehicle for ongoing laments over China's cultural degradation.[76]

Although historical trends are discernable both within and among the various strains at play in the turn-of-the-twentieth-century cultural field, our understanding is not well served by drawing bold lines that occlude cultural complexities. In appropriating from both the ancient past and the modern West, for example, archeomodernists did not establish a sharp East-West binary or overwrite one history with the other. Instead they initiated a dynamic process of cross-fertilization and cultural blending. They represented Ban Zhao as an exemplar of national utilitarianism and Margaret Fuller as a pillar of Confucian virtues. They honored a universal roster of talented women, from Fu Sheng's daughter to George Eliot, for the cultural and social ends their talents served rather than the subjectivities they expressed. They were both unlike contemporary eternalists, in their willingness to embrace Western learning, and unlike the iconoclasts of the next generation, in their continued use of China's ancient past as a cultural resource. They seamlessly assimilated *their interpretation* of Western values into their existing cultural repertoire just as they added Western women to the lineage of Chinese historical exemplars.

Open to the West and respectful of the ancient Chinese past, archeomodernists were, at the same time, dismissive of their own recent history. Although this categorical rejection of the late imperial past deprived them of a fundamental source of self-knowledge, their rhetorically powerful position ultimately prevailed in the field of women's education. This was evident in the prominence of archeomodernists in the founding and running of women's schools and of new-style textbooks in the turn-of-the-century print market. The purpose of these textbooks was to destroy all vestiges of detached aestheticism in Chinese (women's) culture and to create engaged and globally aware new (mothers of) citizens. The woman of talent was the foil for the archeomodernists' politicized mother.

FOUR

Wise Mothers and Mothers of Citizens

> Wu Mengban [d. 1901] explained to her shocked husband
> Gongke [fl. 1900] why she had had an abortion: "If we
> had raised the child, it would have taken at least twenty
> years for him to become a capable person (*rencai*). If
> I apply myself I could develop my [political] abilities
> within five years. How can you show more concern for
> one who would require over twenty years to develop his
> talents than for one who would require less than five?"
>
> *"Daoting yushuo" (Rumors), 1902*

Wu Mengban's passionate reaction to motherhood was one of many voiced at the turn of the twentieth century. In the maelstrom of late Qing cultural and educational debates, maternity was newly valorized, theorized, and politicized. The emphasis on the mother's role reflected the gender paradoxes implicit in nationalist agendas of the period. While it highlighted the centrality of women's reproductive and domestic work to national reform, it also kept women at one remove from politics and history.[1]

Motherhood is linked to nationhood in all late Qing texts on women's education. Even eternalists give the time-honored role of "instructing sons" (*jiaozi*) a new political valence. Authors of the 1904 memorial on women's learning in the home declare maternal teachings the foundation of national education (*guomin jiaoyu zhi diyi jizhi*).[2] Three years later the Education Board repeats this formulation in its regulations on formal female schooling.[3] Meliorists tie motherhood not only to national but to global politics. Wei Xiyuan asserts the relevance of ancient maternal principles to China's international stature in the section on maternal exemplars in the *Illustrated Biographies of Resourceful Women, Past and Present*.[4]

Neither meliorists nor eternalists used the two new maternal constructs prominent in archeomodern materials, however. These constructs, "good wives and wise mothers" (J. *ryōsai kenbo*, C. *liangqi xianmu*) and "mothers of citizens" (*guomin zhi mu*), gave the classic Confucian formulation of the family as microcosm of the polity a heightened racial and national significance.[5] The first, "good wives and wise mothers," a complex amalgam of Confucian principles, Meiji nationalist concerns, and Western influences, entered China from Japan early in the twentieth century. Despite its apparent domestic bias, it served in both Japan and China to legitimate women's education as the basis of national strengthening. It also promoted women's physical education as the foundation of racial strengthening.

The "mothers of citizens" (*guomin zhi mu*) ideal absorbed much of the content of "good wives and wise mothers" but was a sinicized and more openly politicized rendering of it. The mantra of archeomodernists, it was used in their textbooks and polemical essays to establish the biological connection between women and nation, motherhood and citizenship, maternal health and national strength. It also reinforced the importance of female physical training and its close Chinese corollary, foot unbinding.

Late Qing authors appealed not only to current theories but to historical precedents in establishing the relationship between motherhood and nationhood. As in discussions of women of talent, meliorists and archeomodernists appropriated and elided the historical past in distinctive ways. Both groups invoked the venerated ancient mothers of the Chinese cultural tradition, while meliorists alone valorized the achievements of recent maternal exemplars. In a critique that paralleled that of the woman of talent, archeomodernists denigrated these recent women as loving mothers (*cimu*) who were too ignorant and indulgent to effectively raise China's next generation of citizens.

New Theories of Motherhood

The emphasis on motherhood in late Qing materials marks a departure from both ancient and late imperial norms. Despite the importance of childbirth in China's profoundly pro-natalist culture, the maternal role is not highlighted in the classical canon.[6] The five human relationships (*wulun*), the foundation of Confucian society, do not include the bond between mother and child.[7] The *Classic of Filiality* (*Xiao jing*), one of the most widely circulated moral primers from the Han dynasty through the early twentieth century, singles out the father as the prime object of filial devotion.[8] The "Domestic Regulations" section of the *Record of Rites* generally subordinates the mother to the father and even to the woman designated as her child's teacher.[9]

Early female didactic texts, including Liu Xiang's *Arrayed Traditions of Women's Lives*, highlight motherhood but in a doubly reductive way.[10] They reduce womanhood to motherhood by making the bearing and raising of children the highest feminine ideal. And they reduce motherhood to the mothering of great men by focusing exclusively on women who raise exceptional sons.

The maternal role remained marginalized in the late imperial period. Ming-Qing testimonials of merit (*jingbiao*) were overwhelmingly awarded for wifely fidelity rather than maternal devotion, and arches and shrines were established to honor faithful maidens and chaste wives, not upright mothers. While scholars of this period engaged in debates on the faithful maiden cult and wrote countless biographies of chaste women, they discussed maternal virtues only in more private genres such as memoirs or epitaphs.[11] An exception who proves the rule is Luo Rufang (1515–88) of the late Ming dynasty, who emphasized maternal nurturance (*ci*) over chastity and elevated motherly love to the same level as filial piety and brotherly respect.[12]

In the late Qing, the affectionate mothers Luo celebrated were further devalued. As the loving mother was relegated to the dustbin of nationalist history together with the emotive woman of talent, the role of maternal instructress was politicized and often decoupled from wifely fidelity.[13] This new maternal emphasis reflected the rising influence of Social Darwinism and racial theory in East Asia, and the concomitant biologization of the discourse on Chinese society. The new mother who took center stage in late Qing biographies, textbooks, and social debates was not a sentimental nurturer but a physically strong progenitor of able-bodied patriots. A strict moral and political teacher, she was capable of raising not only upright sons but new, globally conscious, and nation-minded citizens.

WISE MOTHERS

Meliorists, who were less in the thrall of foreign ideas than archeomodernists but also less culturally threatened by the "great powers" than eternalists, situated motherhood in a global context. In the preface to his section on maternal exemplars in the *Illustrated Biographies*, Wei Xiyuan uses the language of both international power and cosmology to highlight the importance of motherhood. He asserts that China would be able to compete with the white race only if loyalty to the Qing sovereign and patriotism to the Chinese nation "filled Heaven and earth" (*chongse Tiandi*) and "swept the entire universe" (*hengsao liuhe you yu*). Neither officials nor scholars were capable of teaching these essential values, however. Only wise mothers (*xianmu*) could inculcate them.[14]

Wei's concern in this section is with instructing the wise mothers who would, in turn, educate their sons. The extended metaphor of industrial production he uses to describe this process reflects his commitment to both pedagogical innovation and long-established moral principles. He represents young Chinese women as the raw metal (*tong*) out of which wise mothers of the future would be cast (*zhuzao*). Contemporary schools are the ovens where these metals are fired, and the courses these schools offer are the coals that fuel the ovens. Finally, and of the most importance in the *Illustrated Biographies*, wise mothers of the distant and recent past are the molds (*mu*) from which the mothers of Wei's own day are formed.

Wei's use of the ancient term *xianmu* in putting forward his new conception of motherhood demonstrates the enduring power of the image of the sagacious mother, which dates to at least the Former Han dynasty.[15] It also reveals the dramatic ways that image had changed over time. The fungibility of the term is further apparent in one of the more significant turn-of-the-twentieth-century constructs of idealized womanhood, the "good wife and wise mother" (*liangqi xianmu*).

GOOD WIVES AND WISE MOTHERS

The concept of good wives and wise mothers which developed in Japan in the last decades of the nineteenth century and traveled to China in the early years of the twentieth, connects women and nation, familial and national service, domestic labor and formalized women's education. Because the four-character expression *ryōsai kenbo* or *liangqi xianmu* highlights the roles of wife and mother, however, its full meaning was often misunderstood in its own day and misconstrued in later scholarship.

These misconceptions have been compounded by the instability of the four-character expression, which has taken on different forms and connotations in different East Asian contexts. It appears not only as *liangqi xianmu*—the most common arrangement in late Qing sources—but as *xianmu liangqi* (wise mother and good wife), a mere reversal of the expression's two composite compounds, and as *xianqi liangmu* (wise wife and good mother), a more significant semantic shift that designates the wife who aids her husband, rather than the mother who instructs her children, as wise. To this day, scholars debate whether the four-character expression, however it was ordered, was originally a product of Confucian morality or of modern global concerns. They also dispute whether it was constraining or enabling for women in specific historical contexts.[16] These questions highlight the epistemological and cultural tensions that underlie the concept itself.[17]

One of the earliest Chinese uses of the compound appears in a 1903 issue of the *Educational World* (*Jiaoyu shijie*), the prime Chinese source of information on Japanese education in the early twentieth century.[18] The article that introduces the term is a translated excerpt from a treatise by the prominent Japanese educator Yoshimura Toratarō (1848–1917), *Contemporary Japanese Education* (*Nihon genji kyōiku*).[19] In his section on "Education for Girls and Women," Yoshimura explains that education for girls had not developed as quickly as it had for boys in the Meiji period because women were assumed to be responsible only for matters inside the household. Disputing this claim, Yoshimura insists that, through their moral and intellectual influence on their children, "good wives and wise mothers" in all nations are "the mothers of national enlightenment and civilization" (J. *bunmei*, C. *wenming*).[20]

While the excerpt from Yoshimura's book may have first introduced the term "good wives and wise mothers" into the Chinese discourse, the Japanese educator Shimoda Utako was most responsible for explicating and propagating it in the late Qing. A prominent promoter of the ideology of good wives and wise mothers in Meiji Japan, Shimoda founded the Jissen Women's School (Jissen jogakkō) in 1899, the year after Japanese officials made this ideology a cornerstone of Meiji women's education. The stated objective of Shimoda's school—which would become the principle training ground for Chinese overseas students in the early twentieth century—was to cultivate good wives and wise mothers.[21]

Shimoda's conception of the good wives and wise mothers ideal was culturally hybrid. She had grown up in a family of Chinese learning (Kangaku) scholars and been trained in Chinese learning. She had also experienced "the West" first hand, having lived in England between 1893 and 1895, shortly before she founded the Jissen school. During this two-year stay in England, Shimoda studied Western approaches to women's education, which she would later integrate into the Jissen curriculum. She also developed a keen sense of Japan's—and China's—vulnerability to the West, and began to conceive of women's education as a crucial element in the pan-Asian defense against Western encroachment.

When Shimoda returned to Tokyo in 1895 she collaborated with Japanese and Chinese educators and politicians who shared her determination to strengthen East Asia. They included Meiji officials and a range of politically influential Chinese, from Zhang Zhidong, one of the authors of the 1904 memorial on educating women in the home, to the future revolutionary leader Sun Zhongshan (Sun Yat-sen, 1866–1925).[22] Shimoda's conception of women's education at this time was based on the substance / function (*tiyong*) dichotomy attributed to Chinese educators like Zhang Zhidong. She simultaneously emphasized Westernized practical education, including physical education, to further national utilitarian goals, and East Asian ethical education to cultivate moral and cultural substance.[23]

This substance/function dichotomy reflected China's and Japan's paradoxical position vis-à-vis the West at this historical juncture. Reformers in both countries were simultaneously drawn by Western wealth and power and repelled by aspects of the Western social ethos. This tension was apparent in debates over the origins of the good wives and wise mothers ideal. Most proponents considered its source to have been a classic nineteenth-century European model of femininity that had subsequently been Confucianized. It was first appropriated to East Asian ends by the scholar Nakamura Masanao (1832–91) during a sojourn in Europe in the 1870s, the period when Japan was most intensively engaged with Western ideas.[24] One Chinese journalist maintains that despite its Western origin, the ideal had later been corrupted in the West by notions of sexual equality, individualism, independence, and careerism. Japan, he therefore argues, is the last bastion of an earlier, acceptable version of the ideology.[25]

Other Chinese authors argued, in contrast, that good wives and wise mothers was initially a Confucian Chinese ideal. While proponents of the ideal hoped to make it more attractive to a Chinese audience by linking it to venerable Confucian ethics, opponents attempted to halt its dissemination in China by tying it to increasingly discredited Confucian values.[26] Both groups based their assertions for Chinese origins on ancient textual evidence: the two two-character terms that form the four-character compound—*liangqi* (good wife) and *xianmu*—both appear in Chinese texts dating back as far as the first century BCE.[27]

The Japanese or pan-Asian meaning of the four-character compound as it was used at the turn of the twentieth century differed significantly from its composite Chinese parts, however. The Meiji or late Qing good wife and wise mother was not expected to just "prepare food and wine" in conformity with her ancient ritual roles, but to educate her children, aid her husband, and contribute to the nation.[28] Despite resonances with early Chinese sources and traces of later Western influences, the concept is best understood as a product of its own transnational moment in history. While initially inspired by Western notions, its purpose was to strengthen East Asian society vis-à-vis the West. And while its two-character components were derived from early Chinese texts, they had been appropriated to new global ends.

The global context was palpable in Shimoda's explication of the ideal of wise mothers to her Chinese audience. She asserted that superior maternal instruction was crucial to the survival of both China and East Asia, and that female education was the sine qua non of superior maternal instruction. The quality of this education, she maintained, would determine the quality of Chinese women's minds, bodies, and children, and, ultimately, the strength and vitality of China's citizenry. The Social Darwinian concerns and biological metaphors that infused her argument were typical of turn-of-the-twentieth-century East Asian and Western understandings of the link between healthy mothers and strong citizens. She had conceivably derived these ideas from the British eugenics movement to which she would have been exposed in England in the mid-1890s. Social Darwinism was already prevalent in the Japanese social discourse of the time, however. In Yoshimura's text cited above, for example, he writes that for Japan to hope to join the advanced nations of the world without educating the female half of the population was like expecting a "half paralyzed" invalid to confront a physically robust competitor.[29]

Shimoda's invocation of Social Darwinism made it possible for her to achieve two of her paramount objectives: to tie the fate of China to Japan through a pan-Asian appeal to the survival of the "yellow race," and to link women to the nation indirectly through their biology rather than directly through their intellect.[30] While female education was central to her pan-Asian vision, she did not consider it an end in itself but a means of improving the racial stock. In a lecture delivered to a Chinese audience in Tokyo in 1902 and widely reprinted in Chinese-language journals, Shimoda claims the yellow race was weak because, like all weak nations including Korea, Vietnam, Burma, and Turkey, it had failed to develop education for girls and women. In contrast, because the women of "the white race of Europe and America" are well educated and strong, their sons are knowledgeable and their race powerful. Shimoda encourages the members of her (largely male) Chinese audience to "return home and promote female education as the basis of male education. This will not only enrich your nation," she explains, "it will ensure that our Asia and our yellow race will flourish. Then we will be able to compete with the white race."[31]

Shimoda used several avenues besides public lectures, to convey her ideas to the Chinese. In 1901, she founded a publishing house, the Society for Renewal (Zuoxinshe) in Shanghai, with the assistance of Ji Yihui (fl. 1900), one of China's first overseas students in Japan.[32] Between December 9, 1902, and January 1906, the society published a journal entitled *The Continent* (*Dalu*), which was read not only in Shanghai but in the Chinese provinces.[33] It also published Chinese translations of Japanese books on female education. These include Shimoda's own *Domestic Science* (*Kaseigaku*), the one foreign text that Zhang Zhidong, Zhang Boxi, and Rongqing recommended for inclusion in a new Chinese textbook for girls and women in 1904. They also include *Women's Education* (J. *Joshi kyōiku*, C. *Nüzi jiaoyu lun*) by Naruse Jinzō (1858–1919), which was translated into Chinese in 1901. Both of these texts expounded on the ideology of good wives and wise mothers, and both became foundational texts in Chinese discussions of female education.[34]

Shimoda's influence was also felt through her disciples, a number of whom were active in the private Chinese girls' schools established in the first years of the twentieth century. Kawahara Misako (1875–1945) became one of the nine teachers at the Shanghai School of Fundamental Women's Learning in 1902, for example.[35] Hattori Shigeko (fl. 1904) taught at the Beijing Preparatory Women's School (Beijing yujiao nüxuetang), which she and her husband, Hattori Unokichi (1867–1939), founded in 1905.[36]

Most important, however, Shimoda translated her vision of good wives and wise mothers into the Jissen Women's School curriculum for Chinese overseas students. As the school's name—literally, the "Practical Women's School"—indicates, Shimoda emphasized the development of practical abilities over intellectual talents. She was convinced this form of pedagogy was particularly well suited to her Chinese students. "These women have traveled a great distance," she explained, "and cannot be given a frivolous education."[37] Her curriculum emphasized the cultivation of moral virtues, domestic skills, and physical abilities over the reading and recitation of texts. Shimoda personally taught all ethics classes, using a textbook she had written herself, *Lectures on Ethics for Chinese Overseas Students* (*Shina ryūgakusei no tame no shūshin kōwa*). This text expounds on foundational Chinese and Japanese ethical concepts such as loyalty and filiality, while giving practical instruction on quotidian matters such as health maintenance.[38]

Ultimately, Shimoda placed more emphasis on physical than on moral education. As noted in Chapter 2, she insisted that all Chinese students who entered her school have unbound feet. This would enable them to participate in the calisthenics (*taisō*) classes included in the various Jissen Women's School programs. The overseas students spent three hours each week in these classes—three times more than in their course on ethics.[39] According to this influential turn-of-the-century figure, physical strengthening was imperative if Chinese women were to fulfill their role as mothers of citizens.

MOTHERS OF CITIZENS

As evinced in Shimoda's curricular priorities, the Japanese ideal of good wives and wise mothers was linked to new East Asian nationalist imperatives. The Chinese concept of mothers of citizens made this connection between motherhood and politics more explicit. Because the term *guomin* that was used to denote the Western concept of citizenry in this period signified both an individual within the nation and the entire nation,[40] Chinese women were called upon to mother not only patriotic offspring but the nation itself. The authors of a 1905 *Citizen's Reader* (*Guomin bidu*) explained that the *guomin* and the nation (*guojia*) "cannot be separated from one another. The reputations, interests, honor, and dishonor of the nation and the people are one."[41]

The mothers-of-citizens construct was simultaneously enabling and constraining for women in ways similar to both the Japanese concept of good wives and wise mothers and the French and American ideal of republican motherhood. It simultaneously politicized motherhood and naturalized the potentially denaturing role of women in politics by giving the most elemental of human relationships—that of mother to child—a national meaning.

This new, nationally inflected role legitimized appeals for the development of both women's education and a new feminine bodily hexis.[42] It also allowed for the insertion of women into political theory by emphasizing the outer or public ramifications of women's domestic roles. By granting women an *indirect* political role, however, it made it possible to defer the question of full female political participation and circumvent the more radical idea of "female citizens" (*nü guomin*). It was this displacement of politics through motherhood that was unacceptable to women like Wu Mengban who, as she explains in the epigraph, preferred to become political subjects in their own right.

The genealogy of the concept of mothers of citizens can be traced to reformist writings of the immediate post–Sino-Japanese War period, precisely when the ideology of good wives and wise mothers was gaining prominence in Meiji Japan. Without explicitly using the term, Liang Qichao elucidates much of its content in his 1896 essay on female education. The last two of his four proposals in the essay concern motherhood. In the third he asserts, as Shimoda had, that the relationship between women's education and national strength is critical. He appeals, again like Shimoda, to the Western experience in making this connection: Western mothers are, he states, responsible for 70 percent of elementary education.[43] In his fourth proposal, Liang echoes Shimoda's emphasis on the importance of biology to national strengthening. He insists that the Chinese race has to be invigorated through fetal education (*taijiao*)—the first stage of a child's education in the womb.[44]

Implicit in Liang's argument is the long-held but newly valorized Chinese idea that the family is the microcosm of the polity. Widely developed in turn-of-the-twentieth-century essays and textbooks, this idea formed the local conceptual framework for new global notions of women and nationalism. Compilers of the 1908 *Newest Chinese Reader for Women* remind young female radicals that the relationship between women and the nation is mediated by the family. It is wrong-headed, they assert, for women "to talk extravagantly about patriotism and the salvation of the collective" without realizing that the nation is nothing more than "an aggregate of families." The polity can only be strengthened if women treat household and children as their first priorities.[45]

Overseas female student activists were quite likely among those the editors of the *Newest Chinese Reader* targeted for "talking extravagantly about patriotism." However, several of these young women echoed the *Reader's* assertion that women must serve the nation through their children. Like advocates of good wives and wise mothers, and militant women of the French Revolution, they invested women's domestic roles with a new national significance, calling for the expansion rather than the abandonment of the responsibilities of wives and mothers.[46]

In a preface to the radical pamphlet *A Tocsin for Women (Nüjie zhong)* by Jin Tiange (1874–1947), the female writer Huang Lingfang (fl. 1903) emphasizes the national importance of these domestic responsibilities. "Advances in knowledge and education are dependent on two things," she states. "First, women must advise their husbands in order to benefit society. Second, they must guide their children in order to further education."[47] Wang Lian, who disparaged the woman of talent, maintains that a woman has influence in the outer sphere through the male members of her family. Her love of country inspires patriotism in her husband and sons, and her moral influence determines whether the latter become corrupt officials or national heroes.[48] Cao Rujin (1878–?), who arrived in Japan from Jiangsu Province at the age of twenty-four, asserts that women would be true patriots if only they learned to treat the nation like their own family.[49] Even Qiu Jin, who abandoned her husband and two children, calls on women to strengthen the nation by encouraging their husbands to work for the good of the community, their sons to study abroad, *and* their daughters to pursue an education.[50]

This early-twentieth-century connection between motherhood and nationhood was ultimately subsumed under the new category of "mothers of citizens." The global dimensions of this category were evident from its inception. One of its first occurrences is in the April 1903 issue of the Tokyo-based overseas student *Jiangsu Journal*.[51] It appears in a note appended to a translated entry on female physical education in Europe and America from Shimoda Utako's European travel diary. Allegedly quoting Napoleon, the note declares: "The way to strengthen the nation is through the physical strengthening of the mothers of citizens (*guomin zhi mu*)."[52]

The new category became firmly established in the Chinese discourse by 1904 or 1905, shortly after the concept of good wives and wise mothers was introduced. Absorbing much of the content of the Japanese ideal, the Chinese term ultimately replaced the Japanese in the late Qing discourse. It became the mantra of archeomodern textbooks and a common trope in the mainstream press. An article published in the Japanese-owned *Beijing-Tianjin Times*, in 1905, for example, claims the seven characters in its title "Women Are the Mothers of Citizens"—"Nüzi wei guomin zhi mu"—express reverence for women's education and represent China's only hope for national strengthening.[53]

These sacred seven characters appear in the inaugural line of a number of women's textbooks including Xie Chongxie's *Lower-Level Elementary Female Ethics Textbook*. Because women are mothers of citizens, Xie explains, education for girls is the most pressing project of the day, more urgent even than education for boys.[54] The first chapter of Yang Qianli's *New Reader for Girls and Women,* which features the renowned mother of Mencius, also opens with the declaration that women are mothers of citizens.[55] Like Yang, Wu Tao ties the concept to both ancient models and new political impera-tives. Women educated to be mothers of citizens would develop the elevated morality of the great ancient families and halt the perception that only un-talented women are virtuous, he maintains.[56]

The ultimate target of these textbooks, as the term *mothers* of citizens suggests, was not the female student herself but her male offspring. And the crucial knowledge she would transmit was national knowledge. A mother of citizens was, by definition, a woman who inculcated her sons with patriotism.[57]

All turn-of-the-twentieth-century textbooks—whether labeled ethics primers, Chinese language readers, or teacher-training manuals—convey the new national ethos women were expected to impart to their sons. Many promote a sense of national pride. "The territory of our nation is Shen-zhou, the largest nation in the world," Xu Jiaxing declares in his ethics text-book. "Our race is the flourishing Hua race, which has been superior to all barbarian races from ancient times. Patriotic women must understand this."[58] Other authors temper this sense of chauvinism with an introduc-tion to contemporary geopolitics. Xie Chongxie explains—using a map to visually make his point (see Figure 1)—that although the "Chinese often call China all under heaven, it is only one country in East Asia."[59] Fang Liusheng similarly explains that "China is not alone in the world." In deal-ing with foreigners, it must learn to "study their good methods without becoming enslaved to them."[60]

Fang further explains that the individual is connected to the nation just as local regions are connected to the greater national entity called China. While "I am from Nanxun," he notes, "Nanxun is in the county of Wucheng, which is in the prefecture of Huzhou, which is in the province of Zhejiang, which is in the nation, China." As a result of this geographical embeddedness, "the glory or the shame of China is mine. Whether I am a woman or a man I have a responsibility to protect China."[61] The compil-ers of the *Newest Chinese Reader for Women* offer their female readers an overview of China's various regions from the coast to the hinterland in the guise of the account of a traveler.[62] This introduction to national space is ac-companied by a series of lessons on national time, from the ancient through the modern eras. The more recent accounts discuss crucial moments in the development of Chinese nationalism, such as the 1894–95 Sino-Japanese

War, the 1898 reforms, and the Boxer Rebellion.[63] The *Reader* also includes its audience in the new political imaginary by discussing concepts such as "nation" and "society," and explaining the institutional components of the modern nation-state, from different political systems to assemblies, laws, taxes, and military service.[64] Finally, the *Reader* emphasizes the importance of public morality, which mothers are responsible for communicating to their sons.[65]

The moral and political principles a young woman was required to grasp and eventually impart to her male offspring were, thus, integral to her own schooling. Physical education was, however, the most important aspect of her personal transformation. Consistent with the formation of Japanese good wives and wise mothers, the education of mothers of citizens prioritized strengthening the female body in order to strengthen the race.

This was not the first time biological motherhood and healthy offspring were connected in China. As the science of women's medicine (*fuke*) developed in the late imperial period, the earlier privileging of social over biological mothers—of the woman who morally raised rather than physically bore children—was replaced by a new emphasis on the biological mother's role in the production of fit descendants.[66] Texts from the eighteenth and the turn of the twentieth centuries use resonant agricultural metaphors to describe the relationship between mother and child. While a High Qing essay on female reproductive disorders asserts that "the selection of a female [as a future mother] is just what the selection of soil is to the planter," for example, a turn-of-the-century woman writer Sun Qingru intones that to expect an inferior mother to yield a superior son is "like planting poorly but expecting good sprouts."[67] What is new in the late Qing, however, is the global context. Women are no longer exclusively called upon to produce able sons for the patriline but to provide strong citizens for the nation.

A number of educated women, like Sun Qingru, affirmed the importance of this newly politicized view of biological motherhood. In the preface to an article on the relationship between women and medicine, Yan Bin (1870–?), a medical student at Waseda University and the editor of the *Magazine of the New Chinese Woman*, asserts that the Chinese citizenry could only be strengthened if medical care for Chinese women improved.[68] One of China's first female educators and journalists, Lü Bicheng (1883–1943), declares that the quality of citizens had less to do with the mother's moral or intellectual influence on her children than with fetal education.[69]

Textbooks directly tie the mothering of able-bodied citizens to women's physical education. The sixth chapter of Xu Jiaxing's *Newest Ethics Textbook for Girls and Women* is entitled "Physical Education" (Tiyu) and subtitled "Women Are Mothers of Citizens" (Nü wei guomin zhi mu). Xu opens the lesson by stating that while physical education is important for both males and females, women are the "mothers of citizens. The superiority or inferiority of their physical health is thus linked to the strength or weakness of the citizenry." (See Figure 2 for the accompanying illustration.)[70] Wu Tao similarly elaborates on the concept of mothers of citizens in a chapter on "Exercise" (Yundong).[71]

In addition to these general ethics or Chinese language primers that establish the physical education / mother of citizen link, a number of specialized textbooks devoted to women's physical culture were published in this period. Many were translations, reflecting the newness of the concept of female physical education in East Asia. (Ethics textbooks, in contrast, were never translations.) *Textbook for Girls' Physical Training* (*Nüzi ticao jiaokeshu*), written by the principal of an English girls' high school, Alice R. James, was translated into Japanese by Shirai Kikurō, a famous figure in Japanese sports education, and from Japanese into Chinese by Cai Yun in 1906. In their prefaces, both Cai and Shirai highlight the intimate relationship between women's physical education and the nation (see Figure 29).[72]

The Chinese rapidly became less dependent on foreign expertise in this area, however. From as early as 1905 they were able to train their own physical education teachers and in the next few years, began to write their own specialized textbooks. Xu Chuanlin (fl. 1908), who had published several general textbooks on physical education in the late Qing and early Republic, wrote the *Physical Education Reader for Girls* (*Nüzi ticao fanben*) in 1908.[73]

This textbook emphasis on physical education both reflected and inspired school policy. The earliest Chinese private women's schools, which were often modeled on Japanese schools, included some form of physical education in their curricula. The Shanghai School of Fundamental Women's Learning, where Shimoda's disciple Kawahara taught, even held athletic meets with foot races.[74] The Education Board reinforced this emphasis by highlighting physical education in the 1907 girls' school regulations. Like Shimoda's Jissen Women's School, Chinese schools were to include several hours of physical education instruction a week in their curricula. Lower-level Chinese elementary schools were to allot four out of twenty-six hours of instruction time to physical education classes—twice the number devoted to

Figure 29 Girls' physical training
SOURCE: Alice R. James, 56b

ethics; upper-level elementary schools three out of thirty hours; and normal schools, two out of thirty-four.[75]

This attention to women's physical education became inextricably tied to the early-twentieth-century anti-footbinding movement. Textbook authors present several arguments against footbinding. According to Xie Chongxie, it makes women physically weak by cutting off circulation and obstructing natural growth. It also renders them physically vulnerable by impeding their escape from natural disasters, such as floods or fires, or from human assailants, such as Taiping rebels. The overriding argument against the practice in Xie's textbook and elsewhere is, however, that a woman with bound feet cannot mother strong citizens.[76] The compilers of the *Newest Chinese Reader for Women* expound on the concept of mothers of citizens in a lesson on the founding of an anti-footbinding association in 1908. "Women are the mothers of citizens," the lesson announces. "The strength or weakness of the male body is directly related to the strength or weakness of the female body.

Today women bind their feet and weaken their bodies, and as a result men cannot be strong. This will affect the future of our race."[77] The author of the article on the sacrosanct expression "women are the mothers of citizens," declares that a three-part program for women's education aimed at strengthening the nation would start with the abolition of footbinding.[78]

Maternal Appropriations

Physical education and lessons in global politics were radically new dimensions of women's learning in turn-of-the-twentieth-century China. From ancient times, however, promoters of fetal education had made connections between the bodies of mothers and sons, and didactic texts for women held mothers responsible for their sons' early moral education. Proponents of the various new theorizations of motherhood at the turn of the twentieth century drew on different aspects of this historical legacy. Whether they heralded mothers of citizens or a new notion of wise mothers, all used the cultural stature of historical maternal paragons to forward their new, nationalist views of motherhood. This pervasive use of historical exemplars distinguishes Chinese materials on modern motherhood. Although the mothers-of-citizens idea was indebted to the Japanese ideology of good wives and wise mothers, and both of these East Asian constructs resonated with aspects of Victorian womanhood and republican motherhood, only in China did history remain so integral to newly politicized visions of the mother's role.[79]

ERASURES

Historical erasure was as important as historical appropriation in the archeomodernists' imagining of mother of citizens. Criticizing recent maternal practice just as they had condemned the writings of the late imperial woman of talent, archeomodernists belittled loving mothers (*cimu*) who spoiled their children and were incapable of nurturing either their character or their intellect. They made this deficient mother the stand-in for an alleged lack of moral rigor in the Chinese social ethos, just as the woman of talent was a metonym for obsolete cultural practices. Her maternal pampering was, they deemed, as harmful to the renewal of Chinese culture as the talented woman's sentimental lyricism.

This critical view of the loving mother was consistent with the hierarchy of maternal roles first established in the *Record of Rites*. According to the ritual classic, three kinds of women are responsible for bringing up a child. In descending order of importance, they are, first, the teacher (*zishi*), who is noted for her integrity, respectful bearing, and seriousness, "her carefulness and freedom from talkativeness." Second is the loving mother (*cimu*), and third the guardian mother (*baomu*), both of whose roles are considered less important and described in less detail.[80] Wei Xiyuan maintains this distinction between mother teachers and loving mothers in his meliorist biographical collection. He claims that uneducated mothers love their children with "indulgence" (*guxi*), whereas educated mothers love with the "principles of righteousness" (*yifang*).[81] Unlike his archeomodern counterparts, however, Wei believed there were mothers of this latter principled type in the recent past.

In painting their disapproving picture of recent motherhood, archeomodernists elided the crucial historical and cultural role elite women had played in passing rudimentary classical knowledge on to their children through the tradition of family learning (*jiaxue*). In the Song, a dynasty not renowned for enlightened views on women, many mothers of the educated class taught their sons and daughters to read and introduced them to the elementary texts that were the foundation of a classical education. Women continued to assume the role of maternal instructress throughout the late imperial period.[82] At the turn of the twentieth century, however, male and female archeomodernists adamantly repressed this legacy.

An essay written by members of the Tokyo-based women's organization, the Humanitarian Association, declares that the level of women's education in China was historically so low that mothers were unfit to educate their own children. "While in Europe and America, children learn their habits from their mothers," they state, "in China, the mother's level of knowledge is even lower than that of her children."[83] An article on family education published in an overseas journal and most probably written by a man makes a similar point. It asserts that Japanese and Western authorities understand the importance of motherhood. According to the Japanese, "to build a good family you must first cultivate a wise mother." And according to Napoleon, the "fate of a child depends exclusively on the extent of the mother's knowledge." The situation is different in China, the author laments, where women are ignorant and incapable of self-improvement. "Family education in China has to use a different method," he concludes. "Fathers must take responsibility for educating their children."[84]

Textbooks uphold this narrative of ignorant mothers of the recent past just as they excoriate the woman of talent. In a chapter on "The Limitations of Maternal Authority" (Weimu zhi quanxian), Wu Tao announces that in China, fathers customarily had exclusive responsibility for the education of their sons and daughters. Women did not concern themselves with these matters and were rarely educated.[85]

Several textbook compilers juxtapose inadequate Chinese mothers of the recent past not only with accomplished Western mothers but with ancient Chinese exemplars. Yang Qianli claims, for example, that wise mothers had existed in early Chinese history. From the Zhou through the Qin and Han dynasties, female education flourished and gave rise to the sages and heroes of the era.[86] The woman Sun Qingru, a textbook author and journalist, contends that, rather than use the rites to teach and restrain their young as ancient women had, uneducated women in recent centuries pampered (*niai*) and spoiled their offspring.[87] Wu Tao describes the gentle instruction (*cixun*) these mothers offer their children as lacking all intellectual or moral substance.[88]

While the indulgent mother became a generic category of critique, some archeomodern texts describe specific historical mothers. The section on "Maternal Exemplars" (Muxing) in a school song provides an example from the writings of the Song scholar Cheng Yi (Yichuan, 1033–1107) of a mother who had ruined her son by covering for him whenever he made a mistake. Because of this maternal complicity, the son was disrespectful of authority as a boy and lacking in manners as an adult.[89] The compilers of the *Newest Chinese Reader for Women*, whose explicit objective was to cultivate "excellent wives and wise mothers" (*lingqi xianmu*), include a number of negative lessons on overly lenient contemporary mothers. One was the mother of a certain Yu Qing, who so loved her son that she took him at his word even when he lied or exaggerated. As a result, he lacked moral judgment and was known as a "master of empty talk" (*xuyan jia*).[90]

EXEMPLARY HISTORICAL MOTHERS

Although negative historical exemplars were few in turn-of-the-twentieth-century materials, meliorists and archeomodernists widely invoked past maternal paragons. The distinctiveness of their two positions becomes apparent when we juxtapose their strategies for appropriating these paragons and their divergent uses of the same stories. Their representations of exemplary mothers, nonetheless, share a number of characteristics central to Chinese conceptions of motherhood.

Great Chinese mothers are uniformly celebrated for raising sons—never daughters—whom they sternly instruct rather than lovingly encourage. Their experience of motherhood is portrayed as one of suffering and sacrifice rather than joy and fulfillment, and they often do violence to themselves or to objects around them in order to impress life's crucial moral—rather than intellectual—lessons on their young.[91] They are generally widows who, like many other notable Chinese women, enter the historical record because their husbands are dead, absent, or otherwise unable to perform their normative roles. More than mere biological reproducers, they are also cultural producers credited with giving birth to foundational moments in Chinese civilization.

Among the many celebrated maternal exemplars, certain Ur-mothers stand out in turn-of-the-twentieth-century materials: the three mothers of the Zhou dynasty (Zhou shi san mu), and the mothers of Mencius (Meng Zi, 372–289 BCE) and Ouyang Xiu (1007–72). Their life stories are repeated in the full range of late Qing texts from the *Elementary Learning for Girls and Women* by the eternalist Dai Li to the most self-consciously new textbooks, from meliorist biographical collections to essays in women's journals. Their stories are also the template for biographies of later women who are generally featured only in meliorist texts.

The Three Mothers of the Zhou:
Fetal Education and Cultural Prestige

The turn-of-the-twentieth-century emphasis on the mother's indirect national role is reflected in the prominence of the three mothers of the Zhou in texts of the period. These women, the mothers or wives of the legendary founders of the Zhou dynasty (1122–255 BCE) were: Tai Ren (fl. 1160 BCE), the mother of King Wen, conqueror of the Shang dynasty and founder of the Zhou; Tai Si (fl. 1140 BCE), the consort of King Wen (fl. 1140 BCE); and Tai Jiang (fl. 1122 BCE), the wife of King Wen's son, King Wu (fl. 1122 BCE), the first ruler of the Zhou. Their collective story first appears in early texts including the *Discourses of the States* (*Guo yu*), the *Book of Odes*, the *Records of the Grand Historian*, the *Han History*, and the *Arrayed Traditions of Women's Lives*.

Tai Ren is the prime exemplar of fetal education and biological motherhood. In the *Discourses of the States*, a certain Minister Xu uses her example of impeccable comportment during her pregnancy with the future King Wen to explain the importance of fetal education to Duke Wen of Jin. Xu notes that a child's capacity to learn is determined by his "physical constitution" (*zhi*), which is predetermined by the quality of his education in the womb.[92] In succeeding centuries, Tai Ren's example continued to be used in discussions of prenatal education in family instructional manuals, didactic materials, and influential philosophical texts such as Zhu Xi's *Elementary Learning*.[93] The tradition continues in late Qing didactic materials. Dai Li, whose *Elementary Learning for Girls and Women* is loosely modeled on Zhu Xi's *Elementary Learning*, foregrounds the importance of Tai Ren in her discussion of motherhood.[94] Zeng Yi includes details from Liu Xiang's entry on Tai Ren in the section of the *Exhortation to Women's Learning* on fetal education (without explicitly naming her).[95]

Wei Xiyuan opens the section on maternal exemplars in the *Illustrated Biographies* with Liu Xiang's version of Tai Ren's story in the *Arrayed Traditions*. According to this account, King Wen's unsurpassed talent, virtue, and compassion could be attributed to Tai Ren's extraordinary attentiveness during her pregnancy. She avoided unusual colors or sounds, was careful of her position when she slept or sat, and was vigilant about how her food was cut (see Figure 30). Wei gives this ancient account a contemporary, global relevance in his commentary. "The rise and fall of nations results," he writes, from such careful practices of fetal education.[96]

Archeomodernists introduce the imperative of women's education into the nexus of fetal education and nation. As previously noted, Liang Qichao—whose teacher, Kang Youwei, tied education in the womb to the improvement of humanity—asserts the national importance of fetal education in his essay on female education.[97] Jing Yuanshan promotes formal schooling for girls and women in 1899 by underlining the crucial role women have played in Chinese history. Without Tai Ren and Tai Si, he asks, "how would there have been Kings Wen and Wu?"[98] Writing in a journal devoted to the promotion of women's rights and female education, Sun Qingru similarly invokes the accomplishments of the "three mothers of the Zhou" to posit the relevance of women's learning to China's national survival.[99] Textbook authors make comparable connections. Wu Tao declares, for example, that the culture of the illustrious Zhou dynasty—a model for China's future glory—"was rooted in the inner chambers."[100]

Meliorist texts also feature later mothers who followed Tai Ren's example. The "New Chinese and Foreign Arrayed Traditions of Women's Lives" includes a biography entitled "Mother Li's Fetal Education" (Li Taifuren zhi taijiao), which reiterates that a mother's moral and intellectual influence

Figure 30 Tai Ren's careful practice of fetal education
SOURCE: WXY, VI.1

begins in pregnancy. The subject of the biography is the mother of Wan Chengcang of Nanchang, chancellor of the Hanlin Academy in the Yong-zheng (r. 1723–35) and early Qianlong (r. 1736–96) eras. In the biography, Wan's mother worships daily in a Buddhist temple during her pregnancy (see Figure 7). Rather than pray that her son "will become a high official," she entreats that he "follow in the scholarly tradition of his lineage." Wan eventually enters school at a young age and develops the same passion for the Wang Yangming (1472–1528) style of Confucianism as his ancestors. His love of learning is attributed to his fetal education.[101]

Mencius's Mother: Setting the Context for Civilization

The quintessential maternal exemplar in both ancient and late Qing texts is the mother of the Confucian philosopher Mencius (Meng Zi). Turn-of-the-twentieth-century materials offer specific examples of Mencius's mother's maternal rectitude drawn from the *Arrayed Traditions of Women's Lives* and from another Han dynasty text, *Master Han's Illustrations of the Didactic Applications of the 'Classic of Songs'* (*Han shi waizhuan*). In the first example, which appears only in the *Arrayed Traditions*, Mother Meng moves her home three times—from the vicinity of a graveyard, to the neighborhood of a marketplace, and, finally, close to a temple—to ensure that her son is exposed to the right influences (see Figure 31).[102] The second tale, and the one most frequently represented visually, appears in both the *Arrayed Traditions* and *Master Han's Illustrations*. According to this story, the young Mencius returns from school and announces to his mother that he is going to discontinue his studies. She responds by slashing the piece of cloth she has spent long hours weaving. This dramatic act shows Mencius the irreparable damage he would do to his education by interrupting his lessons.[103]

Figure 31 Mencius's mother finally makes her home next to a temple
SOURCE: Xie Chongxie, 39b.

The third story, from *Master Han's Illustrations*, describes how Mencius's mother teaches her son the value of trustworthiness. When Mencius asks her why their neighbor killed his pig, she lies, saying it is for Mencius to eat. She then buys meat for her son from the neighbor in order to make good on her word.[104]

The various late Qing appropriations of these tales of Mother Meng convey specific political or cultural meanings. Archeomodern authors explicitly politicize this canonical figure. As noted above, Yang Qianli ties her to China's national struggle, opening the three chapters devoted to her in his *New Reader* with the declaration: "Women are the mothers of citizens."[105] Compilers of the *Newest Chinese Reader for Women* also gave this ancient exemplar a new political relevance. While a lesson in the first volume merely recounts the three most familiar anecdotes associated with her, a lesson "On Bravery" (Shuoyong) in volume seven casts her as a national heroine.

The "On Bravery" lesson elaborates on the story of Mencius's mother, the neighbor, and the pig. It describes Mother Meng selling her hairpins and ear ornaments—details that do not appear in the original text—in order to buy the meat for her son. The practice of women selling their personal ornaments to contribute to their family's livelihood was deeply rooted in Chinese history. In the late Qing, however, it was reoriented from the family toward the polity. Women were encouraged to pawn their jewelry or clothing in order to contribute to the government, buy stock in national railways, or otherwise benefit the public welfare.[106] In depicting Mencius's mother engaging in what had become an established early-twentieth-century expression of female patriotism, the compilers simultaneously infused long-standing maternal roles with new political meaning and sanctioned new feminine political practices.[107]

These political resonances are reinforced by the lesson's association of Mother Meng with an international array of exemplars. One of these is a Chinese heroine, the wife of Zheng Yizong of the Tang dynasty, who beats off thieves in order to protect her mother-in-law.[108] Others are contemporary foreign heroines who act selflessly and courageously in turn-of-the-century global political struggles. They include Japanese female patriots who sell their hair to raise money for the army and brave Western social heroines like those discussed in Chapter 2 who "risk their lives . . . following armies [onto battlefields] and caring for the sick and dying" as Red Cross volunteers. What these women, from Mencius's mother to the Red Cross nurses, share, according to the author of the lesson, is a "zeal for the public welfare" (*jigong haoshan*). This commitment enables them to transcend their weak bodies and contribute to national history.[109]

In contrast to archeomodern commentators, meliorists did not take Mother Meng's story in this heroic, nationalist direction. Wei Xiyuan recounts the same three anecdotes found in most textbooks of the period and foregrounds the story of the slashed weaving. He entitles the entry "Halting the Loom to Raise a Sage" (Duanji qisheng) and uses an image of Mencius's mother weaving as the accompanying illustration (see Figure 32). Wei departs from other treatments of Mencius's mother, however, by including a fourth example of her rectitude drawn from the *Arrayed Traditions* but rarely included in turn-of-the-twentieth-century materials. In this episode,

Figure 32 Mencius's mother halts the loom to raise a sage
SOURCE: WXY, VI.2

Mother Meng is no longer the authoritative instructor of her young son but the submissive mother of her adult son. When Mencius explains to her that he hesitates to leave the state where he is serving as an official because of her age, she responds that the decision is entirely his own. In accordance with the ritual principles she taught him, her role is to uphold the thrice following (*sancong*)—the stipulation that a woman successively follows her father, husband, and son throughout the course of her life—and submit to his wishes.[110]

Wei's inclusion of this anecdote about the adult Mencius highlights a second difference between meliorist and archeomodern representations of motherhood. Unique to meliorist texts was the topos of the mother as interlocutor with and advisor to her adult son. These mothers embody different female capacities than did mothers of young boys. While the latter impart basic moral lessons to their young sons, reflecting the archeomodern commitment to new historical departures, the former maintain influence over their adult sons, mirroring the meliorist commitment to cultural continuity. Implicit in these different depictions of motherhood are contrasting idealizations of the relationships between women and citizenship. The influence of mothers of young sons was primarily pre-political and in line with the archeomodernists' disparagement of Chinese women's current intellectual and political abilities. In contrast, mothers who gave ethical and tactical advise to adult sons had an—albeit indirect—influence on politics. This was consonant with the meliorists' valuation of female talent that was properly channeled through the male members of their families toward the greater good.

Several mothers of adult sons that Wei Xiyuan, *Beijing Women's Journal* writers, and other meliorists celebrate first appear in the *Arrayed Traditions*. The mother of General Zifa of Chu (Chu Jiang Zifa) demonstrates not only her good judgment but her knowledge of precedent by drawing on the historical example of King Gou Jian of Yue in convincing her son of the importance of treating his troops well.[111] Tian Jizi's mother successfully admonishes him against political corruption.[112] The mothers of Chen Ying and Wang Ling, both of the Former Han dynasty, are models of political and military understanding.[113] The mother of Jun Buyi teaches her son, a magistrate in the Han capital, the value of being lenient in applying the law.[114] And Lady Wu gives her son, Sun Ce (174–200), sound military advice.[115]

Sage advisors from later periods include Lady Sun, who teaches her son

Yu Ze (fl. 341) the importance of loyalty; the mother of Wang Yifang (615–69), who encourages her son to censor a corrupt official even though this would jeopardize his own career; the mother of Li Jingrang, who offers her son, a general of the Tang dynasty, military guidance; and Lady Cui, mother of the Sui-Tang official Zheng Shanguo (572–629), who listens behind a curtain when her son discusses matters of policy, privately conveying her disapproval to him when he does not act within the bounds of propriety.[116]

The "New Chinese and Foreign Arrayed Traditions of Women's Lives" includes more recent mothers of this type. The mother of the official Yan Zhongcheng (fl. 1750) resolves a problem Yan faces as department magistrate of Pingdu (Shandong) in the Kangxi period. When a flood devastates the community, mother Yan issues granary tickets to the destitute so that they can purchase food. The emperor rewards the family by promoting Yan to prefect and honoring his mother with an imperial title.[117]

As this last example suggests, another difference between melioristists and archeomodernists is their depiction of mothers from the mid- to late-imperial period. While archeomodernists dismiss these women, meliorists celebrate a vast array of them as later incarnations of Mencius's famous mother. These women, like their ancient predecessor, are harsh moral instructresses, not lenient sentimentalists.

Prominent among these strict instructresses are mothers of Song Confucian scholars. Wei Xiyuan depicts men as inherently "barbaric" and their mothers as inherently civilizing in his commentary on the story of the mother of Kou Laigong (961–1023) of the Song dynasty. While all young men crave adventure and thrive on hunting and horseback riding, he notes, it is their mothers' responsibility to restrain these impulses and teach them the importance of study and scholarship. The account itself records an incident resonant with Mother Meng slashing her weaving upon hearing her son's decision to abandon his studies: Mother Kou hurls a hammer at her own foot in frustration over Laigong's preference for hunting over studying. The shocked Laigong—like the chastened Mencius—immediately changes his attitude. He eventually becomes a famous prime minister of the Song dynasty.[118]

Wei also celebrates the mother of a famous adept of the Song Confucian school of principle (*lixue*), Lü Xizhe (1039–1116). He describes the harsh regime to which Mother Lü subjects her son, forcing him to stand in the rain for long periods of time at age ten, for example. Like Mencius's mother,

Mother Lü also attempts to shield her son from corrupt influences. She forbids him to go to tea or wine shops and to read books on inappropriate topics.[119] In conjunction with Mother Lü, Wei commends another Song exemplar, the mother of the famous Cheng brothers, Cheng Hao (Mingdao, 1032–85) and Cheng Yi. Like Mother Lü, Mother Cheng regulates what her sons eat, drink, and wear, and teaches them to restrain their desires. As a result, they become sages of their time.[120]

These and other devoted mothers use their maternal influence not only to raise upright sons but to enrich Chinese civilization. Wei extols women who, like Mother Meng, create the conditions for their sons', and, by extension, the culture's, development. Lady Cheng (fl. 1040) of the Song dynasty, the mother of the famous literatus Su Shi (Dongpo, 1037–1101) and the wife of Su Xun (Mingjiu, 1009–66), makes it possible for the men in her family to study by taking responsibility for all practical matters. Her two sons are thus able to devote their energies to learning and become famous classical scholars.[121] Similarly, the mother of Liang Tingzuo (fl. 1700), Lady Feng (fl. 1650), of the early Qing dynasty, not only helps her immediate family members pursue their studies but purchases land for the establishment of a local school.[122]

One final distinguishing feature of late imperial motherhood in meliorist materials is a tentative departure from the model of the harsh maternal instructress toward a gentler version of the mothers of Mencius or Song dynasty scholars. The representation of the mother of the prominent Han Learning scholar Hong Liangji (1746–1809) in the "New Chinese and Foreign Arrayed Traditions of Women's Lives" is the foremost example of a humanized but not indulgent later maternal figure.[123] The account represents Mother Hong as an heir to Mother Meng. The accompanying illustration depicts her weaving at her loom with the young Liangji reading at a small table by her side (see Figure 33). At the same time, the biography portrays her as a woman of feeling. In the defining incident, her son reads a passage from the *Decorum Ritual* (*Yi li*) aloud that states "the husband is Heaven for his wife." His widowed mother breaks into tears and exclaims, "whom shall I honor?" Hong abruptly stops his reading in order to not upset her further. Hong's later accomplishments reveal this same sensitivity. According to the "New Chinese and Foreign Arrayed Traditions," after serving as a Hanlin compiler, Hong established himself as a painter, poet, and calligrapher. He remained highly virtuous, the legacy of his mother's careful upbringing.[124]

中外新列女傳（一）
洪太夫人
教子成名

Figure 33 Mother Hong weaving at her loom with the young Liangji reading
by her side
SOURCE: "Hong"

Ouyang Xiu's Mother:
Widows in Constrained Circumstances

Mother Meng and later incarnations like Mother Hong were iconic chaste
mothers: women whose singular purpose after the death of their husbands
was to properly raise their sons. This image of the mother who is not only wise
and competent but righteous and pure, is further consolidated in the centuries
after Liu Xiang wrote the *Arrayed Traditions*.[125] In the Yuan dynasty, when
scholars were determined to reassert the primacy of Confucian doctrine under Mongol rule, a new maternal model emerged: the widowed and indigent
mother of the Northern Song official Ouyang Xiu, Lady Zheng (fl. 1010).

First featured in the *Song History* (*Song shi*), Ouyang's mother became
the prototype of the woman who overcame the loneliness of widowhood
and the hardships of poverty in order to raise an exceptional son. In what
became a canonical gesture, Lady Zheng, who could not afford brushes, ink,
or paper, instructed her son by drawing characters on the ground with a reed

(see Figure 34). As the concern with female chastity intensified in the late imperial period, the example of Ouyang Xiu's mother was used to encourage young widows in constrained circumstances to devote themselves to raising the children of their first husband, rather than serving a second.

After the mother of Mencius, with whom she is often paired, the mother of Ouyang is the maternal exemplar most frequently featured in archeomodern textbooks. The second of two lessons devoted to "Maternal Education" (Mujiao) in Xie Chongxie's elementary ethics primer describes Lady Zheng using rush faggots to educate her son.[126] Xu Jiaxing and Wu Tao celebrate the mothers of Ouyang and Mencius in tandem as model mother-instructresses.[127] The song "A Small Collection of Chinese Heroines" ("Zhongguo nüjie xiao yuefu") presents a simplified lyrical rendition of Mother Ouyang's *Song History* biography under the rubric of model mothers.[128]

Meliorists also celebrate Ouyang Xiu's mother. In an entry subtitled "To

Figure 34 The impoverished Mother Ouyang writing characters on the ground
SOURCE: Xie Chongxie, 44b

Teach One's Children with Great Maternal Patience" (Huadijiaozi [lit., To teach the child by drawing characters on the ground with a reed]), Wei Xiyuan praises Lady Zheng for raising her son to follow in his father's footsteps.[129] The "New Chinese and Foreign Arrayed Traditions of Women's Lives" honors a late imperial exemplar, the mother of Wang Tingzhen (1757–1827), née Cheng, whose story echoes Mother Ouyang's. Despite having lost her husband when Tingzhen was twelve, Lady Cheng brings her son up to become a righteous official.[130] The account describes how mother and son were so poor that they often had only one meal a day: the illustration depicts them sharing a single bowl of rice. The quality Mother Cheng exemplifies is profound dignity in the face of poverty. She refuses to tell other people about their plight, feeling it is more shameful to ask for assistance than to be poor. Her self-respect shapes her son's character. He is disciplined in performing his official duties, stern and serious, and always attentive to decorum: "This he owed to his mother's teaching."[131]

The conventions of Ouyang Xiu's mother's biography are even used to overlay meliorist accounts of contemporary women who, like Mother Ouyang, endure poverty and widowhood. One such story involves a beggar woman named Liu. Although she had only a rudimentary education, she is extremely filial. This quality attracts her husband, whom she marries at the age of sixteen and with whom she soon has a son. Shortly thereafter her husband and father both die in a fire. Left with nothing, Liu is forced to beg but uses every spare moment she has to instruct her son. She "breaks a stick and writes on the ground" to teach him how to write, just as Ouyang's mother had. With the money she earns begging, she buys her son books, which he recites as she begs, often earning alms for his cleverness. In 1910, Liu becomes ill and impresses upon her son the importance of learning and upholding the dignity of his ancestors. After she dies he continues to study and becomes the founder of a school for the poor (*pinmin xuexiao*).[132]

Counterpoint: The Case against Motherhood

The various reappropriations of historical models and retheorizations of maternal roles discussed in this chapter reveal the complex ways late Qing authors used motherhood to mediate women's entrée into the public realm and bridge the spheres of family and nation. The connections they drew between domesticity and politics were not completely new in the early twentieth century. Maternal influence had flowed from the inner quarters to the outer world in Chinese gender ideology from at least the time of the *Arrayed Traditions of Women's Lives*. The turn-of-the-twentieth-century concepts of wise mothers, good wives and wise mothers, and mothers of citizens were merely new, racially inflected, and globally situated extensions of this long-standing principle.

Both meliorists, who continued to cast women as wise mothers, and archeomodernists, who self-consciously used the new term "mothers of citizens," emphasized the political ramifications of the biological mother's role. Wei Xiyuan notes in several of his commentaries that women could play crucial, if indirect, roles in strengthening the nation. These roles began in the earliest stages of their sons' lives in utero and continued through their maturity as dynastic officials. Contemporary problems of bureaucratic corruption and military incompetence would be resolved, Wei asserts, if only there are wise women like the ancient mothers of Tian Jizi and Li Jingrang to counsel their sons.

Archeomodernists linked motherhood to an only slightly more activist form of female political engagement. Publicists and textbook authors underscored the links between women's education and national survival by praising Mencius's mother as a patriot and celebrating the role of ancient mothers in establishing Chinese culture. While they used the mother-of-citizens ideal to sanction new spheres of feminine knowledge and a new feminine bodily hexis, they continued to represent the woman's role as setting the context for, rather than directly contributing to, civilization. Female literacy would produce effective mothers and wives by teaching women how to balance household account books, pay taxes on the family's estate, and write letters that would keep sojourning husbands apprised of developments at home.[133] The assumption was that early-twentieth-century women, like the mothers of Su Shi in the Song dynasty or Liang Tingzuo in the Qing, would manage the domestic sphere so that male members of the family could pursue their more consequential roles as scholars or officials in the outer realm. While the authors of these pedagogical texts did emphasize the relevance of scientific and social scientific theories to the domestic arts, this new knowledge—of hygiene and child psychology, for example—ultimately reinforced, rather than transformed existing feminine roles.

Both archeomodernists and meliorists thus linked women to the nation indirectly through motherhood and education. They tied the rise of a new patriotic citizenry to superior mothering and superior mothering to female schooling. Collapsing maternal, nationalist, and educational agendas, they defined the aim of female education as the development of maternal skills, and maternal skill as the effective instruction of China's future *male* citizens.

Presentists vehemently resisted this mediated approach to women's learning and female political engagement. Chen Yiyi (fl. 1909), the male founder of the *The National Women's Journal* (*Nübao*) and a fellow traveler of the revolutionary martyr Qiu Jin, claimed in 1909 that recently founded Chinese girls' schools reduced women to high-level slaves, the "literate maidservants (*shizi zhi binü*) of their husbands and sons."[134] He and other critics understood education as an empowering rather than a utilitarian process, and motherhood as an impediment to, rather than the endpoint of, study. Fully aware of the nationalist imperatives that underlay the new women's education, they insisted that women gain and act on knowledge of global politics themselves. Rather than train to become mothers of citizens, they had to become citizens in their own right.

Wu Mengban, whose words are featured in the epigraph to this chapter, was convinced she could serve the nation more effectively by educating herself rather than raising and instructing a child. Hers is not an isolated case. The revolutionary doctor Zhang Zhujun (b. ca. 1879), a promoter of women's education and professionalization, refused to either marry or have children. She was convinced domestic duties would hinder her from contributing to the national cause.[135] The revolutionary martyr Qiu Jin rejected motherhood after the fact, abandoning her young son and daughter when she left to fulfill her educational and revolutionary aspirations in Japan.[136]

Yan Bin, medical student and editor of the *Magazine of the New Chinese Woman*, was also an outspoken advocate of a new political role for women unmediated by motherhood. In her journal, she promotes the ideal of female citizens (*nüzi guomin*). Premised on a direct relationship between women and politics, this ideal was also, Yan emphasizes, unburdened by history. While eternalists, meliorists, and archeomodernists invested the constructs of wise mothers, good wives and wise mothers, or mothers of citizens with historical resonances, Yan insists that the power of the term "female citizen" lay in its rupture with the past. "From the time when Cang Jie first invented Chinese writing some five thousand years ago," she writes, "these four characters [*nüzi guomin*] have never been used together."[137] It was time, Yan and other presentists asserted, that women overcame their objectification through archeomodern invocations of national motherhood and meliorist notions of maternal virtue and began to write and make history themselves.

PART THREE

New Global Hierarchies of Female Heroism

> Hua Mulan came from a family of high-ranking military officers and would have had some knowledge of military affairs when she joined the army. Joan of Arc, in contrast, was from a family of peasants. Mulan's sole achievement was to replace her father, whom she faithfully served, while Joan defied her father in order to respond to a higher national calling. . . . And, whereas Mulan's name is only known in China, Joan is a global heroine. . . . She never could have achieved what she did as a cloistered woman of the inner chambers.
>
> MEI ZHU, *"Faguo jiuwang nüjie Ruoan zhuan"*
> *(Biography of Joan, the Heroic French Savior)*

Heroism joined talent and virtue as a distinct female quality in the turn-of-the-twentieth-century Chinese discourse. As the epigraph above, from a biography of Joan of Arc (1412–31), indicates, this new quality was understood globally and hierarchically. Late Qing authors who were determined to mobilize their female compatriots for the national struggle, scrutinized, compared, and ranked the heroic achievements of historical Chinese and Western women. While the pseudonymous Mei Zhu declares Joan of Arc superior to Hua Mulan, Jiang Zhiyou proclaims both Mulan and Joan inferior to Harriet Beecher Stowe.[1] Contemporary Chinese women were also pegged on the global heroism index. Less than a month after the execution of the revolutionary martyr Qiu Jin, a "Frustrated Female Worthy" (Mingyi nüshi) wrote that a mere handful of women had risen above the benighted, animal-like female mass in Chinese history. These women, who included the Southern Song patriot Liang Hongyu (ca. 1100–35) and the Ming loyalist

Qin Liangyu (d. 1648), had only struggled on behalf of their families, however. Qiu Jin alone had fought for citizens' rights (like a Western heroine) and shed her blood for the Chinese people.[2]

The decisive stroke against Liang Hongyu, Qin Liangyu, and Hua Mulan in these cross-cultural assessments is their adherence to a cardinal principle of the regime of feminine virtue: service to family. Whereas in the past, women warriors—like Mulan—were praised first and foremost for their familial virtue, the new turn-of-the-twentieth-century code of heroism was defined *against* the regime of feminine virtue. This shift in values is reflected in a linguistic shift. While eternalists and meliorists continued to describe heroines as exemplary women or *lienü*, archeomodernists and presentists only invoked this term derisively. Instead they employed a new complex of expressions to connote women of valor, including *nü haojie, nü yingxiong, nüjie, nü yingci*, and *jinguo zhi jie*.

The presentists' prime mission was to liberate female heroism from Confucian moral constraints, just as the archeomodernists' was to reorient female talent toward the nation, and the meliorists' was to attenuate the excesses of the late imperial regime of virtue. While archeomodernists joined presentists in including women in the new national heroic ethos and invoking Western women as models, they did not share the presentists' commitment to decoupling female heroism from all forms of feminine virtue. Nor did they sanction the presentist belief in individual freedom through often violent political engagement. Continuing to hold a nested view of the polity, archeomodernists believed women's new national roles should be mediated by their long-standing domestic roles. This is evident in their idealization of mothers of citizens rather than female citizens. It is also apparent in their tempering of the achievements of Western social heroines with maternal tropes—including the language of loving mothers (*cimu*), which had lost all currency in discussions of native Chinese mothers. Chapter 5 examines how these competing visions of heroism and nationalism were articulated through presentist and archeomodern representations of Chinese and Western women.

Chapter 6 shifts the focus to late Qing women—from firebrands like Qiu Jin to more muted individuals—who formulated and appropriated the new feminine-heroic ideal themselves. No longer the voiceless objects of a Confucian discourse on heroic female self-sacrifice, these women were new national actors: public writers, social activists, and female educators. Their new roles were not only enabled but constrained by nationalist ideologies, however, and they were fraught with gender paradoxes. The contradictions and disjunctions in women's experience in this period highlight tensions between the archeomodern and presentist positions, and expose aporias in the turn-of-the-twentieth-century Chinese nationalist project.

The Chinese Woman Warrior and the Western Heroine

> All women today know the name of Mulan; it is un-
> necessary to describe or praise her again. While the
> common view is that she was nothing more than a filial
> girl, however, I assert that she was a militant female citi-
> zen of our nation. She stopped at nothing in pursuing
> and killing the northern barbarians, and her deeply felt
> patriotism burst forth in the moment of crisis. Doesn't
> this make her an avid defender of her race? I certainly
> believe it does. Readers—do not just celebrate Mulan's
> filiality. Celebrate her courage!
>
> XU DINGYI, *Zuguo nüjie weiren zhuan*
> *(Biographies of Great Women of Our Country), 1906*

In the account quoted above, Xu Dingyi radically resignifies the story of the great Chinese woman warrior Hua Mulan, a devoted daughter who disguises herself as a man and responds to the emperor's call to arms in the place of her old and infirm father. In his early-twentieth-century retelling, Xu shifts the meaning of this story from filiality to fearlessness, from a dutiful daughter's return home to an ethnic Han nationalist's heroic struggle against threatening foreign—read Manchu—forces.[1] The qualities Xu most praises in Mulan are those exalted in his own day: courage and self-sacrificing patriotism. Using wildly anachronistic language, he describes her as a militant female citizen (*zuguo zhi nü jun guomin*) and an avid defender of her race (*zhongzu zhuyi ciji zhe*) who was driven by a deep love of nation (*aiguo zhi cheng*). More than overlook what was commonly recognized as Mulan's primary virtue—her filiality—Xu challenges his readers to ignore it.[2]

The nationalist qualities with which Xu imbues Mulan's story were generally associated with foreign heroines. As this merging of a Chinese icon with Western-style patriotism suggests, representations of heroic women became a site of cross-cultural blending and global rivalry in late Qing China. In the first years of the twentieth century "the West" prevailed. Influential biographies of American and European women, including Harriet Beecher Stowe and Madame Roland, were printed and reprinted in leading Chinese journals in 1902.[3] Early the following year, two widely read collections of Western heroines were published. The first, *Twelve World Heroines* (*Shijie shier nüjie*), a translation from Japanese, appeared in February; the second, *Ten World Heroines* (*Shijie shi nüjie*), an anonymous Chinese work modeled on the first, a few months later. Western women remained fixtures in the Chinese cultural imaginary in the succeeding years as their stories were integrated into new-style textbooks and celebrated in the popular and women's press.

Not all presentists embraced this Westernization of the Chinese feminine heroic ideal, however. Xu Dingyi openly opposed it. Calling for an end to the "infatuation with Sofia [Perovskaia] and kowtowing to [Madame] Roland," he asserted the rival importance of Chinese exemplars like Hua Mulan.[4] A certain Zhou Dong assured his readers that these native exemplars were no less courageous than the likes of Perovskaia and Roland; they were simply less visible in historical documents. As long as the Chinese remained obsessed with submissiveness and chastity, brave-hearted figures like Mulan would be excluded from the historical record.[5] Presentists were committed to both ending this obsession and altering the way history was written.

Xu Dingyi announces in the preface to his *Biographies of Great Women of Our Country* that his compilation irrefutably demonstrates that Chinese women more than match their Western counterparts.[6] Ding Chuwo proclaims in an introduction to his journal, *Women's World* (*Nüzi shijie*), that the journal celebrates the national essence (*guocui*) rather than Western customs (*Oufeng*) and proves not only that women are as good as or better than men but that *Chinese* women are as good as or better than men.[7] Jin Tiange, in an inaugural essay for Ding's journal, praises the writings, elegance, chivalry, and capabilities of many of the same figures the *Women's World* celebrates: courageous heroines, female knights-errant (*youxia*), and accomplished women writers and artists from the "the 3,000 years of Chinese history." He also berates his audience "for searching far abroad while remaining ignorant of [the value in their own history] near at hand."[8]

Jin had not always been so exclusive in his promotion of heroic female

models, however. In *A Tocsin for Women* (*Nüjie zhong*), which was published the year before his *Women's World* essay, Jin unfavorably compares
contemporary Chinese women to *both* Western heroines like Joan of Arc,
Sofia Perovskaia (1854–81), and Florence Nightingale, and their own illustrious historical predecessors, including Ban Zhao and Hua Mulan.[9] In concluding *A Tocsin*, he provides a composite list of women who could best
serve as models for his female contemporaries: thirteen are Chinese, eight
are Western.[10]

Through Jin's friend Yang Qianli, author of the *New Reader for Girls and
Women*, this blended Sino-Western prototype for young Chinese women
became part of mainstream pedagogy.[11] Yang's textbook features eighteen
Chinese and ten Western exemplars—several of whom figure on Jin's lists.
As Yang explains in his introduction, the two sets of women serve different
but equally important functions: the historical Chinese exemplars are "the
past leaders of the new Chinese female citizen," while the recent Western
heroines "reflect her future image."[12]

The new global models of female heroism that Yang Qianli, Jin Tiange,
Ding Chuwo, Xu Dingyi, and others promoted were thus the product of in-
teractions between familiar tales of historical Chinese exemplars and newly
imported stories of Western heroines. These composite models reshaped
the semantic contours of the Chinese woman warrior tradition personified
by Hua Mulan and her heroic sisters. They also established a new Chinese
repertoire of Western patriots, anarchists, and revolutionaries embodied by
Joan of Arc and her intrepid sisters. These models did not, however, offer a
coherent vision of who the new Chinese heroine should be. Archeomodernists and presentists—the two groups most acutely concerned with defining
a new mode of female heroism—appropriated the deeds of native women of
valor and the exploits of foreign militants to divergent ends. Their representations of Chinese women warriors and Western heroines reveal fissures in
turn-of-the-century views of feminine virtue, cultural accommodation, and
China's national future.

Hua Mulan and Her Heroic Sisters

NON-MARTIAL ANCIENT HEROINES

Not all of Hua Mulan's heroic Chinese sisters were warriors. A number of
turn-of-the-twentieth-century materials represent non-martial exemplars as
national heroines. Two of the more prominent first appeared in the *Arrayed*

Traditions of Women's Lives: Ti Ying (ca. 167 BCE) and the "woman from Qishi in the state of Lu" (Lu Qishi nü). A third is the Han literatus Ban Zhao.

As recorded in the *Arrayed Traditions* and other early texts, Ti Ying's father, a Han dynasty official, Duke Chunyu Yi (b. 205 BCE), had been condemned to corporal punishment. Because he had no sons to come to his defense, the youngest of his five daughters, Ti Ying, courageously petitions the emperor on his behalf. In the petition, she indirectly admonishes the emperor for promulgating laws that made it impossible for a man convicted of a crime to redress his fault. Her clarity of argument persuades the emperor to change his laws and reject corporal punishment. Liu Xiang highlights Ti Ying's eloquence by including her story in the section of the *Arrayed Traditions* devoted to women who demonstrate "Skill in Argument" (Bian tong).[13]

This account had been resignified centuries before the late Qing dynasty. By the late imperial period, Ti Ying had become a paragon not of eloquence, but of filiality.[14] This shift is reflected in illustrations accompanying the story. In the earliest of these, Ti Ying stands or kneels alone, pleading with the emperor. Emphasis is thus on her courage and rhetorical abilities.[15] In late imperial, including late Qing, editions, however, she is always next to her father, who towers above her (see Figure 35).

While this filial emphasis distorts the meaning of the original Ti Ying story, it subtly challenges the regime of feminine virtue by tentatively sanctioning female autonomy. In the Ming and Qing dynasties, the regime had elevated fidelity (*jie*) to husband and service to marital kin over devotion to father or natal family. This is reflected in the removal of the *Classic of Filiality for Women* from Qing dynasty editions of the standard female didactic collection, the *Four Books for Women* (*Nü sishu*), and in the merging of the categories of filiality and fidelity in Qing-period local gazetteers.[16] Turn-of-the-twentieth-century authors and educators began to reverse this trend, returning the *Classic of Filiality for Women* to the curriculum for newly founded private girls' schools, and publishing it in vernacular editions. Textbooks and biographical collections of the period also reemphasize filiality.[17]

These include meliorist collections. Although Wei Xiyuan's *Illustrated Biographies of Resourceful Women, Past and Present* ultimately privileges the marital relationship, it opens with a section on "Filiality to Parents" (Xiao fumu) that celebrates eleven young women for extraordinary service to their *natal* parents.[18] The first is Ying Erzi (ca. 300 BCE), who chose to remain

Figure 35 "Ti Ying Saves Her Father"
SOURCE: Xie Chongxie, 35b

single out of filial devotion to her ill parents.[19] The second is Ti Ying. The illustration accompanying the entry depicts Ti Ying alone, boldly presenting her petition (see Figure 36).

The heroic implications of Ti Ying's filiality remain understated in Wei's meliorist text. They are, in contrast, deliberately drawn out by archeomodernists who link this ancient tale to the new causes of national and legal reform. In Yang Qianli's *New Reader for Girls and Women*, Ti Ying's desire to defend her father is the backdrop to her grander historic accomplishment. After the Han emperor hands down an edict ending corporal punishment, Yang explains, "several thousand years of cruel and sadistic punishment ended. Today, with the exception of capital punishment there is no corporal punishment. This is Ti Ying's achievement."[20] A biography published in the *Beijing-Tianjin Times* similarly declares that "Ti Ying killed two large birds with one stone: she saved her father's life and initiated reform of the cruelest aspects of the law. This was an unprecedented act of courage that left a mark in women's history and legal history. She is a Chinese heroine."[21]

Figure 36 Ti Ying boldly presenting her petition
SOURCE: WXY, I.2

Presentists more vigorously resignified Ti Ying's historic role. The woman author Yi Qin literally brings Ti Ying into the present as a modern-day patriot in an article on the future of Chinese women. Attempting to strip the ancient biography of all references to filiality as Xu had stripped Mulan's story, she declares, "If Ti Ying were to come to life again, she would transmute her love of her father into love of her compatriots."[22] Ding Chuwo and Jin Tiange, who were determined to redeem native heroines from the depths of Chinese history, represent this filial daughter who deferentially petitioned the emperor as a female knight-errant.[23]

The "woman from Qishi in the state of Lu" was also transformed into a new-style heroine in turn-of-the-twentieth-century materials. Originally featured in the "Benevolent Wisdom" (Ren zhi) section of Liu Xiang's *Arrayed Traditions*, she is more patriotic than heroic. Her story, like Ti Ying's, does not involve male guises or extraordinary feats of martial prowess. She, nonetheless, became a symbol of female political commitment in archeomodern and presentist texts.

The biography in the *Arrayed Traditions* opens with the woman from Qishi sobbing. When her neighbors assume she is unhappy because she is still unmarried, she protests that she is grieving for the state of Lu. The ruler is old, she laments, and the heir apparent is young. When her neighbors question what any of this has to do with her, she replies: "Everything." Everyone, she explains, including women and common people, suffers under an old and negligent ruler as they would suffer under a young and foolish successor.[24]

This politically aware paragon became a symbol of patriotism in mid- to late-nineteenth century women's poetry. Wang Caipin (d. 1893) invokes her life story together with Hua Mulan's in a poem on the Ming loyalist woman warrior Qin Liangyu.[25] By the early twentieth century the "Qishi lament" was a standard trope in nationalist writings by and for women. She is trumpeted in archeomodern pedagogy, including a lesson subtitled "Women Have the Responsibility to Be Patriotic" in Xu Jiaxing's ethics textbook.[26] She is also invoked in archeomodern and presentist articles in the women's press.

A lengthy piece published in the *Women's Eastern Times* in July 1911, just months before the 1911 Revolution, is a lament on the dearth of nation-minded women in China. Written by Zhu Huizhen, it introduces a number of contemporary women, including a certain Qi Wanzhen, the central figure. Qi, who came from a good family and had been educated at home by her mother, wants to study the new learning. She seeks out a tutor, a recent girls' school graduate, who not only teaches her history, geography, science, and algebra, but introduces her to ideas of family revolution and free marriage. Qi Wanzhen's greatest preoccupation, however, is with the fate of China. Looking to the past for guidance, she is moved to tears by the story of Mulan. Although she refers to the *Arrayed Traditions of Women's Lives* as "light reading," she ultimately takes the woman from Qishi as her model. Zhu Huizhen thus refers to her as "the second woman of Qishi."[27]

Like her historical predecessor and unlike her more radical contemporaries—including Qiu Jin, who is mentioned in the biography—Qi Wanzhen does not promote or engage in daring acts of violence or self-sacrifice.[28] "The second Qishi" dies of grief for the nation, having internalized the illness that plagued her country. Zhu asks pointedly in her concluding commentary: how many women are as concerned with China's fate as Qi had been?[29]

An article in Chen Yiyi's presentist *The National Women's Journal* uses the example of the woman of Qishi not only to expose the weakness of contemporary patriotic feeling but to legitimate female political participation. The author, a student from Hankou named Zhou Chunying, claims that her most educated female compatriots share the woman of Qishi's depth of national commitment. While Liu Xiang had implicitly compared the ancient paragon with her politically apathetic female peers, Zhou contrasts her own committed female peers with their politically apathetic male compatriots. These men are, Zhou declares, exclusively preoccupied with power politics, official promotions, and private affairs. They are perilously oblivious of national matters.[30]

Ban Zhao, the famed Han dynasty author of the *Precepts for Women* who archeomodernists widely invoked in their writings on female talent, was also redeemed in presentist polemics on female heroism. Xu Dingyi argues that Ban should be recognized as the great sage (*zhisheng*) of all women. Rereading her story in light of recent theories of sexual equality, he asserts that she should be more highly regarded than both Ma Rong (79–166), a contemporary Confucian scholar whom she had instructed in Han era history, and her own father, the illustrious Confucian scholar Ban Biao (3–54). Just as Ban Biao is widely praised for having nurtured the talent of his children, Ban Gu, Ban Chao, and Ban Zhao, Xu argues, Ban Zhao herself merits recognition for having instructed her sister-in-law, Cao Fengshan, and her daughter-in-law, Lady Ding.[31]

Female presentist authors even more dramatically recast Ban's life. In her article on the future of Chinese women, Yi Qin exclaims that if Ban Zhao were alive today, "her love of the sovereign"—manifest in her completion of the *Han Dynastic History* and her tutoring of Empress Deng—would be transmuted into "love of the nation."[32] Stories and dramas published in the new print media literally resurrect Ban as a progressive heroine. In a short story entitled "Repairing the Firmament" (Bu tianshi), the Chinese goddess Nüwa sends Ban back to earth to help reform women. Rather than give lessons in modesty and humility, the reincarnated Ban urges women to abandon old ideas, embrace enlightenment, organize themselves, and adopt a new militancy. Reflecting on her own didactic text, *Precepts for Women*, Ban concedes that while the book was respected in its own day, it had later done tremendous harm and remains deeply flawed from the vantage point of the present.[33]

The following year, the author of a theater script depicted Ban in a court of law presided over by the recently executed Qiu Jin. When Qiu accuses Ban of contributing to the oppression of Chinese women by instructing them to be lowly and meek, Ban defends herself by saying that she was merely responding to the demands of the palace ladies who employed her. Like Nüwa in the previously mentioned story, Qiu gives Ban a chance to redeem herself by returning to earth and using her rhetorical abilities to promote women's rights and female heroism. Once the world becomes fully enlightened on women's issues, Qiu promises, Ban Zhao's past crimes could finally be erased.[34]

THE MARTIAL HEROINE TRADITION

A number of exemplars first featured in the *Arrayed Traditions of Women's Lives* or the earliest dynastic histories were thus appropriated into turn-of-the-twentieth-century discourses on heroism. Most renowned women of valor belonged, however, to an informal tradition of women warriors (*nü yongshi*) that postdated Liu Xiang's *Arrayed Traditions* by some two hundred years.[35] Less formal than the exemplary female tradition generated by Liu's text, this informal tradition neither formed a coherent canon nor became part of official history. A few courageous women were featured in dynastic histories, but they rarely merited their own entries and were only briefly mentioned in the accounts of their husbands or fathers.[36] Other heroines, such as Hua Mulan, were first celebrated in more popular literary forms. A late Qing compiler of tales of heroic women thus had to "journey into the dark recesses of Chinese history" to seek out their scattered traces.[37]

Despite this textual dispersal, a corpus of woman warrior narratives culled from dynastic and local histories, vernacular literature, and scholars' jottings (*biji*) had emerged by the turn of the twentieth century.[38] Distinct in its historical origins, this tradition was also distinctive in its historical trajectory. While archeomodernists ended their lineage of literary paragons in the late imperial period, presentists traced the martial tradition through the Ming and Qing dynasties. Their heroic repertoire included Ming loyalists—whom archeomodernists also celebrated—and both resistors and supporters of the Taiping Heavenly Kingdom.

The defining qualities of these women warriors varied over time. Some were celebrated for their military aggressiveness, others for courageous resistance, and still others for self-sacrificing loyalty. Certain features of heroic female narratives remained constant over the centuries, however. First and foremost, the woman of valor does not act as a natural woman but as a surrogate man. Situated in masculine space—on the battlefield or in the army—she is a stand-in for, often disguised as, and/or works in concert with men. The potential subversiveness of her masculinized and often violent, public feats is tempered by specific narrative conventions. Her violation of the principles of the regime of feminine virtue is represented as transitory and as necessitated by extraordinary circumstances—social or political upheaval—that she helps stabilize. The turning point in her story is not the transgressive moment when she assumes masculine attire or a masculine role, but the moment of return, when order has been restored and she resumes her femininity. Layers of commentaries accrued over the centuries further neutralize the heroine's deeds by underscoring the values of filiality, fidelity, or loyalty these deeds ultimately served.

In the context of China's turn-of-the-twentieth-century national crisis, when bold action was considered crucial to China's survival, women warriors were prominently featured not only in archeomodern and presentist but also in meliorist materials. Wei Xiyuan offers an encomium to Mulan in his *Illustrated Biographies of Resourceful Women, Past and Present*, and the editors of the "New Chinese and Foreign Arrayed Traditions of Women's Lives" celebrate the exploits of the Ming loyalist Shen Yunying (1624–61) in graphic visual detail. Even authors who did not fully embrace the new value of heroism appropriated the new heroic idiom. One such author, who featured faithful and filial (*zhenxiao*), chaste and righteous (*jielie*) exemplars of the kind Xu Dingyi and other presentists disdained, entitled his work *Biographies of Manly Women* (*Jinguo xumei zhuan*).[39]

Archeomodernists who followed Liang Qichao's injunction to cultivate the new qualities of "adventuresomeness" and "militarism," invoked historical women warriors as models for contemporary female nationalists.[40] Textbook authors such as Yang Qianli featured warrior-like heroines in their new-style pedagogical materials, and editors of mainstream newspapers, including the *Beijing-Tianjin Times*, published poetic odes to historical women of valor.

It was presentists, however, who most widely celebrated woman warriors and most radically politicized their stories. Disassociating female heroism from feminine virtue, they liberated intrepid Chinese exemplars from the moralizing overlay that had made their transgressive actions palatable in the past. Ignoring whatever private, familial, or local interests heroic women had historically been made to serve, they turned these submissive agents of patriarchy into daring Han patriots.

Hua Mulan was the martial equivalent of Mencius's mother in the turn-of-the-twentieth-century Chinese cultural imaginary. The most widely invoked woman warrior, she was featured in the full range of late imperial genres from hundred beauties albums and expansions of the *Arrayed Traditions* to textbooks and daily newspapers. Together with Mother Meng, she was also among the few female exemplars to cross over into mainstream publications and boys' textbooks.[41]

Mulan's renown derived neither from the *Arrayed Traditions of Women's Lives*—as had Mother Meng's—nor from a dynastic history entry, but from the popular "Ballad of Mulan," which was recorded in the sixth century but set at the turn of the fifth. In this dramatic story, the young woman is overcome with anxiety when she sees her father's name on all twelve battle-rolls announcing recent conscripts into the Toba Wei army. She knows her father is required to answer the emperor's call, but she is also painfully aware that he is too old to fight and that her brothers are too young to replace him. Mulan thus decides to disguise herself as a soldier and enlist in her father's stead. Concealing her beauty and preserving her chastity, she lives and fights for twelve years in the company of men. When the war finally ends and the emperor instructs members of her victorious regiment to name their own reward, Mulan asks only for a camel to take her back to her family. Upon her return, she resumes her female dress and her weaving.[42]

Mulan's tale, like Ti Ying's, was embellished over the succeeding centuries to emphasize her filiality and modesty. In the Ming dynasty elaboration of the ballad by Xu Wei (1521–93), for example, Mulan not only carries on with her previous domestic roles upon her return home but marries a local scholar.[43]

Meliorist versions of the tale retain this moralistic overlay while imbuing it with contemporary resonances. Wei Xiyuan upholds the conventional privileging of Mulan's devotion to her father over her martial valor by including her in the "Filiality to Parents" section of his compilation and highlighting her daughterly devotion in his commentary (see Figure 6). At the same time, Wei uses Mulan's example to express his support for the anti-footbinding movement. He notes that when he read the "Ballad of Mulan" in his youth, he "was intrigued to find that a woman with bound feet could join the army." He soon realized, however, that women were "healthy and strong" in the past precisely because they had natural feet. The reasoning behind his concluding plea for the abolition of footbinding is ultimately patriarchal, however: women could assist men more effectively with natural feet.[44]

Women's textbooks also emphasize Mulan's daughterly dedication and upright feminine decorum. Yang Qianli devotes three lessons to the famous woman warrior in the *New Reader for Girls and Women*, an honor shared only with Mencius's mother. One of the *Reader*'s two images depicts Mulan riding off to join the army (see Figure 37).[45] In the first lesson, which introduces the "Ballad of Mulan," Yang focuses on the young woman's homecoming: her family's warm welcome, her resumption of feminine dress, and her comrades' astonishment to discover the true gender of their fellow soldier.[46] Xie Chongxie also depicts Mulan riding off to replace her father in an illustration while highlighting her return home in the text.[47] Wu Tao praises Mulan together with Ti Ying and Ban Zhao in a lesson on the spirit of filial piety and sibling love.[48]

The late Qing periodical press offers similar representations of the great heroine. She is featured in several installments of a serial poem published in the *Beijing-Tianjin Times*, "To Sing of Women Officers through the Ages"

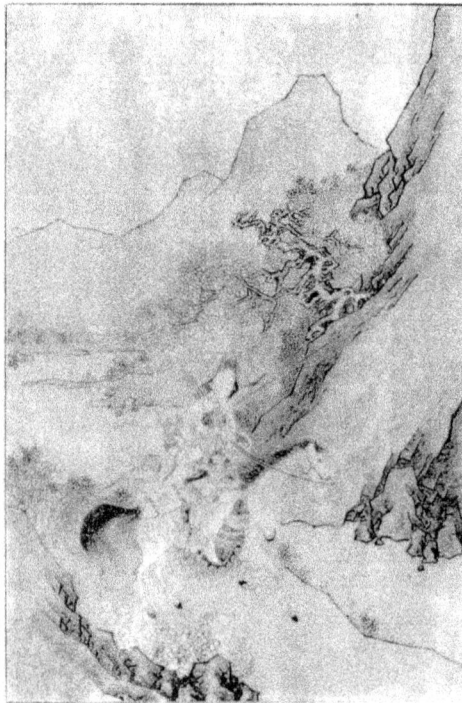

Figure 37 Mulan riding off to join the army
SOURCE: Yang Qianli, *Nüzi xin duben*, frontispiece to vol. 1

(Yong lidai nüjiang). The series celebrates the virtues of individual women warriors from the Eastern Jin through the late Ming dynasties.[49] In one of the poems, Yuan Jisun praises Mulan for upholding the values of the regime of feminine virtue: filially serving her father and chastely masking her beauty.[50]

In contrast to archeomodernists and meliorists, presentists de-emphasize Mulan's filiality and modesty. Using the language of China's national struggle, they trumpet her martial valor instead. Xu Dingyi wrote in this spirit in the passage analyzed in the introduction to this chapter. So did Liu Yazi (1887–1958). In a *Women's World* biography, Liu uses the tale of Mulan to promote a martial spirit (*shangwu jingshen*), the qualities of a militant citizenry (*junguomin zige*), and nationalism (*minzu zhuyi*). He insists that Mulan joined the army not to uphold her family's honor but to "protect our nation" (*bao wo minzu*). He has her boldly proclaim, "Although I am a girl, I am also a citizen" (*guomin yi fenzi*).[51]

In keeping with the late Qing predilection for establishing global hierarchies of valor, the pseudonymous Guardian of Modesty (Baosu) asserts that Mulan was exceptional even on an international scale. In a poem in the *Magazine of the New Chinese Woman*, she writes that none of the "famous beauties of Europe and America" who were all preoccupied with more trivial matters than joining an army could match the Chinese warrior. The Guardian also laments what other presentists attempted to occlude—that China's great heroine ultimately relinquished her martial role. Why, she asks, did Mulan "return to her old adornments" after having achieved such success as a soldier?[52]

The presentists' success in using their refashioned image of Mulan to mobilize their female compatriots is tangible in newspapers from the very last years of Qing rule. A pictorial story published in early 1910 entitled "The Second Hua Mulan" (Hua Mulan dier), describes a prostitute from Foshan who dressed as a man and joined the army in the city of Wuzhou in Guangxi Province. Free of any references to duty to father or emperor, the account asserts that this "second Mulan" deserves her own place in the annals of heroism (see Figure 38).[53] In the months preceding the 1911 Revolution, Mulan's martial image was used to affirm that "young women could serve as soldiers" (*jinguo neng bing*) and to rally them to join newly formed women's armies.[54]

In addition to Hua Mulan, late Qing materials also feature several less well-known martial women of the early and middle imperial periods. One

Figure 38 "The Second Hua Mulan"
SOURCE: "Hua Mulan"

of these was Li Xiu (fl. ca. 350) of the Jin dynasty (280–420), a militant leader from Ningzhou who replaced her deceased father, Prefect Li Yi (fl. ca. 300), in leading local minority forces against bandits in the south (*nanman*).[55] Li's story was given markedly different readings—with different contemporary resonances—in archeomodern and presentist materials. The first woman celebrated in the "Women Officers through the Ages" series, she is heralded for maintaining her chastity and not sullying her father's name while courageously leading thousands of men.[56]

In Xu Dingyi's collection of great Chinese women, this chaste defender of Jin dynasty southern minorities is transformed into a model for the anti-Qing, anti-foreign struggle. Xu praises Li's intelligence, courage, and resourcefulness, describing her roasting mice and gathering grass when her troops are under siege and out of food. His commentary focuses, however, on her ambition "to drive out the foreigners."[57]

Xun Guan (fl. ca. 350), who was first featured in the *Jin History*, appears in a number of turn-of-the-twentieth-century pedagogical materials. What precipitated her entry into history was an attack on the community of Xiangcheng in Henan Province, where her father served as prefect. A mere thirteen years old, she was determined to seek military assistance for him. She broke out of the besieged city at night, violating all rules of propriety, in order to pass a message composed in her own hand to her father's allies.[58]

The author of the preface to a letter-writing manual / ethics textbook, *Copybook of Classified Letters for Women*, praises Xun Guan for being as courageous as Mulan.[59] Other archeomodernists who discussed her achievements in more detail emphasize her loyalty to her father and the letter-writing talents she deployed to serve that loyalty.[60]

In contrast, Xu Dingyi reads a commitment to an *extra-familial* cause into Xun's story. He compares her struggle to protect the people of Xiangcheng with the Han dynasty tale of Yang Xiang, a young woman who rescued her father, Yang Feng, from the mouth of a tiger. Whereas meliorists and archeomodernists widely celebrated Yang Xiang's filiality and bravery, Xu uses her as a negative example to highlight the importance of service to community versus service to family. Unlike Xun Guan, who risked her life to save her community, Yang did not merit an entry in his collection, Xu explains, because she had only saved one man.[61]

Xu did consider Xi Furen (fl. 535) worthy of praise and emulation. First featured in the *Sui History*, Xi had valiantly struggled on behalf of her community in Gaoliang (in present-day Guangdong Province) late in the Six Dynasties period (220–589). When her husband, Feng Bao, who had been responsible for pacifying the Lingnan frontier, died, she continued his work. She first mobilized Lingnan troops in support of the Chen dynasty (557–89) and then led her grandson and others in support of the newly established Sui dynasty. The first Sui emperor granted her the title of Wife of the State of Qiao (Qiaoguo furen).[62]

Poems in the "Women Officers" series praise Xi's leadership abilities and the honors she received, but elaborate little on her story.[63] In contrast, both Yang Qianli and Xu Dingyi foreground ethnic concerns in their narrativizations of Xi's life. Whereas Xi Furen's official biography merely states she was the descendant of a southern leader (*shi wei nanyue shouling*), Yang and Xu present her as the descendant of the chieftain of a tribe of "southern barbarians" (*shi wei manyi jiuzhang, shi wei manzhang,* respectively).[64] Xu states it was fortunate Xi Furen had married a Chinese and quotes a Sui official who was impressed to find a woman of such acumen among the "barbarians."

Giving her story topical relevance in his commentary, Xu concludes that if there were women of such strength among barbarians in his own day, they would shame his female compatriots.[65]

Just as Xi Furen had contributed to the consolidation of the Sui dynasty, the princess of Pingyang (d. 623), daughter of the Tang dynasty founder, Li Yuan (566–635), was active in the establishment of the Tang. Her story is included in the *Old Tang History* biography of her husband, Chai Shao (d. 638). According to the biography, when Chai Shao followed his father-in-law's lead in mobilizing forces to oppose the Sui dynasty, the princess raised money and organized 70,000 troops into a Woman's Army (*Niangzi jun*) under her leadership.[66]

The authors of poems on the princess of Pingyang in the "Women Officers" series praise her loyalty and commend the emperor for rewarding her with special honors after her death.[67] Xu Dingyi, in contrast, does not focus on the princess's contribution to the political and patriarchal order, but on the importance of the Woman's Army. His concern is not, however, to promote the idea of a "*woman's* army"—an army led by a woman, as the Tang princess's was—but of a "*women's* army"—an army of women officers and women soldiers—in the late Qing.[68]

Another great woman warrior who, like the princess of Pingyang, emerged in a period of violent dynastic transition and was briefly mentioned in her husband's biography, is Liang Hongyu. Often paired with Mulan in the turn-of-the-twentieth-century discourse on female heroism, Liang merits one line in the *Song History* entry on her husband, the great general and patriot Han Shizhong (1089–1151). "Lady Liang personally held a drum," the biography states, which she beat to galvanize her husband's troops in the struggle against the invading Jurchen forces.[69] Later authors elaborate on this terse reference. While a Song period literatus questioned Liang's virtue, claiming she had been a prostitute and had initiated her relationship with Han, two Ming dynasty plays sanitize Liang's past and celebrate her martial courage. By the late Ming her renown was such that she became the model for the famous loyalist courtesan Liu Rushi (1618–64).[70]

Liang was a particularly apposite model in the late Qing because she fought against the Jurchens, the forebears of the Manchus. Archeomodern accounts of her story do not accentuate this ethnic element or significantly alter the narrative as handed down from the Ming dynasty, however. Yang Qianli records that Liang had received imperial honors for assisting both Han Shizhong and the famous Song general Yue Fei (1103–41) in defeating the invading Jurchen soldiers.[71] The "Women Officers" poems, commend Liang for protecting Han's troops by frightening away enemy soldiers and ghosts with her drums. They also celebrate her virtue, praising her as a woman of not only remarkable beauty but great modesty.[72]

Presentists more dramatically resignify Liang Hongyu's place in history. The author of a one-act play entitled "Huangtiandang," the name of the stretch of river where Liang had allegedly beaten her drum and driven the Jurchens away, gives Liang a formal military role. Clad in uniform, she is the head of the navy, assisted by four women admirals.[73] Guardian of Modesty similarly elevates Liang's historical importance in her 1907 poem. She credits Liang with the survival of the Southern Song dynasty and bemoans that her critical historical contribution had not been adequately recognized.[74]

Chen Yiyi enters Liang—and Hua Mulan—into the global hierarchy of heroism. He claims their stories dispute conservative foreign gender theories. "According to Westerners," he writes in *The National Women's Journal*, "women can only serve their countries indirectly, while, according to [the principles of] Japanese education, a woman's talents must exclusively be deployed to help her husband in his career, not to advance her own career. The examples of China's Mulan and Liang Hongyu, forcefully refute" these views.[75] Liu Yazi, writing under the name of a woman, Pan Xiaohuang, in the *Women's World*, makes the most forthright connection between Liang's heroic past and present global struggles. Using current rhetoric to describe her exploits, Liu claims that "Liang threw herself into the maelstrom of the nationalist war" (*toushen yu minzu zhanzheng zhi panwo*). More alarmingly, he expresses the wish that Chinese women would emulate Liang and help him "kill members of other races and protect their own race" (*zhu wo sha yizhong bao tongzhong*).[76]

Following Liang Hongyu and Mulan, two of the most widely invoked martial women in turn-of-the-twentieth-century materials are the late Ming heroines Shen Yunying and Qin Liangyu (d. 1648).[77] Shen merits one line in the *Ming History* under an entry on the "Roving Bandit" (Liuzei) Zhang Xianzhong. The entry notes that Shen, the daughter of Shen Zhixu (d. 1643), a second captain in command of the garrison at Daozhou, Hunan (today Dao County), was determined to retrieve her father's corpse when he was killed by Zhang's rebels.[78] Later accounts describe how she succeeds her father as second captain and bravely defends Daozhou, only resigning the command when she hears that her husband, a first captain at Jingzhou, Hubei, had also been killed in a struggle with insurgents. She then returns to her home at Xiaoshan, Zhejiang Province.[79]

A meliorist biography of Shen, which appears almost verbatim in the "New Chinese and Foreign Arrayed Traditions of Women's Lives" and the *Biographies of Manly Women*, describes Shen's loyalty to her father. In a spirit of filial vengeance before retrieving his corpse, she decapitates more than thirty of the bandits who had killed him (see Figure 39). She is also learned in the Four Books, the *Spring and Autumn Annals*, and Tang and Song poetry. The account concludes with a dual emphasis on Shen's talent and allegiance to her native place. After returning home with her father's corpse, she opens a school near the family shrine where she teaches until her death.[80]

Archeomodernists, who so disdained late imperial women of talent, made little mention of Shen's literary abilities. Instead they emphasized her virtue while praising her courage. The author of a poem in the "Women Officers" series intones that it was rare for a woman to display the three qualities of filiality, loyalty, and virtue as splendidly as did Shen.[81] The compilers of the *Newest Chinese Reader for Women* commend Shen for earning

Figure 39 "Officer Shen Courageously Seizes Her Father's Corpse"
SOURCE: "Shen jiangjun"

the title of mobile core commander, but highlight her willingness to die for her father.[82]

Presentists marginalize all references to both Shen's virtue and her talent, and celebrate her heroism as a panacea for China's current global inferiority. In both her poetic narrative *Stones of the Jingwei Bird* (*Jingwei shi*) and her poetry, Qiu Jin extols Shen (often together with Qin Liangyu) for being so fierce in battle that she drove bandits away. Unlike men who were cowardly traitors to both their country and their race, she had the "strength and courage" to fight for China.[83]

Qin Liangyu, who is paired with Shen Yunying in the *Stones of the Jingwei Bird* and other Ming and Qing writings, was one of the few women warriors to merit her own biography in a dynastic history. A native of Zhongzhou, Sichuan Province, Qin had received the same literary and military education as her brothers. She was both wife and military partner of Ma Qiancheng (d. 1615), a native chieftain in Sichuan. The two defended their community against local rebels until Ma's death in 1615, at which time Qin inherited his rank of chieftain. Immediately before the Qing conquest, Qin continued to defend her community from rebels in the west while leading campaigns against the Manchus in the north. In 1620 the emperor ordered her to dispatch a detachment of her troops to Liaodong to fight the encroaching Manchus. In 1630, she led her forces in defending the capital, Beijing. The Ming emperor wrote poems praising her bravery and loyalty, and she was granted the title of Marquis Zhongzhen and Grand Guardian of the Heir Apparent for protecting her hometown from devastation.[84]

An almost identical account of Qin's heroism appears in Yang Qianli's *New Reader for Girls and Women* and Xu Dingyi's *Biographies of Great Women of Our Country*. The account briefly describes Qin's military achievements, including her thwarting of Zhang Xianzhong's advances into her area. It also notes her ability to recite literary works.[85] In his commentary, however, Xu Dingyi adds a presentist layer to Qin's story that directly links it to the late Qing political crisis. He attributes Qin's military success to her focused strategy: rather than disperse her energies by fighting local Han bandits she concentrates on warding off the "northern peoples" (*hu*). Suggesting the need for a unified anti-Manchu strategy in his own time, Xu ends his commentary with a characteristic lament: China of his day needs—and sorely lacks—women of Qin Liangyu's mettle.[86]

While both archeomodernists and presentists celebrated Ming loyalists like Qin Liangyu who had resisted the establishment of the Manchu Qing dynasty, only presentists praised women who had more recently fought against Qing imperial forces. Xu Dingyi announced his racial and implicitly anti-Manchu views in his preface to the *Biographies of Great Women*. The people of our race cannot be faint-hearted, he proclaims. In an effort to discourage Chinese women from becoming slaves to "northerners" as their male compatriots had, he offers examples of women who refused to submit to northern invaders. They include Han Ximeng (fl. 1120), who resisted the Mongols in the Southern Song dynasty, and two female Taiping warriors who fought the Manchus: Hong Xuanjiao (fl. 1860), the younger sister of the Taiping leader Hong Xiuquan (1814–64) and the wife of a lesser Taiping leader, Xiao Chaogui (1820–52); and Xiao's sister, Xiao Sanniang (ca. 1830–ca. 1854).[87]

Xu ends his collection with these Taiping heroines. He presents Hong as a reincarnated Ming loyalist, claiming that anyone who saw her in action could not help but believe that "Qin Liangyu was alive again." He also makes Hong and Xiao Sanniang models for the late Qing revolutionary struggle. They imbibed racialist thinking (*zhongzu zhuyi*) day and night and developed strong antiforeign ideas. Xu concludes with the assertion that any collection of biographies of great Chinese women had to end with these Taiping heroines. Their revived spirit would release the Chinese masses from their torment and inspire them to resist the northerners.[88]

Joan of Arc and Her Intrepid Successors

Unlike Chinese women warriors whom some meliorists honored, Western heroines were almost exclusively celebrated by archeomodernists and presentists. As with the Chinese women warriors, however, the two groups represented Western women of valor in distinct ways. While I draw on a number of sources to highlight this divergence, I focus on the highly revealing differences between two related collections of Western women's biographies published in 1903, *Twelve World Heroines* and *Ten World Heroines*.

As noted in the Introduction, the *Twelve World Heroines* is an early 1903 translation of a Japanese text with exactly the same title. The *Ten World Heroines*, which was published just a few months later, is labeled a translation but, as the anonymous author himself states, is really an original work.[89] The author of the *Ten* claims in his introduction that the *Twelve* had served as his blueprint (*lanben*). At the same time, however, he announces that his text is based on seventeen different sources and that he had seen an advertisement for the *Twelve* and drawn a connection with it *after* having written but *before* the printing of his own collection.[90] The *Ten* ultimately shares only five heroines with the *Twelve*. Most important, its depiction of these five differs dramatically from their portrayal in the "blueprint."

The *Twelve World Heroines* belongs to the genre of Meiji Japanese self-help books inspired by the 1871 translation of Samuel Smiles's 1859 work, *Self Help*.[91] The *Twelve* promotes heroic determination exemplified by Madame Roland's calm resolve in the face of her impending execution.[92] The inspiration for the *Ten*, in contrast, was not Samuel Smiles but Jean-Jacques Rousseau and its purpose was to incite self-sacrifice rather than encourage self-help. The author romanticizes liberty and revolution, and justifies violence in their name. Blood, whether dripping from knives or welling up in women's hearts, is the most prominent leitmotif in this paean to the willingness to die for freedom.

These differences are apparent in the kinds of female attributes the two texts emphasize. The *Twelve* accentuates the qualities of queens and patriots, the *Ten* the traits of anarchists and assassins. The author of the *Ten* explains that he deliberately excluded seven of the women celebrated in the *Twelve*. He left Madame Roland out for technical reasons: her story, he notes, had recently been published in the *New People's Miscellany*. Other women, including three queens—Isabella of Spain (1451–1504), Elizabeth of England (1558–1603), and Louise of Prussia (1776–1810)—were disqualified because he deemed them "insignificant figures."[93] He did retain one queen, however, Catherine the Great of Russia (r. 1762–96) who, he declares, had left a "progressive legacy." Youth and student revolutions unleashed less than ten years after her death and the emergence of secret societies and nihilism at the turn of the twentieth century could be traced to her rule.[94] The exclusion of Joan of Arc goes unexplained but was probably because she was not a heroine of the immediate past.

In addition to Catherine the Great, both collections feature Charlotte Corday (1768–93), Anita Garibaldi (1821–49), Madame de Staël (1766–1817), and Louise Michel (1830–1905). The *Twelve* alone includes Joan of Arc (1412–31), Madame Roland (1754–93), Lucy Hutchinson (1620–80), Queen Isabella, Queen Elizabeth, Queen Louise, and Frances Willard (1839–98). The *Ten* exclusively celebrates the egalitarian, pro-revolutionary British diarist and poet Dorothy Wordsworth (1771–1855), the British suffragette Millicent G. Fawcett (1847–1929), a Russian noblewoman and peace-broker during the Crimean War (1854–56), Dorothea Lieven (1785–1857), Florence Nightingale, and Mary Lyon. The women unique to the *Ten* may not be the most radical in Western history, yet the author infuses their stories with a radical spirit. Millicent G. Fawcett, who was opposed to more militant suffragettes, for example, is depicted in the *Ten World Heroines* as a "fearless officer" (*yongjiang*) in the English struggle for women's rights. Although she is associated with "mothers of enlightenment," the author ties this maternal trope to radical theories of racial and political slavery. Women with a slavish nature will beget a people with a slavish nature, he asserts, and the nation will perish.[95]

The *Twelve* and *Ten* also produced different textual lineages. The *Twelve* became a source for a number of influential textbooks, most notably Yang Qianli's *New Reader for Girls and Women*. Eight of the ten biographies of Western women in Yang's text were simplified versions of biographies in the *Twelve World Heroines*—including five of the seven "insignificant figures" excluded from the *Ten*. Yang, who was a friend of Jin Tiange and, thus, linked to radical circles, may have chosen to use the more moderate *Twelve* as his source because his collection was a textbook.[96] In an introduction to the *New Reader for Girls and Women* published in the *Women's World*, he includes Sofia Perovskaia—who is not included either in the *Twelve World Heroines* or ultimately in his own reader—in the table of contents.[97] Whether he excludes her out of self-censorship or in compliance with the demands of his publishers, he does make a point of referring to her in his biography of the French anarchist Louise Michel. Departing from the original biography in the *Twelve* he equates Michel with the infamous Sofia.[98]

An indication of the influence of the lineage of Western biographies established by the *Twelve World Heroines* and the *New Reader for Girls and Women* is the reappropriation of several of these biographies in other late Qing works. Five of the biographies in Yang's reader—of Harriet Beecher Stowe, Queen Louise, Florence Nightingale, Frances Willard, and Joan of Arc—including three derived from the *Twelve*, are reprinted almost verbatim in the multivolume *Newest Chinese Reader for Women*.[99] A version of at least one of them—the biography of Frances Willard—is also the basis for an account published in the meliorist *Beijing Women's Journal*.[100] The *Twelve World Heroines* is, furthermore, the acknowledged source for a song with the same title published in a popular collection of school ditties, Ye Zhongling's *First Collection of New Songs For Girls*.[101]

In contrast to the *Twelve World Heroines*, which left its mark in a range of pedagogical materials, the traces of the *Ten* can be found mostly in radical journals. The collection was introduced to the public in a June 1903 issue of a publication that would be banned by the Qing government the following month, Chen Fan's *Jiangsu Journal*. The author of the introduction explicitly compares the *Ten* with the *Twelve*, expressing his preference for the former's vivid language and dramatic descriptions.[102] Chen Fan's daughter, the editor of the *Journal of Women's Learning*, Chen Xiefen (1883–1923), shared this enthusiasm. Four months after the introduction to the *Ten* had appeared, and shortly after she and her father escaped arrest and fled to Tokyo, Chen Xiefen announced her intention to serially publish a vernacular version of the *Ten World Heroines* in her *Journal of Women's Learning*.[103] Her objective was emphatically presentist. These biographies would, she explains, teach her female compatriots to embrace a new heroism unconstrained by principles of feminine virtue. Young Chinese women who imitated the first woman in the collection, Louise Michel, would learn to privilege politics over morality and to boldly speak out for righteousness even at the risk of offending others.[104]

The *Journal of Women's Learning* ceased publication after the first installment of the *Ten World Heroines* appeared. Both the *Ten* and individual women celebrated in the *Ten*, including Dorothy Wordsworth, continued, however, to be invoked in radical journals such as Ding Chuwo's *Women's World*.[105]

Differences in archeomodern and presentist conceptions of female heroism emerge through a reading of the biographies of key Western women of valor. These women include Joan of Arc and Madame Roland, who are featured in the *Twelve World Heroines* and in other turn-of-the-century sources. They also include figures celebrated in both the *Twelve* and the *Ten World Heroines*, and often in Yang Qianli's textbook as well: Charlotte Corday, Anita Garibaldi, Madame Staël, and Louise Michel.

Joan of Arc is the Western equivalent of Hua Mulan in late Qing materials. Biographies of her appear in the *Beijing Women's Journal*, the *Twelve World Heroines*, Yang Qianli's *New Reader for Girls and Women*, and the *Magazine of the New Chinese Woman*.[106] Both a religious visionary and one of Europe's first patriots, Joan led French efforts to repulse the British during the Hundred Years' War (1337–1453). Her success on the battlefield thwarted the British Duke of Bedford's claim to the throne of France for his nephew Henry VI and resulted in the coronation of Charles VII in 1429. The British, who despised Joan as a French patriot, had her tried as a religious heretic after finally capturing her in 1430. Charged with contravening a biblical clothing law by cross-dressing, she was burned at the stake in 1431 at the age of nineteen. Twenty-four years later Joan's politically motivated conviction was overturned, and almost five hundred years later she was fully redeemed in the eyes of the Catholic Church. She was declared "Venerable" in 1894, beatified in 1909, and canonized in 1920.[107] Volumes had been written on this remarkable heroine in Western languages by the turn of the twentieth century. Many were translated in the non-Western world, including Meiji Japan, the source of a number of Chinese accounts.[108]

Late Qing authors, from meliorists to presentists, hailed Joan as a national heroine. In an article published in the meliorist *Beijing Women's Journal*, the author uses Joan's ability to mobilize the meager French troops against the more powerful British to inspire loyalty to the Qing dynasty. He is careful to assert his own loyalty at the same time, however, explaining that he was not advocating a sycophantic embrace of all things foreign but the celebration of a woman who fervently loved her own country.[109] The *Twelve World Heroines* heralds this courageous "peasant girl from Domrémy" as "France's savior." Her national self-sacrifice had made her an international icon, a figure that "neither France nor the rest of the world could forget."[110] Yang Qianli presents the young visionary as an intelligent woman who "understood the meaning of patriotism" and was determined to lead her countrymen in the struggle against the British.[111] Mei Zhu, who lauds Joan's "pressing sense of patriotism" in the *Magazine of the New Chinese Woman*, asserts that she had not died in vain: the area north of the Loire River reverted to France shortly after her execution.[112] Qiu Jin declares Joan a fellow traveler in the struggle to restore national glory.[113]

Joan, nonetheless, posed a number of problems for Chinese authors eager to appropriate her story to their own political ends. She was indeed a great patriot, but a divinely inspired great patriot. Moreover, she was a divinely inspired great patriot burned at the stake in male attire, a heroine who did not make the crucial reversion back to her normative female role. Archeomodernists and presentists used similar strategies to dismiss Joan's religiosity. Archeomodernists alone remained troubled by her gender inversion.

The original biography of Joan in the Japanese version of the *Twelve World Heroines* describes her religiosity in detail. She prayed in the local church at the end of every workday, it explains, and at the altar to the Virgin Mary once a week. Regulated by Christian practice, Joan's world was also touched by spirits lodged in the current flowing under the old oak trees in her village on moonlit nights. It was these spirits who first called on her to save France. Throughout her trials both on the battlefield and in the courtroom

Joan's faith remained profound. She prayed to God for protection moments before she was burned at the stake.[114]

Although Zhao Bizhen generally translated the Iwasaki and Mikami biography in the *Twelve World Heroines* faithfully, he established critical distance from Joan's spirituality by inserting comments and translator's notes into his text. He describes Joan's religious beliefs as "inexplicable," particularly to those who did not live in a world defined by the power of the gods.[115] He, nonetheless, attempts to explain her baffling religiosity by stating that she lived at a time when superstition had not yet been trumped by science. Associating her beliefs with Chinese folk legends, he compares them to the familiar tales of the White Snake Fairy (*Baishe*) and the God of the South (*Chidi*). Finally, he asserts that religion was often made to serve politics: crafty rulers manipulate the ignorant with talk of deities and spirits.[116]

Yang Qianli adds another layer of secular skepticism to Joan's story in his adaptation of Zhao's *Twelve World Heroines'* biography. He expands on Zhao's inserted definition of religion as a form of political manipulation by arguing that Joan herself used the so-called divine voices as a ploy. Realizing the difficulty she would have as a sixteen-year-old peasant girl gaining the allegiance of the ignorant and deeply superstitious masses, she contrived to win their confidence by fooling them into believing she was divinely inspired.[117]

Mei Zhu initially makes some concessions to Joan's religious faith in her "Biography of Joan, the Heroic French Savior," which appeared in the *Magazine of the New Chinese Woman*. She notes that Joan strongly believed in the way of the gods (*shendao*).[118] Ultimately, however, Mei Zhu offers a secular interpretation of the story. Disagreeing with those who attribute the actions of great heroes to Heaven or supernatural beings, she states her belief that a strong will can move mountains and fill oceans. "Utmost sincerity can move even the gods" (*zhicheng zhi dao keyi ganshen*), she declares; Joan's will inspired Heaven as much as Heaven inspired her.[119] In her conclusion, Mei Zhu echoes Yang's assertion that Joan invoked divine voices to fool the ignorant masses. All great heroes are forced to resort to trickery, she explains; why should Joan have been any different?[120]

The second problem Joan posed as a model heroine for archeomodernists in particular was her gender bending. Having successfully petitioned the king to wear the equipment of a knight, Joan had achieved all of her military successes dressed as a man. The British feared her life would be spared if she appeared in the courtroom not in a soldier's uniform but in women's dress. According to the official record, the British offered her male garments in prison, which she enthusiastically donned.[121] The *Twelve World Heroines* and the *New Reader for Girls and Women* suggest that Joan's vanity at that moment was her downfall. According to the *Twelve*, as the British attempted to entice her into putting on men's clothing, she reflected on the glorious day when she had presented herself to the king in male guise, a heroic and lovely "beauty in a helmet." This memory of glory prevailed over her knowledge that cross-dressing was a violation of the law.[122] Although the biographies in the *New Reader* were significantly pared-down versions of the tales in the *Twelve*, Yang embellishes the description of this moment, portraying Joan narcissistically dancing and singing in masculine dress. It was at this point, he announces, that the British convicted her of heresy and condemned her to death.[123]

Presentists did not share the archeomodernists' aversion to gender inversion. Mei Zhu notes that Joan was convicted of dressing as a man, but does not disparage her for it.[124] The lens through which she reads Joan's story is more radically secular than the one used in archeomodern materials. It not only strips away the Christian elements from Joan's original story, but any Confucian principles of gender normativity that had accrued in its East Asian retellings.

Mei Zhu states in the passage quoted in the epigraph to Part Three that Joan is a greater heroine than Hua Mulan precisely because she was not constrained by the principles of the Chinese regime of female virtue. She never could have led the French against the British if she had been bound by the rules of gender separation and filial piety. It was her defiance of feminine norms that was the source of her renown. "Who in France today does not know her and worship her?" Mei Zhu asks. And who beyond France's borders has not heard of the great French patriot Joan of Arc?[125]

The revolutionary martyr Madame Roland is another globally renowned French heroine widely celebrated in the late Qing. Both Madame Roland and her husband, Jean Marie Roland de la Platière, were members of the moderate Girondist faction that opposed the excesses of the revolutionary terror. When more radical figures led by Robespierre (1758–94) began to purge the Girondists, Madame Roland calmly awaited her fate, refusing to flee Paris as her cowardly husband did. Tried on fabricated charges of being a royalist, she was guillotined on November 8, 1793. Monsieur Roland committed suicide upon hearing the news of her death two days later.[126]

Liang Qichao introduced this remarkable figure to the Chinese public in

1902.[127] It was because his account had such an impact that the author of the *Ten World Heroines* claimed there was no need to repeat Roland's story in his own collection the following year.[128] The great Girondist martyr was, however, featured in the *Twelve World Heroines*, where she was represented as the exemplar's exemplar, her resolve in the face of the guillotine epitomizing the heroic spirit the collection promoted.[129] Yang Qianli used the *Twelve*'s biography as the basis of two lessons on Roland in the *New Reader for Girls and Women*.[130] She is also widely invoked in presentist writings.

There are marked similarities between Liang Qichao's biography, the *Twelve*'s, and its *New Reader* derivation. All were—directly or indirectly—based on Japanese sources, but not on the same Japanese sources, as transcriptions and details differ.[131] All were politically moderate, and critical of a revolution that had begun to devour its own children. Liang opened his account with the famous line Roland uttered before placing her head on the executioner's block. Bowing to the clay statue of Liberty in the Place de la Révolution, she declared "O Liberté, que de crimes on commet en ton nom!" (Oh Liberty, what crimes are committed in thy name!).[132] Both the *Twelve* and Yang's reader record an equally poignant—if less well-known line—that Roland supposedly delivered with icy laughter at the same historic moment: "You (*gongdeng*) who send me to the guillotine today will soon face the guillotine yourselves."[133]

These moderate biographies emphasize Madame Roland's maternal and feminine qualities. None of the sources describe her as a biological mother—only the *Twelve* mentions in passing the birth of a daughter—but all represent her as a political and social mother.[134] In Liang's account, she had mothered modern politics. She was

> the mother of Napoleon, the mother of Metternich, the mother of Mazzini, the mother of Kossuth, the mother of Bismarck, and the mother of Cavour. In short, all great men of nineteenth century Europe could not but regard her as mother; all civilizations of nineteenth century Europe could not but regard her as mother. Why was this so? Because the French Revolution was the mother of nineteenth century Europe, and Madame Roland was the mother of the French Revolution.[135]

Subsequent biographies built on this maternal metaphor. A twenty-part *Daily Pictorial* biography of Roland published in 1909 opens with the statement, "Madame Roland was the mother of freedom."[136] (See Figure 40.) The *Twelve* describes Roland as a social mother who had inspired such

世界名人歷史畫

羅蘭夫人提倡革命(例)

Figure 40 The "mother of freedom," Madame Roland, advocating revolution
SOURCE: "Luolan"

devotion in her maid and male servant that they risked their lives gathering up and burying her bones and those of her husband. The two servants were ultimately arrested for their loyalty to the reviled Girondists. The young maid was eventually released on grounds of insanity. The male servant was decapitated.[137]

These various accounts also highlight Madame Roland's feminine appearance and demeanor. Although the *Twelve* repeatedly refers to her as a (beautiful) female man (*nü zhangfu*), she does not exhibit any of Joan of Arc's gender ambiguity.[138] Roland blends heroism and grace, with the former never obscuring the latter. Liang makes much of her restraint in expressing her opinions, her inspiring beauty, and her ephemeral appearance—her white silk dress and flowing hair—on the day of her execution.[139] The *Twelve* stresses Roland's elegance, poise (*enuo*), and the same white silk dress and tragic beauty at the moment of death.[140] Although these sources mention that Madame Roland married freely, defying her father's objections, they depict her as the conventional helpmate to her husband.[141] Jean Marie Roland held an official position as minister of the interior, but it was Madame Roland who served, according to Liang, as the shadow leader of the Girondist Party, petitioning for government reform. Similarly, the *Twelve* declares that reports and speeches penned by Madame Roland gained her husband his loyal following.[142]

Finally, Liang and the authors of the *Twelve* use Roland's story to affirm the power of biography by describing the critical role heroic biographies played in Roland's own formation. From the age of nine, according to these accounts, she was an avid reader of *Parallel Lives* by Plutarch (ca. 45 –125). This collection of paired biographies of twenty-five Greek and twenty-five Roman heroes, known in Chinese as *Biographies of Heroes* (*Yingxiong zhuan*), provided Roland with an alternative to Christian doctrine. Liang and the *Twelve* both describe her furtively reading the *Biographies of Heroes* in church, much to her parents' consternation. In the *Twelve* she first commits this transgression during prayers on a holy fast day in 1763. The accounts assert the continued importance of Plutarch as Roland developed her republican ideas and endured the vagaries of politics.[143]

Presentists admired Roland not for mothering but for inciting revolution. They celebrated her historical visibility—the indelible mark her blood had left in the chronicles of the modern world. Overseas female students waxed rhapsodic on Roland's notoriety. He Xiangning lauds her for being a "great figure in history."[144] Wang Lian invokes her "crimson blood" flowing at the time of the French Revolution.[145] Chen Yan'an claims her historic achievements surpassed those of men.[146] A popular song promoting women's education celebrates all twelve world heroines featured in Zhao's translation for having loved their countries, their families, and their race so ardently that their names would be passed on "for ten thousand generations." The song singles Roland out as the quintessential presentist exemplar, however. "If Madame Roland were to live again in the twentieth century," it intones, "she would exhort our female compatriots to immediately rise up!"[147]

Another French Revolution heroine prominent in the late Qing was Charlotte Corday (1768–93). The *Twelve* and the *Ten World Heroines*, Yang Qianli's *New Reader for Girls and Women*, and, most briefly, Xu Jiaxing's *Newest Ethics Textbook for Girls and Women*, all celebrate Corday.[148] Like Madame Roland, Corday supported the moderate Girondists against the radical Jacobins and considered moral transformation to be the Revolution's objective. Her fame rested on a singular violent act: her stabbing of Jean-Paul Marat (1743–93), a Jacobin leader, in his bath in 1793.[149]

The three longer accounts share several similarities. They provide comparable details about Corday's youth, such as her mother's early death, her family's descent into poverty, her father's illness, and her subsequent residence in a convent from 1780 to 1785 or 1786. All emphasize the crucial inspiration Corday derived from the same collection of ancient heroes as Roland, Plutarch's *Biographies of Heroes* (*Parallel Lives*). Charlotte discovers Plutarch while in the convent, falling on her bed in a rapture as she reads it. She takes it with her when she travels to Paris, consults it moments before assassinating Marat, and clutches it at the moment of her execution.[150]

The various versions describe Corday's objective in similar terms: to end the Jacobin evil that Marat had come to personify.[151] All announce that Corday's example would inspire heroism in others and shame men into action.[152] Both the *Ten* and the *Twelve* describe an encounter Corday has en route to Paris with a man who becomes romantically interested in her. The incident underlines Corday's inattention to sentimental trivialities and her resolve to complete her mission. The author of the *Ten* returns to this male figure near the end of the biography to relate how Corday had inspired a similar republican conviction in him. He too was now prepared to shed his blood for the cause.[153]

There are a number of other differences of tone and emphasis between the biographies in the *Ten* and the *Twelve* and Yang's shorter version of the latter. The tenor of the *Twelve* is more resonant with accounts of Chinese women warriors: Charlotte sacrificed herself at a time when "morality and righteousness were floundering" and helped restore moral order.[154] The *Ten*, in contrast, presents Charlotte as the agent of radical historical change. It describes her as a national martyr (*xunguo*) and credits her with the demise of the Terror, the subsequent deaths of its leaders, Georges Jacques Danton (1759–94) and Robespierre, and with the ultimate establishment of the French Republic.[155]

Whereas the *Twelve* and Yang's reader highlight Corday's femininity—suggesting that even frail women could perform great deeds—the *Ten* highlights her heroic blood, intimating that great deeds require bloodshed. The *Twelve* announces that "a delicate hand held a naked blade" and Yang describes how "the majestic Marat died at the hands of a delicate female."[156] The *Ten*, in contrast, opens with a declaration that violence and bloodshed are the seeds of justice and happiness.[157] Blood not only spills at the time of the assassination but becomes the mark of Corday's heroism: she wipes the blood-stained knife she extracts from beneath Marat's clavicle on the pages of Plutarch's *Biographies of Heroes*. She then writes her father just before her execution with the blood of her own finger to inform him that she has left "a momento of Marat" in her copy of Plutarch.[158]

Anita Garibaldi (1821–49), the heroic Brazilian-born wife and comrade-in-arms of the Italian revolutionary Giuseppe Garibaldi (1807–82), is also featured in the *Twelve* and *Ten World Heroines* and in Yang Qianli's textbook.[159] This exceptional woman had left her first husband (a detail *not* included in any of the Chinese accounts) in the Brazilian state of Santa Catarina to join Garibaldi on his ship in October 1839. A Ligurian sailor turned Italian nationalist revolutionary, Garibaldi had fled Europe in 1836 and was fighting for a separatist republic in southern Brazil. Anita fought by his side in Uruguay's wars against Argentina for nine years until the couple returned to Europe to participate in the revolutions of 1848 and to oppose the Austrian empire. In February 1849, Anita joined Garibaldi in the defense of the newly proclaimed Roman Republic against Neapolitan and French intervention aimed at restoration of the Papal State. When Rome fell after a French siege on June 30, Anita fled from French and Austrian troops with the Garibaldian Legion. Sick and pregnant with her fifth child, she died in her husband's arms on August 8, 1849, some seventeen years before the achievement of Italian unification (Risorgimento).

The different late Qing accounts share much including errors, such as the year of Anita's birth (which is given as 1828 rather than 1821), her nationality, and the role of her father (he had abandoned her family but is described in the *Twelve* and the textbook as having trained his daughter in the military arts). The *Twelve* and the *Ten* praise Anita for contributing to the unification of Italy and for her bravery. While Garibaldi was trepidatious about her participation in warfare, she was never fearful. In the end he writes respectfully and lovingly of her in his journal, claiming that he owed half of his achievements to her.[160]

The two main accounts state that Anita was both heroic *and* loving. The *Twelve* lauds her as an affectionate woman and a righteous heroine, while the *Ten* praises her courage and depth of feeling.[161] Even the *Ten* describes her in feminine terms as a natural teacher and mother who tenderly bandaged and nursed wounded soldiers.[162] Both accounts note how struck Garibaldi had been by her beauty.[163] While the *Twelve* suggests a seamless merging of motherhood and heroism, however, with Anita tranquilly giving birth to her first son in a secluded hut, the *Ten* portrays childbirth as bloody, solitary, and difficult. It describes how Garibaldi received a "letter dripping with wet blood in Anita's hand" explaining the trials she had undergone fighting while eight months pregnant, giving birth to a boy, and struggling to care for him under difficult circumstances.[164]

Both texts describe Anita as her husband's comrade-in-arms. Her heroism is more forthright and masculine in the *Ten*, however. The author describes her berating Garibaldi when he gets demoralized, forcing her way into the republican army in South America, dressing as a man, strategizing, and giving rousing speeches. When she and Garibaldi are engaged in battle in Montevideo, Uruguay, she galvanizes him by saying those who do not live like heroes die as ghosts, and that defeat and humiliation breed the passivity of a hedgehog curled up on itself.[165] Whereas the *Twelve* concludes its biography with the statement that Anita must come to mind when one reflects on loving and righteous heroines, the *Ten* closes with the inscription on her tombstone, "Anita, Patriotic Female Knight-Errant."[166]

Madame de Staël (1766–1817), a fierce opponent of Napoleon I (1769–1821), a woman of letters, and an early champion of women's rights, is celebrated in the *Twelve* and *Ten World Heroines* but not in Yang's textbook.[167] The reason for this omission may have been discretion: de Staël was as renowned for her countless lovers as she was for her politics and writings. After a brief and unhappy marriage in 1786 to Baron de Staël-Holstein, a Swedish ambassador, she had affairs with, among others, Count Louis de Narbonne (1755–1813), with whom she had two sons; Count Adolphe-Louis Ribbing (fl. 1790), who masterminded the assassination of Gustavus III, the king of Sweden-Finland; and Benjamin Constant (1767–1830), a writer and influential politician. Brought up in the milieu of Parisian literary salons, she ultimately established one of her own, which became increasingly politicized as the French Revolution approached. After the fall of the monarchy, she sought refuge in Switzerland and returned to Paris a republican in 1795. She was initially hopeful that Napoleon would bring an end to the Revolution, but he soon became suspicious of her. This was the beginning of an ongoing duel between the two that would force her into exile in 1802. She traveled throughout Europe, where she reigned as an exiled sovereign and wrote numerous novels. She returned to Paris when the Bourbons regained power in 1815 and lived there until her death.[168]

The two biographies focus on de Staël's conflict with Napoleon. According to the *Twelve*, she was so powerful in Napoleon's eyes that he "viewed her as an enemy nation."[169] The *Ten* claims Napoleon did not fear oceans, mountains, or snow, and did not wince when confronted with knives or a hail of bullets, but that he was deeply intimidated by the spirited writings produced by this beautiful woman's small and delicate brush.[170] When Napoleon insisted that women have nothing to do with politics and de Staël retorted "France belongs to the French and am I not French?" he forced her into exile.[171] In response to friends and family, who petitioned the emperor to let her return to Paris, Napoleon stated that he would not hesitate if she were a member of the royalist or republican factions. But as she was the driving force behind the powerful salon movement, he could not allow it.[172]

Both accounts highlight de Staël's learning and literary talent, which even Napoleon admitted would surpass men's if properly channeled.[173] By the age of fifteen she was reading *Spirit of the Laws* by Montesquieu (1689–1755). She became a political journalist shortly after her marriage, and effectively wielded her brush to criticize the government and rouse popular opinion.[174] Consistent with other late Qing biographies of foreign women of talent, neither account delves into the content of de Staël's writings. The *Twelve* briefly notes that she had eighteen books to her name, and the *Ten* gives the titles of a number of them.[175]

Only the *Twelve* mentions de Staël's conservative views at the time of the French Revolution. It describes her consternation when the "beautiful name of freedom" was used to justify the execution of Louis XVI and Marie Antoinette.[176] Not a hint of these sentiments can be found in the *Ten*. Rather than criticize those who acted under the banner of freedom, the *Ten* represents de Staël as stirring up feelings of equality and freedom from her exile in England. She declares Napoleon the enemy of freedom, contacts "freedom parties" in other European countries, and dies with the words "I love freedom" on her lips.[177]

Another striking difference between the two texts is the total silence in the *Ten* on de Staël's romantic liaisons. The *Twelve*, which describes these affairs as de Staël's "greatest fault," nonetheless absolves her by explaining that during her life France was in a state of moral chaos. She was a true heroine and it would be foolish to criticize her for these improprieties.[178] The author of the *Ten* completely avoids this subject altogether, although it must have been discussed in some of the seventeen works he consulted. He apparently found such moral details irrelevant to the tale of this enemy of Napoleon and champion of political freedom.

The anarchist Louise Michel (1820–1905) is another French heroine and lover of freedom featured in the *Twelve*, the *Ten* and their derivatives, Yang Qianli's *New Reader for Girls and Women*, and Chen Xiefen's *Journal of Women's Learning*, respectively.[179] The daughter of a serving maid and the son of the house, Michel received a liberal education from her paternal grandfather. From a young age she nurtured a passion for helping the underprivileged, which she later channeled into teaching, works of charity, and revolutionary and anarchist politics. Her involvement in the 1871 Paris Commune resulted in her deportation to New Caledonia in 1873. While engaging with other political prisoners and instructing the natives during her seven years of exile, she began to formulate her anarchist position. She remained politically active through the end of her life, giving impassioned speeches in England and France, and spending periods from months to several years in prison for incitement. She died in Marseilles on January 10, 1905, while on a tour to promote anarchism.

The two principle accounts in the *Twelve* and the *Ten World Heroines* introduce Michel as one of a handful of "female officers of anarchism" in the Western world and use her story to explain anarchism to their audiences.[180] Both collections describe two sources of Michel's politics: her early experience and her grandfather's teachings. As a child, Michel was horrified when she saw other children mistreat animals and encage birds. She would try to persuade them to release the animals, and when they refused she would open the cages herself. At this young age she had learned that when reason fails, force becomes necessary.[181] Her grandfather, who worshipped republicanism, gave Michel a political language to express these natural yearnings. He taught her Rousseau's philosophy and shared both his experience of the French Revolution and his regret that the revolutionary project remained incomplete.[182]

The two biographies used this introduction to Michel and anarchism to different ends, however. For the authors and translator of the *Twelve*, it was to inform the reading public of anarchism's basic principle: the creation of equality through the destruction of the existing social and political infrastructure. Working from the premise that "all deserved to be free," anarchists believed this "natural law and natural principle" of freedom necessitated the abolition of national sovereignty, religious and ethical principles, and the marital and class systems.[183] The author of the *Ten*, in contrast, not only described the principles of anarchism but offered an impassioned plea for their implementation in contemporary China. Michel's story demonstrates, he asserts, that anarchism means more than knives, blood, bombs, and cruel and heartless assassination. The source of anarchist violence, death, and destruction is not a private grudge or a callous disregard for life but a heroic sense of mercy that seeks a better world.[184]

The *Twelve* presents Michel as an unusual creature. Whereas other biographies in the collection make references to the various heroines' beauty, frailty, and femininity, the record of Michel repeatedly alludes to her monstrous ugliness (*yecha*) and unnaturalness.[185] It remarks on the perception that she was illegitimate (claiming that this was only because she had been born so soon after her mother had married).[186] The *Twelve*'s account, nonetheless, ends like all exemplar tales: not only women but men must learn from Michel's story and lead the people toward virtue (*wanliannuoli*).[187]

Michel, who inspired revulsion in some according to the *Twelve*, gave the author of the *Ten* palpitations.[188] He attempts to transmit the passion she aroused in him to his passive compatriots—the most pitiable people on the face of the earth.[189] There is no greater crime than refusing to protect your rights, he rants. The nation will perish if the Chinese do not abandon their slavishness and embrace the struggle for freedom.[190] This biography—the first and most powerful in the *Ten*—establishes the themes of the collection and articulates the central tenets of the presentist position: freedom and blood. Freedom is as essential as air, the author announces: "without air people die, without freedom they also die."[191] Michel's life exemplifies this conviction. She most loved and was willing to fight for freedom: there is no God, she proclaims, only freedom.[192] She believed freedom could only be won with blood, and the author of the *Ten* concurs. Blood's redemptive powers alone, he declares, could destroy evil and save the Chinese nation.[193]

Counterpoint: The Heroic Chastity Martyr

Heroism took on an unprecedented salience in China's turn-of-the-twentieth century national crisis. Different visions of how that crisis should be resolved—through bloodshed and redemption, national utilitarianism, and gradual reform—were articulated through divergent representations of heroic women. Meliorists celebrated Chinese women warriors like Hua Mulan and even a handful of Western heroines like Joan of Arc in order to bolster existing imperial authority. They used Mulan's example to advocate a more active female contribution to the dynasty, and Joan of Arc's to demonstrate that even a small army could defeat a powerful enemy if led by a true patriot.

Archeomodernists and presentists honored a panoply of Chinese heroines who loyally fought to defend existing dynasties and bravely struggled to establish new ones. They also embraced Western women of valor including anarchists, dissidents, military leaders, assassins, and revolutionaries. While the two groups often invoked the same Chinese and Western women, they used these women's stories to different ends, exposing fundamental disparities in archeomodern and presentist political aspirations.

Archeomodernists sought a strengthened nation with greater female participation but without a loss of China's moral and cultural moorings. They simultaneously praised Chinese women warriors for their courage *and* their virtue. In their narratives, Hua Mulan was brave and filial, Liang Hongyu, bold and modest, Shen Yunying daring and loyal. They similarly highlighted the feminine qualities of great foreign heroines. Madame Roland exhibited proper womanly speech and demeanor, and the assassin Charlotte Corday was beautiful, frail, and weak. When foreign exemplars transgressed gender norms, archeomodernists presented them or their times as unnatural. Louise Michel was ugly and illegitimate, Madame de Staël the product of a period of moral disarray. Figures like Joan of Arc who clung to inverted gender roles paid with their lives.

Presentists, in contrast, sought to destroy, rather than bolster, China's faltering ethical infrastructure. Their impulse was to eliminate all moral, cultural, and political constraints on individual freedom through secularization, violence, and bloodshed. They joined archeomodernists in de-Christianizing Western heroines: Joan was inspired not by divine voices but by the need to trick the lowly masses, Roland and Corday by heroic biography rather than biblical verse. At the same time, they forcefully de-Confucianized both Chinese and Western heroines. Extracting the deeds of Chinese women warriors from the moral universes in which they had conventionally been embedded, stripping the didactic overlay from tales of Western heroines, they harnessed these women's stories to new national and racial agendas.

Presentists thus depicted Mulan as fiercely brave and almost regrettably filial, and either occluded or lamented her famous return home. They recast the chaste and filial Li Xiu and the faithful Xi Furen, minority woman leaders of the Eastern Jin and Chen dynasties, respectively, as courageous models for China's anti-Manchu struggle. Presentists subjected the tales of Western heroines to equally muscular resignification. Dismissing the feminine qualities archeomodernists continued to highlight, they praised heroines for their spirit of self-sacrifice: for the hot blood that surged in their veins and the eagerness to shed blood that stirred their hearts. They, therefore, deemed Joan of Arc's cross-dressing, Michel's unattractiveness, and de Staël's infidelity irrelevant. They considered Charlotte Corday, Louise Michel, and Madame de Staël exemplary because these women understood that spilt blood alone—whether of a revolutionary terrorist like Marat or a reactionary leader like Napoleon—would bring political liberation and individual freedom. And they praised Madame Roland not because of her modesty and resolve before she was guillotined but because her blood flowed through history afterward. Self-sacrifice, not self-determination, would save the nation.

Bloody, heroic female self-sacrifice was not new to early twentieth century China, however. A tradition of heroic chastity martyrdom had existed since at least the Mongol invasion in the Southern Song dynasty. While heroic martyrs (*lienü* or *liefu*) were often collapsed with the chaste widows and faithful maidens Xu Dingyi and others derided for their private virtues and particularistic loyalties, their acts were more public and political than those of other female chastity martyrs. These heroic women took their own lives not only to protect personal or familial honor, but to guard the integrity of their communities from outside incursions. Because their heroism was the reactive heroism of resistance, however, turn-of-the-twentieth-century authors determined to actively defend China's honor seldom used them as models.

The figure of the heroic chastity martyr, nonetheless, intruded into public consciousness in the summer of 1900. On August 12, the Joint Expeditionary Forces sent into China to quell the Boxer uprising entered the city of Tongzhou, fourteen miles east of Beijing.[194] Over five hundred "good women" escaped humiliation, rape, and brutalization at the hands of foreign soldiers by drowning themselves in water receptacles or hanging themselves from trees. The views of female heroism and national honor put forward in commentaries on this contemporary incident serve as a counterpoint to discussions of more distant historical or foreign exemplars.

The Joint Expeditionary Forces—consisting of Japanese, Russian, American, British, French, German, Italian, and Austrian soldiers—wreaked such violence and mayhem on the city of Tongzhou that the river that flowed through the city became blocked with corpses. Sixty percent of the population of 4,000 died, thirty percent fled. The remaining ten percent were too old and infirm to move.[195] Among the dead were 570 women who took their own lives.[196]

Observers from the various nations that comprised the Joint Expeditionary Forces recorded the incident, each with their own biases. Although all sources agree that many women had died, there are discrepancies concerning why they had committed suicide, whether or not they had been raped, and which branch forces were most responsible for their violation. According to an American observer, A. Henry Savage-Landor (1867–1924), women committed suicide by jumping from the city wall not because they had been brutalized by Western soldiers but out of despair at having had their homes looted by Boxers and imperial Chinese soldiers.[197] Another American, Luella Miner (1861–1924), of the American Board of Commissioners for Foreign Missions, recorded that hundreds of Tongzhou women killed themselves in order "to escape a worse fate at the hands of Russian and Japanese brutes. Our American soldiers saw them jumping into the river and into wells, in T'ungchow twelve girls in one well, and one mother was drowning two of her little children in a large water jar."[198] The Briton E. J. Dillon (1855–1933) claimed that the non-English- or German-speaking soldiers raped and then bayoneted Chinese women, or raped and abused them to death. "Faithful wives and modest daughters," whom he characterized as Buddhist and Confucian martyrs to chastity, committed suicide in order to escape a worse fate. Young women drowned themselves by holding their heads under the shallow waters of the river, jumping back into the river to die after sympathetic soldiers attempted to save them, hanging themselves from trees, and drowning themselves in garden wells.[199]

These Western reports give us a glimpse into the horror in Tongzhou. The account that was most relevant to subsequent representations of the event in late Qing China, however, was written by a Japanese journalist, Tsuboya Zenshirō (b. 1862). Tsuboya's account, which was probably first filed as a news report for the Japanese press, was subsequently included in a text of reportage, *Observation of the Battles in Northern China* (*Hoku Shin kansen ki*), published in Tokyo in 1901. One of the commentators on the incident, the overseas female student He Xiangning, named Tsuboya's text as her source and it is highly likely that other commentators did as well. Tsuboya details the same carnage as the Western reports. He describes how virgins and women of good families who had been humiliated by Russian and French soldiers threw themselves into water receptacles in the courtyards of their homes. The *Observation* was the only source to give what scholars now accept as the accurate number of women who died, over 570.[200]

These 570 martyrs of Tongzhou belong to a centuries-long lineage of heroic chastity martyrs. They followed conventions of female martyrdom—such as collective drowning—that date to at least the seventh century.[201] And they embodied an exemplar-type that had become a fixture in Chinese historical writing from the Yuan dynasty.[202] Late Qing authors who preferred to exalt the deliberate heroism of the Chinese and Western woman warriors discussed in this chapter did not completely ignore the reactive heroism of historical chastity martyrs. Meliorists appropriated these tales most widely, but archeomodernists and presentists invoked them as well. The principle tension in representations of these martyrs, as in depictions of more militant Chinese and Western heroines, was between virtue and heroism.

The chastity martyrs featured in turn-of-the-twentieth-century sources had generally died either during the Mongol invasion in the Southern Song dynasty or in the chaos of the late Qing Taiping Rebellion. Although the chaste martyr type had reached its apogee in the Manchu Qing conquest, female martyrs of the Ming-Qing transition were largely absent from turn-of-the-century materials.[203] This was perhaps because their virtuous martyr-dom—as opposed to the valiant heroism of late Ming women warriors like Shen Yunying and Qin Liangyu—was harder to dissociate from the taint of the loyalist Ming courtesan.

Wang zhenfu (or Liefu, fl. ca. 1260) of the Southern Song dynasty was captured by a band of Yuan soldiers who had killed both her in-laws and her husband. She successfully repelled the sexual advances of one of her captors before writing her last poetic testament in blood on the side of a cliff and plunging to her death.[204] Wei Xiyuan and Xu Jiaxing include Wang's story in the *Illustrated Biographies of Resourceful Women, Past and Present* and the *Newest Ethics Textbook for Girls and Women*, respectively. The illustrations that accompany these meliorist and archeomodern retellings of Wang's tale reflect divergent emphases on chastity and heroism. In a classic image of refined feminine virtue, the *Illustrated Biographies* presents a dignified Wang zhenfu calmly writing her last testament on a rock with the blood from her finger, the Mongols nowhere in sight (see Figure 41). In contrast, the textbook illustration is in dramatic narrative mode. Underscoring Wang's willingness to heroically defend her honor, it shows her hurtling through space, Mongol soldiers with raised spears on the cliff above her (see Figure 42).[205]

A similar contrast is evident in the same two compilers' representations of Lady Liang of Linchuan. Lady Liang not only chose death over submission to Mongol soldiers as Wang zhenfu had, but sacrificed her own life in order to spare her husband's. Wei Xiyuan highlights Liang's fidelity by praising her

Figure 41 Chaste Lady Wang writing her last testament on a rock with the blood from her finger
SOURCE: WXY IX.15

Figure 42 Chaste Lady Wang hurtling through space, Mongol soldiers with raised spears on the cliff above her
SOURCE: Xu Jiaxing, 72b

for continuing to serve her husband from her grave, appearing in a dream to guide him in choosing a second wife.[206] Xu Jiaxing focuses instead on Lady Liang's heroism. Applauding her decision to separate herself from her husband so he could be spared, Xu describes her boldly berating "the bandits" before taking her own life.[207]

A third Southern Song woman who died resisting the Mongols, Han Ximeng, is featured in an archeomodern and a presentist account. Both a literary and a moral exemplar, Han left a last lyric testament by inserting a suicide poem in the sash of her dress before drowning herself in a river.[208] In his entry on Han in the *Newest Ethics Textbook for Girls and Women*, Xu Jiaxing praises her knowledge of the classics and histories, and her virtue. Invoking one of the conventions of chaste martyrology, he relates that her sexually pure body appeared as if still alive when it was retrieved from the river.[209] Xu Dingyi, who would celebrate Han's talents in his *Guide to Great Women Writers of Our Country*, extols her heroism in his *Biographies of Great Women*. Making her Song-dynasty story relevant to China's late Qing national crisis, he applauds her "well developed anti-foreign consciousness." He laments that the "northerners" continue to display their arrogance on Chinese soil and that, unlike Ximeng, his contemporaries lack the courage to confront them.[210]

While Xu Dingyi's effort to make this tragic tale of a Song talent relevant to the politics of his own day was somewhat forced, the stories of Taiping Rebellion–era heroines had real political immediacy. Representations of Taiping martyrs not only reflected tensions between female virtue and heroism but the spectrum of late Qing views on political virtue and national heroism as well. Predictably, eternalists used these accounts to promote loyalty to the Qing regime, while presentists—including Xu Dingyi, who glorified the female Taiping leaders discussed above—used such stories to oppose the dynasty. The middle ground between these two positions was, however, more ambiguous.

In eternalist accounts, loyalty to the Qing regime trumped adherence to the regime of feminine virtue in instances where men became traitors to the empire. Three such stories later collected in the *Draft History of the Qing Dynasty* featured women from Anhui Province who committed suicide after their husbands or fathers-in-law surrendered to the Taipings. In one of the accounts, a lower-degree holder from Tongcheng who had joined Hong Xiuquan's soldiers returned to his native place with a Taiping band in 1861. His wife, Lady Zhao, greeted him with a harsh rebuke. Had he forgotten he was the descendant of officials, not rebels? she asked sardonically. She then drowned herself together with her young son.[211]

Wei Xiyuan chose not to include one of the many widely circulating stories of Taiping martyrs loyal to the Qing regime in his *Illustrated Biographies*. Instead he featured a woman victimized by Qing soldiers, Huang Shuhua (ca. 1850–67). Huang was only four years old when her native Shangyuan in Jiangsu Province fell to Taiping forces in the early 1850s. Some thirteen years later, government soldiers who "liberated" Shangyuan acted with a brutality that rivaled that of the rebels. They killed most of Shuhua's family, only sparing her because they planned to sell her in their native Hunan. Three months later, en route to the place of sale, Huang poisoned one of her two captors and stabbed the other before hanging herself at a Xiangtan inn. Like Wang zhenfu and Han Ximeng, Huang left behind a written testament ostensibly scribbled on the wall of the inn and later transcribed by two travelers. In his short commentary on the biography, Wei praises the courage, tenacity, and steadfast virtue of this seventeen year old.[212]

An archeomodern account entitled "Biographies of Four Loyal Women" (Si zhongnü zhuan) highlights heroic allegiance to the Qing dynasty. The account features three women who committed suicide after failed attempts to kill or trick the Taiping leader Yang Xiuqing (d. 1856), and a fourth who poisoned her rebel captors before killing herself. The author aligns these women with the Chinese heroic tradition, comparing them to Wang Qi of Lu who died resisting the state of Qi at a tender age in the Spring and Autumn period.[213] He also infuses their stories with the familiar conventions of female martyrology, describing the supernatural qualities that emanated from their sexual purity. Some seventeen years after one of the four, Zhao Biniang of Anhui, died, she returned as an apparition and ended an epidemic in Nanling.[214]

The often implicit politicization of female martyrdom in commentaries on the Taiping Rebellion was more explicit in interpretations of the Tongzhou incident. Three women offered analyses of the incident in various organs of the late Qing press: the Japanese educator and promoter of the ideology of good wives and wise mothers Shimoda Utako; Revolutionary Alliance member He Xiangning; and the pseudonymous "Jin Xia" or Female Knight-errant. Working from divergent assumptions about feminine virtue, female heroism, and current political imperatives, each of these commentators invested the Tongzhou suicides with national meanings. All used the incident to signal what they considered to be a necessary shift in both understandings of female heroism and national political practices at the turn of the twentieth century.

Shimoda Utako, perhaps the most influential foreign woman in late Qing China, praised the Tongzhou martyrs in a transcribed and widely reprinted lecture on Chinese female education. Well versed in Chinese learning, committed to Confucian values, and preoccupied with the political fate of East Asia, Shimoda took a meliorist stance on the challenges China faced at the turn of the twentieth century: "I heard that at the time the Joint Expeditionary Forces attacked [the Beijing region]," she states, "the men generally surrendered whereas women who had been humiliated by foreigners all killed themselves. This exemplifies the most beautiful quality Chinese women possess." Merging Confucian principles with new nationalist concerns, she continues: If only these women could learn to "love their nation as they loved their own bodies," to transmute their personal virtue into national virtue, they would become exemplary patriotic subjects.[215]

He Xiangning did not consider the feminine attributes Shimoda so praised to be assets in China's struggle for international preeminence. Referring to Tsuboya's *Observation of the Battles in Northern China*, she describes the incident as one of humiliation: "When the Joint Expeditionary Forces entered [the Beijing region]," she records in the overseas student journal *Jiangsu*, "[soldiers] brazenly slaughtered civilians and shamelessly raped women in Tongzhou. Respectable women were so ashamed that they threw themselves into rainwater receptacles [and drowned]. In Tongzhou alone," she states, inflating Tsuboya's numbers, "over 1,000 killed themselves." Unlike Shimoda, who considered this self-sacrifice the "most beautiful quality" of Chinese women and a source of national dignity, He interprets it as a marker of Chinese passivity and national degradation. Why, she asks, were her fellow Chinese not outraged by the foreign soldiers' heinous acts? Why were her female compatriots not active nationalists but passive victims who remained ignorant of national affairs "until they personally felt the shame of rape or the tragedy of death?"[216]

Jin Xia took a markedly presentist stance on the incident in the *Magazine of the New Chinese Woman* in 1907. The point of departure for her commentary was Shimoda's narrativization of the events in Tongzhou. "According to Shimoda Utako," she writes, "when the Joint Expeditionary Forces entered [the Beijing region], many men surrendered, whereas women who had been humiliated by foreigners all committed suicide. They were females but they had a male nature."[217] Whereas Shimoda's concern was to nationalize women's chastity, Jin Xia sought to masculinize it. Where Shimoda sought to preserve the virtue of female self-sacrifice, Jin Xia considered it redeemable only as a new brand of heroic masculinity.[218]

These three commentaries present an array of preoccupations from masculinizing acts of female heroism, to overcoming martyrdom as a response to national humiliation, to maintaining the sanctity of female virtue in the age of global politics. All, however, use this instance of female suicide to signify politics. Just as the authors discussed in this chapter appropriated the stories of Chinese and Western heroines to political ends, Jin Xia, He Xiangning, and Shimoda used the martyrs of Tongzhou as vehicles for their own national aspirations.

One last terse comment on the incident from a local gazetteer reminds us that the 570 Tongzhou victims were not just figments of national imaginings but historical individuals who had suffered an unspeakable fate at the hands of foreign soldiers. "Lady Wei Pei was the wife of Wei Tingyu," the gazetteer entry records. "When the Joint Expeditionary Forces entered

[Tongzhou] in 1900, she threw herself into a well and died. She was twenty-one years old."[219]

Only when we encounter this poignant image of a drowning young wife, are we forced to reflect on the thwarted lives subsumed under the rubric of "female martyrdom." Only when we try to penetrate Lady Wei's world are we confronted with the silence of the "chastity martyrs"—and "woman warriors"—who stood in for an array of national ambitions in the ever-shifting hierarchies of global heroism.

It was this silence that China's new-style heroines were determined to overcome at the turn of the twentieth century.

SIX

The New-Style Heroine
and the Paradoxes of Feminine Time

> Women must become the equals of men in their am-
> bition and their ardor. They too will bear daggers to
> defend the nation.
>
> YI QIN, *"Lun Zhongguo nüzi zhi qiantu, xu"*
> *(The Future of Chinese Women, Continued)*

Yi Qin and other turn-of-the-twentieth-century women who lived abroad and published in new-style journals were determined to end the silence of their historical predecessors and overcome the objectification of Chinese women as paragons of virtue, talent, or chaste martyrdom. Assuming a new feminine-heroic subject position, they were no longer bound by the codes of female virtue so derided by Xu Dingyi and other presentists. Their aim was to transcend private, life-cycle-bound feminine time and insert them-selves into public, linear, masculine time—to join men in bearing daggers to defend the nation.[1] Among the most outspoken and influential women of their generation, these new public writers and activists were not representa-tive of all late Qing women. Their lives did, however, embody the conditions of possibility that existed for Chinese females at this crucial juncture in their nation's history. They also highlight tensions both between the archeomod-ern and presentist positions, and within the late Qing nationalist project.

The new-style heroines used recently circulating categories for coura-geous Western women to define themselves. Neither *lienü*, *cainü*, nor *liefu*, they were *nüjie*, *nü haojie*, and *nü yingxiong*—terms that graced the titles of recent publications and suffused the political and women's press.[2] Their adopted pseudonyms convey their "ambition and ardor." The revolutionary Qiu Jin used the pen-names Female Knight-Errant of Jian Lake (Jianhu nüxia), Vying for Heroism (Jingxiong), and Qiu Who Struggles (Qiu Jing).[3] Yan Bin, the editor of the *Magazine of the New Chinese Woman*, used the pseudonym Smelting Stones (Lianshi), an allusion to the goddess Nüwa's heroic feat of mending the earth's damaged firmament.[4] Other anonyms, such as One Who Struggles on Behalf of the Collective (Jingqun), express the same sense of fortitude and courage. In one instance, an author replaced the masculine second character of the commonly used compound for hero, *yingxiong*, with the character denoting female birds or animals, *ci*, to make the new compound *yingci*.[5]

This new feminine-heroic subject position was an effect of the early-twentieth-century national crisis, and a mark of archeomodern and presentist responses to that crisis. Many of the new heroines considered their personal aspirations inseparable from broader national aspirations. Following prominent archeomodernists, they asserted this connection through the new language of the periodical press, engagement in patriotic organizations, and the promotion of women's education.

This new ethos was, however, riven with gender paradoxes. Heroines claimed their new historical role both as representative females and as surrogate males, simultaneously embracing and rejecting the identity of "women."[6] In pursuing their personal ambitions to become recognized national actors, they distanced themselves from the illiterate mass of Chinese women—ignorant playthings, in their characterization—"as stupid as vulgar rustics" and as "dull as wood and stone."[7] In fulfilling their national ambition to strengthen and renew China, however, they were committed to mobilizing their "two hundred million female compatriots"—a new trope that had both rhetorical weight and real political potential.[8]

These tensions within the archeomodern position were compounded by tensions from without. As disjunctions between the promise and the limitations of nationalism became apparent, women realized that this male-driven discourse could not contain the range of aspirations they had for themselves, for womanhood, or for the broader culture. Many responded by prioritizing women's education over political struggle. A handful openly questioned the enterprise of joining masculine time. Still others attempted to write a presentist history of women's oppression that transcended topical political categories. The aporias between masculine and feminine temporalities, national and personal ambitions, the quest for community and the desire for autonomy were rarely unambiguously resolved, however, either in the pages of new-style journals or the lives of particular individuals. Ambivalence and paradox remained defining features of the new feminine heroics.

The New Feminine-Heroic Ethos

NATIONALISM: THE SETTING

The sense of national crisis in China at the turn of the twentieth century not only prompted male reformists to theorize the woman question but enabled female activists themselves to establish a new relationship between women and temporality. These activists used the rhetoric of political crisis to justify extending the timeless roles of daughters, wives, and mothers to include the unprecedented roles of female students, journalists, and nationalists. Evoking the aura of urgency that defined the era, they declared that we, the women of China, "must act before the land of our ancestors is divided like a melon and its people enslaved."[9] They insisted that the national present, rather than the cultural past or the progeny of the future, was the most meaningful context for female self-definition.[10]

In distancing themselves from all-embracing domestic roles, these writers did not attack the regime of feminine virtue as an evil in itself. Instead, they identified it as one of the sources of national decline. "The Chinese race has been weakened," one writes, because of the perpetuation of such sayings as "the husband regulates the wife" and such practices as women adopting their husbands' surnames. The social fabric of a country in which "men are their wives' representatives, and women are their husbands' appendages," she argues, would inevitably be weak.[11]

Following Liang Qichao, these new heroines tied the sense of national peril to the imperative of female education. The overseas student Chen Yan'an announced that if parochial, uneducated, and dependent women represent half the nation's population, "how can the country but perish? . . . The relationship between female education and national survival is crucial."[12] Wang Lian claimed to value her education in Tokyo not for enhancing her personal development but for raising her national consciousness. Earlier, in China, Wang writes, "I did not understand what a nation was or what the importance of female education was. When I came to Japan, I often heard people talk about the nation . . . and I finally began to understand. . . . All people belong to a nation, and all must make the nation their own." If women don't understand national matters, Wang continues, "they must study books and read newspapers. . . . Once women become stronger and more intelligent, the nation will become more powerful and more advanced."[13]

OVERSEAS STUDY: THE CATALYST

Women like Wang Lian and Chen Yan'an went to Japan to study both because Chinese political exigencies linked national survival to women's education, and because Chinese gender principles ruled that female students could only be educated by female teachers.[14] Since the instruction of Chinese girls and women in the late nineteenth century had been almost exclusively conducted in the home or in missionary schools, which few elite girls attended, China lacked female teachers competent to impart the new women's education in the early twentieth century. It, therefore, had either to import teachers—which it did in great numbers—or to export students, which it did in even greater numbers. This overseas study experience reinforced the sense of epochal change and national crisis central to the new feminine heroic ethos.[15]

Between 1901 and 1905, there were an estimated 103 Chinese students enrolled in girls' schools in China, while approximately twice that number, 210, were educated at Shimoda Utako's Jissen Women's School alone in Tokyo.[16] The number of Chinese female students in Japan—the majority of whom enrolled in Shimoda's school—continued to increase even after the Education Board approved formal female schooling in 1907. In that year, there were close to 100 female overseas students in Tokyo; in 1908, 126; in 1909, 149; and in 1910, a slight drop to 125. Sixty-seven Chinese women graduated from Jissen in 1909 and 1910, considered the peak years for female overseas study in Japan.[17] In 1911, out of 116 Chinese graduates from the five main women's schools in Japan, 94 were from the Jissen School.[18]

The popularity of the Jissen Women's School among Chinese students was due to Shimoda's leading role in women's education in Japan and her high reputation among officials in China. Having opened Jissen in 1899 to educate elite Japanese women in the ideology of good wives and wise mothers, Shimoda accepted her first Chinese students in 1901. She established a Chinese Female Division (Shinkoku joshibu) that offered accelerated one- or two-year teacher-training and handicrafts courses the following year.[19] After two Chinese students (including Chen Yan'an) graduated from the school in 1904, provincial missions started sending groups of students for teacher training. By 1905 the Chinese division was large enough to require its own two-story building with a dormitory on the upper floor.[20]

Shimoda's practical pedagogical principles and ethical vision conformed to the expectations Chinese officials and parents had for female overseas study. She limited the Chinese students' formal instruction to the domestic arts and early childhood education, and, as evinced by her reaction to the Tongzhou suicides and her understanding of the roles of good wives and wise mothers, was attuned to Confucian gender principles. She attempted to restrict the students' involvement in politics outside of the school by insisting they reside either with male relatives or in closely supervised dormitories. In her address at the first graduation ceremony for Chinese students in 1904, she asserted that the primary objective of overseas study was the cultivation of domestic skills, not political activism. A number of women who attended Jissen—Qiu Jin, Zhang Hanying (Huifen, 1872–1915), and Tang Qunying (1871–1937) among them—nonetheless became leaders in protests against the Japanese government, in late Qing revolutionary politics, and in the early Republican women's suffrage movement.

As Shimoda rightly feared, the life-changing lessons Qiu, Zhang, Tang, and many other Chinese students learned in Tokyo were learned outside the classroom. Acquiring more than basic literacy or homemaking skills, these overseas students gained a new understanding of historical time and a new sense of gendered space. Their awareness of Meiji Japan's successful political development and of what various Japanese media represented as China's arrested cultural development heightened their sense of the present as a turning point in global history. At the same time, the opportunity to interact with male members of the highly politicized overseas community in Tokyo shaped their feminine-heroic and radical nationalist aspirations.

Women who traveled from China to Japan often represented their voyage in geographic space as a passage in historical time toward a more advanced stage of human civilization. The founders of the Association of Chinese Female Students in Japan (Zhongguo liu-Ri nü xuesheng hui) declared the female overseas movement "an important milestone" that would empower "Chinese women to abandon the old society and enter a new era."[21] In a poem addressed to the supervisor of Hunan overseas students in Japan, Zhang Hanying portrays women's education in Tokyo as a powerful historical force that would enable China to ascend the world stage, build a new empire, and become the dominant force in East Asia (*dongfang*).[22]

Late Qing literature underlines the historic role of the female overseas study experience. Two female characters in a 1907 theater script declare the overseas student movement a catalyst in advancing Chinese women beyond their current degraded state as "pitiful and unlearned," crippled and "corrupted" creatures.[23] In *The New Story of the Stone* (*Xin shitou ji*), the tragic cultural icon Lin Daiyu is able to break with her unfulfilling past through study abroad. Rather than die when Jia Baoyu marries her rival, Xue Baochai, Lin goes to Japan where she eventually becomes a professor at Kang Youwei and Liang Qichao's School of Great Unity (Datong xuexiao) in Yokohama. When Baoyu rushes to Japan to see her, she makes it clear that scholarship is now more important to her than romance. The progressive ethos of the new citizen requires leaving all sentimental talk of love and feelings behind.[24]

The students did not always experience life in Japan as an exhilarating advance, however. Their encounters in Tokyo often highlighted global disparities between an archaic past and an evolved present that they mapped onto the spatial distinction between China and Japan. Zhang Hanying described the awkwardness she felt residing in the liminal zone between the "old" China and the "new" Japan at a lunar New Year celebration with Japanese colleagues. As part of the festivities, Zhang recited a Song dynasty poem that described the Chinese New Year's day custom of hanging scrolls on either side of a household doorway to expel ghosts and spirits. The dean of the school derisively responded that the Japanese had abandoned all such superstitious customs at the time of the Meiji Restoration. Zhang then started to nervously chant a new song about breathing in enlightenment (*wenming*) in Japan before returning home. This time her audience applauded in approval.[25]

Observations of their female Japanese counterparts heightened the Chinese overseas students' awareness of a Sino-Japanese cultural gap. Chen Yan'an notes that "it has only been thirty years since the Restoration and already young girls and women can be heard reciting texts throughout the nation." Unlike these literate, independent, and worldly Meiji women, she complains, her Chinese counterparts are apathetic about their studies, reliant on others, and ignorant of their relationship to China's national survival.[26] Wang Lian relates that the example of literate women in Tokyo shamed her into studying diligently. "At home," Wang explains, "I didn't study much. It was not until I got to Japan that I realized all Japanese women could read, all could write letters and peruse the newspaper. This made me feel extremely ashamed. Now I attend school every day."[27]

This sense of inferiority was reinforced by representations of Chinese women as culturally backward in various Japanese media including the Japanese-owned Chinese-language newspaper the *Beijing-Tianjin Times*. According to one article, the Chinese students were more concerned with their appearance than with hygiene. They used the same water to wash their faces and their teacups, their hands and their bowls, and went to bed at night without changing their clothes. They were not used to cleaning their rooms, carelessly spit pumpkin seeds on the floor, and were just getting over their fear of bathing.[28]

Japanese museums and expositions singled out footbinding as the signpost not only of Chinese women's but China's underdevelopment. The Tokyo Imperial Household Museum (Teishitsu hakubutsukan), which was on the circuit of Chinese visitors to Meiji Japan at the turn of the twentieth century, featured bound feet, together with opium pipes, as signifiers of Chinese customs.[29] The depiction of footbinding that had the most profound impact on young Chinese, however, was a display booth planned for the 1903 Osaka Exposition (Ōsaka hakurankai), a showcase of diverse cultures and recent technological developments.[30] On March 8, 1903, two Japanese newspapers announced that the "Races of Man Pavilion" would introduce premodern customs of the Chinese, the Ainu, the aborigines of Taiwan, and the inhabitants of the Ryukyu Islands, Korea, India, and Java. Twenty-one women with bound feet, one smoking opium, would exemplify Chinese customs. This projected display aroused such outrage in the overseas community that it was ultimately cancelled. Because of Taiwan's status as a Japanese colony, however, the Taiwan exhibit was mounted as planned. It featured "elaborately ornamented women with bound feet" in one of its displays and had two "small-footed women" serving in the pavilion's tea shop.[31]

The sense of degradation this incident generated was tangible in the writings of female overseas students who decried footbinding for contributing to the objectification of Chinese women as useless playthings.[32] This feeling of shame ultimately extended well beyond the overseas student community and became a principle of mainland pedagogy. A women's ethics primer published two years after the Osaka Exposition explains that when the Japanese mounted an exhibition, they included footbinding in the "barbarian" (yeman) section. "Is this not humiliating?" the author asks his female readers.[33]

The overseas study experience offered not only a new sense of global historical time by exposing "barbaric" Chinese practices like footbinding, but a new sense of gendered space by eroding China's "barbaric custom" of gender separation. Wang Lian, who arrived in Tokyo in 1902 from Hubei Province, describes her journey from China to Japan as a gradual naturalization of her relations with men. At her first stop, in Hankou, she was uncomfortable with the idea of traveling with male companions. By the time she got to Shanghai, however, she was a little more accustomed to her male fellow travelers. On the boat from Shanghai to Kobe, as she shared meals with male passengers and allowed them to help her embark and disembark along the way, she felt even more at ease. Once settled in Tokyo she became even less conscious of gender differences. She viewed the ten or so friends of both sexes who visited her every day like brothers and sisters who treated each other with mutual "respect and love." Wang contrasts this feeling of naturalness with "the barbaric Chinese custom of not letting men and women see one another."[34] When male students from her native Hubei graduated from the Kōbun Academy (Kōbun shoin) and the Cadet School (Shikan gakkō) in Tokyo and were about to return to China in 1903, Wang gave a speech at their farewell gathering, a mark of how integrated she had become into the overseas student community.[35]

Wang Lian's speech honoring her male colleagues was delivered at a Western-style restaurant, the Seiyōrō, in the Ueno section of Tokyo, one of the many public spaces in the city where Chinese men and women were able to meet.[36] Even allegedly segregated spaces, including the relatively well-guarded women's dormitories where the majority of the Chinese female overseas students lived, were not impermeable.[37] Sakaki Mitsuko (1883–1975), teacher and dean of the Department of Chinese Overseas Students (Shina ryūgakusei bu) at Shimoda Utako's Jissen Women's School, reported that despite a strict curfew and injunctions against visitors, some students allowed male "guests" into their rooms. As a result, there had been a number of miscarriages among the students and one case of a woman dying in childbirth.[38]

The new spaces where young women and men were able to meet in Tokyo were not only sexually but politically charged. The Chinese overseas community consisted of a politically engaged group of exiled publicists, revolutionaries, and tens of thousands of male Chinese students. They formed a radical elite that hailed from all over China and would play key roles in the 1911 Revolution and its aftermath.[39] Female students came into contact with this community at public meeting places like the Chinese Overseas Student Hall (Zhongguo liuxuesheng huiguan) and even within their own homes.[40] He Xiangning left a school dormitory in 1903 to live with her husband, Liao Zhongkai (1877–1925), in a house that served as a front for Sun Zhongshan's Revolutionary Alliance. She formally joined the alliance, one of the first women to do so, in her own home in 1905, the year it was founded.[41]

NEW WRITING: THE MEDIUM

Women who entered male political space in Tokyo also entered male dis-cursive space: the new field of overseas student, reformist, and translation journals. Many female students, including He Xiangning, Wang Lian, and Chen Yan'an, published essays in overseas student journals. Others, how-ever, wrote for and/or edited women's journals. These women's journals created a transnational imagined community in the first years of the twen-tieth century with Shanghai and Tokyo as its two principal hubs. Editors of women's journals published in Shanghai were closely attuned to the ac-tivities of overseas students in Japan, while writers living in Tokyo were preoccupied with social and political change on the Chinese mainland.[42] This Shanghai / Tokyo print nexus also had reverberations well beyond these two urban polestars. Overseas students from places as diverse as Guang-zhou (Guangdong Province), Liling (Hunan), and Shangyuan (Jiangsu), and young women living in China, from Changsha (Hunan) to Fuzhou (Fujian), wrote essays in Tokyo-based periodicals. The most influential of these journals reached audiences in the Chinese hinterland from Fengtian in the northeast to Yunnan in the southwest.[43]

An estimated forty-four women's journals were published in China and Japan between 1898 and 1911.[44] The magnitude of this number only be-comes apparent when properly contextualized. Given the lower recorded rates of female-to-male literacy and female-to-male school attendance in both the overseas community in Japan and in China, the number is strik-ing.[45] Whereas the ratio of female-to-male overseas students in Tokyo was one to forty, the ratio of women's journals to male-run journals was one to ten.[46] The total number of women's journals to male-run journals pub-lished in China and Japan—approximately one to five over the period 1898 to 1911—was also significantly higher than the number of women's schools to boys' schools in China proper: one to seventy-seven in 1907, the year female education was sanctioned, and the number of girls' schools was on the rise.[47] The more successful women's journals also rivaled mainstream publications in their circulation. Before the Japanese government forced its closure in 1907, the circulation of the *Magazine of the New Chinese Woman* was estimated to be as high as 10,000, a figure that compares favorably with the major journals of the day.[48]

There are many possible explanations for this proportionately high number of women's journals. It may imply higher rates of female liter-acy than previously assumed. It also suggests that the audience for these journals extended beyond the targeted community of female students to include older women and young women educated at home who read the periodical press, as new-style textbooks exhorted them to, without leaving the household. It further seems to confirm the contention that men, who founded and supported several women's journals, were, either through displacement, voyeuristic fascination, or genuine concern with women's issues, among their most avid readers.[49]

Regardless of the precise reason, the significant number of these journals underlines the prominence of the woman question in cultural and political discourse at the turn of the twentieth century. Furthermore, it reflects the widely held conviction in this period that the press would foster a new historical role for women. Tang Qunying, who was involved in several journals in Japan and China both before and after the 1911 Revolution, declared that newspapers and journals—rather than girls' schools or vocational training—would most effectively prepare women to join the struggle for China's survival.[50]

Women like Tang who wrote for the new-style press at the turn of the twentieth century were not the first in Chinese history to defy the long-standing injunction against words from the inner chambers reaching the outside world (*neiyan buchu*).[51] Rather than align themselves with any strand of the extensive female literary legacy discussed in Chapter 3, however, these new-style authors defined themselves against women writers of the past. While they followed Liang Qichao in denouncing the late imperial women of talent, their critique had a personal edge the metonymic male discourse lacked. In criticizing the constrained writings of past women of talent, they highlighted the global reach of their own journalistic essays. In belittling the circumscribed circulation of the woman of talent's poetic rumination, they foregrounded the breadth of their own audience, the ever-widening, anonymous late Qing reading public.[52]

There were, nonetheless, certain formal continuities between late imperial and turn-of-the-twentieth-century literate female culture. New-style women writers often relied on their male colleagues for entry into the new print field, just as past female poets had depended on male relatives to disseminate their writings. Of the two earliest Chinese women's journals, the first was established by male reformers as one of a constellation of new-style institutions, and the second appeared as a supplement to a male-run journal.[53] Prominent early-twentieth-century female authors or editors generally gained their first journalistic experience writing for "male-stream" publications. Members of the female overseas student organization the Humanitarian Association, including Hu Binxia, a future editor of the Republican-era *Ladies' Journal* (*Funü zazhi*), and Lin Zongsu (fl. 1905), who would edit such late Qing publications as the *Daily Alarm* (Jingzhong ribao), published their maiden essays in the overseas student *Jiangsu Journal*.[54]

Even as women entered this new journalistic print world, their writing continued to be marked as female. They followed past women writers (or men posing as women writers) in inserting the characters signifying a woman or a woman of learning (*nüshi*) between their surname and given name. And their essays were generally included under gender-specific rubrics in male-run publications.[55] Most significant, women's journals were explicitly gendered. Whereas titles of publications targeting a male or a general audience reflected topical concerns or regional affiliations, titles of journals published for a female audience almost uniformly included the term *nü* (female).

All women's journals included a literary section that published the poetic forms typically associated with the woman of talent.[56] The *Magazine of the New Chinese Woman*, for example, a journal considered so politically incendiary that it was eventually shut down by the Japanese authorities, regularly featured a literary column. Male-run overseas student publications also included women's poetry. A seven-verse poem by Wang Lian appeared in the first issue of *Students of Hubei* (*Hubei xuesheng jie*) in 1903 (followed by her tirade against the woman of talent in the following issue).[57]

These traces of earlier literary practices were more formal than substantive, however. Journals founded by or for women differed most from past women's writing in their heightened sense of temporality, their preoccupation with gender and cultural change, and their adoption of new, politicized genres. They offered their readers socially engaged poetry, galvanizing essays and biographies of the Western female icons discussed in preceding chapters. Each journal issue opened with a lead editorial (*shelun*) that introduced a topic of immediate importance and often exhorted readers to take action.

The rousing tone of these topical essays was echoed in the "new poetry featured in the most classical literary section of women's journals."[58] Conventional in form but new in content, this poetry conveyed reflections on current problems, critiques of gender norms, and chivalric female aspirations.[59] Wang Lian declared in verse that only when belief in the incompatibility of women's virtue and talent was shattered could "the seeds of enlightenment" be scattered and the women of China awakened to the possibility of freedom.[60] Qiu Jin offered impassioned laments on China's degraded state in such poems as "Moved by the Times" (Gan shi) and "Moved to Indignation" (Gan fen) in her *Chinese Women's Journal* (*Zhongguo nübao*).[61]

Unlike past women authors who wrote exclusively for their literary peers, editors of women's journals were committed to communicating with all "two hundred million" of their female compatriots, including those not literate enough to read the often allusive "new poetry" or erudite political essays. Women's journals therefore featured articles written in both the literary and vernacular (*baihua*) languages.[62] The well-educated women who wrote for these publications were capable of composing in the literary style, but they were also among the earliest and most effective practitioners of the vernacular.[63] Reflecting these new heroines' dual objective of joining the masculine political discourse and creating an inclusive feminine discourse, several women's journals used the literary and demotic languages in distinct sections. The editors of the 1898 *Women's Journal* decided, after much debate, to use the literary language in 30 and the vernacular in 70 percent of every issue.[64] The regulations of the *Magazine of the New Chinese Woman* stipulated that essays would be in written in literary Chinese and lectures recorded in the vernacular.[65] Other journals, including Qiu Jin's *Vernacular [Journal]* (*Baihua*) and *Chinese Women's Journal*, were composed exclusively in the vernacular.

ACTIVISM: THE ACTUALIZATION

This commitment to engaging their less educated female compatriots distinguished the new women writers' from past women warriors. Whereas historical women of valor acted alone, guided by a hierarchical sense of service to sovereign, patriarch, or husband, their late Qing counterparts were increasingly driven by a horizontal, cooperative spirit and the desire to make a place for all women in China's national history.[66] Inspired by Western models, they combined the political ambition of Madame Roland with the reformist zeal of Frances Willard or Millicent Fawcett. Their new activism—from the early years of the overseas study movement through the early Republican suffrage movement—continued, however, to be shaped and constrained by male political agendas. While the new heroines were anxious to establish a collective of engaged Chinese women, their initiatives were often in response to male prompts and driven by the desire to join masculine time.

One of the first Chinese organizations to reflect this tension between new feminine and dominant masculine agendas was the Humanitarian

Association, a woman's organization founded in Tokyo on April 8, 1903, with roughly a dozen members. Some three weeks later, on April 29, 1903, members of the association joined what has been described as the first large Chinese nationalist demonstration (the impetus for Yang Qianli's coda to his biography of Florence Nightingale discussed in Chapter 2). Led by overseas students in Tokyo, the demonstration protested Russia's refusal to withdraw the troops it had been amassing in northeast China since the Boxer Rebellion.[67] When male students announced the founding of the Volunteer Corps to Resist Russia (Ju-E yiyong dui), members of the Humanitarian Association responded with a call to organize a parallel women's organization.

Hu Binxia, the association's founder, first took the podium, followed by eight other students—including Chen Yan'an, Wang Lian, Lin Zongsu, and Gong Yuanchang. Together with four other women, these nine joined a Chinese wing of the Japanese Association of Dedicated Nurses (Tokushi kangofu kai) and announced that they would follow the volunteer corps to Manchuria.[68] Not satisfied with their small, Tokyo-based contingent, these aspiring nurses further attempted to establish a broad-based organization by mobilizing women in China. In a telegram sent to students of the Shanghai School for Girls and Women (Shanghai nü xuexiao), they declared: "Women are also a part of the nation, members of the universe." They, too, must embrace their responsibilities.[69]

The Humanitarian Association became increasingly radicalized in 1904 when Qiu Jin arrived in Tokyo and took over its leadership. Qiu renamed the organization the Humanitarian Association for Practical Action (Shixing gongai hui) to emphasize its shift toward a more activist stance. The new association called for Chinese women to come to Japan both to study and to join the growing revolutionary movement.[70]

Like members of the Humanitarian Association who were committed to following the male students' volunteer corps in confronting the Russians in Manchuria, members of the Humanitarian Association for Practical Action followed their male compatriots in protesting a more immediate affront to Chinese patriotism. On November 2, 1905, the Japanese government published a series of Control Laws (Torishimari kisoku) that Chinese students interpreted as a paternalistic attempt to control their activities in Tokyo. Qiu Jin, who was the appointed female student representative for the protest, called for a general student strike, and female students at a number of women's schools in Tokyo, including the Jissen Women's School, responded. The movement received its most dramatic impetus when the renowned male revolutionary activist Chen Tianhua (1875–1905) expressed his despair over the treatment of the Chinese students in Japan by drowning himself in a Tokyo bay. As feelings of anguish and humiliation intensified in the overseas community, some two thousand Chinese students left Japan. They included thirty women led by Qiu Jin.[71]

In China proper, female activism was ideally restricted to participation in moderate, male-run organizations. This is reflected in a women's textbook that promotes patriotism by depicting both men and women at a meeting of a commercial association. The seated members of the association are flanked by banners that read "Restore National Strength through Organization" and "Resolutely Boycott American Products."[72] (See Figure 43.) This restrained and ancillary female activism was apparent in women's efforts to join specific national struggles, such as the movement to recover China's

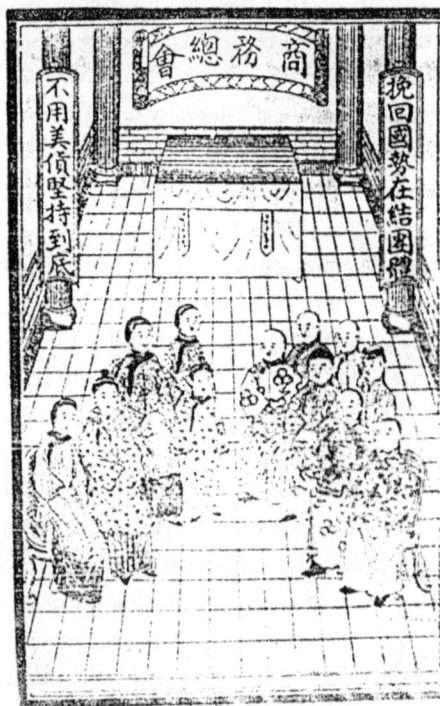

Figure 43 A group of female and male patriots committed to "Restoring National Strength through Organization" and "Resolutely Boycotting American Products"
SOURCE: Xie Chongxie, 49b

rights to the Suzhou-Hangzhou-Ningbo Railway in 1907. Female activists followed men in buying stock in the railway and forming parallel railway recovery organizations, such as the Women's Railway Protection Association (Nüjie baoluhui).[73] They also attempted to institutionalize female contributions to the national cause through such foundations as the Female Citizen's Fund (Nü guomin juan).[74]

Women who participated in these various organizations conformed to an archeomodern vision of female social activism. Others—who generally had had some experience in Japan—took more militant action. Fang Junying (1884–1923), for example, one of the earliest Chinese graduates of the Tokyo Senior Women's Normal School (Tōkyō joshi kōtō shihan gakkō) and the sister of the future revolutionary martyr Fang Shengdong (1886–1911), served as part of the revolutionary rearguard in Hong Kong and south China in the last years of the Qing dynasty. Together with a number of other overseas students, including Qiu Jin and Chen Xiefen, Fang had been trained in the use of explosives by a Russian nihilist in Yokohama. She had also belonged to an assassination squad (*mousha tuan*) organized by Wang Jingwei (1883–1944) in 1908. In 1909 Fang went to Hong Kong where she served over the next two years as part of the rearguard for a series of attempted uprisings and assassinations in China. She and her sister-in-law, Zeng Xing, also participated in the planning of the Guangzhou Uprising of April 27, 1911. When the uprising was crushed, Junying's brother, Fang Shengdong, was among the seventy-two "revolutionary martyrs of Huanghuagang." Junying, who took her own life in 1923, never fully recovered from Shengdong's violent and early death.[75]

After the Wuchang Uprising on October 10, 1911, more women became active in the revolution as both supporters and combatants. Eight students in Japan, including Tang Qunying, organized a Women's Red Cross Army (Nüzi hongshizi jun). On October 19, 1911, they left Japan and joined forces with the Cantonese doctor and revolutionary Zhang Zhujun, who was organizing a Red Cross Association in Shanghai.[76] On October 24, these Japanese returned students, together with Zhang and some twelve other women and twenty men, traveled to Wuhan to support the revolutionary forces.[77] Tang Qunying was also among the women who directly engaged in revolutionary warfare. Together with Zhang Hanying she organized the Shanghai Women Commandos (Nüzi beifa gansidui).[78]

Both before and after the revolution, many women, including Tang, were also involved in fledgling women's organizations whose programs were not explicitly determined by male agendas. These included the Association of Chinese Female Students in Japan, founded by a student from Hubei, Li Yuan, in September 1906, with the aim of struggling on behalf of Chinese women. The association boasted some seventy members, a significantly larger number than the more militant Humanitarian Association. Those in positions of responsibility included the editor of the *Magazine of the New Chinese Woman*, Yan Bin, together with Tang Qunying, and Wang Chang-guo (1880–1949).[79] In March 1911 Tang helped organize a similar association, the Study Society of Female Students in Japan (Liu-Ri nü xuehui), and was editor and publisher of its organ, the *Magazine of the Study Society of Female Students in Japan* (*Liu-Ri nü xuehui zazhi*).[80]

After the 1911 Revolution had succeeded with the support of Tang Qunying, Zhang Hanying, Fang Junying, Zhang Zhujun, and countless others, many women, including Tang and Zhang Hanying, were no longer content with auxiliary women's associations. When the Ministry of the Army prohibited the further engagement of women in military activities in February 1912, they joined Lin Zongsu and Wang Changguo in focusing their energies on the struggle for women's suffrage.[81] For these four individuals and their associates, the right to vote would signal formal recognition for women's contributions to the 1911 Revolution and ensure them a voice in Republican politics. Lin Zongsu had already organized an Association of Female Comrades for Women's Political Participation (Nüzi canzheng tongzhi hui) in November 1911.[82] On February 20, 1912, this organization merged with four others (three of which had also been formed by overseas students) to form the Female Suffrage Alliance (Nüxing canzheng tongmeng hui).[83]

When the March 11, 1912, Provisional Constitution of the Republic of China failed to give women equal status, members of the Female Suffrage Alliance, including Zhang, Tang, Lin, and Wang, began what would become an infamous protest campaign. Together with some twenty other women, they approached the parliament in Nanjing three times between March 19 and 21, breaking windows and forcing their way past guards.[84] Having earned little save social opprobrium for these dramatic gestures, they retreated from political confrontation and reorganized the suffrage alliance in April of 1912 as the Women's Suffrage Alliance (Nüzi canzheng tongmeng hui). The alliance adopted a nine-point resolution that underscored the new heroines' dual agenda: the first resolution was to promote equal rights for men and women; the second to disseminate women's education.[85]

By 1913 Yuan Shikai's government made it increasingly difficult for women to be active in any sphere of public life other than education. In October of that year, a few months after the failure of the Second Revolution, which claimed the life of Zhang Hanying's husband and political fellow traveler Li Faqun (1873–1913), the Ministry of Internal Affairs ordered the disbanding of the Nanjing women's suffrage movement. In March 1914 Yuan announced a Public Order Regulation that prohibited women from joining political organizations or attending public discussion meetings. Tang and Zhang reluctantly returned to their hometowns of Hengshan and Liling, respectively, having little choice but to devote their energies to local schools.[86]

EDUCATION: SOCIAL REPRODUCTION

As Tang and Zhang found in the early Republic, the strong Chinese bias against female political involvement—manifest in the 1914 Public Order Regulation, the 1907 girls' school regulations, and the 1904 memorial on female instruction in the home—made education the only consistently sanctioned sphere of public female engagement. The new women's education was not exclusively a fallback position for women with more grandiose political ambitions, however. It was also an integral component of the feminine-heroic program.

Archeomodernists and presentists tied female education to heroism in various organs of the mainstream and women's press. Chen Yiyi argued in 1909 that the objective of women's education "is not to produce wise mothers and good wives. Rather it is to create heroic and outstanding women (*nü yingxiong nü haojie*)."[87] The overseas female student Lin Shiying echoed Chen Yiyi's language two years later. "If heroic and outstanding women (*nü yingxiong nü haojie*) wish to enlighten the benighted women [of China]," she wrote, "they must receive teacher training and promote universal education."[88] Newspapers extolled late Qing women who heroically devoted themselves to education. In 1904 the *Beijing-Tianjin Times* hailed a niece of Zeng Guofan (1811–72) as a heroine (*nüzhong zhi jie*) for single-handedly raising the money to found the Jingshan Girls' School (Jingshan nü xuetang) in Hunan.[89] In 1906 the same newspaper declared the Manchu bannerwoman and martyred founder of the Women's School of Purity and Progress, Huixing, a true heroine (*nüzhong haojie*).[90] Biographies of the period similarly praised foreign women not only for shedding their blood in revolutionary movements, but for advancing women's education. The American founder of Mount Holyoke College, Mary Lyon, was acclaimed in the *Magazine of the New Chinese Woman* as a "beloved hero."[91]

This coupling of women's education with heroism marks a significant change in Chinese conceptions of female talent at the turn of the twentieth century. From the ancient through the late imperial periods women's learning had been understood in tension, but also in tandem, with women's virtue. According to the normative view upheld by turn-of-the-twentieth-century eternalists and meliorists, the purpose of female instruction was to prepare young women for their moral and practical roles as wives and mothers. Archeomodernists began to shift the purpose of female education from private, moral concerns to public and national imperatives in the late 1890s, making education the first duty of mothers of citizens. Presentists reinforced this political emphasis and further shifted the goal of women's education from motherhood to the formation of autonomous national actors.

Despite the range of these visions of women's education, all required training Chinese female educators to staff the growing numbers of early-twentieth-century girls' schools. This entailed not only sending young Chinese women abroad to study, but establishing teacher-training programs in China and sanctioning education as an acceptable female career choice. From 1904—the year high officials memorialized the court on restricting female learning to the home—authorities in several provinces began to arrange for young women to study in Japanese normal schools. In China, the Education Board approved the founding of teacher-training schools together with elementary schools in 1907. As the number of girls' schools continued to rise in subsequent years, so did the need for female teachers. When the early Republican government endorsed secondary-level female education in 1912, upper-level teachers' schools grew faster and were in greater demand than regular women's middle schools.[92]

In the first years of the twentieth century only a few of the early Chinese private schools, such as the School of Fundamental Women's Learning in Shanghai, attempted to develop teacher-training programs.[93] A few normal schools were also established in both the south and the north.[94] These programs were insufficient to meet the need for teachers in private girls' schools prior to 1907 and in the increasing numbers of private and public schools thereafter. Although some of these schools employed men, the 1907 regulations attempted to end this by stipulating that female schools could only hire upstanding, highly educated women as deans, principals, teachers, and dormitory heads. If no Chinese women were available, schools were required to hire foreign female graduates of higher-level normal schools.[95]

Early in the twentieth century local educational authorities who recognized the need to train their own female teachers rather than depend on either foreign women or Chinese men began to look to Japanese schools. In November 1904 officials in Hunan Province were the first to make formal arrangements with Shimoda Utako's Jissen Women's School through the intermediary Fan Yuanlian (Jingsheng, 1876–1927), a male overseas student.[96] This Hunan initiative was of particular historical significance. It served as a template for other provincial programs and produced a number of new-style heroines, both teachers and activists, including Zhang Hanying.

Fan Yuanlian, who knew that two Chinese women had graduated from the Jissen School the previous July, asked Shimoda to accept twenty young Hunanese women in 1905. She agreed, establishing a program for Chinese students that included a one-year accelerated teacher-training course (extended to a full three-year course in 1907), a general two-year course, and a one-year accelerated handiwork course.[97] Later in 1904 the Chinese government formally approved the female overseas study initiative and in early 1905 Fan gave a lecture in Shanghai promoting Shimoda's accelerated teacher-training course.[98]

The twenty Hunanese students arrived at Shimoda's school in late July 1905. Ranging in age from fourteen to forty-eight, they came from several counties in Hunan and included four women from outside of the province.[99] Thirteen of the twenty enrolled in the accelerated normal course and seven in the accelerated handiwork course. Fan Yuanlian and others acted as interpreters in the classroom in an effort to overcome one of the greatest difficulties the Chinese students faced in Tokyo: the Japanese language.[100]

The Chinese and Japanese press showcased the successful students. It recorded their enthusiasm for their studies in Japan and their commitment to teaching when they returned to China. Zhu Jingyi (b. 1888), from Jingzhou in Hubei Province, was seventeen years old when she arrived in Tokyo in the summer of 1905 (see Figure 44).[101] Her brother Zhu Yongzhen, who had preceded her in Tokyo as a student at the University for the Study of Law and Politics, had told Jingyi that Japan was the most advanced of nations, particularly in academics. Jingyi reports that she found all classes at the Jissen School challenging. She most enjoyed physical education, singing, and composition, which were a great contrast to the more limited reading, calligraphy, and embroidery instruction she had received in China. Zhu's tentative aim upon returning to China was to work in the field of childcare (*yuying*).[102]

Figure 44 The overseas student Zhu Jingyi
SOURCE: Jissen joshi, file no. 1132. Courtesy of the Jissen
Women's University Library.

Zhu Jingyi's fellow student, Huang Guohou (b. 1881), who was from the
provincial capital of Changsha and had enrolled in the Jissen accelerated
teacher-training program at the age of twenty-three, was more ambitious.
The top student in the program, she declared with conviction in an interview with the *Beijing-Tianjin Times* that she would become an educator
when she returned to China.[103]

Other provinces followed Hunan in sending women to train as teachers
in Japan both at Shimoda's Jissen Women's School and at other institutions
in Tokyo.[104] Given the high rate of attrition for female overseas students due
to linguistic, cultural, or personal difficulties, a remarkable number completed their studies and became girls' school founders and/or instructors
upon their return to China.[105] Incomplete data preclude calculating the precise figure, but a sense of the relative numbers emerges when we examine
specific groups of women who studied in Tokyo. Of the twenty students
who entered the Jissen Women's School in 1905 as part of the Hunan initia-

tive, one-fifth became active in women's education: twelve of the thirteen Chinese women who had enrolled in the accelerated teacher-training course graduated in 1906, and at least four started their own schools.[106]

Among these four was Zhang Hanying, who made her first contribution to Chinese female education while still a student in Japan. When Zhang returned to Tokyo in 1906 after having left in protest over the new Japanese regulations for Chinese students the preceding year, she did not go back to Shimoda's Jissen School. Instead she founded the Chinese Female Student Department (Shina jogakusei bu) at the Women's School (Seijo gakkō). Together with her collaborator, Kuang Junyi, a male overseas student from Hubei, Zhang established five programs for Chinese students, including one accelerated and two three-year teacher training courses.[107] These programs reflected feminine-heroic aspirations more closely than did the Jissen school's: their stated objective was not to form good wives and wise mothers but to train women to assume their national responsibilities alongside their male compatriots and to teach in girls' schools upon their return to China.[108]

The first group of Chinese female students to enroll in the program on December 16, 1906, included Zhang herself, Tang Qunying, who had also previously been a Jissen student, and the textbook author and *Magazine of the New Chinese Woman* contributor Sun Qingru.[109] Twelve students, including Tang, graduated from the Chinese Female Student Department's accelerated teacher-training program in December 1907.[110] After this pedagogical success in Japan, Zhang contributed to developments in female education in Changsha and Liling both before and after the 1911 Revolution.[111]

Wang Changguo, who was active in the early Republican suffrage movement together with Zhang, became the principle of the Pingxiang School of Fundamental Women's Learning (Pingxiang Wuben nüxiao) after returning to Hunan from Tokyo.[112] Other teachers trained through the Hunan initiative included Huang Guohou, who had announced her commitment to teaching in the 1906 *Beijing-Tianjin Times* interview cited above. In 1916, Huang became dean of the Hunan Number One Girls' Normal School (Hunan diyi nüzi shifan xuexiao) in her native Changsha. She taught home economics at the same school the following year and was involved in women's vocational education on the eve of the May Fourth Movement.[113] Li Qiaosong (1872–1933) from Pingjiang County, who had arrived in Japan at age thirty-three, established the Private Enlightenment Girls' School (Sili qiming nüxuetang) with her husband, Ling Rongzhong (1874–1929), sometime between 1905, the year of Li's graduation, and 1908, when she sent Shimoda a photograph of herself with a group of Enlightenment Girls' School students.[114] Li's school was particularly successful. In 1916, administrators applied to the Education Board for accreditation as a teacher-training school.[115]

Various sources provide disparate references to other returned students, some named, many not, who served in girls' schools in diverse regions of China in the early twentieth century. A number taught at the famous Shanghai Patriotic Girls' School. The educator Chen Yongsheng (1900–1997), who was a student there in the early Republic, recorded that all of her teachers had studied in Japan.[116] Returned students also found employment at various physical education schools in Shanghai.[117] Cao Rujin, a former Jissen student, younger sister of the future Vice-Minister of Foreign Affairs Cao Rulin, and a participant in the 1903 anti-Russian protest in Tokyo, was involved in a number of informal educational activities in her native Shanghai upon her return to China. In winter 1906, she founded a music lecture society for girls and women, and by 1910 had established a home for poor girls that offered instruction in childcare.[118]

Returned students were also employed in Beijing schools, which generally developed later than those in Shanghai. Several became teachers at the three Institutes of Teaching and Learning (Chuanxi suo) established by Jiang Kanghu (1883–1954) from 1905. Jiang's wife, who was in charge of the Beijing Inner City Institute for Women's Education (Beijing neicheng nüxue chuanxi suo), actively sought graduates from Japan to teach in the school. In 1907 she wrote to Yan Bin, editor of the *Magazine of the New Chinese Woman*, in Tokyo, asking her to hire teachers on the school's behalf.[119] By 1909 six women who had studied in Japan taught a range of subjects at the three schools.[120] Zhili Province also engaged returned female students as teachers and school administrators. A Miss Liao was hired as school superintentent at a girls' school in Baoding that opened in the winter of 1907. Her name is known to us because she was dismissed from her job for insisting on bringing her female students to a graduation ceremony at the local army school.[121] Japan-trained students were also important in Guangdong Province. Chen Yongsheng taught at a school, for example, whose principal, the elder sister of He Xiangning's husband, Liao Zhongkai, had studied in Japan.[122]

The Paradoxes of the New Feminine Heroics

The experience of those who returned to China and devoted themselves to teaching is more difficult to trace than that of women who catapulted themselves into the historical narrative by smashing the windows of parliament or plotting assassinations. Women like Tang Qunying, Zhang Hanying, and Qiu Jin were prototypical new heroines because they were involved in both education *and* politics. They helped lay the foundation for a new feminine culture and a new feminine temporality by promoting overseas study in Japan, women's education in China, and a new female life course. Their ultimate aim was, however, to synchronize this new time with masculine time. Education, which they trumpeted in their journals as integral to the new feminine-heroic ethos, often served either as their default mode or as a cover for their political activism. Zhang Hanying and Tang Qunying founded numerous new schools in the early years of the Republic, but they did so most intensively when the Yuan Shikai regime had disabled their efforts to pursue their suffrage agenda. Qiu Jin's educational activities, which are discussed below, were primarily a front for her anti-Manchu activities.

These women exemplified fundamental tensions in the feminine heroic ethos: between *educated heroines* advancing China's political struggle and *heroic educators* promoting schooling for girls and women, between striving to *join* or straining to *transcend* the national masculine time of archeomodernism.

THE PROBLEM OF MASCULINE TIME
AND THE STRUGGLE WITH HISTORY

Some women who studied abroad, wrote for new print media, and promoted female education did not embrace the male-driven nationalist project. These skeptics voiced their critique from three perspectives: gender difference, male weakness, and anarchism.

Gong Yuanchang was a politicized overseas student from Hefei in Anhui Province who had joined the Humanitarian Association in 1903, the Revolutionary Alliance in 1905, and the Association of Chinese Female Students in Japan in 1906. She was also a proto-"difference feminist." Unlike Yi Qin and others who called for women to be the equals of men, Gong believed talk of sexual equality was naïvely reductive. In making masculinity the norm, it perpetuated the oppression of women. She encouraged her female compatriots not to follow men but to cultivate their own uniquely feminine abilities and assume responsibilities in fields most appropriate to their gender. She defined these as education and the fine arts.[123]

Fang Junji of Fujian Province, a cousin of Fang Junying's, warned against adopting what she considered a distorting masculinity. "Those who advocate women's rights today," Fang complains, insist that women blindly follow men. This means imitating even their gravest faults, including unruliness and immorality.[124]

He Zhen, an anarchist and the nominal editor of the journal *Natural Justice* (*Tianyi*), was not only wary of women's efforts to join national time but opposed to nationalism. Collapsing this new ideology with Confucianism and other male discourses that reproduced gender inequality, she rejected the nationalist-based rationale for the development of female literacy. She also ridiculed her female compatriots for embracing male militancy by celebrating martial heroines as exemplars. Until women are able to access, develop, and use knowledge without appealing to a masculine system of values, she argued, they would be condemned to subordination.[125]

The new heroines, who held conflicted views of masculine time, were equally ambivalent about historical time. Like other presentists and archeomodernists, they both stridently rejected and strategically reappropriated the past. Pressing for a radical disengagement from enduring traditions, they nonetheless continued to cling to the precious raft of history in negotiating China's, and their own, transformation.

The new heroines' critical engagement with the past distinguishes them from previous female literati. Ban Zhao, author of a section of the *Han Dynastic History*, was perhaps the only woman in Chinese history to have earned the credentials of a true historian. While some turn-of-the-twentieth-century writers fantasized about resurrecting Ban and mobilizing her talents for the present, many feminine-heroic authors viewed her as the irredeemable source of nearly two millennia of women's oppression, the nemesis of—rather than a model for—Chinese womanhood. Yan Bin declared Ban's famous didactic text, the *Precepts for Women*, one of the most damaging works in the history of Chinese women.[126] He Zhen dismissed the great literatus as a traitor to Chinese womanhood for not only internalizing but perpetuating the patriarchal Confucian discourse.[127]

Critics like He Zhen and Yan Bin viewed more recent Qing women who engaged in the exegesis of historical texts as hopelessly pedantic and politically irrelevant. These authors who focused their scholarly abilities on collating and glossing Liu Xiang's *Arrayed Traditions of Women's Lives*, often modeled themselves on Ban Zhao, one of the first scholars to expand on and annotate Liu Xiang's text.[128] They include a near-contemporary of the feminine-heroic authors, Xiao Daoguan (d. 1907), whose *Collected Annotations to the Arrayed Traditions of Women's Lives* (*Lienü zhuan jizhu*) was compiled in 1892 and published in 1907.[129] In her preface, Xiao situated herself within a lineage of female scholars of the *Arrayed Traditions* that extended from Ban Zhao through Liang Duan (1757–1825) and Wang Zhaoyuan (1763–1851) of the early nineteenth century.[130]

The new-style authors' historical approach departed radically from Wang's, Liang's, and Xiao's. Rather than confirm prevailing norms by treating the past with eternalist reverence or a meliorist sense of historical continuity, they disputed these norms in a critical presentist spirit. Yan Bin recounts how when she and a former classmate and close friend, Luo Ying, had studied history (*shijian*) together, both had been struck by the representation of women as lowly, weak, and inferior. They were determined to expose this historical bias but were immediately thwarted by the continued power of male authority. Luo's father, with whom they shared their reactions, silenced them with the accusation that they were "slandering the ancients." The sense of historical injustice this incident aroused in Yan drove her to establish the *Magazine of the New Chinese Woman* as a platform for her views. The magazine would disseminate new perspectives on women's issues and counter the inequities embedded in the Chinese past.[131]

If women were to overcome their status as objects of history, Yan Bin and other feminine-heroic authors believed, they had to themselves become politically engaged practitioners of history. This involved reappropriating historical models in socially and politically significant ways, as many of the authors discussed in earlier chapters had done. It also meant charting a genealogy of female oppression.

As discussed in Chapter 5, the pseudonymous Guardian of Modesty attempted to elevate women's status and galvanize her female compatriots by drawing on the accomplishments of past Chinese exemplars. She argued that Hua Mulan was a world-class heroine and Liang Hongyu the single-handed savior of the Southern Song dynasty.[132] She also expressed trepidation about the institution of marriage by invoking the story of another Chinese exemplar, Ying Erzi of the Warring States period. In the Guardian's retelling, Ying Erzi had shunned marriage not only out of devotion to her ill parents—the conventional interpretation of her story—but out of indignation over female subordination. "Half of the reason" she intended to withdraw and never marry, the Guardian has Ying explain, "is illness in the family. Half of the reason is the [deterioration of women's rights]."[133]

The Guardian traces the historical process through which these rights had deteriorated in order to inspire women to reclaim them. "Alas," she announces, the day the traces [of sovereign rule] were extinguished and the royal odes ceased to be made was precisely the day male power (*nanquan*) was unleashed."[134] She comments on the first part of this passage (from the *Mencius*) in an interlinear note: "When Confucius edited the *Odes*, he initially discussed the empresses' virtues." Women were, thus, not yet treated with contempt. It was only "from the Warring States period that women's rights (*nüquan*) began to deteriorate."[135]

By locating the origin of women's oppression at a particular moment in history—"the day the traces [of sovereign rule] were extinguished and the royal odes ceased to be made" in the Guardian's poem—the new women writers were able to historicize this oppression. And by historicizing this oppression they were able to prove that the subordination of women was not an eternal and insurmountable feature of Chinese culture. It had a beginning, and thus could have an end.

If female oppression had a history, it also had to have a prehistory. Redeeming that prehistory became one of the presentists' most pressing tasks. They did not seek to *establish* women's rights in imitation of the West—just as many of them balked at kowtowing to foreign icons like Madame Roland. Instead they sought to *recover* rights that had existed deep in the Chinese past—in the same way Xu Dingyi, Ding Chuwo, and others sought to recover the stories of Chinese heroines. Just as knowledge of forgotten women warriors like Li Xiu and Xun Guan would mobilize young women to become militant nationalists in the present, knowledge of the prehistory of women's oppression would galvanize those committed to ending it.

This task of redeeming women's lost rights was integral to the platforms of almost all late Qing women's organizations and journals. The Humanitarian Association declared the recovery of women's "special rights" the first step in creating nation-minded female citizens.[136] The anarchist journal *Natural Justice* was published by a society devoted to the "reinstatement of women's rights" (Nüzi fuquan hui).[137] At the same time, male supporters of the feminine-heroic ideal admonished women to reclaim the rights they had possessed in primitive Chinese society.[138] Many female activists acknowledged these men as necessary allies in this struggle.[139] Lin Zongsu hailed Jin Tiange, the male author of *A Tocsin for Women*, for example, as the driving force behind the revival of women's rights.[140]

These rights that had to be reclaimed had been lost for millennia. The "Inaugural Statement" to the *Magazine of the Study Society of Female Students in Japan* explains that "for several thousand years . . . women had been dependent on others for their livelihood, and their duty had been to serve."[141] The pseudonymous Jin Xia laments that men had suppressed the spirit of China's women "for several thousand years."[142] Yi Qin refers to one thousand years of oppression during which the rights that women like Hua Mulan had enjoyed "in antiquity" had been lost.[143]

These critics generally attributed millennia of oppression to ancient philosophical developments, rather than socioeconomic or historical forces—assuming the former shaped the latter. Only one male author and feminine-heroic fellow traveler, Chen Yiyi, describes female oppression as the product of distinct historical stages—of "Slavery" (Nuli shidai), "Dependence" (Congshu shidai), "Harmonious Relations" (Hele shidai), and "Independence" (Duli shidai)—but he does so in the translation of a Darwinist-inspired work.[144] Chen's essays on Chinese women were, in contrast, clouded with vague historical notions. In a critical discussion of ethical prescriptions for women's conduct, for example, he collapses the ancient thrice-following with the Ming-Qing chastity cult, as if they were part of one long, dark historical moment.[145]

Female presentists were equally nebulous in charting the history of women's oppression. They traced this oppression to distant cultural, rather than recent social or political sources thus both avowing the tremendous weight of this oppression *and* revealing their own tentativeness about confronting male power. Claiming the sources of female subordination lay in pre-Confucian, Confucian, or post-Confucian ideology, they avoided both the contentious issue of anti-Manchuism and the risk of alienating their radical male compatriots.

Xiao Yin, a fellow student of Yan Bin at Waseda University in Tokyo, claimed that the oppression of Chinese women was rooted in the cosmological concepts of *yin* and *yang*. Originally signifying the opposing forces of darkness and light, night and day, these concepts had later given rise to notions of female and male, wife and husband, and ultimately to the particularly restrictive Chinese conception of the family. Xiao unfavorably contrasted this *yin/yang*–based formulation with theories of human relations in the West. In Western society, she announces, the individual—not the family—was the point of origin of all communal and national formations.[146]

Many authors held Confucius responsible for the low status of women in China. A number pointed to a particular passage from the *Analects* (17: 25)—"women and mean people are difficult to cultivate" (*nüzi yu xiaoren nanyang ye*)—as the source of female subordination. The pseudonymous One Who Struggles on Behalf of the Collective (Jingqun) laments in a poem that these poisonous words had made women objects of hatred since antiquity. She declares that this statement was also profoundly unfilial as it rendered Confucius's "own pitiful mother" the "victim of his unjust charge."[147] An author who called herself Mover of the Earth (Zhuan kun) also links the subordination of Chinese women to statements in Confucian texts. In addition to the line from the *Analects* quoted above, she cites an excerpt from a poem entitled "Lu'e" in the *Book of Odes*, a text that Confucius had allegedly edited: "A father can conceive [a child] but not nurse it, a mother can nurse [a child] but not teach it" (*fu neng shengzhi buneng yangzhi, mu neng yangzhi buneng huaizhi*).[148]

The anarchist He Zhen forcefully denounced Confucianism as the source of female oppression. In a learned and sophisticated essay, she asserts that Confucians had created an elaborate discursive web that trapped women in a position of inferiority. She recounts how, in early Confucianism, the great teacher Mencius threatened to divorce his wife—following a custom allegedly introduced by Confucius—on the grounds that she did not greet him properly on his return home one day. Later Confucians, such as the authors of the Han *Discussions in the White Tiger Hall* (*Baihu tong*), continued to twist words and force interpretations in advancing their selfish prerogatives. They declared that when Heaven created humanity, it favored males. Therefore, anything associated with the masculine *yang* was good and anything associated with the feminine *yin* bad. This ensured the female's subordinate status and legitimized a system that allowed one man to have several wives. Confucians realized that women might not accept this arrangement, and so they created the discourse of submission whereby it was the woman's responsibility to be faithful to one husband all her life. Preempting any protest, they gave women duties but no rights and prohibited them from leaving their husbands, remarrying, or expressing jealousy.[149]

Other turn-of-the-twentieth-century writers exempted Confucius himself from responsibility for Chinese women's degradation and exclusively blamed later scholars for distorting the Master's original teachings. The Guardian of Modesty contends, in the poem cited above, that it was not until after Confucius had finished editing the *Book of Odes* that women were demeaned.[150] The Heroine of Chubei (Chubei yingci) defends the great sage who she claims had acknowledged women's rights when he referred to them together with men in the phrase "a man and a woman" (*pifu pifu*). It was Han dynasty literati, she insists, who were responsible for first denying women their rights.[151] A certain Pei Gong was one of many who concurred with this view. She asserts that ancient social concepts such as the three bonds (*sangang*) had been misinterpreted by pedantic later scholars, with devastating results for Chinese gender relations.[152]

Whether they blamed Confucius or later thinkers for the subjugation of Chinese women, feminine-heroic writers consistently focused—as did archeomodernists—on two specific manifestations of this oppression: limited access to education and footbinding. Historicizing what had become essentialized feminine characteristics—ignorance and bound feet—they hoped to eradicate these obstacles to the advance of Chinese womanhood.

Late Qing female authors traced the origins of female illiteracy—like the loss of female rights—back at least a millennium. Some suggested women had not been educated since the dawn of Chinese civilization. Chen Yan'an writes of "4,000 years without education for girls and women."[153] Others intimated that women had been educated in the pre-imperial period. The overseas student Huang Lingfang laments that Chinese women had been deprived of education for "the past 2,000 years."[154] Still others followed archeomodernists in regarding women's ignorance as a post-Han dynasty development. The pseudonymous Foqun asserts that the examples of Fu Sheng's daughter and Ban Zhao prove that Chinese women had been well-educated in the period before the narrow-minded view that only a woman without talent was virtuous prevailed.[155] Some authors conceded that women had been educated up through the recent past, but only in a highly didactic and meaningless way. Yan Bin complains, for example, that for several millennia Chinese women had only been exposed to the "old teachings."[156]

Following Liang Qichao and other archeomodernists, the feminine-heroic authors tied women's education to footbinding, and footbinding to national weakness. While female illiteracy was not unique to China at this point in world history, through the eyes of the Japanese and of Western missionaries before them, footbinding had become the global marker of Chinese backwardness.[157] New women writers like Wang Lian and Chen Yan'an who were committed to exposing this humiliation were also determined to expunge it by identifying footbinding's historical origins. As Qiu Jin declared, it was time for women to examine their own past and finally call to account those responsible for perpetuating this debilitating practice.[158]

A few turn-of-the-twentieth-century authors claimed ancient or early imperial roots for footbinding. One asserted that the description of the gait of the woman of Handan in the *Records of the Grand Historian* made it possible to date the practice to the late Zhou dynasty. Another contended that it could be traced to Pan Shu, wife of Donghun Hou, who ruled as emperor of the Qi dynasty from 499 to 501.[159] Qiu Jin herself blamed the practice on Chen Houzhu (Chen Shubao, 533–604), the last emperor of the Chen dynasty near the end the period of division (220–589).[160] Overwhelmingly, however, the new-style heroines contended that footbinding was neither an ancient Chinese practice nor an element of classically defined feminine deportment (*rong*).[161] This was consistent both with their discourse on the recovery of women's rights and with available historical data.

These authors traced the origin of the practice to the Five Dynasties period (907–60). According to this view, the first woman to bind her feet was Yaoniang, a lady in the court of the last emperor of the Southern Tang dynasty, Li Yu (937–78, r. 961–74).[162] Poems in the *Journal of Women's Learning* describe how Yaoniang's golden lotuses had contaminated Chinese women's history. One announces that her incurably diseased feet were the "source of the infirmity" that continued to afflict Chinese women.[163] Another explains that even the Manchu Shunzhi Emperor (r. 1644–62) had been powerless to eliminate the unrelenting disease Yaoniang had unleashed.[164]

EMBRACE AND REJECTION OF THE
IDENTITY OF "WOMEN": THE CASE OF QIU JIN

The eradication of footbinding and the promotion of women's education were central to the feminine-heroic ethos. Turn-of-the-century female authors rejected the past—and present—unlettered and crippled identity of Chinese women in order to embrace a new enlightened and empowered identity. This tension between refusing and concentrating on the identity of "women" was evident in all practices in which the new heroines engaged. It was manifest in their efforts to transform Chinese women by writing the history of their oppression, in their ambivalent self-positioning as educated heroines or heroic educators, in their founding of female associations prompted by male agendas, and in the double—classical/vernacular—register of their public pronouncements. This fundamental tension is also salient in the essays and lives of particular late Qing women.

In a 1903 article, Hu Binxia first disdainfully rejects, and, then, hopefully embraces the identity of "women." "What pains me most are the 200 million women [of China]," she writes. "Not only are they regarded by others as playthings but they consider themselves playthings. Is this not lamentable? . . . How can we find it strange that people call them inferior beings?" Hu, nonetheless, goes on to describe her derided female compatriots as China's future hope. "If from this moment on all of the women of China make China's suffering their own personal suffering and regard China's corruption as their own corruption . . . then the nation would flourish."[165]

The tension is perhaps most prominent in the dramatic life of Qiu Jin (Figure 45). Modern China's most renowned female revolutionary, Qiu was also an accomplished poet, essayist, and orator, and an ardent promoter of women's education. Her writings and activism were central to the theorization and actualization of the feminine-heroic ethos.[166]

Qiu Jin self-consciously adopted a heroic identity shortly after leaving her husband and children to study and pursue her political destiny in Japan. In Tokyo she dropped the distinctively feminine middle character of her name, Gui, and adopted the heroic noms de plume, the Female Knight-Errant of Jian Lake and Vying for Heroism.[167] She framed her aspirations within the revolutionary project: she joined organizations devoted to overthrowing the Qing government and trained in bomb-making. Assuming the public roles women had been taught to shun, she excelled at public speaking and moved crowds of men and women with her galvanizing speeches about China's fate.[168] Shortly after her return to China from Japan, she was implicated in a failed attempt to assassinate the governor of Anhui Province. She was executed by the Qing government in 1907.

Qiu Jin's greatest aspiration was to transcend the identity of "women" by shocking her male compatriots and leaving a mark in national history. This was manifest in her highly self-conscious acts of cross-dressing. In 1904 she both appeared in public in Beijing and had herself photographed in a Western man's suit (see Figure 46).[169] In 1906, when she returned to China, she donned a Chinese man's long gown and jacket, again had herself photographed, and wrote a poem reflecting on her image, "Inscribed on a Photograph of Myself Dressed as a Man" (Ziti xiaozhao nanzhuang) (see Figure 47).[170] While living in Tokyo from the summer of 1904 to the spring of 1906, Qiu adopted not male but Japanese female dress. She did, however, accessorize her kimono with a small dagger that became the focal point of this famous pose which she, again, had photographed (see Figure 48).[171] Qiu used this last photograph as the frontispiece of the second issue of the journal she founded in Shanghai in early 1907, *Chinese Women's Journal*. The caption for the photograph highlighted the aura of the dagger, "Photo of Ms. Qiu Jin, the Female Knight-Errant of Jian Lake."

Many who knew Qiu in China and Japan commented on her distinctive femininity that transcended the various layers of male guise she adopted

Figure 45 An early image of Qiu Jin
SOURCE: Zhonghua shuju, n.p.

Figure 46 Qiu Jin in a Western man's suit
SOURCE: Wang Canzhi, n.p.

Figure 47 Qiu Jin in male Chinese dress
SOURCE: Zhonghua shuju, n.p.

Figure 48 "Photo of Ms. Qiu Jin, The
Female Knight-Errant of Jian Lake"
SOURCE: *Zhongguo nübao*, 1:1 (February 1907)

(see Figure 49). None, however, disputed her success in adopting characteristically masculine skills, from riding astride on horseback to powerful oratory.[172] She publicly defied her gender even in death. While the customary fate of women criminals was to be dismembered or hanged, Qiu Jin was beheaded, like a man.[173]

Qiu Jin tied her preoccupation with entering history to contemporary politics and channeled her heroic yearnings through the cause of nationalism. This was evident in a conversation recorded by Hattori Shigeko, a Japanese educator living in Beijing who would accompany Qiu Jin to Tokyo in 1904 and facilitate her entry into Shimoda Utako's Jissen Women's School. Immediately before announcing to Hattori that she had decided to go to Japan to study, Qiu explained that her ambition in life was to shock. She refused "to live without spirit" and was committed to pushing herself to the limit in order to surpass men. Qiu then repeated the revolutionary mantra: "China belongs to the Chinese, not to those foreign barbarians the

Figure 49 Hattori Shigeko's feminine rendering of Qiu Jin in the man's suit
SOURCE: Hattori, "Shū," 39

Manchus." Revealing how her personal struggle gained meaning through the national struggle, she asked, If we only fear for ourselves, what are our lives worth?[174]

Qiu suggested in this last statement that her main concern was not to equal men but to surpass them. In her embrace of the figure of the female knight-errant and her sartorial shifts from (Western) male, to (Japanese) female, and back to (Chinese) male dress, she was less intent on denying her femininity than on defying all prescribed gender norms. This was further evident in a famous essay addressed to her two-hundred million female compatriots, a manifesto of the new feminine-heroics. In the essay, Qiu encourages her Han Chinese sisters to exceed both the standard expectations for women and the past achievements of men. It was women, she announces, who had to take responsibility for China's future and overcome the past errors of male civilization. "We all know the nation is about to perish and men are incapable of saving it. Can we still think of relying on them?"[175]

Qiu's individual, woman warrior-like aspirations, thus, coexisted with a commitment to mobilizing her female compatriots to join the national cause. She understood that Chinese women first had to be liberated from patriarchal subordination before they could take on their new historical role. In the company of her close female friends, she asserted that revolution had to begin with the family. Wu Zhiying remembered her saying, "Today young people talk excitedly about 'Revolution! Revolution!' but I say revolution has to start with the family and equality of the sexes."[176]

Qiu's own life was a testament to "family revolution." She was China's own Nora who had slammed the door on a constraining domestic existence.[177] Her daring behavior and personal encouragement inspired her female contemporaries to do the same. There are well-known and less well-known examples of this. In Japan, Qiu publicly shamed her good friend Chen Xiefen, daughter of *Jiangsu Journal* editor Chen Fan, into refusing an arrangement by which she would become the concubine of one of Chen Fan's friends.[178] Qiu further convinced Chen Fan's two concubines to leave him, rallying other Zhejiang students to pay the women's tuition so they could attend school. One of the ex-concubines, Chen Xiangfen, later participated in the 1911 Revolution.[179] Qiu was also renowned for saving a number of women from forced marriages to local bullies while teaching in Zhejiang shortly before her death.[180] A less well-known incident involved a young Japanese woman Qiu had met on the ship from Tianjin to Kobe in the summer of 1904. Qiu rebuked the woman for her despondency over an aborted love affair in China and told her that it was more meaningful to die than to live feeling sick at heart. The next day the Japanese woman jumped off the side of the ship.[181]

Qiu also took an institutional approach to improving women's lives. She founded two vernacular journals that targeted a female readership: *Vernacular [Journal]*, a monthly published in Tokyo from August 1904 to 1905, and the *Chinese Women's Journal*, founded in Shanghai in early 1907.[182] In essays published in these and other journals, in her speeches, and in her daily life, Qiu was an avid promoter of women's education and female overseas study in Japan. In a June 6, 1905, letter addressed to students at a women's normal school in Hunan and published in the *Women's World*, she encouraged all Chinese women to travel to Japan to study.[183]

Qiu's commitment to women's education was, however, riven with the feminine-heroic tensions between individual and collective, political and educational aspirations. While she genuinely believed in the need to uplift her female compatriots, she instrumentally used the cause of female education to advance her own political agenda. This was apparent in a trip she made in the spring of 1905 to Shaoxing from Tokyo in the midst of her overseas studies. The visit was both crucial to Qiu's revolutionary career and a high point in her agitation for female overseas study. In Shaoxing, she secretly joined the revolutionary Restoration Society (Guangfu hui) and made her first contact with Xu Xilin (d. 1907), who would be her coconspirator and co-martyr in the plot to assassinate Anhui governor Enming in 1907.[184] Qiu also openly promoted study in Japan, in particular, at Shimoda's Jissen Women's School, during the trip. Given the timing of the campaign and the intense dissatisfaction Qiu had otherwise expressed with Shimoda's school both before and after her 1905 visit, this pro-Jissen campaign most probably served as a cover for Qiu's Restoration Society activities.

Qiu Jin had privately and publicly criticized almost all aspects of the Jissen school, from the cost and quality of the dormitory food to the knowledge and competence of the teachers.[185] On her return visit to China in 1905, however, she mimeographed copies of the regulations for the school's accelerated normal and handicraft courses for Chinese students, appended an enthusiastic essay of her own, and distributed the document in Jiangsu and Zhejiang Provinces.[186] Her appended essay underlines the imbrication of education and politics in the feminine-heroic ethos. Signed Qiu Who Struggles, it declares that Japan's women's school courses were "not only good for Chinese women but for the future of China." It encourages those with limited time or money but with unfulfilled ambitions to "pack up light suitcases and leave the obscurity of the inner chambers in order to board the steamship of joy, breathe the air of freedom, and flock to Japan to pursue their academic studies."[187] Despite this rhetoric of self-liberation, Qiu was relatively unconcerned with the personal experience Chinese women would gain abroad. Instead, she was anticipating the contribution these women would eventually make to schools in China, and through these schools to the revolutionary struggle.[188]

When Qiu returned to China definitively in December of 1905 in protest over the Japanese governments' new regulations for Chinese students, she was again simultaneously engaged in female education and anti-Qing politics. And again, the former seems to have served as a cover for the latter. In May 1906 administrators at the Xunxi Girls' School (Xunxi nüxue) in northern Zhejiang Province, where Qiu had taught Japanese, hygiene, and science since March, forced her to leave on the grounds that she was promoting revolution among the students.[189] Almost a year later, in February 1907, she became the principal and physical education teacher at a school founded by Xu Xilin and Tao Chengzhang (1878–1912) to train revolutionaries, the School of Great Unity (Datong xuetang) in Shaoxing.[190] Symbolically, it was here, on the school grounds, that Qiu was arrested by Qing soldiers on July 11, 1907—the penultimate act in her dramatic quest to leave her mark in the national narrative and bring women into Chinese history.[191]

Qiu's complex and tension-ridden aspirations—her desire to reject *and* embrace the identity of "women," to engage in the male-defined project of national salvation *and* a female-centered project of redemption and edification—were reduced to one order of meaning after her death and particularly after the 1911 Revolution, with which her name became inextricably tied. As her story became integral first to a triumphant revolutionary history and only secondarily to a more tentative women's history, her singular act of martyrdom overshadowed the ambivalence that suffused her recorded conversations, her often tormented poetry, and her involvement in women's causes.[192] Even her female contemporaries overwrote these complexities by underscoring Qiu's devotion to political revolution. As noted in the opening to this Part, the pseudonymous "Frustrated Female Worthy" entered Qiu into the new global hierarchy of militant heroines less than a month after her execution.[193] Wu Zhiying who focused on Qiu's commitment to social change in the first of five biographical sketches she wrote between 1907 to 1912 delineated a more decisive and coherent political trajectory in the sketches written after the revolution.[194] In most later historical accounts, Qiu's proto-feminist impulses were presented as intrinsic and subordinate to her revolutionary aspirations.

Through this political signification of her life story, Qiu Jin did, however, achieve what she and other radical women most craved. She left a mark not in paradigmatic female history but in political male history. Her crimson blood flowed, as had Madame Roland's, in the chronicles of the modern world. At the same time, however, like Roland and historical Chinese martyrs, Qiu was remembered to the extent that her life merged with the dominant political narrative. She became an icon of the late Qing revolutionary struggle just as Madame Roland stood in for the French Revolution, Southern Song martyrs embodied Han resistance to barbarism, and the chaste Li Run sanctified the Hundred Days' Reforms. Li Run's and Qiu Jin's stories could only become part of late Qing History through the marginalization of their actions on behalf of other women. Feminine-heroics were only readable as heroism, the new feminine temporality only perceptible in its intersection with masculine time.

Counterpoint: The Case of Chen Yan'an

Chen Yan'an, whose life was not characterized by martyrdom, rousing oratory, or shocking male guises, was excluded from the grand national narrative. Her traces remain, as a result, fragmented and underdetermined.[195] They, nonetheless, form a revealing counterpoint to the feminine-heroic ethos, not because Chen's experience was radically distinct from the new heroines', but because the two were intimately linked at one juncture. An early advocate of joining masculine time, Chen later embraced what the new heroines reviled as cyclical feminine time. Her life trajectory could be neatly reconstructed as a linear progression from passionate archeomodernist to subdued meliorist, from radicalized student to conservative good wife, kindergarten teacher, and lifelong disciple of Shimoda Utako. Imposing such coherence, however, obscures the rich paradoxes Chen's story brings to light and the insights they provide into the late Qing moment.

Chen, who was from Shangyuan in Jiangsu Province, was one of the first Chinese women to study in Japan and one of the earliest graduates of the Jissen Women's School. She had been part of a small contingent of students who left China in June 1902 with Wu Zhihui (1865–1953), a young fire-brand whom the Meiji government would expel almost immediately upon his arrival in Tokyo.[196] Chen herself soon became involved in radical politics while at the Jissen School. A member of the Humanitarian Association, she supported the 1903 protest against Russia's presence in Manchuria, volunteering to serve as a nurse on the Manchurian front.[197] Her political profile in Tokyo was such that Qiu Jin considered her a kindred spirit when they met at the Jissen school in 1904. In a poem dedicated to Chen and a certain Sun Duokun with whom Chen was about to return to China, Qiu laments the brevity of their time together. She encourages Chen and Sun to devote themselves to uplifting their downtrodden Chinese sisters upon their return to the mainland.[198]

Chen ultimately conformed to Shimoda Utako's rather than Qiu Jin's aspirations for her, however. Shimoda, who had close ties to the Qing government, strongly disapproved of the activism that had won Chen Qiu Jin's respect. A public speech she delivered at Chen's graduation ceremony may have been directed at Chen herself. Shimoda stated that she did not want her students to become "radical proponents of popular power" (*gekietsu na minken ronsha*) or "rebels" (*ranshin zokushi*), but good wives, wise mothers, and devoted elementary-level teachers.[199] Despite likely early tensions, however, Chen and Shimoda developed a long-lasting and close relationship once Chen had abandoned the pursuit of "popular power" in favor of the roles of kindergarten teacher and devoted wife. On March 23, 1918, Chen addressed Shimoda as her respected teacher in a poem she signed with her husband's surname.[200]

Chen's marriage was crucial to her life course. Unlike Qiu Jin, who left her husband, Tang Qunying, who was widowed after two short years of marriage, or Zhang Hanying, who had a companionate marriage, Chen Yan'an assumed the role of the new-style good wife. While in Japan, she was engaged to the Chinese student Zhang Zongxiang (Zhonghe, 1877–ca. 1940). A native of Zhejiang Province, Zhang had passed the first level of the civil service examinations in 1895 and was awarded a scholarship to enroll in the law program at the Imperial University in Tokyo in 1897.[201] As one of China's earliest students in Japan, he commanded a certain authority in the Chinese overseas student community and was the author of a widely used student handbook. Unlike his future wife, however, Zhang maintained his distance from the increasingly nationalistic elements in this community. He opposed the founding of the Anti-Russian Volunteer Corps that Chen actively supported, characterizing it as a "makeshift" army that would only antagonize the Qing government.[202]

In spite of these differences, Zhang and Chen were married sometime after they both returned to China. Chen left Tokyo in 1904 and Zhang returned to Beijing shortly thereafter. The law degree he had earned in Tokyo won him the status of a metropolitan graduate (*jinshi*) and a post in the Law Revision Office in 1905.[203] A wedding photo of the couple was published in one of the early issues of the *Women's Eastern Times* in 1911, probably several years after their marriage (see Figure 50). Almost every issue of the *Women's Eastern Times* included wedding photos that often juxtaposed "old-" and "new-style" (or *wenming*) marriages.[204] The photograph of Chen and Zhang is of a new-style couple. Chen is not veiled nor are her in-laws included in the photo, as in representations of old-style marriages. At the same time, her experience abroad is highlighted. The caption describes her as an overseas student and she is dressed in a kimono. Seated with Zhang standing above her, however, she does not appear as self-possessed as the woman in the photo opposite, Pan Ying, a sericulture expert, who is standing next to her

Figure 50 Wedding photos: Zhang Zhonghe and Chen Yan'an (right), Pan Zhixi and Pan Ying (left)
SOURCE: FNSB 1 (May 13, 1911)

husband, Pan Zhixi, both in Western dress (see Figure 50). There were clear gradations even within the category of *wenming*.

Zhang Zongxiang continued to have both a successful ministerial career in the Qing and Republican government and close ties with Tokyo: in 1916 he was appointed China's ambassador to Japan.[205] Chen accompanied Zhang on his official missions. This allowed her to maintain her relationship with Shimoda, which Zhang strongly encouraged. He lavishes great praise on Shimoda and her school in an essay written in the early Republic. Likening the reconciliation between Shimoda and Chen to one between mother and daughter, he describes how Shimoda had cared for Chen when she injured her foot in a rickshaw accident in Tokyo. He concludes that the bond between female teacher and disciple was stronger than the tie between male instructor and student.[206]

The sources suggest, however, that Chen Yan'an had harbored ambiguous views of women's education in Japan. In 1903 she published a manifesto entitled "Exhortation for Female Overseas Study" (Quan nüzi liuxue shuo). In passages cited earlier in this chapter, she contrasts the sorry state of women's learning in China with the high level of female literacy in Japan. Encouraging her female compatriots to improve themselves by studying abroad, she outlines the advantages of overseas study in Tokyo: geographic proximity, a similar writing system, and relative inexpensiveness.[207]

The following year, however, Chen presented a radically different assessment of female education in Japan at a meeting between a group of overseas students and a Chinese emissary, Hu Yujin, who had been sent to observe the state of Meiji education.[208] In a speech Chen gave at the meeting, she criticized the level of women's education in Japan and insisted that it would be more advantageous to establish women's schools in China than to send more students to Tokyo. Hu, who had read Chen's essay in *Jiangsu Journal* the year before, concluded that her understanding of the situation in Japan had improved since the article was published.[209]

At least two other explanations for Chen's antithetical views on Meiji female education are plausible, however. It is possible that she, like Qiu Jin, had had private reservations about women's education in Japan but felt compelled to publicly promote it as the best educational option for Chinese women at this time. It is also possible that her 1904 critique of Japanese women's education was largely strategic. She may have felt that if Qing officials became convinced of the inadequacies of Meiji girls' schools, they would be forced to develop women's education in China. Unfortunately, there is no further documentation to suggest how Chen's views on either Japan or Japanese women's education evolved through the Republican period, when she lived in Tokyo as the Chinese ambassador's wife. Nor do we know what her feelings were during the May Fourth Movement, when Zhang was labeled a pro-Japanese traitor and beaten by patriotic protesters.[210]

Chen's teaching career presents further ambiguities. The expectation when she graduated from the Jissen Women's School was that she would return to China, marry, and possibly teach at the pre-school or elementary level, as Shimoda had prepared her students to do.[211] According to some accounts, Chen had wanted to open a kindergarten or elementary school for girls, and one source claims she was responsible for all kindergartens in Beijing.[212] There is hard evidence of her role as the head of the Number One Kindergarten (Diyi mengyang yuan) in Beijing in 1908.[213] Established the year after the Education Board had officially promulgated women's elementary and normal school education, the kindergarten was supported by members of the Qing government. The Manchu noble Zhen Beizi contributed funds and appointed three officials—Zhang Zongxiang among them—to administer the school.[214] Unlike Zhang Hanying, Tang Qunying, and other women who struggled to found and finance their own schools, Chen was able to take part in an educational initiative blessed by the authorities, supported by her own husband, and subsidized by the Qing court.

Most remarkably, Chen made no mention of her teaching career in an interview in Japan in the early Republican period.[215] The preface to the interview includes an anecdote from Chen's early years as a student at the Jissen Women's School that highlights her domestic diligence. When students and teachers were moving to a new location, Chen was the last to leave the old dormitory. She was later discovered cleaning the doorbolts of the sliding doors long after the other students had left. According to the preface, this fastidiousness was a mark of the "beautiful virtue of East Asian woman."[216] Chen did nothing to dispel this image in the interview. She claims she was most concerned with domestic matters. If she had to leave the house on a social call, she only did so reluctantly. Being away from the house all day made her feel she had not accomplished anything and left her dissatisfied.[217]

This leads to the final paradox in Chen's life story: her initial rejection and ultimate embrace of the conventional East Asian identity of "women." In her 1903 *Jiangsu Journal* article, Chen had urged her female compatriots to join the national struggle. She demanded they become more globally aware, more independent and focused in their studies, and more directly responsible for China's fate.[218] Not an echo of these former aspirations can be heard in the Jissen interview. Reflecting on her time as a Jissen student, Chen claims that her favorite course had been domestic science. She makes no mention of her membership in the Humanitarian Association or her participation in the anti-Russian protest. Rather than credit her experience in Japan with opening her eyes to the world—the almost inevitable result of her involvement in the nationalist overseas community—she claims that what had sustained her most from her student days was Shimoda's teaching that women "manage small matters." She states that she was fond of cleaning the house and cooking for her family, that she preferred to do domestic chores herself rather than take the time to explain them to a maidservant, and that she had personally cared for her father-in-law.[219]

Although Chen rejected the new identity of women advanced by her feminine-heroic counterparts in favor of the long-standing identity of women as dutiful daughters-in-law, wives, and caregivers, her life was not a simple reiteration of eternal feminine roles and Confucian verities. Her marriage to Zhang Zongxiang was progressive by some criteria. Husband and wife had both studied abroad, as the *Women's Eastern Times* photograph emphasizes, and Chen was an active assistant to her husband not only in the inner but the outer realm, where she headed a kindergarten that he administered. She did not become an independent career woman, but her world departed radically from that of her immediate historical predecessors. The defining difference between her generation and theirs was access to schooling and the possibility of a teaching career.

The new education was one of the most potent forces of change for women in turn-of-the-twentieth-century China. This was, in part, because it accommodated the widely divergent visions of femininity that coexisted in this period and encompassed both women's own aspirations and the aspirations others had for them. Eternalists and meliorists mandated that girls' schools would counter destabilizing social forces by reproducing female ritual knowledge and domestic roles. Archeomodernists and presentists deemed new schools the crucial training ground where young women would become nation-minded "mothers of citizens" and revolutionary-minded new patriots, respectively. These varied conceptions of female education continued to coexist in the Republican period. "Virtuous and chaste girls' schools" existed through and beyond Chiang Kai-shek's New Life Movement in the 1930s.[220] And the connection between new schools and political radicalism—symbolized by Qiu Jin's arrest at the Datong School in 1907—intensified in the succeeding decades. The Chinese Communist Party was founded in a Shanghai girls' school in 1921.[221]

A new social space, girls' schools also contributed to the reorientation of feminine time toward a more secular future. The language of the regime of feminine virtue was usurped even in eternalist and meliorist discourses by new idioms—including wise mothers, good wives and wise mothers, mothers of citizens, and martial heroines—that tied female education to national politics. Offering instruction in reading and writing, practical handiwork, and political literacy, women's schools in Japan and China also trained young women to become teachers, the most broadly sanctioned and widely practiced female profession in early-twentieth-century China.[222]

For women like Chen Yan'an, Qiu Jin, Tang Qunying, and countless others who were among China's first teachers, education not only provided access to new bodies of knowledge, but to a new mode of life. As students, these women admired Japanese teachers and Western educators both for their devotion to education and for their self-sufficiency. As China's first school teachers, they too were able to become social, and no longer exclusively familial, beings. Although the careers of many, such as Chen Yan'an, remained circumscribed by their relationships with their husbands, teaching could release women from a life course defined as successive stages of reliance on father and husband.[223] It could also liberate them from the third of the thrice followings as a career in education became—particularly in larger early-twentieth century urban centers—a sanctioned alternative to the patriarchal and national imperative to produce male descendants.[224] In conjunction with this social autonomy, teaching allowed for female romantic and erotic autonomy—from extramarital affairs, to divorce, and female same-sex love.[225]

The nascent women's culture that was intimately linked to women's education created a new feminine temporality that was neither cyclical and bound to the biological life course nor fully synchronized with linear visions of national progress. This culture was still governed by fundamental principles of the regime of feminine virtue. Women teachers—from agitators like Qiu Jin to preschool caregivers like Chen Yan'an—continued to serve society and educate the next generation. The next generation was, however, no longer coded as male.

Conclusion

From The Turn of the Twentieth Century to the Turn of the Twenty-First

> People today constantly reflect on the earth-shatter-
> ing changes in Chinese cities. However, they overlook
> aspects [of urban life] that are fixed and not subject to
> qualitative change even as the streets are quantitatively
> transformed.
>
> O u N i n g , *"Da zha lan ji hua: Chuanye chengshi fudi"*
> *(The Da Zha Lan Project: Crossing into the Heart of the City),* 2006

The Guangzhou/Beijing documentarian and graphic designer, Ou Ning
(b. 1969), traces conflicts "caused by the imbalance between modernization
and tradition" in contemporary Chinese urban "renewal" projects. In his
reflections on the "slow and relentless undercurrent" of social meanings that
flow beneath these vast demolition and building projects, he draws parallels
between urban life at the turn of the twenty-first century and at the turn of
the twentieth. One of his sources for establishing this connection is Beijing's
Awakening Pictorial (*Xingshi huabao*), published in the same year (1909) and
similar in form and content to one of the journals used in this study, the
Shanghai *Daily Pictorial.*[1]

Ou Ning's historical point of reference, the turn of the twentieth century, was—as both the *Daily Pictorial* and *Awakening Pictorial* attest—a
period of pluralistic modernities and heterogeneous temporalities. Individuals staked out their political positions by resignifying the past, invoking
Chinese or Western icons, and establishing divergent hierarchies of heroism. In highlighting this richness and complexity, the preceding chapters
have attempted to overcome reductive characterizations of the late Qing as
at worst feudal and monolithic, at best a transitional antecedent to the May

Fourth Movement of the late 1910s. They also offer a way of understanding this richness and complexity by delineating a series of processes through which Chinese modernity continues to unfold: de-Confucianization and re-Confucianization, globalization and nationalist retrenchment, temporalization and ultrastabilization of the past.[2]

As Ou Ning has recognized, this highly textured late Qing period, rather than the more frequently invoked May Fourth era, should serve as our benchmark for understanding contemporary China.[3] These two turn-of-the-century moments emerged out of periods of political trauma—imperialist wars and internal rebellion in the late nineteenth century, the "ten lost years" of the Cultural Revolution in the late twentieth. Both instigated calls for far-reaching reforms by educated, relatively young critics of the state that resulted in government crackdowns in 1898 and 1989. Without fundamentally altering the course of reform that was already in motion, these bloody crackdowns diminished and dispersed the states's critics—who in both cases were accused of representing Western political values—and placed control of "new" nationalism more firmly in the hands of the imperial and communist leaders. The 1901 New Policies abolished the civil service examination system and launched constitutional reform (while auguring the demise of the dynastic order). The post-Tiananmen policies of the Li Peng regime accelerated the process of economic restructuring and globalization begun in 1978 and promoted rapid top-down commercialization (while auguring the demise of the Communist order).[4] These respective reforms were driven by and further provoked widespread reassessments of the fixed relations among China, its past, and the West in the prevailing ideologies of Confucianism and Maoism. Involving both new appropriations of the foreign and new quests for historical roots, they produced a myriad of cultural formations that were more intricately blended and less categorically antagonistic than the "tradition-modernity" dichotomy of the May Fourth period.[5] Central to these new cultural formations was the woman question, which had first been ignited in the late 1890s and which was forcefully reignited in the post-Mao and post-1989 eras.

In both eras, the woman question and these broader cultural formations are marked by foreign ideas, which are, however, even more pervasive in the later period. Translation projects today are less ad hoc than in the late Qing, and more systematic in their introduction of Western masterworks in particular fields.[6] Japan has been supplanted as the prime route of transmission of Western ideas as new media from television to the increasingly ubiquitous Internet expose Chinese audiences to Western images, ideas, and lifestyles.[7] Despite these differences, the fundamental issue raised by this rapid and widespread infusion of foreign influence remains the same: How should China define its culturally specific but inevitably globally determined modernity?

Just as Xu Dingyi was loathe to kowtow to Madame Roland and determined to locate the sources of a (Western-style) feminine heroic modernity in the Chinese past, turn-of-the-twenty-first-century authors have resisted Western cultural logic and "mindless" globalization through new "root-searching" (*xungen*) efforts. Authors, including Ah Cheng (b. 1949), Mo Yan (b. 1956), and Wang Anyi (b. 1954), seek to rescue Chinese modernity from triviality by linking it to the Chinese past.[8] At the same time, promoters of a Neo-Confucian revival—from the post-Mao state to Harvard University professor Tu Wei-ming (b. 1940)—see Confucianism not as an antidote to Western-style modernity but as an integral component of Chinese modernity.[9]

I focus in this conclusion on three turn-of-the-twenty-first-century figures or sets of figures that have direct bearing on the closely related historical and woman questions. Each highlights one aspect of Chinese modernity—secularization, globalization, and temporalization—and each reflects aspects of one of the chronotypes analyzed in previous chapters—meliorism, archeomodernism, and presentism. The first is a 1990s female exemplar, Liu Huifang, the heroine of the popular television soap opera *Aspirations* (*Kewang*, also translated as *Yearnings* and *Expectations*). Liu's meliorist commitment to certain principles of the regime of feminine virtue provoked passionate and historically resonant debates over the relationship between female self-sacrifice and the nation. The second is a "global signifier of Chinese women," Li Xiaojiang (b. 1951), the founder of the women's studies movement in China.[10] Li's selective appropriation of Western feminist ideas and her concomitant assertion of the uniqueness of the Chinese women's movement builds on—and challenges—archeomodern notions of cultural blending. The third is an early-twenty-first-century artistic representation of paragons from the two-millennia-long Chinese female biographical tradition, *National Shame: Guang Lienü Zhuan* [*Biographies of Exemplary Women*] by Wu Weihe and Bai Chongmin. The artists' reductive resignification of that tradition through a politicized retrospective lens is reminiscent of early-twentieth-century presentist dismissals of the Confucian past.

A Televisual Female Exemplar of the 1990s: Liu Huifang

The soap opera *Aspirations* aired in the post-Tiananmen period of moral and political disillusionment, first appearing on local stations and then on Chinese Central Television in December 1990.[11] A modern-day morality tale written to promote traditional values, it charted the dramatic tensions between two families, the worker Lius and the intellectual Wangs, from the height of the Cultural Revolution in 1969 through the 1980s.[12] The program was a tremendous and unexpected popular success. Its estimated 900 million viewers chose to watch *Aspirations* over foreign shows with which it competed for prime air time.[13] Broadcasting stations responded by moving the series from three times a week to every night for three hours, ultimately airing all fifty episodes in one month.[14]

The Communist Party, which was caught off-guard by the show's success, scrambled to endorse it for promoting "socialist ethics and morals."[15] Intellectuals, who were no less surprised if significantly less approving, debated the meaning of the phenomenon in arts journals and intellectual forums.[16] The show's prime audience—popular viewers—looked to the program for moral guidance, seeking answers in the episodes of this Western-style melodrama to century-old Chinese questions: What would replace Confucian spiritual and ethical values? How should the content of Chinese nationalism be defined? Who could serve as national heroes and heroines?[17] Their ruminations—and those of intellectuals and officials—on these questions became focused on the figure of Liu Huifang, a paragon of virtue, self-sacrifice, and self-denial.

Liu is a late-twentieth-century version of such a paragon. She asserts her free will in marriage, works outside of the home, and makes her greatest sacrifices for an adopted daughter rather than a son. At the same time, aspects of her selfless behavior mimic that of past female martyrs. Like the faithful maiden Lady Jin of the Qing dynasty, she devotes herself to raising a child she did not bear, a young girl named Xiaofang, who had been abandoned at a bus station in the chaos of the Cultural Revolution. Like a modern-day mother of Ouyang Xiu, she diligently raises Xiaofang despite the straitened circumstances in which she lives, relinquishing the opportunity to continue her own education, jeopardizing her health, and alienating her husband, who does not acknowledge the baby. When Xiaofang's rightful parents are discovered, Liu willingly hands the child—for whom and with whom she has suffered for more than a decade—over to them.[18]

Reactions to the character of Liu Huifang were as varied as reactions to chastity martyrs at the turn of the twentieth century. She became something of a 1990s pop icon whose image was used—like the images of righteous widows and faithful maidens in late Qing popular pictorials—to promote ethics (on the cover of the official magazine *Observation* [*Liaowang*], for example), but also to sell luxury goods.[19] At the same time, she became a metonym for the national character in intellectual debates on Chinese identity. Her defenders praised the redemptive power of the private, traditional values she embodied in an age of moral disarray, just as late imperial literati had celebrated chaste widows as spiritual beacons in times of political chaos. In contrast, her critics bemoaned—in language resonant with that of early-twentieth-century presentists—the nationally crippling effect of Liu's self-sacrifice, compliance, endurance, and forbearance. (Liu is literally crippled at the end of the show.)

Those who publicly praised Liu Huifang followed eternalists in invoking timeless principles as a bulwark against destabilizing change. Their commentaries on the show melded Confucian virtues with Communist values to form a bedrock of Chinese authenticity capable of withstanding the post-socialist challenges of globalization, bourgeois liberalization, and commercialization.[20] Li Peng (b. 1928), the much-reviled premier at the time of the Tiananmen Massacre, praised the show as "a matter of moral education which includes education in Communist ideology, Communist morality and traditional Chinese virtues." It would contribute, Li declared to "the reconstruction of spiritual civilization."[21]

Critics of Liu decried the implications of her role for both Chinese women and the Chinese nation. Spokeswomen for the official All China Women's Federation (Zhonghua quanguo funü lianhe hui) broke ranks with the likes of Li Peng and complained that *Aspirations* pushed the liberation of Chinese women back fifteen years.[22] Women who considered themselves ungendered intellectuals often sympathized with Liu Huifang but adamantly rejected her as a model.[23] Fearing that her character would efface the public sacrifices they and other woman had made for the nation, they denigrated her as an embodiment of the ideal of good wives and wise mothers, and, by extension, of male fantasies of submissive women.[24] (A commonly expressed male desire at the time the show aired was to find a Liu Huifang for a daughter-in-law.)[25] Applying this critique of Liu's submissiveness to the nation, others claimed she exposed the most deviant aspects of the Chinese national character.[26] In the words of one intellectual, she evinced how entangled the Chinese collective unconscious remained with the mindless roots of Confucian thinking.[27]

Li Xiaojiang: A Global Signifier of Chinese Women

The television character Liu Huifang thus provoked a cacophony of reactions reminiscent of responses to exemplary Chinese women at the turn of the twentieth century. In contrast, the self-positioning of Li Xiaojiang, an academic and the founder of the Chinese women's studies movement, brings clarity to two fundamental aspects of the woman question that remained unsettled in the turn-of-the-twentieth-century archeomodern and presentist discourses.

The first is the dilemma that plagued late-Qing new-style heroines: whether to embrace or reject the identity of "woman." Having lived through the state-mandated erasure of gender differences in the high Communist Cultural Revolution, Li Xiaojiang focuses on the distinctive identity of woman. Undeterred by charges of essentialism and resistant even to the notion of gender studies, which she fears would efface the specificities of the woman question, Li embraces womanhood in its most concrete physicality.

Li also unravels the fuzzy archeomodern blending of China and the West, of ancient Chinese exemplars and Western heroines who absorb one another's characteristics as Ban Zhao becomes a national utilitarian, Margaret Fuller Ossoli a good Confucian, and Western social reformers, loving mothers. Despite her own commitment to understanding and disseminating the classics of Western feminism, Li asserts the incommensurability of the Western and Chinese woman's movements.[28] Her clarity falters, however, when she attempts to reposition the Chinese women's movement in relation to China's own history.

Unlike her near-contemporary, the feminist critic Dai Jinhua (b. 1959), who believes the truth of women must remain unresolved, Li Xiaojiang's purpose is to recover women's natural, feminine singularity.[29] Distant taproots of her position can be found in the writings of late Qing women like the proto-difference feminist Gong Yuanchang. Li is responding, however, to the radical culmination of the turn-of-the-twentieth-century trend toward male-mandated sexual equality that Gong resisted. Li exposes the chasm between Chinese Communist Party (CCP) rhetoric of total social, sexual, political, and legal equality and the profound inequalities Chinese women face as working wives and mothers.[30] She also reveals the gulf between CCP policy and female subjectivity, between the party's claim to have "always, already" liberated Chinese women and Chinese women's as yet unformed sense of autonomy.[31] Most poignantly, she highlights disjunctions between the erasure of the female body—which endured even after the Cultural Revolution in Marxist humanist "asexual" (*feixinghua*) consciousness—and the physicality of the female procreative body.[32]

More openly concerned with female corporality than women writers at the turn of the twentieth century, Li is also less torn by a dual commitment to womanhood and nationhood. Her cause is unambiguously the woman's cause. She has been involved in female pedagogy and activism, but intellectual work is her preferred mode.[33] Despite daunting political and academic obstacles, she established the first nongovernmental institute of women's studies in China at Zhengzhou University in 1985. In 1987 the institute became a formal women's studies center, an important alternative to the CCP's All China Women's Federation. The center has promoted national interest in academic women's studies by hosting public lectures, organizing conferences, and compiling a women's studies book series.[34]

Like her archeomodern predecessors and unlike many of her anticapitalist contemporaries, Li is not opposed to globalization.[35] She believes the global commercial economy provides opportunities for Chinese women.[36] And she has willingly joined the international intellectual economy, accepting Ford Foundation grants, publishing in English, and following the United States, European countries, and Japan in launching women's studies in China.[37]

Li's work is nonetheless marked by the century-old tension between transnational trends and national imperatives. While she believes the woman question to be fundamentally universal, she considers national differences to be as profound as gender differences.[38] She is, therefore, attentive to the distinct historico-political contexts from which the Chinese and Western feminist movements emerged and sensitive to linguistic manifestations of these differences. She points out, for example, that the Chinese language has two separate terms for Western feminism and Chinese feminism. The former, *nüquan zhuyi*, or literally doctrine of women's rights, has clear political resonances. The latter, *nüxing zhuyi*, or feminology, is more academic in tone.[39] She also explains that the Western feminist slogan "the personal is political" is anathema to leaders of the Chinese women's movement, whose primary struggle is to free female subjectivity from the reach of the state.

And she asserts that the Communist Party's term for its liberation (*jiefang*) of Chinese women cannot be translated by the English words freedom or liberty: women's liberation under the CCP means a lack of freedom.[40] In 1994, participants in Non-Governmental Organization panels held in Beijing in conjunction with the Fourth United Nations World Conference on Women recognized that such divergences in the Chinese and Western experience that Li underscores challenge the international hegemony of Western feminism.[41]

Li and other turn-of-the-twenty-first-century feminists are, thus, more cautious vis-à-vis the West than their forebears who indiscriminately invoked—while variously reinterpreting—the tales of foreign heroines. At the same time, they share the archeomodernists' ambiguous stance toward the Chinese past, which they both reject as "feudal history" and attempt to reclaim as national history. In some instances, Li Xiaojiang echoes the harshest late Qing feminine-heroic diatribes against their illiterate and crippled, past and present female compatriots. She asserts that Chinese women have no history and contributed nothing to history, having spent the millennia since the fall of matriarchy "vegetating" in their natural-historical roles as daughters, wives, and mothers.[42] She also concedes, however—as did turn-of-the-twentieth-century women writers committed to tracing the genealogy of women's oppression—that "feudal history" is a "venerable history" embedded in national conditions and endowed with its own unique power.[43] Losing touch with this history, she acknowledges, means losing touch with ourselves.[44]

"National Shame: Biographies of Exemplary Women"

The tendency to categorically dismiss the past, which Li Xiaojiang ultimately resists, can be traced to the turn-of-the-twentieth-century archeomodern repudiation of the recent past—articulated through the critique of the late imperial woman of talent—and the presentists' blanket rejection or radical resignification of the past. Although presentist authors like Xu Dingyi continued to use indigenous cultural resources, they reinvented the stories of Chinese heroines —Li Xiu of the Eastern Jin dynasty, Hua Mulan of the Wei, Xi Furen of the Sui—in Western ideological terms. Stripped of the historical meanings they had once possessed, these women warriors became paragons of Western racial and nationalist thought.

These temporal trends mark the beginning of what Dai Jinhua has termed

China's "internal exile" from its own culture.[45] This alienation would inten-
sify with the May Fourth intellectuals' attack on traditional Chinese culture
(which Dai identifies as its starting point) and reach its apogee in the Red
Guards' violent destruction of old books, historical artifacts, and the lives of
those identified as carriers of "feudal thought."

In subsequent decades, root-searchers, Neo-Confucians, and others have
struggled to redeem their own versions of the Chinese past. The Chinese
cultural imaginary continues to be haunted, however, by "allegories of the
ruins and wastelands of . . . traditional culture."[46] A powerful example
is the 2001 multimedia art project *National Shame: Guang Lienü Zhuan
[Biographies of Exemplary Women]*. In the sculpture component of the project, the female artist Wu Weihe and her male collaborator Bai Chongmin
cast historical exemplars in stone—reducing their manifold potential meanings and layered transformations to one indurate form (see Figure 51). The
artists celebrate this reductiveness. They describe their "main intention" in

Figure 51 Tomb figures of female exemplars from *National Shame* exhibit
SOURCE: Wu Weihe and Bai Chongmin, 47. Courtesy of the artists, We Weihe and Bai Chongmin.

creating these sculptures as "[reducing] the gesture and form of the figures to their most basic extreme." They "use the female body to express the effects of being collectively controlled." The stone figures' covered heads symbolize "their passive position in marriage, lack of clarity in individual identity, and preconditioned state of remaining unawakened."[47]

Wu and Bai take the same approach in the painting component of the project. They impose new layers of material onto a representation of the text of the *Biographies of Exemplary Women* in order to destroy old rather than create new meanings. "The Chinese text [of the *Biographies*] is duplicated, they explain, broken up by red editing marks, or scorched by fire, obstructed, covered, cut into pieces, and then sutured back together." The artists might also "paint directly over the text to the point of destruction."[48]

Wu Weihe's stated aim in *National Shame* is highly personal. She is determined to trace the sources of what she describes as the "absurd morals" that prevented her from freely "thinking, moving, or breathing" as a young unmarried woman in turn-of-the-twenty-first-century China. Together with her male partner, Bai, she has set out to examine and understand "the past afresh" to uncover how "a certain 'ideology' was purposefully legitimated through historical editing—the creation of a particular version of woman."[49]

Wu and Bai's "fresh" look at the past, while intriguing from the perspective of contemporary feminist art, ultimately offers little in the way of historical understanding. Their terra cotta rendering of a static female biographical tradition contravenes the Chinese practice of preserving the past through the fluidity of succeeding generations rather than the immobility of inanimate objects.[50] Their assertion of a singular historical "version of woman" is also at variance with the polysemic, mutable, and porous biographical repertoire found in the various sources examined in this book. While the artists effectively convey their sense of current injustices in *National Shame*, their representation of the Chinese past as a "space of failure" obliterates any traces of former subjectivities, historical possibilities, and potential sources of self-knowledge.[51]

Fragments of these subjectivities and possibilities can be reclaimed, not by reiterating how oppressed "Chinese women" were as chastity martyrs, good wives and wise mothers, or selfless nationalists, but by examining how particular individuals assumed, manipulated, or transcended these identities. The heterogeneity of Chinese temporalities and the layered complexity

of the Chinese woman question are revealed in the ways these various actors—from meliorist biographers and new-style heroines at the turn of the
twentieth century, to root-searching authors and soap opera viewers at the
turn of the twenty-first—sought refuge in and continuously recrafted the
precious raft of history.

Abbreviations

Page numbers in reprinted journals are indicated by [ ].

BD I	Ho, Clara Wing-chung, ed. *Biographical Dictionary of Chinese Women: The Qing Period, 1644–1911*. Editors-in-Chief, Lily Xiao Hong and A. D. Stefanowska. Armonk, NY: M. E. Sharpe, 1998.
BD II	Lee, Lily Xiao Hong, ed. *Biographical Dictionary of Chinese Women: The Twentieth Century, 1912–2000*. Editors-in-Chief, Lily Xiao Hong and A. D. Stefanowska. Armonk, NY: M. E. Sharpe, 2003.
BJNB	*Beijing nübao* 北京女報 (Beijing women's journal). Beijing, 1905–9.
DFZZ	*Dongfang zazhi* 東方雜誌 ("The Eastern Miscellany"). Shanghai, 1904–49.
DGB	*Dagong bao* 大公報 ("L'Impartial"). Tianjin, 1902–16.
FNSB	*Funü shibao* 婦女時報 (The women's eastern times). Shanghai, 1911–17.
HB	*Hubei xuesheng jie* 湖北學生界 (Students of Hubei). Tokyo, Jan. 29, 1903–May 27, 1903. Rtp., Taipei: Zhongguo Guomindang, Zhongyang weiyuan hui, Dangshi shiliao bianzuan weiyuan hui, 1968.
HS	*Hansheng* 漢聲 (Voice of the Han). Tokyo, June–July 1903. Continuation of *HB*. Rpt., Taipei: Zhongguo Guomindang, Zhongyang weiyuan hui, Dangshi shiliao bianzuan weiyuan hui, 1968.
JS	*Jiangsu* 江蘇 (Jiangsu journal). Tokyo, April 27, 1903–May 15, 1904. Rpt., Taipei: Zhongguo Guomindang, Zhongyang weiyuan hui, Dangshi shiliao bianzuan weiyuan hui, 1968.
JYZZ	*Jiaoyu zazhi* 教育雜誌 (Educational review). Shanghai, Jan. 1909–Dec. 1948. Rpt., Taipei: Taiwan Commercial Press, 1975.
LNZ	Liu Xiang 劉向. *Lienü zhuan* 列女傳 (Arrayed traditions of women's lives). Ca. 34 CE.

NQYDSL   *Jindai Zhongguo nüquan yundong shiliao 1842–1911* 近代中國女權運動史料 1842–1911 (Historical materials on the modern Chinese movement for women's rights, 1842–1911). Ed. Li Yu-ning 李又寧 and Chang Yü-fa 張玉法. 2 vols. Taipei: Taibei zhuanji wenxue she, 1975.

NZSJ   *Nüzi shijie* 女子世界 (Women's world). Shanghai, Jan. 1904–July 1907. Rpt., *Zhongguo jinxiandai nüxing qikan huibian* 中国近现代女性期刊汇编 (Compilation of modern and contemporary Chinese women's journals). Beijing: Xianzhuang shuju, 2006.

QBLC   *Qing bailei chao* 清稗類鈔 (Drafts of legends from the Qing dynasty). Ed. Xu Ke 徐珂. Vol. 23, *Zhenlie lei* 貞烈類 (On virtue), 1–86. Shanghai: Commercial Press, 1928.

QKJS   *Xinhai geming shiqi qikan jieshao* 辛亥革命时期期刊介绍 (An introduction to periodicals from the period of the 1911 Revolution). Ed. Ding Shouhe 丁守和. 5 vols. Beijing: Renmin chubanshe, 1982.

SB   *Shibao* 時報 ("The Eastern Times"). Shanghai, 1904–39.

ShB   *Shenbao* 申報 (Shanghai journal). Shanghai, 1872–1949.

STSB   *Shuntian shibao* 順天時報 (Beijing-Tianjin daily). Beijing, 1901–30.

THRB   *Tuhua ribao* 圖畫日報 (Daily pictorial). Shanghai, 1909. Rpt., 8 vols., Shanghai: Shanghai guji chubanshe, 1999.

TY   *Tianyi* 天義 (Natural justice). Tokyo, 1907–8. Vols. 1 and 2, Tokyo: Shūkō sha, 1907. Vols. 11–12, 15–19, rpt., Tokyo: Daiyasu, 1966.

WXY   Wei Xiyuan 魏息園 (Xiyuan waishi 息園外史), comp. *Xiuxiang gujin xiannü zhuan* 繡像古今賢女傳 (Illustrated biographies of resourceful women, past and present). 9 fascicles. Shanghai: Jicheng tuhua gongsi dianshizhai, 1908. (No pagination; in notes fascicle number given in roman numerals followed by chapter number; fascicle number alone refers to the preface to that section.) Rpt., Beijing: Zhongguo shudian, 1998.

XNJZZ   *Zhongguo xin nüjie zazhi* 中國新女界雜誌 (Magazine of the new Chinese woman). Tokyo, Zhongguo xin nüjie zazhi she, 1907. Rpt., Taipei: Youshi wenhua shiye gongsi, 1977.

XZSL   *Zhongguo jindai xuezhi shiliao* 中国近代学制史料 (Historical materials on the modern Chinese educational system). *Jiaoyu kexue congshu* 教育科学丛书 (Compendium of sources on education). Ed. Zhu Youhuan 朱有瓛. 2 vols. Shanghai: Huadong shifan daxue chubanshe, 1983–86.

XZYB   *Xuezhi yanbian* 学制演变 (The evolution of the educational system). *Zhongguo jindai jiaoyushi ziliao huibian* 中国近代教育史资料汇编 (Compendium of sources on the history of Chinese modern education). Ed. Chen Yuanhui 陈元晖. Shanghai: Shanghai jiaoyu chubanshe, 1991.

ZGFNS *Zhonggguo funü shi lunji* 中國婦女史倫集 (Essays on the history of Chinese women). Ed. Pao Chia-lin 鮑家麟. 5 vols. Taipei: Daoxiang chubanshe, vol. 1 (1979) 1999; vol. 2 (1971) 1999; vol. 3, 1993; vol. 4, 1995; vol. 5, 2001.

ZJC *Zhejiang chao* 浙江潮 (Tides of Zhejiang). Tokyo, Feb. 17, 1903–Dec. 8, 1903. Rpt., Taipei: Zhongguo Guomindang, Zhongyang weiyuan hui, Dangshi shiliao bianzuan weiyuan hui, 1968.

Notes

Introduction

1. According to the author, the title of Li Run's biographical work was *Lichao lienü zhuan* (Arrayed traditions of women's lives through the ages). Hu Wenkai (262) lists it as *Lidai lienü lun* (Female exemplars through the ages). Hu had not seen the text, and I have not been able to find it in Chinese or Japanese libraries.

2. On Yang Jisheng's story, see Goodrich, 2: 1503–5. On Yang's admonition to his wife not to commit suicide, see Bossler.

3. The original *Qingyi bao* biography was reprinted in the 1925 *Qing bailei chao* (Drafts of legends of the Qing [dynasty]), "Li Run." A slightly different version appears in Yi Zongkui, 315b–16a.

4. Ono, 38.

5. I have adapted the idea of "historical imaginary" from Charles Taylor's (6) concept of "social imaginary." I define it as the way Chinese at the turn of the twentieth century imagined the histories they inhabited and sustained.

6. The removal of God or religion is not the only meaning of secularization. Charles Taylor (93–94) defines radical secularity as "a shift in the understanding of what society is grounded on" and argues that the etymology of the term reflects "the way human society inhabits time"—processes that resonate with those I examine in the book. The term "secularization" has been previously used in the Chinese context to refer to the decline of correlative cosmology and the undermining of Neo-Confucianism's "monopoly on intellectual life" by evidentiary scholarship in the late imperial period. See Furth, "The Patriarch's," 207, on the work of John Henderson and Benjamin Elman. I argue that this monopoly was further undermined in the social and cultural spheres in the early twentieth century.

Lijiao literally means ritual (*li*) as teaching (*jiao*). For an extensive historical analysis of the concept, see Cai Shangsi. The term *wenming*, which represents new, generally Western-derived values and ideas, is a return graphic loan—a term derived from classical Chinese, used in the modern Japanese language, and re-imported into China at the turn of the twentieth century. See Masini, 204; Lydia H. Liu, 308–9.

7. Cai Shangsi, "Xulun," 1. Vincent Goossaert (309) describes "Chinese fundamentalism" as a "distinct field of thought and practice dealing with rituals, devotion, and salvation." On the prime functions of ritual, see Sivin, 24. Correlative

cosmology assumes an alignment between the human and cosmic realms. In Confucianism, the natural and human worlds constituted an organism of multitudinous interconnected parts. Heaven presided over this organic whole and was a force for harmony and balance. Arthur F. Wright, 5. See also Henderson.

8. Chen Chi-yun.

9. Goossaert (309) describes the embedding of Chinese religious life in its socioeconomic context. Shang Wei (14) refers to "dualistic ritual": ritual as the source of ultimate value and significance, and as the legitimate means of enforcing sociopolitical order.

10. The most recent and sophisticated treatment of the encounter between China and the "great powers" is Huters, *Bringing*.

11. Xie Chongxie, 48b; Levenson, 98–104.

12. Education was variously linked to processes of secularization in early-twentieth-century China. Daoist and Buddhist temples were taken over to serve as new schools. See Goossaert; Duara, *Rescuing*, chap. 3. In 1906 the Qing court decreed that the new Education Board (founded the previous year) would supersede the Ministry of Rites in the administrative hierarchy. Elman, *A Cultural History*, 609.

13. Legge, trans., "The Nei Tse," 478–79.

14. On the extent of women's learning from the Song dynasty through the Qing, see Ebrey, *The Inner*; Dorothy Ko, *Teachers*; Mann, *Precious*.

15. Xiong, "Degrees," 34.

16. The mapping of temporal onto spatial relations was common between non-Western and Western societies. See, for example, Felski, 14.

17. Referring to the Ming-Qing transition, Lynn Struve (4) has written that "disrupted *times*, that is ones of disrupted *time*, reveal [the resources of time perception] most vividly in drawing upon them most exigently." See Jörn Rüsen (15) for a discussion of critical moments when concepts of time change.

18. See Osborne (200) for a discussion of the political significance of different temporalizations.

19. We have been overcoming these binaries at least since Benjamin Schwartz's seminal 1972 article, "The Limits." For two recent books on the late Qing and early Republican periods that recognize the limits of these binaries but continue to use them, see Reed and Mittler, and a review essay discussing these books: Judge, "The Power," 236–38.

20. Walter Benjamin (Susan Buck-Morss, 110) was struck by the fact that "when modern innovations appeared in modern history they took the form of historical restitutions." Other theorists similarly develop this idea. Peter Osborne (xii) asserts that modernity produces the old as well as the new; Rita Felski (59) argues that the imagining of the past was the counterpart of modernity's widely acknowledged imagining of the future; and Charles Taylor (129) writes of how the new imaginary owes a debt to a more archaic one.

21. On the importance of examining what modernity represses, see Gross, 135.

22. On the idea of history "[brushed] against the grain," see Benjamin, "On the Concept of History," 392.

23. The expression *funü wenti*, a translation of the English phrase "woman question" which had circulated in Europe for centuries, became prevalent at the outset of the New Culture movement from 1915. Wang Zheng, 3. The term *nüzi wenti* was, however, in circulation in the late Qing. See, for example, Mulan tongxiang (discussed later in the Introduction), who claims reformers had categorically ignored the woman question (*nüzi wenti*) in formulating their political agendas.

24. Felski, 59.

25. Kandiyoti, "Afterword," 271–72.

26. Sangari and Vaid, 18. Prasenjit Duara has also noted for a period slightly later than the one examined here that historical rather than spatial representations have framed Chinese women as figures of authenticity in Chinese modernity. Duara, "The Regime," 300.

27. Taylor, 146–47.

28. Mary Clabaugh Wright (60–62) made a similar point in describing the belief among Chinese that they could "leapfrog over the stages of the development of other countries."

29. A careful reading of the main texts of the Enlightenment in France, England, and the colonies reveals that the relationship between women and the state remained largely unexamined. Kerber, "The Republican," 42. On France, see Ozouf, 260–61.

30. While Tani Barlow (*The Question*) interrogates the singular category of "women" in late imperial and modern China, the range of competing subcategories better reveals the complex materiality of the era and the stakes involved in various positions on the woman question.

31. The English term "biography," which corresponds to the Western tradition at least since Plutarch (ca. 46–ca. 120) of portraying an individual's life in its fullness, does not accurately reflect the content of Chinese life-story narratives or *liezhuan*. These thumbnail moral sketches present selective details relevant to specific incidents in an individual's life. I follow Stephen W. Durrant (xix–xx) who translates *liezhuan* as "arrayed traditions," and, therefore, refer to female life-story narratives, *lienü zhuan*, as "arrayed traditions of women." Dennis Twitchett (25) and Burton Watson (120–21) translate *liezhuan* as "connected traditions" and "memoirs" respectively. For the sake of clarity and brevity I will, however, continue to use the term "biography" when referring to *lienü zhuan*, but urge the reader to keep the difference between the Western and Chinese concepts in mind.

32. Although my use of "technology of the self" resonates with Foucault's "technologies of the self" in that it is related to the ways the self is formed (through the reading of biographies) and becomes an object of knowledge (through the writing of biographies), he is most interested in the relationship between interdictions and the self (in pagan and early Christian practices), rather than models for the self. See Foucault, *Technologies*, 16–49.

33. Huang Chun-chieh, "'Time,'" 34; Arthur F. Wright, 9; Shang Wei, 17. Sima Qian's *Shi ji*, which introduced the concept of "praising virtue and condemning evil" (*shan shan e e*), was the first Chinese work to use biographies to underline the moral lessons of history. See Shang Wei, 121.

34. I have adapted the idea of parabiography from Gérard Genette's idea of the paratext. See Genette, *Paratext*.

35. Genette, *Palimpsests*.

36. "Shijie." *Baofa* is a metaphor for Buddhist teachings that transport individuals to the shores of enlightenment. See Fong, "Female," 20.

37. John Bender and David E. Wellbery (4) define chronotypes as "models or patterns through which [historical] time [assumed] practical or conceptual significance." Huang Chun-chieh ("'Time,'" 20–21), suggestively discusses Supertime as the paradigmatic in Time, that which patterns Time into the meaningful human tapestry called history. He does not, however, discuss the politics that drive this designation of Supertime.

38. Pierre Bourdieu (*Masculine*, 82–88) writes of the structure and corresponding principles of the sexual division as the product of a labor of eternalization.

39. I am grateful to William Sewell, Jr., for suggesting the term "meliorism" for this stream. According to the *Oxford English Dictionary*, "meliorism" is the compromise between optimism and pessimism "which affirms that the world may be made better by rightly directed human effort."

40. See Ryckmans, 8–9. Similarly, the great *jinwen* (modern script) school proponent Kang Youwei (1858–1927) declared Confucius a reformer. See Gray, 189, 198–203.

41. Walter Benjamin ("Paris," 148) describes an "archeomodern" process through which the recent past is dismissed as obsolete and wishful fantasies or images direct the imagination "which has been activated by the new back to the primeval past." Elements from the past thus "mingle with the new to produce [a vision of] utopia." Benjamin developed this point in *The Arcades Project*, where he writes that the "utopian images that accompany the emergence of the new always concurrently reach back to the ur-past"; cited in Buck-Morss, 116. The term "archeomodern" (written as archaeomodern) has also been used by Jacques Rancière (24–40) in discussing Benjamin's historical thinking.

42. Walter Benjamin has written of how history is meaningful not when filled by the chronological, homogonous time of the historicists but by messianic now-time (*Jetztzeit*). Benjamin, "On the Concept," 395.

43. Cyclical and linear time have often been juxtaposed as the time of nature and the time of civilization. Henri Lefebvre (231–32) has written, for example, that we "know that [cyclical time scales] have their origins or their foundations in nature; they are connected to profound, cosmic, vital rhythms. [Linear time scales] are connected to knowledge, reason, and techniques: they correlate not with vital rhythms and processes, but rather with processes of economic and technological growth." Julia Kristeva ("Women's") has interpreted this juxtaposition in gendered terms,

contrasting the masculine, linear time of history with a cyclical or monumental feminine temporality.

44. As David Schaberg (18) has written, individuals and events can embody generalities "without ever disappearing into them."

45. The counterpoints highlight what Dipesh Chakrabarty (36–37) has called "disruptive histories": evidence which does not easily fit our categories, thus revealing the limitations of our methods for translating complex histories.

46. Felski (26, 209) recommends a multi-genre approach because different genres tell different stories about the same culture at the same moment.

47. "Xuebu zouding nüzi shifan," 666.

48. "Xuebu zouding nüzi xiaoxue," 658.

49. A 1904 memorial called for the compilation of an official textbook that would include selections from earlier instruction books for women, most prominently the *Nü jie* and the *Lienü zhuan*, but also the *Nü xun* (Women's instructions) of Cai Yong (Bojie, 133–82) and the *Jiaonü yigui* (Sourcebook on women's education, 1742), the Qing-era compilation of earlier didactic texts by Chen Hongmou (1697–1771). It would also include excerpts from mainstream texts that continued to be used at the elementary level for boys, such as the *Xiao jing* (Classic of filial piety) and the *Si shu* (Four books). Rongqing, Zhang, and Zhang, 395–96. The authors of the Education Board's 1907 regulations recommended drawing on an even longer list of historical didactic books for women. In addition to the *Nü jie*, the *Lienü zhuan*, the *Nü xun*, and the *Jiaonü yigui*, they included the *Jia fan* (Family model) by Sima Guang (1019–86) and two texts from the Ming compilation, the *Nü sishu* (Four books for women): the *Nü xiaojing* (Women's classic of filial piety) and the *Nei xun* (Inner instruction). They also made specific reference to two texts included in Chen Hongmou's *Jiaonü yigui* (in addition to the already-mentioned *Nei xun*), the *Gui fan* (Exemplars of the inner quarters, 1590) by Lü Kun (1536–1618), and the *Wen shi muxun* (Recorded teachings of the mother of Mr. Wen Huang). Finally, the regulations included three Qing dynasty texts: *Nüjiao jingzhuan tongzuan* (Compilation of classics and histories for the instruction of girls and women), by Ren Qiyun (1670–1744); *Nü xue* (Teachings for girls, preface dated 1712–13), by Lan Dingyuan (1680–1733); and "Fuxue" (Women's education), by Zhang Xuecheng (1738–1801). "Xuebu zouding nüzi shifan," 669.

50. The *Elementary Learning for Girls and Women* was approved as an ethics textbook in women's normal schools and as a reference text for general female ethics classes. It was distributed by both the Xue bu tushuju shoushuchu (Book Sales Division of the Education Board) and by the Commercial Press office in Beijing. Zhang Jinglu ("Jiaokeshu," 236) has noted that many women's normal schools used Dai Li's text.

51. Dai Li, "Zixu," 1a. Dai also aligned her *Elementary Learning for Girls and Women* with the Song-dynasty *Elementary Learning* (*Xiao xue*) written by the famous Confucian scholar Zhu Xi (1130–1200), via Lan Dingyuan's *Teachings for Girls*. Dai noted that Lan's *Teachings*—which was itself modeled on Zhu Xi's *Elementary Learning*—had been her greatest source of influence. Ibid., 1b.

52. Zeng was from a scholar-official family and married her cousin, Yuan Youan of Changzhou, Jiangsu, who was commissioner of judicial affairs in Hunan. She was the author of three volumes of poetry, including the *Guhuanshi shici ji* (Collected poems from the Guhuan studio; Changsha, 1907) and six works on medicine collected in *Zeng nüshi yixue quanshu* (Complete medical works of Madame Zeng). On Zeng's life and writing, see Hu Wenkai, 484; *BD* I, 288–89.

53. Zeng Yi, "Zixu," 5b.

54. Katherine Carlitz ("The Social," 126) has coined the term "*lienü zhuan* expansion" to refer to this genre. Chinese designations include *Xu lienü zhuan* (Continued arrayed traditions of women's lives), *Lienü zhuan zengguang* (Enlarged arrayed traditions of women's lives), and *Guang Lienü zhuan* (Expanded Arrayed traditions of women's lives). While one of the first expansions was *Gujin lienü zhuan* (Arrayed traditions of ancient and recent women's lives) by Jie Jin (1369–1415), the most widely reprinted were *Gui fan* by Lü Kun, and *Huitu lienü zhuan* (Illustrated arrayed traditions of women's lives) by Wang Geng (fl. 1600), which was initially printed in the early 1600s and republished in 1779. On the *Guifan*, see Handlin, 13–38. On the *Huitu*, see Raphals, *Sharing*, 116; Carlitz, "The Social." Perhaps the last expansion to appear before the turn of the twentieth century was *Guang lienü zhuan zhuan* (Expanded arrayed traditions of women's lives) by Liu Kai (1781–1821).

55. Late Qing expansions compiled by women that appear to no longer be extant include one by Xiao Daoguan (d. 1907), author of *Lienü zhuan jizhu* (Collected annotations to the Arrayed traditions of women's lives) (n.p. [1892] after 1907) and teacher of Dai Li (Hu Wenkai, 594); another was by Li Run, whose story opens this Introduction.

56. We know little about Wei except that he was from Xiang County, Hunan Province, and that he was responsible for levying taxes in Suqian County in northern Jiangsu Province at one point in his career. Wang Zhenda, 1. Wei was the author of 101 palace poems reprinted in Wu Shijian, 22–41. He was also an avid supporter of the 1901 New Policies reforms, particularly legal reform. See Wei Xiyuan. I am deeply indebted to Martin Heijdra of the Gest Library, Princeton University, for his invaluable assistance in tracking down sources related to Wei. For more on Wei, see Judge, "Exemplary."

57. Wei drew on Yan Xiyuan's *Baimei xin yongtu zhuan*, a High Qing collection that includes women of the pleasure quarters together with empresses, court ladies, literary or musical talents, goddesses, and immortals. Wei's indebtedness to this text is suggested by his style name, which is homophonous—including tones—with Xiyuan, the given name of the *Baimei*'s compiler. It is further apparent in a number of markedly similar biographical narratives in the two texts. The image of Mulan that Wei takes from Yan was originally from Jin Guliang, *Wu shuang pu* (A record of famous personages), an early Qing dynasty work (1690) featuring woodblock prints of eminent persons in Chinese history.

58. Carlitz ("The Social," 139–41) refers to expansions as an object of conspicuous consumption or an artifact in the connoisseurship of women. Wei added two new parabiographical elements to each entry in his collection: a poem of four lines,

which praised the virtues of the celebrated individual, and what appear to be ink drawings—most likely lithographs—usually of foliage or flowers accompanied by poetic inscriptions often penned by Wei himself. The sense of moral purpose in the text is also apparent in Wei Xiyuan.

59. In descending number of biographies, the sections in the compilation include: "Education of Sons" (Jiaozi; nineteen biographies), "Kindness and Benevolence" (Cihui; fourteen), "Filiality to Parents" (Xiao fumu; eleven), "Diligence and Frugality" (Qinjian; eleven), "Assistance to Husband" (Xiangfu; ten), "Service to in-laws" (Shi jiugu; eight), "Fraternal Love" (Youai; eight), and "Harmony with Sisters-in-law" (He disi; four).

60. Thanks to Qian Nanxiu for confirming my reading of these prefaces and the introduction.

61. On the Jicheng tushu gongsi (Compendium book company), which published the *Illustrated Biographies*, see Lufei, 213; Xiong, *Xixue*, 667; Zhang Jinglu, "Jiaokeshu," 236.

62. Wei Xiyuan, VI; VI: 18, VI: 16.

63. *SB* (October 1, 1910). The title given for the work advertised, *Huitu daban gujin xiannü zhuan* (Illustrated large edition of biographies of resourceful women, past and present), is slightly different from Wei's, but "Huitu daban" could have been used descriptively. The rest of the description mostly fits Wei's text. The advertisement notes, however, that the collection was published by Wentong shuju; it is possible there was more than one publisher or distributor for the text at the time. Also the advertisement announces the price for each of the "eight volumes (*ben*)," while the Jicheng edition was in nine *juan* and four volumes.

64. The *Daily Pictorial* was the first and only pictorial to be published as a daily. It appeared from August 1909 to August 1910 in 404 issues. On the journal, see Liu Huating; and Shi He, Yao, and Ye.

65. Xiong, "Dazhong," 489, 493.

66. On the *Daily Pictorial*'s commitment to national reform, see ibid., 490.

67. The *Daily Pictorial* was not averse to introducing and promoting foreign ideas, products, and people, including foreign women, however. The section of the newspaper entitled "Shijie mingren lishi tu" (Historical illustrations of famous world figures) included a 23-part biography of Madame Roland, for example, which ran from issues 113 to 137 (December 1909).

68. On Liu's appropriation of exemplar stories from the *Zuo zhuan* and the *Guo yu*, see Zhou Yiqun, 39–42.

69. Chen Kangqi, who was from Yin County in Zhejiang Province, received his metropolitan degree (*jinshi*) in 1871. He was frustrated in his ten-year tenure as vice director of the Ministry of Justice because he did not receive the promotions he thought he deserved (ergo the title of his text, *Chronicles of an Unpromoted Official*). He therefore resigned from his post and asked to be reassigned to a position in the provinces. Jin Shi, 1. Chen's jottings, like the *suibi* and *wenji* (collected writings) of many late imperial literati, included sketches of renowned figures, acquaintances, and family members. Feng Erkang, 397. The *Daily Pictorial* journalists

most probably used a Xuantong era (1908–11) edition of Chen Kangqi's jottings, which were first published in the 1880s and widely disseminated in the late Qing and early Republic. Jin Shi, 3.

70. Xie Chongxie's lower-level elementary female ethics textbook was published in Shanghai by the Zhongguo jiaoyu gailiang hui and distributed by Wenming shuju, Kaiming shuju, Xinxue huishe, Shizhong shuju, Kexue huishe, and Guan shuju, in all provinces, for example.

71. The *Hanyu da cidian* does not give a locus classicus for the term *jiaokeshu* (providing an example from the 1920s or 1930s), nor is the term analyzed either in Masini or Lydia Liu. The compound most probably entered China from Japan, where the term *kyōkasho* was in circulation from the early 1870s and prominently used from the 1890s. It was used in the Meiji Education Act (Gakusei) of 1872 (Yamazumi, 781) and first appears in a Japanese-English dictionary in 1888 (Sōgō, 109). Although the term *jiaokeshu* appears in the Chinese newspaper *Shenbao* as early as 1873, authors of the first Chinese-produced textbooks in the late 1890s did not use it, generally labeling their texts *keben* (lesson books) or *duben* (readers). With the introduction of educational reforms and the wide translation of Japanese textbooks into Chinese in the first years of the twentieth century, however, *jiaokeshu* became the generic term for pedagogical texts written by Chinese. The label was most consistently applied to elementary-level instruction books, while *duben* continued to be used in materials for more advanced students. The first Chinese textbook listed in Zhang Jinglu's "Jiaokeshu" (227) that includes the words *jiaokeshu* in the title was published in 1902. On the translation of textbooks from Japanese, see Sanetō, Tam, and Ogawa; Abe, *Chūgoku*, 45–49; Reynolds, 117–21.

72. Xiong (*Xixue*, 667) discusses how gradation was a mark of all new-style textbooks.

73. Written in the Song Dynasty, the *Sanzi jing* opens with the ideologically charged story of Mencius's mother. See Wang Yinglin, 13.

74. Xu Jiaxing, "Liyan," 1a.

75. Xu Jiaxing.

76. The lack of information on artists who illustrated textbooks is a serious lacuna in our knowledge of late Qing print culture. Front matter to textbooks rarely includes any mention of the illustrators and recent scholarship does not probe the issue. Wang Jianjun, who provides a relatively thorough examination of late Qing textbook publishing, makes no mention of illustrations, for example.

77. Carlitz ("The Social," 120, 127) discusses this use of pre-drawn elements in Ming dynasty woodblock illustrations.

78. See Wu Youru. Wu was the head illustrator of China's first pictorial journal, the *Dianshizhai huabao* (Stones-into-gold studio pictorial), founded in 1884. His "One Hundred Beauties" was first published in his own pictorial journal, *Feiyingge huabao* (Pavilion of flying shadows pictorial; 1890–93), and posthumously reprinted in *Wu Youru huabao* in 1908. On the *Feiyingge huabao*, see Reed, 95–96.

79. Liang Qichao, "Lun nüxue," 869–70. "General Discussion of Reform" appeared serially in *Current Affairs* (Shiwu bao) from 1896 to 1897. Other essays in the

series were on such topics as schools, the civil service examination system, study societies, teacher training, kindergartens, translation, Manchu-Han relations, and banks.
See Liang Qichao, "Bianfa." On the place of this essay in Liang's work, see Tang, 3.

80. Judge, *Print*, 44.

81. Yan Fu ("Lun," 880) emphasized the need for women to cultivate *yueshi*.

82. Xie Chongxie, 43b.

83. Guang, Guang, and Chen, 8: 13a–14b; Liang Qichao, "Lun baoguan." According to the lesson, for a minimal daily expense, newspapers would broaden
young women's understanding of new theories and keep them apprised of domestic
and international political developments.

84. Yang Qianli, Nüzi.

85. Jiang Weiqiao had studied in Japan before 1902. Under the Republic he held
a number of educational appointments. For a brief portrait, see Wang Jianjun, 116.

86. Sun's textbook was entitled *Nüzi shifan jiangyi* (Lectures for women's normal
education). See "Xuebu shending." A brief biography of Sun, who was from Yunnan Province, is in the preface to her article; see Sun Qingru. She also contributed
to the third issue of the *XNJZZ*.

87. The *Chinese Girls' Progress* ran for twelve issues from July to October 1898.
See Nanxiu Qian, "Revitalizing," on the editor Xue Shaohui's opposition to Liang
Qichao's critique of the woman of talent (425–26).

88. *Beijing Women's Journal* was a daily that ran from August 20, 1905, until at
least as late as January 15, 1909. Its targeted audience not only included students in
new schools—of whom there were not as many in the north as in the south—but
housewives, officials, merchants, scholars, and common people. The most authoritative source on the journal is Jiang Weitang and Liu, 35–72.

89. Xiefen and her father fled to Japan following the court's indictment of Chen
Fan's *Jiangsu Journal*—to which the *Journal of Women's Learning* was initially printed
as a vernacular supplement—in what is known as "the *Subao* case." Kuang; Beahan,
389–90. On the confusion of Chen Xiefen's *Nü xuebao* with the 1898 *Nü xuebao*, see
Nanxiu Qian, "The Mother."

90. *Women's World* was established in Shanghai in 1904 by a man, Ding Chuwo,
but women, including Qiu Jin, also served as writers and editors. Sang Bing, 264;
Xu Yuzhen; Beahan, 395–98. Beahan mistakes Ding for a woman.

91. Nanxiu Qian ("Qingji," "Borrowing Foreign Mirrors") has done extensive
and fascinating work on this text as part of her project on Xue Shaohui.

92. Liang Qichao, "Jinshi." The Japanese source for Liang's text was a serialized
biography of Madame Roland that ran from December 1893 to February 1894 in
Katei zasshi (Family journal; September 1892–August 1898). See Matsuo, 265–78.
While many Japanese-language biographies that were sources for Chinese biographies were published in Meiji journals, others appeared in book-length biographical works. At least 41 of the 229 Meiji period book-length biographical works on
women listed in the catalog of the National Diet Library in Tokyo featured Western
women; see Kokuritsu, 1: 83–99. Of these 41, a handful became prime sources for
late Qing biographies.

93. Iwasaki and Mikami, *Sekai*; Iwasaki and Mikami, *Shijie*. Zhao, who was from Wuling in Hunan Province, was establishing himself as a prolific translator of Japanese texts, including several on socialism, at precisely this time. See Li Yu-ning, *The Introduction*, 13–14.

94. Yang Qianli was from Zhenze in southeastern Jiangsu (now Wu County). According to Zhang Jinglu ("Jiaokeshu," 228), the *Nüzi xin duben* was published in 1902, although 1904 is given as the date of first printing on the actual textbook. Han Xifeng (2095) lists a 1906 edition.

95. Guang, Guang, and Chen, vols. 7, 9, 10.

96. Ye Zhongling, 52–58.

97. Liu Mei Ching, 299.

98. Mulan tongxiang, 30.

99. Xu Dingyi, *Zuguo nüjie weiren*. Xu, whose style names included Juxue luzhu ren and Juxue zi, was from Shanhua in Hunan Province. In Tokyo he attended Qinghua [buxi] xuexiao (Chinese Preparatory School). Fang Zhaoying, 35.

100. *Shijie shi*, "Xu," 1.

Part One

1. According to the *Book of Ritual* (*Yili*), a woman wore mourning clothes for three years for her husband, but only one year for her father. See Chang So-an, "Murder," 10. A woman's spirit was honored after death in her husband's rather than her natal home, and her ancestral tablet resided at the alter of her marital family. Mann, *Precious*, 54. The role of wife was also privileged in didactic texts for women. As Sherry Mou (31) notes, only one of the 104 core biographies in the *LNZ* featured a girl who was not married either before or during the course of the biography (*LNZ*, 6:15). Ban Zhao's *Nü jie* was based on the premise that marriage was the destiny of all women.

2. These principles correspond to what Susan Mann ("Widows," 49) describes as "community gossip shaped by the elite discourse on chastity," and what Rey Chow (61) calls a "monitoring social system."

3. Xu Zihua, 137–38. The two women whose suicides Xu lamented were Wu Qide, from Guangdong Province, and Jiang Yunhua, from Jiashan, Zhejiang Province, both of whom were attending school in Shanghai when they were slandered. Wu committed suicide by swallowing opium, Jiang by ingesting poison. Many thanks to Hu Ying for bringing this source to my attention.

Chapter 1

1. Chaste women honored in the *LNZ* include Tao Ying, a chaste widow who lived on (*LNZ*, 4:13; Zhang Jing, 159–60); Qi Liang, a chaste widow who committed suicide (*LNZ*, 4:8; Zhang Jing, 147–48); and the wife of Xuan of Wei, a faithful maiden (*LNZ*, 4:3; Zhang Jing, 135–36).

2. The term "cult of chastity" has no Chinese language referent but was inspired by Republican-era Chinese scholars such as Liu Jihua and Dong Jiazun who

emphasize the religious aspects of chastity-related practices. This emphasis has been maintained by scholars, such as Zhou Wanyao, and disputed by Weijing Lu (*True*, Introduction), who claims it vitiates female agency. See also Theiss, *Disgraceful*, 13.

3. On shrines, see Theiss, *Disgraceful*, 31–33.

4. Theiss, "Managing"; Theiss, *Disgraceful*; Weijing Lu, *True*; Ropp, Zamperini, and Zurndorfer; Sommer; Chang So-an, "Shiba"; T'ien Ju-k'ang; Elliott.

5. Theiss (*Disgraceful*) focuses on state policy and Mann ("Widows," 50–51) draws on articles and gazetteers from the 1930s, for example.

6. According to Luo Suwen (150), chastity remained the "most sacred foundation of female morality" in the late Qing.

7. Dai Li, 1a. "Tian" as a synecdoche for "tiandi" was one of the most common concepts applied to the cosmos. Sivin, 5n1.

8. Dai Li, 1a.

9. Rongqing, Zhang, and Zhang.

10. Cong, 52.

11. Chaste widow homes, which were variously referred to as Xuli hui (Widow relief association), Qingjie tang (Hall of purity), Zhenjie tang (Hall of virtue), Jingjie tang (Hall of chastity), or Guangren tang (Hall of great benevolence), were established to protect marriageable and potentially reproductive widows from greedy relatives or local bullies. While these institutions had been in existence from the late eighteenth century, their number increased dramatically toward the end of the Qing dynasty. See Leung. The 1904 memorial proposed using orphanages (*yuyingtang*) to the same purpose.

12. Rongqing, Zhang, and Zhang, 394.

13. Japanese women were instructors at the School for Revering Chastity. Zhang Zhidong.

14. Huixing's biography was included in the *Draft History of the Qing Dynasty*. Zhao Erxuan, 46: 509, 14082. Her story has been analyzed by Chinese scholars of women's history, most notably Xia Xiaohong, "Wan-Qing nüxue," and by recent American scholars of the Manchus, including Rhoads.

15. "Buji."

16. "Baqi xieling gongcheng"(Colonel of a Regiment of the Provincial Manchu Garrison makes a public appeal), cited in Xia Xiaohong, "Wan-Qing nüxue," 235.

17. The memorial was reprinted in "Nüjie xinwen," *BJNB* (July 9, 1906). By the early seventeenth century, the system of granting state rewards for virtuous acts, which can be traced to the Han dynasty, had become both routinized and increasingly focused on women who preserved their sexual purity. Elvin, 307–16; Weijing Lu, *True*, 76 [throughout the Notes page citations to this work are from the manuscript]; Zhao Fengjie, 118; Theiss, *Disgraceful*, 25. The Qing awarded more *jingbiao* than any other dynasty and there was an extremely sharp gender imbalance in favor of women. Weijing Lu, *True*, 79.

18. Founded the month of Huixing's death, December 1905, the Education Board responded to the petition in place of the Ministry of Rites, which it was to supersede in the administrative hierarchy.

19. Huixing's husband was named either Jishan (according to most sources, including the *Draft History of the Qing Dynasty*) or Jizhi ("Buji," 1450) and was a licentiate of the first degree. There is also some discrepancy in the sources concerning the age at which Huixing was widowed. According to "Buji" (1450) and "Hangzhou," she was nineteen *sui* when her husband died, while according to an Education Board official document (cited in Xia Xiaohong, "Wan-Qing nüxue," 251) she was twenty.

20. "Xuebu Libu," cited in Xia Xiaohong, "Wan-Qing nüxue," 251.

21. Zhao Erxuan, 46: 509, 14082. The entry did go on to mention Huixing's martyrdom for her school and claimed she was granted the posthumous title *zhenxin yili* (pure and resolute).

22. The quotation is from "Buji."

23. The passage is from the "Xiangyin jiuyi" (The meaning of the drinking festivity in the districts) section of the *Record of Rites*. Legge, *Li Chi*, 2: 437.

24. WXY, IX.

25. Ibid., 20.

26. There are numerous earlier examples of the supernatural ramifications of chaste virtue. For examples in the *Jin History* (*Jin shu*), see Mou, 102; for the Yuan-era drama "Dou E yuan" (The injustice done to Dou E), see Liu Jung-en. On the supernatural powers of the chaste and virtuous, see Weijing Lu, *True*, 109–10.

27. WXY, IX.20. Wei included several other examples (IV.1; IX.13) of the links between sexually pure women and the cosmos.

28. Ibid., IX.4.

29. Ibid., 1. Wei voiced this same criticism in ibid., VI.1.

30. Ibid., IX.1.

31. Ibid. This kind of bamboo became known as the "Xiang queens' bamboo."

32. Ibid., 17.

33. While the early Qing rulers continued the Ming dynasty practice of glorifying chaste widows, they were much more reluctant to honor chastity martyrdom. The Kangxi emperor officially banned widow suicide in 1688 and Yongzheng supported this policy with further edicts. These directives were, however, largely ineffective. Weijing Lu, *True*, 74, 80; Theiss, "Managing," 74. The Qing emperors' opposition to widow chastity was often for ethnic rather than philosophical reasons. Elliott, 42–47, 53.

34. On Kangxi's 1688 edict, see Elvin, 322.

35. "Lun Liu."

36. The widow of Liang (*LNZ*, 4:14, Zhang Jing, 160–62) cut off her nose to deflect pressure to remarry. A disfigured woman could not make ancestral sacrifices with an "unwhole" body. Fong, "Signifying," 106.

37. Weijing Lu, *True*, 199–200.

38. For Wei's views on judicial torture, see Wei Xiyuan; on extreme expressions of filial piety, WXY, IV.6. Other meliorists criticized the practice of *gegu* as well. See "Gerou."

39. WXY, IX.5. Legge, *The Works*, 311 (Bk. 4, pt. 1, Ch. 21).

40. WXY, IX.5.

41. WXY, IX.6. On Song Lian's (1310–81) glorification of Lady Xiahou, see Weijing Lu, *True*, 200.

42. Wei Jingyu's wife is mentioned in the Tang dynasty text *Taiping guangji* (Expanded record of great peace), *juan* 270, "Furen" (Women).

43. WXY, IX.12. This ideal of genuine love was first expressed in the fifth century narrative poem "A Peacock Southeast Flew" (Kongque). See also Birrel.

44. WXY, IV.6.

45. Ibid., IX.14. In his commentary Wei recounts the story of a beautiful, virtuous widow named Li who was only able to stop a recurrent dream about a man pressuring her to marry him when she cut her hair and dirtied her face.

46. Faithful maiden practice can be traced to the *Arrayed Traditions of Women's Lives* (*LNZ*, 4:3; Zhang Jing, 135–36), but it was not until the Southern Song dynasty that it was sanctioned with government awards, and not until the Ming that it took on cultic proportions. On the practice in the Ming and Qing dynasties, see Weijing Lu, *True*; Theiss, "Managing," 60, 29–30.

47. Weijing Lu, *True*, 157; Sommer, 69.

48. Legge, *Li Chi*, 1: 311–42. On uses of the "Zengzi wen,"see Chang So-an, "Murder," 17–20.

49. Only a few defenders of the cult, including Zhu Yizun (1629–1709), appealed to the discourse of feeling. Weijing Lu, *True*, 234–35.

50. Ibid., 228.

51. Ibid., 242.

52. "Shouzhen."

53. Ibid. For the views of "reformist literati" such as Gui Youguang and Wang Zhong on the tension between *renqing* and the dictates of *lijiao*, see Rowe, *Saving*, 432. Wang Zhong was the author of one of the most important documents in the *zhennü* debate; see Mann, *Precious*, 84–85; Kai-wing Chow, 205–7; Weijing Lu, *True*, 243. Zhang Wenhu of Nanhui (now part of Shanghai), had worked in the office of Zeng Guofan and was the founder of the Jinling shuju (Nanjing publishing house). Xiong, *Xixue*, 532–33

54. "Shouzhen."

55. Ibid.

56. "Wang jiemu."

57. Chen had modeled himself on two Qing scholars, Qian Daxin (1728–1804) and Yu Zhengxie, both of whom had argued against the late imperial faithful maiden cult. For Qian's views on women, see Qian Daxin; for Yu's, see Yu Zhengxie; on Qian and Yu's views of chastity, see also Hu Fagui. According to Weijing Lu (*True*, 221–67), Qian's position on the *zhennü* cult was ultimately ambiguous.

58. Gui was a member of the Ming-loyalist Return to Antiquity Society (Fushe) and a leader of resistance to the Manchu invasion in the early Qing. Hummel, 427.

59. Gui Zhuang. Zhou Wanyao (215) questions whether Gui was really on the opposing side of the debate.

60. Chen Kangqi, "Wang shi."

61. In 1749 the Qianlong emperor approved the establishment of collective arches, and by 1845 chaste widows could only be honored with such arches. Elvin, 331; Theiss, "From Model Subjects," 4–5.

62. Chen Kangqi, "Wang shi."

63. Ibid.

64. They did not include the Su Wu analogy, for example, which they may have considered too erudite for the *Daily Pictorial*'s audience.

65. "Wang jiemu."

66. WXY, VI.17. Faithful maidens were the only unwed women who could legally adopt, and they often did so in order to fulfill their highest obligation to their husband: to ensure that his descent line would be continued and that an heir would be able to perform the requisite sacrifices to his spirit. See Weijing Lu, *True*, 192–96. On the notion of social versus biological motherhood, see Bray, 335–68. The story of Lady Jin is recorded in the *Zhejiang tongzhi* (Zhejiang gazetteer), *juan* 215, *Lienü* 14, but Jin is only referred to as "Mou shi" (Lady So-and-so).

67. The heroine's name in this semi-historical popular drama was Qin Xuemei. For details, see Weijing Lu, "True," 179–81.

68. WXY, VI.17. On Yu's critique, see Weijing Lu, "True," 243.

69. WXY, IX.21.

70. On these views, see Weijing Lu, "True," 261–64; Mann, *Precious*, 84–85.

71. WXY, IX.21.

72. Ibid., 23.

73. Boyi and Shuqi were princes of a small kingdom and sons of Guo Zhujun. On Wang Wan's use of this analogy, see Weijing Lu, "True," 231–32.

74. Peng and Yin, 1031. There are, however, details in the gazetteer account that Wei does not record, such as Jingqing's given name, Quansheng (Jingqing is her style name), family relations, and, most intriguingly, a second engagement, which her parents imposed on her and which, according to the gazetteer, was the event that ultimately precipitated her suicide.

75. WXY, IX.23.

76. Weijing Lu, "True," 256–67.

77. For a meliorist critique of chastity in the early Republic, see, for example, Shi Shuyi. Shi was the author of a 1922 anthology of women's poetry, which Ellen Widmer ("The Rhetoric," 215) has characterized as "conservative" while noting its relatively diminished emphasis on virtue. On Shi's writings for the *Ladies' Journal* (*Funü zazhi*), see Hu Hsiao-chen, 185–88.

78. Yosano.

79. Hu Shi; Lu Xun, "Wo zhi"; Lu Xun "My Views." See also Zhang Yihe and Chen Chunlei, 298–99.

80. The idea of fidelity was honored, however, in a textbook for boys that encouraged men to be as faithful as women. The example given was of Liu Tingshi, who insisted on marrying his betrothed even after she went blind and her family offered to end the engagement. The story was taken from *Su Dongpo ji* (Works of

Su Dongpo). Gao Fengqian, Cai, and Zhang, *Zuixin xiushen jiaoke shu, jiaoshou fa*, 4: 9a–9b.

81. Xie Chongxie, 58b.

82. Xu Jiaxing.

83. Xu Jiaxing, "Lieyan," 1b.

84. Xu Jiaxing, 71a.

85. Ibid., 70a.

86. Ibid., 71a (there are two pages 71a and b in the text, clearly a printing error). In the original story, Jiao's wife drowned herself. For the poem, see Birrel.

87. Xu Jiaxing, 78b–79a.

88. Xu Dingyi, "Fanli," *Zuguo nüjie weiren*, 1.

89. *Shijie shi*, "Xu," 1.

90. Takano.

91. While a number of newspapers, including the *Beijing-Tianjin Times* and the *"The Eastern Times,"* published news of official rewards, the *Shanghai News* directly reprinted *jingbao* excerpts. See Mittler, 202–3.

92. "Jingbiao."

93. "Guifan."

94. "Zhenjie."

95. "Liefu hanbei."

96. "Zouwei."

97. Weijing Lu, *Truth*, 99–102.

98. "Chen Huizhen." These shrines were first instituted by the Yongzheng emperor. Weijing Lu, *True*, 107–8.

99. "Jiefu fa." On cutting off hair as a cultural gesture of making a pledge, see Weijing Lu, *Truth*, 17.

100. "Zhenfu."

101. "Jiefu yin."

102. Rowe, *Saving*, 432. Rowe adds Chen Hongmou to this list of "literati reformers," but Chen did not, to my knowledge, make a specific contribution to the chastity debate.

103. WXY, IV.6.

104. Lu Xun, "My Views," 16.

105. Hu Shi, 298.

Chapter 2

1. Examples include Ti Ying of the *LNZ*, who petitioned the emperor on her father's behalf because he had no sons to come to his aid, and Hua Mulan, who replaced her father in the army when he was too old and infirm to fight. See Chapter 5 on both of these women. Another example is Huang Chonggu, a talented woman who passed herself off as a male official of the Shu kingdom (908–25). Ko, *Teachers*, 130.

2. Rongqing, Zhang, and Zhang, 393–96.

3. "Gongbu."

4. "Xuebu zouding nüzi shifan," 668.

5. Dai Li, "Zixu," 2b.

6. Zhang Qin, 1a.

7. "Zicha." For other newspaper reports on this incident, see Bailey, "'Unharnessed,'" 342. Most extant new-style textbooks contain discussion of free marriage, suggesting the ineffectiveness of these government bans.

8. "Xiangguo." Zhang further advised the Ministry of Foreign Affairs to negotiate with the country in question in order to halt the importation of more copies.

9. Xue and Chen, "Yili" (Translation note), in Xue and Chen, 1a. This disagreement is discussed in Nanxiu Qian, "'Borrowing,'" 64–65.

10. Zeng Yi, 6b–7b.

11. Ibid., "Zixu," 5a.

12. Xu Jiaxing, 88b.

13. See, for example, "Nü xuesheng shang."

14. "Chuangshe wanguo."

15. "Yingguo," 41.

16. Yang's reader was published in 1904. On this incident and the nationalist sentiment it inspired among overseas students, see Harrell, *Sowing*, 131–39; Rhoads, 13, 285.

17. Yang Qianli, *Nüzi*, 2: 16a. These courageous Chinese "Nightingales" included members of the Humanitarian Association and the Association of Dedicated Nurses in Tokyo, and students at the Patriotic Girls' School in Shanghai, all of whom had volunteered to serve as nurses in the struggle against the Russian incursion. While the editors of Guang, Guang, and Chen (8: 24b–25a) reprinted Yang's version of Nightingale's biography verbatim in 1908, they excluded Yang's parabiographical exhortation because the issue of Russia's encroachment had subsided by this time. This underlines how topical concerns drove the signification of Western women's biographies in these materials.

18. Edward T. James, 3: 617.

19. Yang Qianli, *Nüzi*, 2: 9b–11b; Guang, Guang, and Chen, 9: 14b–15b.

20. Liu Gengzao, 345.

21. Ibid., 346.

22. Wu Tao, 39b.

23. Jiang made this declaration not in the biography itself but in a speech recorded in the *Journal of Women's Learning*. See Jiang Zhiyou, "Aiguo." The biography ([Jiang Zhiyou], "Wuyue") was first published in *Xuan bao* (Digest magazine) in 1902, and reprinted in both *Women's Journal* and *New People's Miscellany* in July of the same year. I am using the latter version. While Jiang's biography was the source for biographies of Stowe included in both Yang Qianli's and Guang, Guang, and Chen's textbooks, the source for Jiang's biography is unclear. The potential sources were numerous. Stowe was widely featured in Meiji Japanese collections of Western women's biographies including Katō and Nemoto, neither of which was the precise source. Westerners had also introduced Stowe to the Chinese audience; see Hanan, 441. On Beecher Stowe in the late Qing, see Xia Xiaohong, "Ms. Picha."

24. [Jiang Zhiyou], "Wuyue," 9; Yang Qianli, *Nüzi*, 2: 14a; Guang, Guang, and Chen, 7: 16b.

25. [Jiang Zhiyou], "Wuyue"; Yang Qianli, *Nüzi*, 2: 14a; Guang, Guang, and Chen, 7: 16b.

26. While the textbook biography is quite faithful to Jiang's original, this detail was added. Yang Qianli, *Nüzi*, 2: 14a.

27. "Nüshi Du."

28. "Xiangshan."

29. Lyon was often the single educator among ten to twenty women with various accomplishments featured in Japanese collections of Western heroines. See Nagayama; Katō; Nemoto. She is not featured in any Chinese textbooks I have seen.

30. Lingxi, "Meiguo da jiaoyujia."

31. I am referring here not to the biological/social distinction between mothers who bore/raised children, but to the distinction between mothers who raised—biological or non-biological sons—for the patriline, and women who were metaphorical "mothers" of social movements.

32. See, for example, *Shijie shi*, 52, 57.

33. Yang Qianli, *Nüzi*, 2: 15b.

34. "Chuangshe wanguo," 71; Lingxi, "Meiguo da jiaoyujia," 67–68. Egyptian biographies of Florence Nightingale from precisely this period (1909) also describe her as caring for soldiers in the Crimea "just like a mother" (Booth, "'May,'" 875). This raises the intriguing question of whether there was a stock pool of Western female biographies that circulated in the non-Western world in the early twentieth-century.

35. "Pujiu zhu" is the title of the biography of Nightingale in *Shijie shi*, 47.

36. "Yingguo," 40.

37. *Shijie shi*, 47, 52.

38. Xia Xiaohong, "Ms Picha," 246.

39. Liu Gengzao, 344.

40. [Jiang Ziyou], "Wuyue," 9; Yang Qianli, *Nüzi*, 2: 13b.

41. Nemoto, 82.

42. Lingxi, "Meiguo da jiaoyujia," 70.

43. Shoujuan.

44. *Shijie shi*, 57.

45. Ibid., 54–55.

46. In addition to assuming new roles, many women continued long-standing public roles as actresses and courtesans. See Cheng Weikun, "The Challenge"; Catherine Yeh, "Creating"; Catherine Yeh, *Shanghai Love*.

47. On the Association of Dedicated Nurses, which was formed in the heat of the northeastern struggle in 1903, see "Liuxue"; on the Women's Red Cross Army, which left Japan on October 19, 1911, and joined forces with Zhang Zhujun's embryonic Red Cross Association in Shanghai, see Sun Shiyue, 119–20. The revolutionary Qiu Jin attempted to advance such activities in China by translating a Japanese Red Cross nursing guide, *Nihon Sekijūjisha kangogaku kyōtei* (The Japanese Red Cross

course on nursing) into Chinese as *Kanhuxue jiaocheng* (A course in nursing) in 1906. The first two installments were published in her *Chinese Women's Journal*, and reprinted in "*The Eastern Times*" shortly after her death. Qiu Jin, "Kanhuxue"; *SB*, July 24, 27, 28, 1907.

48. See Yan Bin's discussion of the Zhongguo furenhui in *XNJZZ* 3 (April 5, 1907), 107–14. The Female Citizen's Fund was established by Wu Zhiying (1867–1935) to institutionalize female contributions to the national cause. See Yan Bin, "Benbao duiyu"; Xia Xiaohong, *Wan-Qing wenren*, 98.

49. Lu Xun, *Lu Xun*, 303. See also Eileen J. Cheng, 1, 5, 7, 8, 9, 23.

50. While numbers of female students were small, they rose dramatically over the course of the first decades of the twentieth century, thus fueling concern. According to what are certainly incomplete statistics, there were approximately 103 female students enrolled in China and over 210 enrolled in a single school in Japan, Shimoda Utako's Jissen Women's School, between 1901 and 1905; see Liao Xiuzhen, 225; Sechiyama and Kihara, 281. Numbers increased over the first decades of the twentieth century with the government's approval of women's schools in 1907. In 1907 there were 420 recorded women's schools and 14,658 female students. By 1912 the number of students had increased tenfold to 141,130. Liao Xiuzhen, 226–27; Chen Dongyuan, 362; Xia Xiaohong, "Wan-Qing funü," 269; Bailey, "Unharnassed," 330–31. From 1907 through the end of the Qing, there were between 100 and 150 Chinese female students enrolled in Japan each year. Zhou Yichuan, *Chūgokujin*, 84.

51. In 1904 there were, however—again according to incomplete statistics—a mere 26 schools with some 494 students. Liao Xiuzhen, 224–26.

52. Rongqing, Zhang, and Zhang, 396.

53. "Xuebu zouding nüzi shifan," 668.

54. See, for example, "Lun Shanghai."

55. Articles on enlightened marriage began to appear in the Chinese press around 1902, reached a crescendo between 1905 and 1907, and continued well into the Republican period. It was a subject of discussion, for example, in *FNSB* from early 1911 through 1917.

56. For examples of *wenming* ceremonies, see a series of articles entitled "Wenming jiehun" that appeared in *STSB* on August 23, September 10, and September 13, 1905. See also Xia Xiaohong, "Wan-Qing funü shenghuo," 308–9.

57. This marked the emergence of a discourse on "eugenic sexuality" based on the idea that freer unions produced healthier offspring and ultimately a stronger nation. See Barlow, *The Question*, 7.

58. "Wenming jiehun," *STSB* (September 13, 1905).

59. On footbinding as concealment, see Ko, *Cinderella's*, 109–225.

60. "Shanghai funü."

61. Xia Xiaohong, "Wan-Qing funü," 261–62.

62. Liang Qichao, "Lun nüxue," 875.

63. The Patriotic Girls' School had similar regulations. Xia Xiaohong, "Wan-Qing funü," 268.

64. Wu Ruoan, 603.

65. "Xuebu zouding nüzi xiaoxue," 658. In 1902 the Empress Dowager Cixi had issued an edict abolishing footbinding. Pao Tao Chia-lin, 170. On the Manchus earlier prohibition attempts, see Ko, *Cinderella's*, 266n49.

66. "Xinshu."

67. See, for example, Xie Chongxie, 51a; Guang, Guang, and Chen, 9: 5b–6b; Fang Liusheng, 19b.

68. Fang Liusheng, "Fulu," 4a–b.

69. Chen Yan'an, "Quan," 155 [0585]. On this theme, see Ko, *Teachers*, 149; Larson, 77.

70. Wang Lian, "Tongxiang," 114.

71. Ko *Cinderella's*, 11. Ko (*Cinderella's*, 47–48) does, however, provide evidence of older women who attempted to unbind their feet.

72. Wang Lian, "Tongxiang," 114.

73. Anti-footbinding critics included Gu Hongming. See Ko, *Cinderella's*, 30–37.

74. This incident was discussed in newspapers in China and Japan, including the *Shanghai News*, the Fengtian *News* (*Tongbao*), and the Tokyo-based *Magazine of the New Chinese Woman*. See, for example, "Shen Zhongli"; "Jiangsu"; "Tianzu"; Hui Xin.

75. "Nüshi fangzu."

76. "Huaixuhai."

77. On dress as both a signifier and a constituent of social difference, and on sartorial regulation, see Ko, *Cinderella's*, 182–86, quotation on 183. Demeanor (*rong*) was one of the four womanly attributes (*side*), which also included virtue (*de*), speech (*yan*), and meritorious deeds (*gong*). First described in the *Zhou li* (Rites of Zhou) they were elaborated upon by Ban Zhao in the *Nü jie's* fourth chapter, "Fuxing" (Womanly behavior). See Swann, 86; Mann, "Learned," 30.

78. "Wuben nü xuexiao," 593. Articles calling for the regulation of female students' dress, include "Qing ding"; "Nü xuesheng ying"; "Nü xueshi."

79. "Xuebu zouding nüzi shifan," 674.

80. "Xuebu zou zunni."

81. "Shibiao you kui" (The failure of models for emulation), *DGB* 2233, 1/10 1908, cited in Fong, "Alternative," 34–35. See also Qiu Liu.

82. "Lun Shanghai."

83. "Maochong." Similar comments can be found in the periodical press and official documents up through the 1930s. John Fitzgerald has alerted me to a document from 1933 in which the magistrate of Huaxian County called on the Guangdong Eastern District Commission "to rule that prostitutes should not be allowed to solicit for trade while wearing school uniforms": "Guangdong nanqu dierci suijing huiyi ge shenchazu shencha ti'an baogao" (Investigations, proposals, and reports of each investigation group of the second conference of the Guangdong southern regional pacification commission), undated (ca. mid. 1933). Archival document. Guangdong Zhongshan shengli tushuguan wenxiangguan, K 0.47.5/3938, 30.

84. "Wansheng gongchang fang'ai nüxue zhi jiaoshe" (Negotiations over a public

brothel hindering women's education in Anhui), *ShB* (January 25, 1913), cited in Bailey, "Unharnassed," 351.

85. "Nü xuejie."

86. "Shanghai nü xuexiaozhang."

87. "Shijin." The same phrase *shangfeng baisu* was used in a number of spurious criticisms of girls' schools. See, for example, "Hunan," which recounts how a man who had been spurned by a student at a local school had the school closed.

88. "Shuchang."

89. "Qing ding."

90. See, for example, "Kan women nüzi bei renjia chixiao" (See how our women are ridiculed), *DGB* (June 27, 1912), cited in Bailey, "Unharnassed," 352.

91. *Beijing ribao* (August 11, 1910), cited in Cheng Weikun, "Going," 128.

92. "Datong."

93. On this topic, see Tze-lan Sang.

94. Shan Zai.

95. Ibid.

96. This understanding of female education was evident in the section on "Educating Sons" in WXY.

97. See, for example, the complaints of the textbook authors Zhuang Yu and Jiang Weiqiao in "Zhi Nanyang." Zhuang and Jiang refer explicitly to the need for women to cultivate the qualities of good wives and wise mothers.

98. "Sichuan."

99. On the Zhongguo furenhui, see *XNJZZ* 3 (April 5, 1907), 107–14; Yan Bin, "Benbao duiyu"; Xia Xiaohong, *Wan-Qing wenren*, 98.

100. "Sichuan."

101. Qu's style name was Bogang; he was from Pinghu County in Zhejiang Province.

102. "Sichuan." Du published another response to Qu in *NZSJ*; see Du Chengshu. As a result of this incident, Qu, who according to the testimony of his friends was a respectable individual, not the lecher of Du's description, was forced to discontinue his studies at the Translation Bureau. On the incident, see also "Xuesheng."

Chapter 3

1. This privileging of virtue over talent was evident in the earliest didactic texts for women. See Zhou Yiqun, 39–42, on Liu Xiang's choice of stories in the *LNZ* that highlight virtue. Even tales of reasoning and wise women were what Lisa Raphals (*Sharing*, 23) has called "intellectual virtue stories."

2. On female literacy in this era, see Ko, *Teachers*. On the courtesan as model for the woman of talent, see Kang-i Sun Chang, "A Guide," 146.

3. The phrase can be traced to the writings of Feng Menglong (1574–1646), but he was articulating an idea already in circulation. Wang Guangyi, 148. See also Chen Dongyuan, 188–202; Ko, "Pursuing," 9, *Teachers*; Ho.

4. Zhang Xuecheng, "Fuxue," 10b; Zhang Xuecheng, "Fuxue," trans. On the

"querelle" between Zhang and Yuan, see Mann, *Precious*, 83–94; on the "Fuxue" itself, see Mann, "'Fuxue'"; and Mann, "Learned."

5. On Wanyan and her anthology, the *Guochao guixiu zhengshi ji* (Correct beginnings: Women's poetry of our august dynasty), see Mann, *Precious*, 94–117; Widmer, "The Rhetoric," 195–99; Kang-i Sun Chang, "A Guide," 145.

6. "Xuebu zouding nüzi shifan," 669.

7. Swann, 86.

8. The most renowned example of this is the "willow-catkin" poet Xie Daoyun (fl. 350) who is discussed more fully later in this chapter.

9. Dai Li, "Zixu," 1b.

10. Ibid., 1a.

11. Zhang Boxi, 2b.

12. Zeng Yi.

13. Ibid., "Zixu," 5b.

14. Quoted in Nanxiu Qian, "Revitalizing," 425–26.

15. I have discussed certain aspects of this critique of the woman of talent in "Talent," and "Re-forming."

16. Mann, "Women's"; Mann, "Womanly"; Kang-i Sun Chang, "Women's."

17. Kang-i Sun Chang, "Women's," 1.

18. On Li Qingzhao, see Idema and Grant, 204–43.

19. Mann, "Women's"; Mann, "Womanly"; Kang-i Sun Chang, "Women's."

20. On the uses of this same strategy in current Islamic women's biographical writing, see Booth, "'May.'"

21. Mann, *Precious*, 78.

22. Widmer, "The Rhetoric."

23. See for example, Yan Fu, "Lun"; Jing Yuanshan, "Quan."

24. On the serial essay that appeared in *Current Affairs* (Shiwu bao) from 1896 to 1897, see Liang Qichao, "Bianfa"; Tang, 3. On the disparagement of the woman of talent in Liang's essay, see also Hu Ying, *Tales*, 6–8.

25. Liang Qichao, "Lun nüxue," 870.

26. Yan Fu, "Lun," 880. This is possibly a reference to women like Liang Duan and Wang Zhaoyuan, who wrote annotated versions of the *LNZ* in the nineteenth century. Liang Qichao directly criticizes Liang and Wang in "Ji Jiangxi," 119. Both women are discussed in Chapter 6.

27. Kang. On the appearance of the article in *Nüxue bao*, see Nanxiu Qian, "Revitalizing," 417.

28. Kang, 878. This saying about the hen first appeared in the *Shang shu* (Book of documents).

29. Ibid.

30. He Xiangning, "Jinggao."

31. "Gongai."

32. Wang Lian, "Tongxiang," 114 [0288]. Wang's views echoed both Liang Qichao's critique of the woman of talent and his later call for a literary revolution. For a discussion of Cui and Dai, see Waltner.

33. Wu Tao, 4b, 10a–b.

34. Xie Chongxie, "Xuyan," 1a.

35. Wu Tao, 10a.

36. Yang Qianli, Nüzi, "Daoyan," 1: 1b–2a.

37. Kang, 878.

38. Ibid. Italics mine.

39. Two of Ban Zhao's texts are included in the *Hou Han shu* biography: a memorial she wrote advising the empress to grant her exiled and aging brother retirement, and the full text of the *Nü jie*. On the biography, see Mou, 79–86. For translations of the two texts and an insightful introduction to Ban's life, see Idema and Grant, 17–42.

40. On the classical revival of Ban, see Mann, *Precious*, 80–81.

41. Kang, 878.

42. Yang Qianli (Nüzi, 1: 11a–b) commends Ban for writing the *Nü jie* and continuing a tradition of family learning by completing the *Han shu*. Xie Chongxie (46a) praises the *Nü jie* for teaching women to sew, cook, and weave, but concludes with Ban's role as an instructress at court. Wu Tao and Biaomeng also note Ban's learning.

43. Kang, 878.

44. Ibid. The story of Fu Sheng's transmission of the *Shang shu* first appeared in Sima Qian's "Rulin zhuan" in the *Shi ji*. The story of his daughter mediating the transmission of his text was a later accretion credited to Yan Shigu (581–645) of the Tang dynasty. On representations of Fu Sheng's daughter in the High Qing, see Mann, *Precious*, 212.

45. Kang, 878.

46. Zhang Xuecheng recounts the story of Lady Song in the "Fuxue." See Mann, *Precious*, 81.

47. See the song "Nü zhuzuo" (Women writers), which celebrates four women: Ban Zhao, Lady Zheng, Song Ruohua, and Empress Changsun of the Tang, author of a text called the *Nü ze* (Female regulations). Ye Zhongling, 30. Theresa Kelleher (827) argues that while Song Ruohua wrote the *Analects for Women*, her sister Song Ruozhao propagated it. For the celebration of these women in High Qing texts, see Mann, *Precious*, 81, 213; Zhang Xuecheng, "Fuxue," trans., 791.

48. Yang Qianli, "Daoyan," 3a, 1: 12a–b.

49. Qizhan. The biography was a translation from Nemoto's collection.

50. Ibid., 54–55.

51. Lingxi, "Meiguo da xinwenjia." Lingxi translated the biography from Nemoto Shō's collection.

52. The biography does not mention Fuller's influential feminist tract, *Women in the Nineteenth Century*, or the out-of-wedlock birth of her son. It is of course highly likely that Lingxi was herself ignorant of these details. *Women in the Nineteenth Century* was, however, mentioned in the contemporary Xue and Chen (4: 21a–21b). The illegitimate birth was not.

53. *Analects*, 7: 18, Legge, *Confucius*, 201.

54. *Analects*, 15: 18, Legge, *Confucius*, 300; Zhang Xuecheng, "Fuxue," trans., 786.

55. Lingxi, "Meiguo da xinwenjia."

56. Wanyan Yun Zhu privileged virtue in *Guochao guixiu zhengshi ji* (Correct beginnings: Women's poetry of our august dynasty) as did Shan Shili (1858–1943) in her sequel to the anthology. Mann, *Precious*, 94–117; Widmer, "The Rhetoric," 213.

57. WXY, III.1. Gao Qizhuo held various governorships and governor-general-ships in southern China. On Cai Wan, see Min, 3265; Chang and Saussy, 445; Hummel, 735.

58. WXY, IX.11. On Guan Panpan, see Carlitz, "Desire," 116, 125.

59. WXY, IX.23.

60. Ibid., 22. On Huang's poems, which were collected as the *Surviving Poems of Heroic Woman Huang* (*Huang lienü yishi*), see Hu Wenkai, 503; Fong, "Signifying," 121–28.

61. On the position of Xie Daoyun in the High Qing, see Mann, *Precious*, 17, 76, 83, 91, 213; on Zhang's views of her, see Zhang Xuecheng, "Fuxue," trans., 790–91.

62. WXY, IX.3.

63. Ibid., 24.

64. Ibid., 25. On Ye Xiaoluan, see Hu Wenkai, 149–50; Ko, *Teachers*, 82, 100, 138, 161, 166–68, 187, 201–2, 211–12; Idema and Grant, 390–406.

65. WXY, IX.24, 25.

66. Ibid., 24.

67. Ibid., 25. Idema and Grant, 400–406.

68. "Ruan." For a brief biography of Kong Luhua, see Li Junzhi, 3: 664. On Ruan, see Vissière; Hummel, 399–401.

69. When Ruan Yuan was director of education under Bi Yuan, governor of Shandong from 1794, the two men pledged to unite their children in marriage. Their shared respect for the ancients and esteem for Confucianism rendered them worthy of mingling their bloodlines with those of the great sage Kongzi. "Bi Ruan."

70. "Ruan."

71. A recent article situates Xu's guide among Republican histories of women's literature by Xie Wuliang (1916), Lei Jin and Lei Jian (1916), Tan Zhengbi (1930), and Liang Yizhen (1932); see Lin Shuming, 257–58. The entries on each woman in Xu's guide varied in length but were generally no more than a few lines. They gave basic biographical information on lineage and native place and recorded the titles of the woman's major writings.

72. Xu Dingyi, *Zuguo nüjie wenhao*, "Xu," 1a–b; "Fanli," 1a.

73. The greatest number of entries in Xu's guide, 106 of the 365, were women from the Qing dynasty. In addition, sixty-nine women of the Ming were included, eighteen from the Yuan, one each from the Jin and the Liao, fifty-eight from the Song, six from the Five Dynasties, forty-nine from the Tang, six from the Sui, eleven from the Period of Division, twenty-six from the Eastern Jin, and fourteen from the Qin-Han dynasties.

74. Because of Cai Yan's remarriage, scholars, including Liu Zhiji (661–721) of the Tang dynasty, questioned whether her story should have been included in the *Hou Han shu*. Mou, 87.

75. Xu Dingyi, *Zuguo nüjie wenhao*, "Xu," 1b.

76. Leftist critics in the 1920s and 1930s and Communists in the following decades associated national weakness with the woman of talent's excessive individualism, lack of social commitment, realism, and patriotic fervor. They based their visions of a revitalized Chinese polity on the elimination of her lyrical traces. See Larson, 140–46, 165, 170–72; Judge, "Talent," 802–3.

Chapter 4

1. On a similar formulation of the place of motherhood in Western modernity, see Felski, 55.

2. Rongqing, Zhang, and Zhang, 396.

3. According to the 1907 regulations, the "education of girls and women was the foundation of citizens' education." See "Xuebu zouding nüzi shifan," 668.

4. WXY, VI. The section dedicated to mother instructors is the second largest in Wei's compilation, with nineteen exemplars following the section on "Virtue" with twenty-five. Similarly, five of the eleven biographies in the *Daily Pictorial*'s "New Chinese and Foreign Arrayed Traditions of Women's Lives" feature remarkable mothers.

5. The idea of family as microcosm is most clearly set forth in the classic Confucian text the *Daxue* (The great learning). A similar emphasis on the public ramifications of women's private roles is evident in many of the biographies in the *LNZ*.

6. On this high estimation of childbirth, see Furth, "Concepts," 9.

7. Yu-yin Cheng, 103. These five relationships were between ruler and subjects, father and sons, husband and wife, among brothers, and among friends.

8. Ebrey, "The *Book*," 47.

9. In the "Nei ze," the mother is generally referred to in conjunction with her husband unless he has died or when brief reference is made to her confinement during pregnancy. In the first months of the child's life, he is handed over to three surrogate mothers, the most important among them being his teacher. Legge, *Li Chi*, 453, 471, 473.

10. The first section of the *LNZ* includes fourteen exemplars of "Muyi" (Maternal rectitude). On motherhood in the *LNZ*, see Shimomi.

11. For an analysis of a number of these epitaphs, see Hsiung, "Constructed."

12. Yu-yin Cheng, 103–16. Another exception was Li Qing (1602–83), author of the *Nü shishuo* (Women's shishuo), who exalted the cultural value of motherly love. In Li's view, *ci* should be considered "the most fundamental and universal value of the human world." Nanxiu Qian, "Milk," 209.

13. The one place the loving mother was valorized was in accounts of Western social heroines, discussed in Chapter 2, another example of how archeomodernists used values considered outmoded for Chinese women to make foreign women appear less threatening.

14. WXY, VI.

15. The term appears in the "Zhaoce" (Zhao record) section of the *Zhangguo ce*

(Intrigues of the warring states) and thus dates to at least the Former Han dynasty (206 BCE–8 CE). Lü Meiyi, 15–16.

16. For the most recent review of the literature on the concept of good wives and wise mothers throughout East Asia and a critique of its collapse with Confucian women's education, see Jin Jungwon.

17. For a fuller exploration of the Sino-Japanese dimensions of the concept, see Judge, "The Ideology."

18. *The Educational World* was founded by Luo Zhenyu (1866–1940) in May 1901.

19. Yoshimura, *Nihon*. An important figure in the Meiji educational world, Yoshimura was the second head of the Tokyo Women's Academy (Tōkyō jogaku kan), and in 1898 he established the Women's School (Seijo gakkō).

20. Yoshimura, "Riben," 19. Chinese and Japanese scholars of the good wives and wise mothers ideal have apparently been unaware of this translation of Yoshimura. They claim the expression first appears in Chinese in 1905 and 1906 in the Japanese-owned and -operated newspaper *Beijing-Tianjin Times*. Lü Meiyi, 17; Sechiyama and Kihara, 287–91; Takamure, 545.

21. Abe, *Chūgoku*, 98–99. Following its victory over China in the war of 1894–95, the Japanese government sought both to maintain its status in a rapidly militarizing and industrializing world, and to preserve social stability and fundamental East Asian values by linking motherhood to nationalism. This new validation of motherhood was concretized in the Education Ministry's ordinance of 1898 mandating higher education for girls. Katayama, "Meiji yonjū," 1; Uno, 39–42; Sechiyama and Kihara, 286–87; Takamure, 555.

22. The Meiji officials included Kanō Jigorō (1860–1938), Konoe Atsumaro (1863–1904), and Inukai Tsuyoshi (1885–1932). Abe, *Chūgoku*, 99.

23. Katayama, "Meiji yonjū," 4; Abe, *Chūgoku*, 98–99.

24. Most current Japanese scholars continue to uphold the theory of Western origins. Takamure, 544, 547; Katayama, "Meiji yonjū," 9. Nakamura used the concept in one of the last issues of an important journal of the period, *Meiroku zasshi* (*Meiji Six Journal*) (March 1875). Sievers, 22–23.

25. "Lun nüxue yi xianding," 131–32.

26. For a recent example of a critique of the concept based on its association with Confucian ideas, see Liu Ningyuan, cited in Jin Jungwon, 200.

27. *Liangqi* was first used in the "Weishi jia" (Chronology of the family of Wei) section of Sima Qian's *Shi ji*. See Lü Meiyi, 15–16.

28. Ibid., 17.

29. Yoshimura, "Riben," 19. There were, however, important differences in how the eugenics movement was used in Britain and Japan. In Britain, feminists claimed that women's racial responsibilities authorized their equality in the public sphere, whereas Shimoda and others in Japan and China used racial arguments to emphasize the importance of the woman's domestic roles. On the British case, see Burton, 49.

30. On pan-Asianism, see Duara, "The Discourse."

31. "Huazu," 11 [39].

32. Ji Yihui was also Shimoda's teacher of modern Chinese. Liu Mei Ching, 154.

33. The majority of the journal's staff writers and editors were young Chinese who had been overseas students in Japan and shared Shimoda's interest in educational issues. It ran for forty-seven issues and was distributed in Sichuan, Hubei, Hunan, Guangdong, and Fujian provinces. Jissen joshi gakuen, 101; Ko Shimoda, 428; Huang Mo. Huang does not mention that the journal was founded by Japanese.

34. Naruse, *Joshi*; Naruse, *Nüzi*. Naruse's text was written in 1896.

35. Wu Ruoan, 606; Abe, *Chūgoku*, 99.

36. Uenuma, 85.

37. "Shu jiaoyu."

38. Shimoda, *Shina*.

39. Jissen joshi gakuen, 113–16.

40. As Peter Zarrow ("Introduction," 18) has written, the term *guomin* "straddled the distinction between a mere 'national' and a full-fledged 'citizen.'" For a fuller discussion of these issues, see Judge, "Citizens," 31–37.

41. Chen Baoquan and Gao Buying, 1: 1–2.

42. Bodily hexis includes the physical shape of the body and its deportment, and is assumed to express a person's true nature. Bourdieu, *Masculine*, 64.

43. Liang Qichao, 871. For similar arguments, see Jing Yuanshan, "Zhi," 881; Kang Tongwei, "Nüxue," 877.

44. Liang Qichao, "Lun nüxue," 871–72.

45. Guang, Guang, and Chen, 1: "Dayi," 1b.

46. Lynn Hunt (123) has demonstrated that, at the time of the French Revolution, even the most militant women subscribed to the ideal of republican motherhood.

47. Huang Lingfang, 133 [943].

48. Wang Lian, "Tongxiang," 115.

49. Cao. Cao was the younger sister of the male student Cao Rulin (1876–1966), with whom she traveled to Japan. This view of family as a microcosm is repeated in a number of other overseas female essays. See, for example, "Zhina," 67 [0385].

50. Qiu Jin, "Jinggao Zhongguo."

51. The West was the distant inspiration for the concept in Liang's "Lun nüxue" and later writings. One author claimed in 1907 ("Lun nüxue yi xianding," 129) that Westerners had first declared "that women are the mothers of citizens."

52. Shimoda, "Ou-Mi," 91.

53. "Nüzi wei guomin."

54. Xie Chongxie, 1a.

55. Yang Qianli, *Nüzi*, 1: 1a.

56. Wu Tao, 9b–10b.

57. This again resonates with the ideal of republican motherhood. Linda Kerber ("The Paradox," 268) has written that in republican America women could claim political participation only if they implicitly promised to keep their politics in the service of the men in their family.

58. Xu Jiaxing, 86b–87a.

59. Xie Chongxie, 49a.

60. Fang Liusheng, 4a–b.

61. Ibid., 1b–2b.

62. Guang, Guang, and Chen, 5: 2b–3b.

63. Ibid., 7: 9b; 8: 16b–17a; 9: 10a–b.

64. See examples in ibid., vols. 4, 6, 7, 8, 10.

65. Ibid., 7: 17b–18a.

66. Furth, *A Flourishing*, 131, 307; Furth, "Rethinking," 144.

67. Dikötter, 43; Sun Qingru, 4.

68. Yan made this statement in the preface to Xiao Yin, 19.

69. Xia Xiaohong, *Wan-Qing wenren*, 94.

70. Xu Jiaxing, 4b. Xie Chongxie (16a) also emphasizes the importance of physical activity, citing the authority of Western doctors and noting the difference between exercise for girls and boys.

71. Wu Tao, 13b–14b.

72. Shirai, 2b; Cai Yun, 1b. It is unclear when the text was first published in English or translated into Japanese.

73. I have gleaned this information on Xu's textbook from "Shaojie." See Zhang Jinglu, "Jiaokeshu," 243, 244, 247, 249, on textbooks Xu published in the early Republic.

74. See, for example, "Wuben nüshu zengshe," 594–95; "Wuben nüshu ji"; Chen Xiefen, "Ji Wuben," 599.

75. "Xuebu zouding nüzi xiaoxue," 661–65; "Xuebu zouding nüzi shifan," 671–72.

76. Xie Chongxie, 28a, 29a.

77. Guang, Guang, and Chen, 9: 5b–6b. Other textbooks make the same connections among motherhood, the nation, and footbinding. See, for example, Fang Liusheng, 19b.

78. "Nüzi wei," 607.

79. The Spartan mother was an inspiration for conceptions of republican or patriotic motherhood in America and France. Kerber, "The Republican," 42. She was, however, a singular example, whereas the Chinese worked with a full and complex repertoire—which included the Spartan mother (see, for example, Liu Yazi, "Lun," 574). The Japanese also tended to draw on more recent exemplars rather than on figures from deep in the past.

80. Legge, "The Nei Tse," 473.

81. WXY, VI.16.

82. On mother-instructresses in the Song, see Ebrey, *The Inner*, 185–86; for the seventeenth century, see Ko, *Teachers*; on the eighteenth, see Mann, *Precious*, 101–8; on the Ming-Qing, see Hsiung, "Constructed," 94–95, 97, 99, 108.

83. "Gongai," 160.

84. "Lun jiating," 47 [801].

85. Wu Tao, 28a–29a.

86. Yang Qianli, *Nüzi*, I: 1a.

87. Sun Qingru, 2.

88. Wu Tao, 28b.

89. Ye Zhongling, 24.

90. Guang, Guang, and Chen, 7: 12a–13a. For another example, see 9: 12a–13a.

91. Rare maternal paragons living under exceptional circumstances did take responsibility for their son's intellectual education. An example was the mother of Yu Ji (1272–1348), Lady Yang (fl. 1280), who was celebrated in both WXY, VI.16, and Xu Dingyi, *Zuguo nüjie wenhao*, 24a, for orally instructing her two sons, Ji and Pan, on canonical Confucian texts in the midst of the chaos of the Mongol conquest. Both of her sons became great scholars.

92. Despeux, 70–71.

93. Ibid., 95–97.

94. Dai Li, 4: 1a.

95. Zeng Yi, 1: 8b–9a.

96. WXY, VI.1.

97. In his utopian social treatise, the *Great Unity* (*Datong shu*) Kang even advocated the establishment of institutes for prenatal education. Despeux, 96.

98. Jing Yuanshan, "Zhi," 882.

99. Sun Qingru, 6.

100. Wu Tao, 2b.

101. "Li taifuren." According to the unpublished conference version of Despeux, Mother Li's fetal education was discussed in late imperial didactic texts.

102. *LNZ*, 1:11; Zhang Jing, 35–40; O'Hara, 39–40.

103. *LNZ*, 1:11; Zhang Jing, 36; O'Hara, 40; Hightower, 290.

104. Hightower, 290.

105. Yang Qianli, *Nüzi*, I: 1.

106. The *Reader* also includes a lesson on members of the Women's Railway Protection Association (Nüjie baolu hui) who pawned their "hairpins, ear ornaments, and clothing in order to buy stock in and help China maintain control over the Suzhou-Hangzhou-Ningbo railway." Guang, Guang, and Chen, 4: 11a–12a. Essay topics in the 1910 *Longjiang Women's School Model Essays* (*Longjiang nüxue wenfan*) include "The Policy of Casting Off Jewelry and Establishing a Bank"; see Chen Dongyuan, 348.

107. Guang, Guang, and Chen, 7: 2a–b.

108. See entries on Zheng Yizong in Guang, Guang, and Chen, 1: 12a–b; WXY, IV.5.

109. Guang, Guang, and Chen, 7: 2a–b. Other late Qing authors used Mother Meng's example in similar ways. Sun Qingru tied the story of her moving three times to the projects of women's education and national strengthening. [Sun] Qingru, 3. Drafters of regulations for a school for Chinese female overseas students in Japan noted that Mencius's mother made a great "contribution to the nation (*guojia*)." "Riben Dongya," 145.

110. WXY, VI.2.

111. Ibid., VI.3; "Zifa."

112. WXY, VI.4.

113. Ibid., VI.5. In the *LNZ* Chen's and Wang's mothers are featured in separate entries (8:5 and 8:6), whereas Wei's text celebrates them together.

114. WXY, VI.6; "Jun."

115. WXY, VI.7.

116. Ibid., VI.8, 9, 10, 11.

117. "Yan taifuren." This story first appeared in Chen Kangqi, *Langqian jiwen chubi*, 1: 1, 142–43.

118. WXY, VI.12.

119. Ibid., VI.13.

120. Ibid.

121. Ibid., VI.15.

122. Ibid., VI.18.

123. On the phenomenon of strict late imperial mothers who, nonetheless, had a strong emotional bond with their sons, see Hsiung, "Constructed," 94, 104.

124. "Hong." The central incident in this account was repeated in the *Draft History of the Qing Dynasty* biography of Hong's mother. The biography includes two verbatim phrases and the same quotation about the husband being Heaven but gives its source as the *Li jing* (Ritual classic). Zhao Erxuan, 46: 508, 14025. On Hong Liangji, see Hummel, 373–75; Elman, *From Philosophy*, 106, 121, 123; Hsiung, "Constructed, 95–96. For details of Hong's childhood and his mother's influence in his early education, see Jones, 30–42, esp. 32.

125. In the seventh century *Sui Dynastic History*, for example, all good mothers were chaste widows. Mou, 121.

126. Xie Chongxie, 45a.

127. Xu Jiaxing, 15b–16a; Wu Tao, 30a.

128. Ye Zhongling, 25.

129. WXY, VI.14.

130. Wang Tingzhen became a presented scholar (*jinshi*) in 1789 and later president of the Board of Ceremonies. See Hummel, 776.

131. "Cheng taifuren."

132. "Liu gaifu."

133. On functional female literacy, see Wu Tao, 38b–39b; Fang Liusheng, 27b–28a. There were also specialized textbooks on letter writing, including Biaomeng.

134. Chen Yiyi, "Nanzun."

135. Ma, 3.

136. Qiu Jin did not visit her children when she returned to China from Japan in 1905 and 1906. Nor did she tell her close collaborator and colleague in 1906 and 1907, Xu Zihua, that she had children. Qiu is discussed in Chapter 6.

137. Yan Bin, "Benbao duiyu," 43.

Part Three

1. Jiang Zhiyou, "Aiguo," 2a–2b.

2. Mingyi. "Mingyi" is one of the sixty-four trigrams from the *Book of Changes*. By the late Qing it had taken on the meaning of a sage frustrated in his ambition.

Chapter 5

1. Mulan's ethnicity is ambiguous in the original ballad, which is set during the rule of the Toba Wei house, a northern people, at the turn of the fifth century. Mann, "Presidential," 846; Wu Pei-yi, 167.

2. Xu Dingyi, *Zuguo nüjie weiren*, 23.

3. Jiang Zhiyou's biography of Harriet Beecher Stowe was published in *Digest Magazine* (*Xuanbao*) in 1902 and reprinted in the *Women's Journal* and the *New People's Miscellany* (*Xinmin congbao*) in July of that year; Liang Qichao's biography of Madame Roland was published in *New People's Miscellany* in October 1902 and reprinted in the *Women's Journal* several months later.

4. Xu Dingyi, *Zuguo nüjie weiren*, "Zixu," 4. This conviction that truly great heroines existed in the Chinese past and did not have to be imported from the West is resonant with the formula of "Chinese sources of Western knowledge" (*Xixue Zhongyuan*). Huters, 23–42; Xiong, *Xixue*; Quan. While this formula is often interpreted as integral to the conservative project of asserting Chinese cultural authority in the face of new Western knowledge, in this instance it is used to sanction radical change.

5. Zhou Dong.

6. Xu Dingyi, *Zuguo nüjie weiren*, "Zixu," 4.

7. Ding Chuwo.

8. Jin Tiange, "Nüzi." Ding had given specific examples of women from these various categories. Courageous exemplars include Feng Liao (Former Han dynasty), Hua Mulan, Liang Furen, and Qin Liangyu. Female knights-errant include Ti Ying, Nie Jie (fl. 395), and Pang E (Later Han dynasty). Women accomplished in the literary and fine arts include Ban Zhao and Zuo Fen (255–300). Ding Chuwo.

9. Jin Tiange, *Nüjie*, 4–5. There are at least two possible reasons Jin wrote favorably of Western women here but not in his later *Women's World* essay. He may have been disturbed by the rising prominence of biographies of Western women in the interim as manifest in the publication of the *Twelve* and *Ten World Heroines*. Or he may have simply followed Ding's editorial preferences.

10. Ibid., *Nüjie*, 82–83.

11. According to Xia Xiaohong, both Jin Tiange and Yang Qianli were from Wujiang (according to the back matter in the *New Reader for Girls and Women* Yang was from Zhenze, now in Wu County). Yang inscribed the characters for the title of Jin's *Nüjie zhong*, and his sister Yang Gonglan wrote one of the prefaces in the treatise, "Tongyi." Xia Xiaohong, "Wan-Qing nüxing dianfan," 42n18.

12. Yang Qianli, *Nüzi*, "Daoyan," 1: 2a.

13. *LNZ*, 6:15; Zhang Jing, 258–61; O'Hara, 183–85. Ti Ying's story was also included in the *Records of the Grand Historian* and the *Han History*.

14. Raphals, *Sharing*, 47–48, 133–36.

15. See three images in ibid., 134–35.

16. Du and Mann, 238.

17. Even in Dai Li's eternalist *Elementary Learning for Girls and Women*, two of the four sections emphasize women's roles before marriage. See also Wu Tao.

18. Five of WXY's nine categories, representing 66 of the total number of 106 biographies (62 percent), are directly related to service to husband or marital family.

19. Ying Erzi, who was from the state of Qi, was first commemorated in the "Qice si" section of the Former Han dynasty text the *Intrigues of the Warring States* (*Zhanguo ce*).

20. Yang Qianli, *Nüzi*, 1: 2a–b.

21. "Zhongguo nüjie." This biography was possibly written by Qiu Jin. According to "Ji Shanyin," Qiu wrote a biography with an almost identical title: "Zhongguo nüjie yiyongjia Ti Ying zhuan" (A biography of the righteous and courageous Chinese heroine Ti Ying).

22. Yi Qin, "Lun Zhongguo, xu," 130 [940].

23. Ding Chuwoi; Jin Tiange, "Nüzi."

24. *LNZ*, 3:13; Zhang Jing, 121–24; O'Hara, 95–97.

25. Mann, "Women's Poems," 15. This was not the only poem of Wang Caipin's to invoke the woman of Qishi.

26. Xu Jiaxing (86b) praises the woman of Qishi together with a widow from the *Zuo zhuan* who did not worry about her weaving but about dynastic decline.

27. Zhu Huizhen. It is unclear whether Qi Wanzhen or the author of this article even knew that the woman of Qishi's story first appeared in the *LNZ*.

28. Zhu records one discussion between Qi, her tutor, and a friend on the subject of Qiu Jin. Their collective assessment of the recent martyr was ambiguous.

29. Zhu Huizhen.

30. Zhou Chunying.

31. Xu Dingyi, *Zuguo nüjie weiren*, 7–9. On Ban's instruction of Ma Rong, see Idema and Grant, 27.

32. Yi Qin, "Lun Zhongguo, xu," 130 [940].

33. Wa Hun, discussion of *Precepts*, 3: 174.

34. Bei Qiu (Grieving Qiu [Jin]), "Shei zhi zui xiqu" (Whose crime? A drama), 2–3 (December 1908), cited in Xia Xiaohong, "Gudian," 97–98.

35. Martial women are prominent in dynastic, local, and informal histories from the Wei through the Tang dynasties, and at least one remarkably intrepid woman emerged from the chaos at each dynasty's end from the Tang through the Ming. See Carlitz, "Mixed," 7.

36. See Wu Pei-yi (138, 156, 161) on the terse mention of women like Liang Hongyu in the *Song History*.

37. Xu Dingyi, *Zuguo nüjie weiren*, "Zixu," 1.

38. It is apparent that several turn-of-the-twentieth-century authors and compilers used the same sources on women warriors. The *Biographies of Manly Women* and the "New Chinese and Foreign Arrayed Traditions of Women's Lives" present almost identical biographies of the late Ming warrior Shen Yunying; see, for example, *Jinguo*, 41–42; "Shen Jiangjun." Similarly, several entries in the *Biographies of Great Women of our Country* were similar to those in Yang's reader, and at least one, the biography of Qin Liangyu, was identical; see Xu Dingyi, *Zuguo nüjie weiren*, 32–33; Yang Qianli, *Nüzi*, 1: 8b–9a.

39. The compiler insisted that these women were the corollary of intrepid men, including heroes (*haojie*), sages (*shengxian*), and luminaries (*wenren*). *Jinguo*, "Xu," 1a–b. No author or date is given for the text, but contemporary advertisements suggest that it was published around 1910.

40. On Liang's call to heroism, see Liang Qichao, "Xinmin." See also Judge, *Print*, 91–96; Tang, 80–116, passim.

41. Mulan is praised in a lesson on filial devotion in Gao Fengquian, Cai, and Zhang, *Zuixin xiushen jiaokeshu*, 7: 1a.

42. The original ballad is featured in a number of late Qing sources including WXY I.13; Yang Qianli, *Nüzi*, 1: 4a–b.

43. Mann, "Presidential," 847.

44. WXY, I.3. Other authors also used Mulan's example to bolster their arguments against footbinding. See, for example, "Zhili chuangban," 38.

45. This same image of Mulan appears in the *NZSJ* in March of 1904 in conjunction with another biography of her (Liu Yazi, "Zhongguo").

46. Yang Qianli, *Nüzi*, 1: 3b–5a.

47. Xie Chongxie, 36a.

48. Wu Tao, 6a.

49. Jin Shuxi.

50. Yuan Jisun.

51. Liu Yazi, "Zhongguo diyi."

52. Baosu, 132.

53. "Hua Mulan."

54. See, for example, Tongxiang; Qingjiang. On the uses of Mulan as a galvanizing model for women's military participation, education, employment, and political rights, see Edwards, *Men*, 89, 112.

55. I have only been able to find one terse reference to Li Xiu in the 24 Histories, "Zaiji."

56. Zhu Dianyi.

57. Xu Dingyi, *Zuguo nüjie weiren*, 12.

58. "Xun Song."

59. Biaomeng, "Xuyan," 1a.

60. Yang Qianli, *Nüzi*, 1: 5a–b.

61. Xu Dingyi, *Zuguo nüjie weiren*, 13. Textbooks that feature Yang Xiang include Yang Qianli, *Nüzi*, 1: 9a–10a; Xie Chongxie, 34a. She is also featured in WXY, I.4.

62. "Qiaoguo." The region referred to as Lingnan in the text now corresponds to the Guangdong–Guangxi region.

63. Zhu Dianyi; Wang Yingkun.

64. "Qiaoguo"; Yang Qianli, *Nüzi*, 1: 7b; Xu Dingyi, *Zuguo nüjie weiren*, 17.

65. Xu Dingyi, *Zuguo nüjie weiren*, 17–19.

66. "Chai Shao."

67. Yuan Jisun; Wang Yingkun; Qian Wenbin.

68. Xu Dingyi, *Zuguo nüjie weiren*, 22–23.

69. "Han Shizhong," 11361.

70. Wu Pei-yi, 161–64. On Liu Rushi, see Ko, *Teachers*, 274–83.

71. Yang Qianli, *Nüzi*, 1: 8a–7a.

72. Huang Di; Wang Yingkun; Zeng Fuqian.

73. Cited in Wu Pei-yi, 165.

74. Baosu, 132.

75. Chen Yiyi, "Nanzun," 682.

76. Liu Yazi, "Zhongguo minzu," 22, 24. Xia Xiaohong ("Wan-Qing nüxing dianfan," 36) convincingly argues that Liu Yazi wrote this essay although Pan Xiaohuang is given as the author. Pan is described as "a girl from Songling," and Songling is an alternate name for Wujiang County in Jiangsu Province, where Liu Yazi was from.

77. Shen and Qin were often featured together but also appeared individually. A 1751 play features both women. Hummel, 168–69.

78. "Li Zicheng," 7975.

79. Hummel, 168–69.

80. "Shen Jiangjun"; *Jinguo*, 41–42.

81. Zeng Fuqian. Another poem in the series, by Wang Yingkun, is laced with allusions to a Daoist immortal in the Tang dynasty who shared Shen's given name.

82. Guang, Guang, and Chen, 6: 16a–b.

83. Qiu Jin, *Jingwei*, 135. See also Qiu Jin, "Man jiang hong," in Kang-i Sun Chang and Saussy, 653–54.

84. *Ming shi*, 270/6944–98. See also Hummel, 168–69.

85. Either Xu had drawn on Yang's textbook account, which appeared in Shanghai two years before his own volume was published in Yokohama, or both authors drew on the same source. Yang Qianli, *Nüzi*, 1: 8b–9a; Xu Dingyi, *Zuguo nüjie weiren*, 32–33.

86. Xu Dingyi, *Zuguo nüjie weiren*, 33.

87. Ibid., "Zixu," 3. For a very brief description of Hong Xuanjiao, see Ono, 17, 18. Xiao Sanniang was an erroneous name for Su Sanniang. Xu Dingyi also misrepresents Su's lineage, describing her as the sister of Xiao Chaogui and thus the sister-in-law of Hong Xuanjiao. On Su Sanniang, see *BD* I, 197–99.

88. Xu Dingyi, *Zuguo nüjie weiren*, 36–38.

89. *Shijie*, "Liyan," 1. The *Ten World Heroines* is undated. It was, however, introduced in the June 12, 1903, issue of *Jiangsu Journal* and so probably appeared in April or May of that year.

90. *Shijie*, "Liyan," 1, 2. Given the different transcription of a number of personal and place names in the *Ten* and the *Twelve*, it is apparent that the author of the former did not draw exclusively on the latter.

91. On the connection between the *Twelve World Heroines* and Samuel Smiles's *Self-Help* (London, 1859), which Nakamura Masanao translated in 1871, see Xia Xiaohong, "Wan-Qing nüxing dianfan," 43n35.

92. Iwasaki and Mikami, *Sekai*, "Jo"; Iwasaki and Mikami, *Shijie*, "Xu," 1–2.

93. *Shijie*, "Liyan," 1.

94. *Shijie*, 65.

95. Ibid., 31–35. Thanks to Heather Jackson for helping identify Wordsworth.

96. On Yang's friendship with Jin, see Xia Xiaohong, "Wan-Qing nüxing dianfan," 42n18.

97. Yang Qianli, "Nüzi," 83.

98. Yang Qianli, *Nüzi*, 2: 5a. Yang also compares Michel to an Italian anarchist whom I have not been able to identify. Biographies of Sofia Perovskaia appear in radical overseas student journals including *Zhejiang chao* and *Min bao*; see Hu Ying, *Tales*, 111–17, and more broadly, 105–52.

99. Guang, Guang, and Chen: the biography of Stowe was published in 7: 5b–7a; Queen Louise, 7: 15a–b; Florence Nightingale, 8: 14b–15b; Frances Willard, 9: 14a–15b; Joan of Arc, 10: 15b–17a. The biographies of Stowe and Nightingale were not originally from the *Twelve*.

100. "Yanshuo Fulanzhisi."

101. Ye Zhongling, 52–58.

102. "Shijie."

103. On the attempted arrest of Chen Fan, see Rankin, *Early*, 86–95.

104. Chen Xiefen, "Shijie," 55–56.

105. A glowing endorsement of the *Ten* (Qianzhu) that ends in a call to arms to Chinese women as defenders of the Han race appears in the *Women's World* in late 1904. Wordsworth is mentioned, for example, in Liu Yazi, "Ai." The *Twelve* is also mentioned in *NZSJ*, however. See Jing Han.

106. "Aiguo"; Iwasaki and Mikami, *Shijie*, 31–42; Yang Qianli, *Nüzi*, 2: 5a–7a, repeated in Guang, Guang, and Chen, 10: 15b–17a; Mei, 53–82.

107. On Joan of Arc, see Pernoud; Warner.

108. On Joan in Egypt, see Booth, "The Egyptian." In 1866 two biographies of Joan, one clearly a translation, were published in Japan, and others would follow through the early twentieth century. See, for example, Asakura; Tuckey.

109. "Aiguo."

110. Iwasaki and Mikami, *Shijie*, 41–42.

111. Yang Qianli, *Nüzi*, 2: 5b.

112. Mei, 82, 81.

113. Qiu Jin, "Mian."

114. Iwasaki and Mikami, *Sekai*, 51–52, 63–64.

115. Iwasaki and Mikami, *Shijie*, 33.

116. Ibid., 35, 36.

117. Yang Qianli, *Nüzi*, 2: 5b; repeated in Guang, Guang, and Chen, 10: 16a.

118. The use of the term *shendao* suggests that this text also drew on a Japanese source as this was the term for the Shinto religion.

119. Mei, 60, 63.

120. Ibid., 81–82.

121. Recent scholarship suggests, however, that Joan was most probably raped in prison and that she resumed male dress either to protect her chastity or because the British provided her with nothing else. On the discussion of Joan's male attire at court, see Pernoud, 220.

122. Iwasaki and Mikami, *Shijie*, 40–41.

123. Yang Qianli, *Nüzi*, 2 6b; Guang, Guang, and Chen, 10: 17a.

124. Mei, 81.

125. Ibid., 62, 53–54, 55, 59.

126. Madame Roland was born Manon Jeanne Philipon. For an insightful discussion of her place in the late-Qing cultural imaginary, see Hu Ying, *Tales*, 153–96.

127. Liang Qichao, "Jinshi."

128. *Shijie shi*, "Liyan," 1.

129. Iwasaki and Mikami, *Sekai*, "Jo"; Iwasaki and Mikami, *Shijie*, "Xu," 1–2. The biography of Roland appears in Iwasaki and Mikami, *Shijie*, 42–50.

130. Yang Qianli, *Nüzi*, 2: 7a–8b.

131. The Japanese source for Liang's text was a serialized biography of Madame Roland that ran from December 1893 to February 1894 in *Katei zasshi* (Family journal; September 1892–August 1898). See Matsuo, 265–78.

132. Liang Qichao, "Jinshi," 1. For a perceptive analysis of how Liang used Roland as a vehicle for his own ambiguous views on revolution, see Hu Ying, *Tales*, 173–74.

133. Iwasaki and Mikami, *Shijie*, 49; Yang Qianli, *Nüzi*, 2: 8a.

134. For the reference to Roland's daughter, see Iwasaki and Mikami, *Shijie*, 42. Hu Ying (*Tales*, 179–86) discusses a *tanci* version of Roland's story that explores her relationship with her daughter.

135. Liang Qichao, "Jinshi," 1.

136. "Luolan."

137. Iwasaki and Mikami, *Shijie*, 49–50; Yang Qianli, *Nüzi*, 2: 8b.

138. See, for example, Iwasaki and Mikami, *Shijie*, 46.

139. See Hu Ying's analysis of the sexualization of the martyred woman (*Tales*, 176–79).

140. Iwasaki and Mikami, *Shijie*, 45, 49.

141. Ibid., 46–48; Yang Qianli, *Nüzi*, 2: 7a.

142. Iwasaki and Mikami, *Shijie*, 48. See also Hu Ying, *Tales*, 176.

143. Liang Qichao, "Jinshi," 1–3; Hu Ying, *Tales*, 174–76; Iwasaki and Mikami, *Shijie*, 43, 44–45; Yang Qianli, *Nüzi*, 2: 7a.

144. He Xiangning, "Jinggao."

145. Wang Lian, "Zagan," 106 [0116].

146. Chen Yan'an, "Quan," 155 [0585]. See also Yongli, 241.

147. Foqun, "Nü xuexiao," 138.

148. Iwasaki and Mikami, *Shijie*, 1–9; *Shijie*, 9–16; Yang Qianli, *Nüzi*, 2: 1a–2a; Xu Jiaxing, 79b.

149. On Corday, see Schama, 729–31, 735–41.

150. Iwasaki and Mikami, *Shijie*, 2, 4, 5, 8; *Shijie*, 10, 11, 13, 15; Yang Qianli, *Nüzi*, 2: 1a; Xu Jiaxing, 79b

151. Iwasaki and Mikami, *Shijie*, 3, 7; Yang Qianli, *Nüzi*, 2: 1b–2a; *Shijie*, 13.

152. Iwasaki and Mikami, 1, 7.

153. *Shijie*, 15.

154. Iwasaki and Mikami, *Shijie*, 1

155. *Shijie*, 16.

156. Iwasaki and Mikami, *Shijie*, 1, 5; Yang Qianli, *Nüzi*, 2: 1b–2a.

157. This was allegedly a "Western maxim." *Shijie*, 9.

158. Ibid., 13, 14, 15.

159. Iwasaki and Mikami, *Shijie*, 9–18; *Shijie*, 37–45; Yang Qianli, *Nüzi*, 2: 2a–3b.

160. Iwasaki and Mikami, *Shijie*, 16.

161. Ibid.; *Shijie*, 44.

162. *Shijie*, 37, 39.

163. Iwasaki and Mikami, *Shijie*, 10; *Shijie*, 38.

164. *Shijie*, 40.

165. Ibid., 41, 38, 39, 43.

166. Iwasaki and Mikami, *Shijie*, 18; *Shijie*, 45.

167. Iwasaki and Mikami, *Shijie*, 18–26; *Shijie*, 21–24.

168. On de Staël, see Ozouf, 64–87.

169. Iwasaki and Mikami, *Shijie*, 18.

170. *Shijie*, 10.

171. Iwasaki and Mikami, *Shijie*, 24.

172. *Shijie*, 24.

173. Iwasaki and Mikami, *Shijie*, 25.

174. *Shijie*, 22.

175. Ibid., 24.

176. Iwasaki and Mikami, *Shijie*, 23.

177. *Shijie*, 23, 24, 25.

178. Iwasaki and Mikami, *Shijie*, 25–26.

179. Ibid., 26–32; *Shijie*, 1–8; Yang Qianli, *Nüzi*, 2: 3b–5a; Chen Xiefen, "Shijie."

180. Both mention two other female anarchists, the American Emma Goldman and an Italian woman.

181. Iwasaki and Mikami, *Shijie*, 28–29; *Shijie*, 3; Yang Qianli, *Nüzi*, 2: 4a–b.

182. Iwasaki and Mikami, *Shijie*, 29; *Shijie*, 4.

183. Iwasaki and Mikami, *Shijie*, 26–27.

184. *Shijie*, 2–3.

185. Iwasaki and Mikami, *Shijie*, 28, 27; Yang Qianli, *Nüzi*, 2: 4a.

186. Iwasaki and Mikami, *Shijie*, 28. This reflects a pattern in late Qing biographies of Western women, which repress unsavory personal details such as Anita's first marriage and Margaret Fuller Ossoli's child born out of wedlock.

187. Iwasaki and Mikami, *Shijie*, 21.

188. *Shijie*, 2.

189. Ibid., 8.

190. Ibid., 1–2.

191. Ibid., 7.

192. Ibid., 5, 4.

193. Ibid., 6, 5.

194. The Joint Expeditionary Forces, an army of about 200,000 international soldiers, left Tianjin on August 4, 1900, and raised the Boxer siege of Beijing on August 14. On the Boxer Uprising, see Cohen. On the role of the Joint Expeditionary Forces, see Li Dezheng, Su, and Liu. It is unclear if there was one incident in Tongzhou, which some authors referred to as Beijing as it was in the Beijing region, or incidents in both cities. The most reliable contemporary Japanese source, Tsuboya, does not mention suicides in Beijing. Other sources do, however. See "Lianjun," [3952]; Zhonghua Minguo, 277; Zhao Erxuan, 46: 510: 14140.

195. Li Dezheng, Su, and Liu, 230–31. A recent encyclopedia article (Beijing, 354) gives a slightly lower figure for the number of dead—1,178—compared to Li Dezheng's approximately 2,400.

196. Tsuboya, 225.

197. Savage-Landor, 1: 379.

198. Cited in Cohen, 184.

199. Dillon, 21–22.

200. Tsuboya, 225. The most comprehensive scholarly Chinese treatment of the incident (Li Dezheng, Su, and Liu, 231) cites Tsuboya and uses his figure of 570 female suicides.

201. Mou, 124. Collective drowning had been a part of Tongzhou *lienü* lore well before the 1900 incident; see Zhao Erxuan, 46: 511: 14180.

202. Fong, "Signifying," 122.

203. On late Ming martyrs as symbols of localty, see Carlitz, "The Daughter," 38; Theiss, "Managing," 49. In the early Republic, these women could be formally celebrated; see Zhao Erxuan, 46: 510, 14108–15.

204. Fong, "Signifying," 122.

205. WXY, IX.15; Xu Jiaxing, 72b.

206. WXY, IX.16

207. Xu Jiaxing, 71a.

208. Fong, "Signifying," 122.

209. Xu Jiaxing, 74a.

210. Xu Dingyi, *Zuguo nüjie wenhao*, 17a–18; Xu Dingyi, *Zuguo nüjie weiren*, 30–32.

211. Zhao Erxuan, 46: 511: 14175.

212. WXY, IX.22. Huang's story is recorded in her own *Extant Poems of Heroic Woman Huang*, in an 1874 gazetteer of her native place, and in Min, 3342–45. The version in Min is longer than Wei's. On Huang's story and the gazetteer, which most likely served as the source of Wei's biography, see Fong, "Signifying," 121–28.

213. Wang Qi's story was recorded in the *Commentary of Mr. Zuo* and the *Record of Rites*; see Legge, *Li Chi*, 1: 185.

214. "Si zhongnü."

215. "Huazu," 12–13 [40–41].

216. He Xiangning, "Jinggao," 144 [762].

217. Jin Xia, 8.
218. Jin Xia.
219. Xu Bai, 343.

Chapter 6

1. On cyclical and linear, feminine and masculine time, see Lefebvre, 231–32; and Kristeva.

2. These terms are also used in popular fiction including Luo Pu's *Heroine of Eastern Europe* (Dong'Ou nü haojie, 1902), and Zhan Kai's (Siqi zhai) *China's New Heroines* (Zhongguo xin nühao, 1907).

3. Jingxiong could also be translated as "Challenger of men" or "To emulate male bravery." Rankin, "The Emergence," 52.

4. Nüwa became something of a feminist icon in early-twentieth-century China. She is the subject of a story discussed in Chapter 5 (Wa Hun), and of a popular unfinished novel, *Nüwa's Stone* (*Nüwa shi*), advertised in the press from the spring of 1905. See *SB*, May 2, April 5, 1905; and Liu Huiying, 167–70. Nüwa's image also graces the first issue of *TY* and issues 2 and 3 of *XNJZZ*. On the uses of Nüwa in *TY*, see von Sivers.

5. Chubei. In the essay itself, the author laments that language coded females as weak and subservient. See also Liu Mei Ching, 240.

6. On this tension in Western feminism, see Riley, 17.

7. Hu Binxia, "Lun Zhongguo."

8. Male reformers like Liang Qichao and female activists like Qiu Jin used this trope. See, for example, Qiu Jin, "Jinggao Zhongguo."

9. Hu Binxia, "Hu nüshi," 149 [0381].

10. Mary Poovey (196) discusses the process by which individuals embrace the nation as the most meaningful context for self-definition.

11. Chubei, 96 [270].

12. Chen Yan'an, "Quan," 156 [0586].

13. Wang Lian, "Tongxiang," 115.

14. All positions of authority in government schools had to be filled by women. "Xuebu zouding nüzi shifan," 673.

15. For a detailed discussion of these developments, see Judge, "Between"; Judge, "Beyond."

16. For the number of Chinese female students in Chinese schools, see Liao Xiuzhen, 225; at the Jissen School in Japan, see Sechiyama and Kihara, 281. Both of these numbers are, I suspect, low.

17. Jissen joshi gakuen, 119; Zhou Yichuan, "Qingmo," 59–60. Forty students graduated in 1909, twenty-seven in 1910.

18. Sun Shiyue, 101.

19. The length of these courses was expanded in 1908 as the result of new regulations for Chinese students aimed at increasing student seriousness and decreasing political agitation. Jissen's middle-level and teacher-training courses were expanded to three years and its handicrafts courses to two. Zhou Yichuan, *Chūgokujin*, 82.

20. Ibid., 70.

21. Cited in Tan Sheying, 13.

22. Zhang Hanying.

23. "Nüzi chuyang."

24. Yan Ansheng, 70–71. On *The New Story of the Stone*, see David Wang, *Fin-de-Siècle*, 5, 29; David Wang, "Jia Baoyu." Other late Qing novels, such as Zhan Kai's *China's New Heroines*, feature overseas students committed to developing Chinese women's education as heroines. See Widmer, "Inflecting," 147–51. This early-twentieth-century equation of female study in Japan with epochal change has been upheld in recent Chinese and Japanese scholarship. Zhou Yichuan (*Chūgokujin*, 95) describes the overseas experience as a crucial milestone in Chinese women's history. Ishii Yōko (48) declares it a historical turning point on a par with the 1911 Revolution and the May Fourth Movement. Wang Qisheng (31) claims that it allowed Chinese women to finally throw off "feudal ways" and embrace liberation and modernization.

25. Yan Bin, "Liu-Ri," 83–84. The poem was "Yuan dan" (New Year's day) by Wang Anshi (1021–86).

26. Chen Yan'an, "Quan."

27. Wang Lian, "Tongxiang," 115.

28. "Zai-Ri," 1256; Ishii, 34. For more on these representations of Chinese women, see Judge, "Between," 127–32; Judge, "Beyond," 372–80.

29. The Tokyo National Museum (Tōkyō kokuritsu hakubutsukan) was founded in 1872, and had its name changed to the Teishitsu hakubutsukan (Imperial Palace Museum) in 1900; see Shiina. The museum is described in the travel diaries of Chinese visitors to Japan at the turn of the twentieth century. See, for example, Zhu Shou, 16a–17a; Lin Bingzhang, 5b–6a. Zhu and Lin describe the museum differently, however. Zhu describes numerous departments, each represented by one exhibition room, while Lin describes five largely different departments. Both accounts note the inclusion of Chinese women's shoes for bound feet, but in Zhu's account they are in a room displaying customs of all nations and in Lin's account in the reference section. It is possible the museum was reorganized between Zhu's visit in 1899 and Lin's in 1903.

30. Harrell, *Sowing*, 127–29.

31. On the overseas students' reactions to the Exposition, see "Bolan"; "Riben Daban."

32. See, for example, Chen Yan'an, "Quan," 155 [0585].

33. Xie Chongxie, 51a.

34. Wang Lian, "Tongxiang," 114–15.

35. Wang Lian, "Tongxiang."

36. Ibid., 113. On this and other public spaces where male and female students congregated, see Judge, "Between," 122–27; Judge "Beyond," 362–71.

37. In 1909, for example, one of the peak years for female overseas study in Japan, roughly thirty of the more than fifty-five students at the Jissen Women's School lived in the dormitory, while twenty-five lived with family members. Ko Shimoda, 406.

38. Sakaki's comments on this subject are, understandably, cryptic and other sources of the period are, unfortunately, silent on this subject. Sakaki, "Sakaki," 6.

39. There were as many as 13,000 male overseas students in Japan in 1906. On male overseas study in Japan, see Sanetō, *Chūgokujin*; Huang Fu-ch'ing, *Qingmo*; Huang Fu-ch'ing, *Chinese*; Harrell, *Sowing*.

40. On the hall, see Judge, "Between," 124; Judge, "Beyond," 366–67. Qiu Jin had attended Japanese classes, joined weekend discussion sessions, and frequently given lectures at the student hall. In her *Vernacular Journal*, Qiu reports on debating sessions held regularly at the building on Sundays. Liu Mei Ching, 291, 295.

41. He Xiangning, "Wo de huiyi," 15–20; He Xiangning, "When," 135–43. According to some sources, He Xiangning was the first female member of the Tongmeng hui; see, for example, Sun Shiyue, 118. Others claim this honor goes to Tang Qunying; see, for example, *BD* II, 505. Zhou Yichuan (*Chūgokujin*, 90) has concluded that the two were "among the earliest members."

42. The sixth issue of *NZSJ* includes a photo of students from Shimoda's Jissen School, for example, and other issues include news of the overseas students.

43. The *XNJZZ*, for example, was distributed by individuals and women's schools in almost every Chinese province. See list on back page of issues of the journal.

44. Maeyama, "Fu 3." Charlotte Beahan's pioneering article on the women's press published in 1975 estimates (387) there were only seventeen women's journals published between 1902, when she claims the first such journal was published, and 1911.

45. Evelyn Rawski (140) estimates that in China in the 1800s 30–40 percent of males and 2–10 percent of females were literate.

46. Ishii, 43, 46.

47. Given the sparse data, these numbers are less than precise. For the ratio of journals, I compare the number of women's journals on Maeyama's list to the total number of male-run journals included in Ding Shouhe's five volume *QKJS*. Many of these were daily newspapers, however, which are not comparable to women's journals: the ratio of women's journals would be higher if newspapers were excluded. At the same time, it is highly unlikely that Ding included every journal published in this period. The ratio of female to male schools is found in Liao Xiuzhen, 229.

48. The figure of 10,000 was published in a Singapore journal, *Zhongxing ribao* (February 13, 1909: 23), cited in Li Yu-ning, "*Zhongguo*," 241n71. Other estimates are not as high, however. Charlotte Beahan (405) claims a monthly print run of 7,000 copies, making it the second largest Chinese paper in Japan, but this statement is not footnoted. According to Xiong Yuezhi ("*Zhongguo*," 566), the journal's own announcement in issue 4 (which is not included in the reprint I have seen) states that circulation had reached 5,000 by the third issue. Fang Hanqi (20) also refers to the number 5,000.

49. Based on an interview with the editor-in-chief of *FNSB*, Perry Link (250) has recorded that less than 10 percent of the readership for that journal was female. Barbara Mittler (310) concludes that "men apparently read women's magazines as much, if not more, than women did."

50. [Tang Qunying], "Duiyu nübao zhi ganyan" (Rousing words on women's journals), cited in Li Junling, 686.

51. This statement is found in the "Neize" section of the *Li ji*; Legge, "The Nei Tse,", 1: 455.

52. Ellen Widmer (*Beauty*, 253) notes that a sea change occurred in women's writing in the late Qing when female authorship became a point to celebrate rather than hide. She dates this change for women novelists to 1904, a little later than when women began writing for the periodical press.

53. The 1898 *Nüxue bao* ("Chinese Girls' Progress"), or the "mother *Nüxue bao*" in Nanxiu Qian's terms, was part of a cluster of institutions put into place by male Chinese reformers, including Jing Yuanshan and Liang Qichao, together with Chinese women and Western men and women. Qian, "Revitalizing," 401. Chen Xiefen's *Nübao* (later entitled *Nüxue bao* [Journal of women's learning]), the "daughter *Nüxue bao*," was initially published by the Subao guan (the *Jiangsu Journal* office, which published Chen's father's journal, *Subao*, and it was distributed as a supplement to *Subao*. On the relationship between these two journals, see Nanxiu Qian, "The Mother."

54. Hu Binxia arrived in Japan in June 1902 from Jiangsu Province at the age of fourteen. On her activities as an overseas student in Tokyo, see Sun Shiyue, 107, 114; Zhou Yichuan, "Qingmo," 51–53; Ishii, 107–8. Hu later traveled to America as an overseas student in 1907, where she eventually graduated from Wellesley College. See Weili Ye, 136–40.

55. The series of essays by Gongai hui members published in Jiangsu, for example, is grouped under the headings "Nüxue lunwen" (Essays on women's education) and "Nüxue wencong" (Collection of writings on women's education). *JS* 3 (June 25, 1903): 155–58 [0585–88]; 4 (June 25, 1903): 141–46 [0759–64].

56. These literary columns, generally entitled "Wenyi" (Belles-lettres) or "Wenyuan" (Writer's garden), were included in most overseas student and women's journals with the exception of *Youxue yibian*, which was mostly a journal of translations, and He Zhen's *TY*. Mainstream newspapers, including *STSB* and *SB*, generally included literature sections as well. On the "Wenyuan" column in the *Ladies' Journal*, see Hu Hsiao-chen. A number of women's journals including the "Chinese Girls' Progress," *XNJZZ*, and *FNSB* also featured "traditional"-style women's painting as front matter.

57. Wang Lian, "Zagan"; Wang Lian, "Tongxiang," 114.

58. Liang Qichao had defined this new kind of poetry in 1899. Michelle Yeh.

59. He Zhen ("'Qiu Jin,'" 342–43) describes Qiu Jin's poetry in this way.

60. Wang Lian, "Zagan," 105 [0116].

61. See, for example, *Zhongguo nübao* 2 (March 4, 1907), 39, 40.

62. While a number of mainstream journals, including the *STSB*, include vernacular columns, there are significantly more articles in the vernacular in women's journals.

63. One of the earliest vernacular journals, *Wuxi baihua bao* (Wuxi vernacular journal), was founded by a woman, Qiu Yufang, and her uncle, Qiu Tinglian, on

May 11, 1895. *BD* I, 179–80. On vernacular publications in this period, see Cai Dongsu. The commitment to accessible language among editors of women's journals in the late Qing is one of the rarely acknowledged sources of the *baihua* movement that would reach its apogee some ten years hence. Hu Shi, who has been widely credited with founding the movement in 1917, claimed that he received his training in writing the vernacular from 1906 to 1908 at a school that Qiu Jin allegedly helped establish in Shanghai, the Zhongguo gongxue. Liu Mei Ching, 298. I have not, however, seen mention of this school elsewhere.

64. Nanxiu Qian, "Revitalizing," 413–15.

65. Li Yu-ning, "Zhongguo," 207.

66. On the mode of action of past woman warriors, see Edwards, *Men*, 101–2.

67. This conflict is briefly discussed in Chapter 2 in relation to Florence Nightingale.

68. "Liuxue." The four other students who mounted the podium were Qian Fengbao, Cao Rujin, Fang Junji, and Hua Gui.

69. "Liuxue."

70. Sun Shiyue, 108, 116–19; Ishii, 41–44. Chen Xiefen was director of the Humanitarian Association for Practical Action.

71. On Chen's suicide, see Huang Fu-ch'ing, *Chinese*, 235. On the departure of the female students after this incident, see Sun Shiyue, 108, 116–19; Ishii, 41–44.

72. Xie Chongxie, 49b, 50a.

73. See, for example, "Nüjie baolu"; "Ji Shanghai"; "Jinggao"; Guang, Guang, and Chen, 4: 11a–12a. On the railway rights recovery movement, see Judge, *Print*, 183–86.

74. On the Female Citizen's Fund, see Yan Bin, "Benbao duiyu"; Xia Xiaohong, *Wan-Qing wenren*, 98. See also Chapter 2.

75. Li Yu-ning, "Xinhai"; Cai Yuanpei; *BD* I, 36.

76. Sun Shiyue, 119–20.

77. On the Chinese Red Cross, founded in 1911, see Xu Huiqi, Liu, and Xu, 520–32. On Zhang Zhujun's activities, see ibid., 526–27. Zhang Zhujun remained active in the medical field after 1911, as chancellor of the Nanshi Hospital in Shanghai, for example, but her involvement with the Red Cross seems to have ceased around 1912. See also *BD* I, 310–13.

78. In December 1911 Tang and Zhang helped set up a Nüzi houyuan hui (Women's rearguard association) in Shanghai. Members of the society traveled to other provinces and prepared supplies for the Northern Expedition Army. The two women also established the Nüzi beifajun jiujidui (Women's auxiliary of the Northern Expedition Army). *BD* I, 290.

79. Ishii, 44.

80. The journal was published from April 1911. Zhou Yichuan, *Chūgokujin*, 88–90.

81. *BD* I, 290–91.

82. Ono, 80.

83. The other four organizations included Wang Changguo's Nü guomin hui (Female citizens' association), Wu Mulan's Nüzi tongmeng hui (Women's alli-

ance), Tang and Zhang's Women's Rearguard Association, and Shen Peizhen's Nüzi shangwu hui (Women's militant association). See Zhou Yichuan, *Chūgokujin*, 93.

84. For a detailed description of this campaign, see Ono, 80–89.

85. Ibid., 85–86.

86. In 1913 Zhang founded the successful Liling nüzi xuetang (Liling girls' school). *BD* I, 292–93. Tang continued both local educational work and suffrage activism until her death in 1937. *BD* II, 508–9; Zeng Qiqiu.

87. Chen Yiyi, "Nanzun," 683.

88. Lin Shiying, "Lun nüzi dang ju duli zhi xingzhi" (Women must be independent), *Liu-Ri nüxue hui zazhi* (May 1911), cited in Li Junling, 687.

89. "Nüzhong."

90. "Buji," 1450.

91. Lingxi, "Meiguo da jiaoyujia," 70.

92. "Jiaoyu," 669; Cong, 181.

93. The Wuben School announced a normal school preparation course in 1905; see, for example, *SB* (December 17, 1905).

94. These normal schools included the Shanghai Accelerated Normal Handicraft Teacher-Training Institute for Girls (Shanghai sucheng nügong shifan zhuanxi suo); see, for example, *SB* (April 7, 1905); and the Beiyang Women's Normal School (Beiyang nüzi shifan xuetang), which was founded in early 1906 and later called the Zhili diyi nüzi shifan xuetang (Zhili number one women's normal school); see *XZSL* 2: 2 687–93; McElroy. Another women's normal school was founded in Fengtian Prefecture in 1906; see Cong, 56.

95. "Xuebu zouding nüzi shifan," 673. From 1844, when Western women missionaries established the first girls' school in China, foreign women played a critical role in the development of Chinese female education. On the role of missionary schools, see Luo Suwen, 56–83. Japanese female teachers taught at some of the earliest indigenous Chinese schools. They include Shimoda Utako's disciple, Kawahara Misako, who was hired as the one female among nine teachers at the School of Fundamental Women's Learning in 1902. Abe, *Chūgoku*, 191–93; Harrell, "The Meiji," 132–33. In 1904 the Jingshan Girls' School in Changsha employed Japanese women to teach Western languages; see "Nüzhong." In 1909, two years after China had begun to train its own women teachers in government-sanctioned public schools, there were, according to what is certainly a low estimate, twenty-three Japanese women instructors in China; see Taga, 74; Abe, *Chūgoku*, 189–90. Even a cursory reading of the late Qing press yields numerous references to Japanese teachers in Chinese girls' schools. See, for example, "Nüxue jianxing"; "Yu xiannü."

96. Fan followed Liang Qichao to Japan in 1898, where he first enrolled in the School of Greater Unity, then in a Japanese normal school. He later established accelerated courses in law and politics for Chinese students. From 1906 he was employed in the Qing Education Board and later in the Republican Ministry of Education. He edited a language textbook for girls in 1914. Liu Shaotang, 1: 117–18; Zhang Jinglu, "Jiaokeshu," 247.

97. On the establishment of the Chinese department, see Jissen joshi gakuen, 96–121; on Fan Yuanlian's role, see ibid., 102.

98. "Chuangshe liuxue."

99. The Hunanese students came from Changsha, Xiangtan, Shanhua, Liling, Pingjiang, and Hengshan. Those from outside the province were from Shangyuan, Jiangsu Province, and Jiangling in Hubei. On the arrival of the students in Tokyo, see "Zhongguo nü liuxuesheng"; on their graduation, see "Ji Dongjing." See also "Zhongguo liudong"; Sun Shiyue, 66–68; Abe, *Chūgoku*, 100–101.

100. Chinese students often had to seek additional language instruction outside of the schools they attended. Qiu Jin took Japanese language classes at the Institute for Japanese Language Study (Ribenyu jiangxi suo) in the Chinese Overseas Student Hall; see Hirano, 112–13; Guo Zhanghai and Li, 128. He Xiangning, who had been forced to leave the first school she had enrolled in because of her poor Japanese, eventually improved her language competence with the help of the head of the Japanese Women's University (Nihon joshi daigaku), Naruse Jinzō. See He Xiangning, "Wo de huiyi," 12; Zhou Yichuan, *Chūgokujin*, 58. Students less linguistically successful than Qiu Jin and He Xiangning were limited to taking courses in music and handicrafts. Many left Japan without having made significant academic progress. Yan Bin, "Liu-Ri," 84–85.

101. There is some confusion in the sources as to how long Zhu stayed in China. According to Xie Zhangfa (274), she withdrew from the Jissen school in July 1905, some two weeks after enrolling. This is clearly false as she was later photographed and interviewed as a Jissen Women's School student. Wang Huiji (269) claims she graduated in 1909, but her class would have graduated no later than 1907.

102. "Zai-Ri," 1256–57. The interview states that Zhu wanted to teach English (*yu Ying*) but the second character is certainly an error. She made no reference to English-language instruction and students in the Jissen normal school courses were trained to teach at the preschool and elementary levels, that is, in the field of child-care or *yuying*.

103. "Ji liuxue." According to Wang Shize (228), Huang lived well into the Communist era and worked at the Beijing shi wenshi yanjiu guan (Beijing municipal research institute of culture and history).

104. In 1905, the head of the Fengtian Bureau of Agricultural and Industrial Affairs, Xiong Xiling (1870–1937), arranged to send fifteen students each year from Liaoning to Shimoda's school. The first twenty-three arrived in Tokyo in 1907. Zhou Yichuan, *Chūgokujin*, 73–74; Sun Shiyue, 68. Ten students from Jiangxi Province entered the Jissen Women's School and several from Jiangsu, including Hu Binxia, were sent to other programs in Tokyo. Uenuma, 80; Sun Shiyue, 68; Zhou Yichuan, "Qingmo," 54. Elsewhere (*Chūgokujin*, 74) Zhou notes, however, that the Jiangxi students may not have actually arrived. Other normal school programs included a Chinese Female Overseas Students' Short-Term Normal School that was added to the East Asian Women's School (Tō-A jogakkō) in March 1905. Jissen joshi gakuen, 104; Abe, *Chūgoku*, 105. From December 1906 the Chinese Female Student Department (Shina jogakusei bu) of the Women's School (Seijo gakkō) also offered

a three-year normal school program. Ishii, 39; Zhou Yichuan, "Qingmo," 55; Abe, *Chūgoku*, 105. The Seijo program is discussed later in this chapter. The Tokyo Senior Women's Normal School accepted Chinese students as well; see Ishii, 39. It became the present-day Ochanomizu Women's University. There were other Japanese schools that offered general and specialized programs for Chinese students; see Judge, "The Ideology," 236.

105. According to Sun Shiyue (326), between 1909 and 1922 most returned female students went into careers in education.

106. According to Ko Shimoda (405), three started their own schools. However, I have found evidence for a fourth.

107. Other courses were a two-and-one-half-year general course and a two-year handicrafts course. Kuang, who was a student at the University for the Study of Law and Politics (Hōsei daigaku), and Zhang had secured some official support for their initiative. Supervisors of overseas students for each province had agreed to pay tuition for the first term with the understanding that students would support themselves thereafter. See Zhou Yichuan, *Chūgokujin*, 75.

108. Yan Bin, "Liu-Ri," 84.

109. Ibid. Tang had enrolled at Shimoda's school in 1904, shortly after the death of both her daughter and her husband, Zeng Chuangang, a cousin of Zeng Guofan. Sun Shiyue, 83.

110. Zhou Yichuan, *Chūgokujin*, 75.

111. On Zhang's educational activities, see ibid., 94; *BD* I, 292–93.

112. Wang Shize (228) notes Wang's role in the Pingxiang school but does not give dates.

113. In 1918 Huang taught handicrafts at the Yifang Girls' School (Yifang nüxiao), and in 1919 was head of the Hengcui Girls' Vocational School (Hengcui nüzi zhiye xuexiao).

114. Ko Shimoda, 431. In both "Zhongguo nü liuxuesheng" and "Zhongguo liudong," Li's surname is given as Ling, her husband's surname, and her age is given as twenty-three instead of thirty-three.

115. Cong, 91.

116. Chen noted that the training provided by these returned students included physical education courses in gymnastics, ball games, martial arts, and the use of batons and weights. Wang Zheng, 265.

117. One physical education teacher trained in Japan was a certain Tang Linren, who taught at the School of Physical Education for Girls and Women (Nüzi ticao xuexiao) founded in Shanghai in 1908; see "Shanghai Zhongguo." Designed to train female teachers of physical education, such schools also taught standard courses such as ethics, Chinese language, education, arithmetic, and music.

118. The music lecture society was advertised in *SB* (December 16, 1906).

119. "Canguan."

120. "Sancheng." The Beijing Outer-City Institute for Women's Education hired a graduate of the Japanese School of Fine Arts (Bijutsu gakkō), a Miss Wang, for example, to teach drawing. See Fang Cheng.

121. While Miss Liao believed this field trip would enhance her students' respect for the army and their martial spirit, the school principal opposed it as a violation of the principle of gender separation. When Liao was fired, the students went on strike in protest. "Zhili nü."

122. Wang Zheng, 267. I have only found reference to a younger sister of Liao who studied in Japan, Liao Yongyun.

123. Gong Yuanchang. Gong had traveled to Japan in 1902 with her husband, Kuai Shoushu (Ruomu), and would return to China in 1910. On her life and activities in Japan, see Zhou Yichuan, "Qingmo," 52, 53; Guo Zhanghai and Li, 229; Saeki, 18. On the position of difference feminists in the West, see Scott, *Only*, 173.

124. Fang Junji.

125. He Zhen, "Nüzi," 17–20. Little is known about He Zhen. For the fullest treatment of her to date, see Zarrow, "He Zhen." Xia Xiaohong is currently working on a study of her.

126. Yan Bin, "Luo Ying," 54.

127. He Zhen, "Nüzi," 17–22.

128. Ban had added the eighth fascicle of supplementary biographies to the *Arrayed Traditions* (Xu Xingwu, 917) and had also annotated the collection. See Mou, 27. Wang Duanshu (1621–after 1702) apparently engaged in a different kind of historical writing, but this work is no longer extant. See Widmer, "Selected."

129. Xiao Daoguan. Xiao's husband, Chen Yan (1856–1937) published the text after her death. The original title recorded by Hu Wenkai (584) is *Lienü zhuan jijie*. Chen Yan changed it in order to make an explicit connection with Liang Duan and Wang Zhaoyuan's texts. See Chen Yan,1a.

130. Xiao Daoguan, "Lienü zhuan jijie zixu," 2a. Liang Qichao ("Ji Jiangxi," 119) condemned Liang and Wang as retrograde women of talent. See also Hu Ying, "Naming," 186–87. Liang Duan's *Arrayed Traditions of Women's Lives: A Collated Reader* (Lienü zhuan jiaoduben) was initially published in 1831, reprinted in 1875, and again in 1910. Wang used the most up-to-date evidential scholarly methods in her *Supplementary Notes to the Arrayed Traditions of Women's Lives* (Lienü zhuan bu-zhu), which was published in 1812, reprinted in 1833, and at least once again in 1917. Wang had been committed to restoring Ban Zhao's lost annotations to Liu Xiang's text. See Zhao Erxuan, 46: 508, 14052.

131. Yan Bin, "Luo Ying," 54.

132. Baosu, 132.

133. Ibid., 131–32.

134. Ibid., 132. The reference is to *Mencius* bk. IV: II, ch. 21: 1; Legge, *The Works*, 327. The passage refers to the extinction of the royal rule of Zhou and the degeneration of the Ya portion of the *Book of Odes*. From that time, no additions were made to the Ya odes, and they degenerated into mere records of the past rather than descriptions of the present.

135. Baosu, 132.

136. "Riben liuxue," 167.

137. Kōtoku Shūsui ("Furen," 50), a Japanese anarchist closely associated with *Natural Justice*, encouraged its readers to struggle to reclaim their original rights.

138. Liu Yazi, "Ai."

139. See, for example, Yi Qin, "Lun Zhongguo," 143 [761].

140. Lin Zongsu, 132 [942].

141. Cited in Tan Sheying, 18.

142. Jin Xia, 14.

143. Yi Qin, "Lun Zhongguo," 143 [761].

144. Chen Yiyi, "Nülun." Chen does not give the title of the article he is translating in English; he gives its original title in Chinese as "Furen lun" (On women). It is therefore, unclear if he has translated it from a Western language or, more likely, from Japanese.

145. Chen Yiyi, "Bo nüzi wucai shi de zhi wangyan" (A refutation of the absurd statement that women without talent were virtuous), *Nübao* 3 (n.d.), 139, cited in Liu Jucai, 503–4.

146. Xiao Yin, 19.

147. Jingqun.

148. Zhuan Kun, 34.

149. He Zhen, "Nüzi," 17–20.

150. Baosu, 131–32.

151. Chubei.

152. Pei, "Nannü pingdeng de zhenli," 30.

153. Chen Yan'an, "Quan," 156 [0586].

154. Huang Lingfang, 133 [943].

155. Foqun, "Xing," 12.

156. Yan Bin, "Fakanci," 1.

157. On the Western missionaries' critique of footbinding, see Drucker; Pao Tao.

158. Qiu Jin, "Jinggao Zhongguo," 134.

159. These earlier datings are discussed in "Jie chanzu."

160. Qiu Jin, "Jinggao Zhongguo," 134.

161. On footbinding's origins, see Ko, *Cinderella's*, 109–44.

162. "Jie chanzu." Anti-footbinding officials also referred to Yaoniang. See, for example, "E Fu"; "Shuntian fu."

163. Guiji, 52.

164. "Nüjie jinbu," 522. Shunzhi had first tried to eliminate the practice in 1645.

165. Hu Binxia, "Lun Zhongguo."

166. The literature on Qiu Jin is vast in Chinese, Japanese, and English. Recent and canonical works include: Kong; Lingzhen Wang, 27–60; Pao, "Qiu"; Rankin, "The Emergence"; Takeda.

167. Rankin, "The Emergence," 52.

168. Qiu Jin was one of the more effective speakers—male or female—in the revolutionary movement. She was also a theorist of the power of oratory. See Qiu Jin, "Yanshuo." On female orators in this period, Qiu and Tang Qunying in particular, see Strand.

169. For a description of Qiu in the suit, see Hattori Shigeko, "Shū," 40–41.

170. Opinions vary on the dating of this poem, and whether it was written for this photograph or for the one in which Qiu wore the Western suit. For evidence that the poem was written for this photograph with Qiu in Chinese male attire, see Guo Yanli, *Qiu Jin yanjiu*, 119; Guo Yanli, *Qiu Jin shi wen*, 94–95.

171. The famous kimono was probably part of Qiu's Jissen Women's School uniform, which all students were required to buy. Jissen Women's School dean Sakaki Mitsuko (Sakaki, "Shimoda," 2, 5) explained that the pattern of scattered arrow-shaped figures known as *yagasuri* on the students' kimonos reflected the school's ideology of "good wives and wise mothers": mothers of upright sons had to be as straightforward as the arrows in the pattern. The inspiration for the dagger Qiu is holding in the photo also seems to have been Japanese. Some accounts (Pao, "Qiu Jin," 373) state Lu Xun gave Qiu the knife, and a fellow Chinese male student, Wang Shize (227), claimed that Qiu had bought the dagger herself. One of the many poems Qiu wrote on daggers, "Riben Lingmu wenxueshi baodao ge" (Ode to [Professor] Suzuki's precious dagger), suggests, however, that her initial fascination with daggers could be traced to Suzuki Shintarō, with whom she had studied Japanese in Beijing. Nakamura, 247.

172. On Qiu's feminine demeanor, see Hattori, "Shū," 39; Hirano, 246.

173. Xia Xiaohong, "Wan-Qing ren," 436.

174. Hattori, "Shū," 48.

175. Qiu Jin, "Jinggao Zhongguo," 134–35.

176. Wu Zhiying. Hu Ying ("Writing," 121) suggests that Wu Zhiying emphasized Qiu Jin's social rather than her political activism in this and other early memoirs published shortly after Qiu's execution in order to exonerate her. It is also possible Qiu prioritized political or social revolution at different moments and in different contexts.

177. The reference is to Ibsen's Nora in *A Doll's House*, which would be introduced in China in 1918. See Xu Huiqi, "Nala."

178. This incident is briefly described in Beahan, 394.

179. Pao, "Qiu," 365.

180. Ibid., 373.

181. According to Hattori ("Shū," 47), Qiu was deeply pained by the possibility that her own words had provoked the suicide.

182. On the publication of the *Vernacular* [*Journal*] in Japan, see Xu Shaungyuan, 209.

183. Pao, "Qiu," 364.

184. On Qiu's activities in China at this time, see Kong, 124; Rankin, "The Emergence," 52. Qiu's membership in the Restoration Society (Guangfu hui), the single revolutionary organization that maintained a separate identity after the formation of the Revolutionary Alliance in 1905, was allegedly the source of Sun Zhongshan's hostility to her memory. Gilmartin, 204–5.

185. Qiu had complained to Hattori Shigeko in September 1904 that the food at the Jissen Women's School was both bad and expensive, and in mid-November

that the teachers were neither knowledgeable nor competent. Hattori simultaneously learned from the school manager that Qiu had sent Shimoda a letter outlining her complaints and then left the school in late 1904. Qiu reentered Jissen in August 1905, after which her criticism became even more vociferous. According to letters Hattori received from contacts in Tokyo, Qiu stood at the side of the road at Suidōbashi (Suidō Bridge) and publicly criticized female education in Japan, Shimoda Utako, and the Jissen teachers. Her outbursts were so disruptive that she attracted the attention of the police. Hattori, "Shū," 48–49.

186. Qiu Jin, "Shijian." See also Ōsato, 13.

187. Qiu Jin, "Shijian."

188. Ōsato, 13.

189. Kong, 125. Qiu was forced to leave Nanxun together with Xu Zihua, the school principal, and Xu Yunhua, Zihua's sister and a student at the school.

190. Ibid., 127. Qiu had allegedly planned to establish a physical education school (the Datong tiyu xuetang [Great Unity School of Physical Education]) on this site by joining her own physical education association with the Datong School. Pao, "Qiu," 371–72. While at the Datong School, Qiu also managed the Mingdao nüxue (Enlightened way girls' school). Pao, "Qiu," 371; Rankin, "The Emergence," 59.

191. Pao, "Qiu," 353.

192. I leave the interpretation of Qiu's poetry to scholars of literature. See the excellent work of Wang Lingzhen, 27–60; and Eileen J. Cheng, "The Menacing."

193. Mingyi.

194. Hu Ying, "Writing," 124–38.

195. Although fragmented and contradictory, Chen's reconstructed "biography" is fuller than the life stories of most returned overseas students who became teachers in China. This is, in part, because of her ongoing relationship with Shimoda and the careful preservation practices of Jissen Women's School library archivists.

196. Xie Zhangfa, 272. Wu was expelled from Japan in August 1902 for his involvement in the Seijō School Affair. See Harrell, *Sowing*, 114–20.

197. "Liuxue."

198. The poem is entitled "Wang haichao" (Watching the ocean tides); in Qiu Jin, *Qiu Jin ji*. 107. Sun was from Anhui Province.

199. Ko Shimoda, 399–400.

200. Chen Yan'an, "Chū-Nichi."

201. Harrell, *Sowing*, 62–63.

202. Ibid., 134.

203. Ko Shimoda, 432; Harrell, *Sowing*, 67.

204. Marriage practices in general and the new enlightened marriage in particular were subjects of sustained discussion in the journal *FNSB* from early 1911, when it was founded, through 1917, when it ceased publication.

205. Zhang was minister of justice in 1914 and a translator for a Chinese educational mission to Japan at approximately the same time. In 1916 he was appointed minister of agriculture and industry before becoming ambassador to Japan.

206. Ko Shimoda, 432–34. The date for Zhang's essay is given as early Taisho, which corresponds to the early Republic.

207. Chen Yan'an, "Quan."

208. On Hu and the many Chinese educational, official, and business missions sent to Japan in the first years of the twentieth century, see Harrell, *Sowing*, 40–59. The meeting with Hu was held at the Jiangsu Provincial Society Office in the Ushigome section of Tokyo.

209. Hu Yujin, 39.

210. Zhang was beaten when protesters broke into Cao Rulin's home and found him there. See Fogel, *Nakae*, 39–41.

211. Ko Shimoda, 399.

212. Saeki, 18.

213. "Ji jingshi," 4.

214. Ibid. Beizi was the fourth rank for princes and nobles of the imperial clan. Other financial contributors included the Liangjiang governor Duanfang (1861–1911), and a leading Japanese legal scholar, Okada Asatarō (1868–1936), who was a legal adviser to the Qing government and involved in drafting the late Qing civil code. "Ji jingshi," 3.

215. The date of the interview is unclear. It is filed in the Jissen archive as from 1943 but the actual interview is dated "between 1908 and 1916." It probably took place when the couple returned to Japan in 1916 with Zhang as ambassador. "Jūsan."

216. Ibid., 1–2.

217. Ibid., 3–4.

218. Chen Yan'an, "Quan."

219. "Jūsan," 3–4.

220. On the virtuous and chaste girls' schools, see Duara, *Sovereignty*, 136. Chiang reasserted the importance of the ideology of good wives and wise mothers in the 1934 New Life Movement.

221. The girls' school, which was located in the French Concession of Shanghai, was empty in the summer when the CCP was founded. Jerome Ch'en, 515; Meisner, 34.

222. A number of vocations were tentatively opening up to women at this time, including sericulture, medicine, and publishing, but teaching was the most important among them. Wang Zheng. 130.

223. This became increasingly true in the early Republic when young women trained and inspired by this first generation of independent teachers had greater opportunities to establish their independence from the patriarchal familial order. The famous May Fourth writer Lu Yin (1895–1934) was able to distance herself from her kin and finance her college education by teaching in the inland provinces after graduating from a Beijing normal school. See Cong, 157–58. Similarly, Lu Lihua (1900–1997) saved enough money to start her own school by working at five teaching jobs, and Chen Yongsheng remained single throughout her life, supporting herself by teaching in various Chinese cities and even in Burma. Wang Zheng, 153–54, 259–86.

224. While certain segments of Chinese society began to accept women who chose teaching over motherhood at this time, however, enduring familial and social structures did little to accommodate those who may have wanted both. Women with families were rarely able to sustain their teaching careers beyond the age of twenty-five, finding it almost impossible to balance child-rearing and household and teaching responsibilities, even with domestic help. On these difficulties, see Cong, 87–94. Childless women such as Chen Yongsheng and Lu Lihua were most successful in sustaining lifelong careers as educators.

225. Chen Yongsheng never felt compelled to marry, and Lu Lihua had two brief marriages and a number of informal relationships. While Lu's romantic life was subject to humiliating social scrutiny, her teaching career was never seriously impeded. Wang Zheng, 183–84. Female same-sex love was discussed in Chapter 2.

Conclusion

1. "An Evening"; Ou Ning.

2. Ultrastability was both the mark of the Chinese epistemological tradition that privileged unity and, according to critics of the post-Mao period including Su Xiaokang, creator of *River Elegy* (Heshang), the outcome of the tyrannical cycle of oppressive Chinese rule. See Jing Wang, 175, 54.

3. Jing Wang (47–48) compares cultural discussions in the 1980s to debates in the May Fourth period, as do many of the authors and critics she examines, including Su Xiaokang (52). Turn-of-the-twenty-first century critics including Li Zehou generally use May Fourth as the starting point in periodizations of the modern. Barlow, *The Question*, 271.

4. On transformations in China since 1989, see Wang Hui.

5. This dichotomous view of May Fourth also needs to be challenged, however.

6. On one such systematic translation project, see Jing Wang, 50.

7. Televisions reached 78 percent of the Chinese population by the late 1980s. Rofel, 703.

8. On the root-searching movement, see Jing Wang, 180–86 and disparate references elsewhere in her book; David Wang, *Fictional*, 299–301; Dai Jinhua, 191.

9. On state efforts to revive Confucianism, see Jing Wang, 49–50; on the broader Confucian revival, see 64–78. On Tu Wei-ming's idea of Neo-Confucianism of the third stage, see Tu.

10. Tani Barlow ("International," 1104) describes Li in these terms.

11. Barmé, 101. Rofel (700) claims the show aired in January 1991; Wang Yi (224) in late 1990 and early 1991.

12. On the intentions of the show's five script writers, two of whom were well-known novelists, see Barmé, 104; Rofel, 704.

13. Wang Yi, 233.

14. Rofel, 700.

15. Barmé, 101, 103.

16. The *Aspirations* phenomenon was debated in the arts journal of the Shanghai Academy of Social Sciences, *Shanghai Literary Criticism* (*Shanghai wenlun*), and

in forums organized by the Shanghai Academy of Social Sciences and the leading Shanghai newspaper, *Wenhui Daily*. Ibid., 105; "Huashuo."

17. "Huashuo," 10–11; Rofel, 701.

18. For a synopsis of the soap opera, see Rofel, 705–6.

19. Barmé, 104; Wang Yi, 237.

20. Barmé, 106.

21. Quoted in Wang Yi, 238.

22. Dai Jinhua, 197.

23. "Huashuo," 12.

24. Rofel, 714.

25. "Huashuo," 12.

26. Ibid.

27. Barmé, 106.

28. For a recent example of Li's engagement with Western feminism, see Li Xiao-jiang, "Shijimo."

29. Barlow, *The Question*, 253, 306.

30. Li Xiaojiang, "My Path," 114–18.

31. Li Xiaojiang, "With," 266–69. On Communist state policy toward women, see Edwards, *Women*, especially 61.

32. Li Xiaojiang, "With," 269; Barlow, *The Question*, 300.

33. Barlow, *The Question*, 276. On Li's educational involvement at the Henan Women's Cadre School, for example, see Li Xiaojiang, "Creating," 84–85.

34. Li Xiaojiang and Zhang Xiaodan, 141–43; Li Xiaojiang, "Creating."

35. Dai Jinhua, for example, engages in an anticapitalist politics of utopian resistance. See Barlow, *The Question*, 306.

36. Li Xiaojiang, "From," 1276.

37. Li Xiaojiang, "My Path," 118–22; Li Xiaojiang and Zhang Xiaodan; Barlow, "International," 1104.

38. On Li's belief in the universality of the woman question based on shared physiology and a shared historical trajectory from matriarchy through slavery to liberation, see Barlow, *The Question*, 272, 283; on national difference, 278.

39. Li Xiaojiang. "The Development," 4–5; Li Xiaojiang and Zhang Xiaodan, 148.

40. Li Xiaojiang, "With," 275, 273.

41. Esther Ngan-ling Chow, 191.

42. Barlow, *The Question*, 287.

43. Li Xiaojiang, "With," 264; Barlow, *The Question*, 288.

44. Li Xiaojiang, "With," 264.

45. Dai Jinhua, 192.

46. Dai Jinhua (191) describes male cultural production in the 1980s in these terms.

47. Wu Weihe and Bai Chongmin, 51.

48. Ibid.

49. Ibid., 50.

50. Pierre Ryckmans describes this practice, developing the insights of the French

poet, sinologist, and archeologist Victor Segalen (1878–1919). Segalen wrote that the relative absence of ancient monuments in China reflects the belief that eternity should inhabit not the building but the builder.

51. Ironically, Chinese often have an eye to the Western gaze when they represent their own past as a space of failure. See Dai Jinhua, 192. At a discussion of the *National Shame* installation held at a conference on Chinese feminism at Fudan University in Shanghai in 2004, a Chinese woman journalist accused the creators of the work (who were not in attendance) of giving in to Western views of "traditional China."

Glossary and Character List

Ah Cheng (b. 1949)		阿城
Aiguo		愛國
Aiguo nü xuexiao	Patriotic Girls' School	愛國女學校
aiguo zhi cheng		愛國之誠
Analects for Women	*Nü lunyu*	女論語
Arrayed Traditions of Foreign Women's Lives	*Waiguo lienü zhuan*	外國列女傳
Arrayed Traditions of Women's Lives	*Lienü zhuan*	列女傳
Association of Chinese Female Students in Japan	Zhongguo liu-Ri nü xuesheng hui	中國留日女學生會
Association of Dedicated Nurses	Tokushi kangofu kai	篤志看護婦会
Association of Female Students in Japan	Liu-Ri nü xuesheng hui	留日女學生會
Association to Recover Women's Rights	Nüzi fuquan hui	女子復權會
baguwen		八股文
Bai Chongmin (b. 1970)		白崇民
Bai Guowen (d. ca. 1846)		白國穩
Baihu tong	*White Tiger Hall*	白虎通
baihua		白話
Baihua	*Vernacular [Journal]*	白話
baimei		百美

Baishe		白蛇
Ban Biao (3–54)		班彪
Ban Gu (32–92)		班固
Ban Zhao [Cao Dagu] (ca. 48–ca. 120)		班昭 [曹大家]
Bao Canjun (414–66)		鮑參軍
bao wo minzu		保我民族
baofa		寶筏
baomu		保姆
Baoying		寶應
"Baqi xieling gongcheng"		八旗協領公呈
Bei Qiu		悲秋
"Beifen shi"		悲憤詩
Beijing nübao	*Beijing Women's Journal*	北京女報
Beijing ribao	*Beijing Daily*	北京日報
Beijing shi wenshi yanjiu guan	Beijing Municipal Research Institute of Culture and History	北京市文史研究館
Beijing-Tianjin Times	*Shuntian shibao*	順天時報
Beijing Women's Journal	*Beijing nübao*	北京女報
Beijing yujiao nü xuetang	Beijing Preparatory Women's School	北京豫教女學堂
Beiyang nüzi shifan xuetang	Beiyang Women's Normal School	北洋女子師範學堂
ben		本
Bi Zhu [Taowen] (fl. 1643)		畢著 [韜文]
"Bian tong"	Skill in Argument	辯通
biji		筆記
Bijutsu gakkō	School of Fine Arts	美術學校
Biographies of Great Women of Our Country	*Zuguo nüjie weiren zhuan*	祖國女界偉人傳
Biographies of Heroes [Plutarch's *Parallel Lives*]	*Yingxiong zhuan*	英雄傳

"Bo nüzi wucai shi de zhi wangyan"		駁女子無才是德之妄言
Book of Changes	*Yi jing*	易經
Book of Documents	*Shang shu*	尚書
Book of Odes	*Shi jing*	詩經
Boyi		伯夷
bubi caiming jue yi		不必才明絕異
bunmei		文明
Catherine [the Great of Russia] (r. 1762–96)	Jiasaileng	加塞冷
Cai Wan [Jiyu] (1695–1755)		蔡琬 [季玉]
Cai Yan [Wenji] (fl. 170)		蔡琰 [文姬]
Cai Yong [Bojie] (133–82)		蔡邕 [伯喈]
Cai Yurong (1633–99)		蔡毓榮
caihua		才華
cainü		才女
Cang Jie		蒼頡
Cao Dagu [Ban Zhao] (ca. 48–ca. 120)		曹大家 [班昭]
Cao Fengsheng (fl. 80)		曹豐生
Cao Jialin (fl. 1905)		曹家麟
Cao Rujin (b. 1878)		曹汝錦
Cao Rulin (1876–1966)		曹汝霖
Cao Wenshu (Han dynasty)		曹文叔
Chang Shi shi		常石氏
Changsun (fl. 900?)		長孫
Chen (dynasty)		陳
Chen Fan (1860–1913)		陳範
Chen Hongmou (1697–1771)		陳宏謀
Chen Houzhu [Chen Shubao] (533–604)		陳後主 [陳叔寶]
Chen Huizhen (fl. 1900)		陳惠貞

Chen Maoxie [Chen Yan'an] (b. ca. 1833)		陳懋虒 [陳彥安]
Chen Pu		陳溥
Chen Tianhua (1875–1905)		陳天華
Chen Xiangfen (fl. 1911)		陳湘芬
Chen Xiefen (1883–1923)		陳擷芬
Chen Ying (Former Han dynasty)		陳嬰
Chen Yongsheng (1900–97)		陳永聲
Cheng furen (fl. 1040)		程夫人
Cheng Hao [Mingdao] (1032–85)		程顥 [明道]
Cheng Yi [Yichuan] (1033–1107)		程頤 [伊川]
Chengzhi nü xuetang		承志女學堂
Chidi		赤帝
"Chinese Girls' Progress"	*Nüxue bao* (Xue Shaohui)	女學報
Chinese Reader for Girls	*Nüzi guowen duben*	女子國文讀本
Chinese Women's Journal	*Zhongguo nübao*	中國女報
Chinese Women's School	Zhongguo nü xuetang	中國女學堂
chongse tiandi		充塞天地
Chu Jiang Zifa (Han dynasty)		楚將子發
Chubei yingci		楚北英雌
Chunyu Yi (b. 205)		淳于意
ci	prose poem set to music	詞
ci	maternal nurturance	慈
Cihui		慈惠
cimu		慈母
cixun		慈訓
Classic of Filiality	*Xiao jing*	孝經
Classic of Filiality for Women	*Nü xiaojing*	女孝經
Commentary of Mr. Zuo	*Zuo zhuan*	左傳

Commercial Press	Shangwu yinshu guan	商務印書館
Congshu shidai		從屬時代
congyi er zhong		從一而終
The Continent	*Dalu*	大陸
Copybook of Classified Letters for Women	*Nüzi fenlei chidu fanben*	女子分類尺牘範本
[Corday], Charlotte (1768–93)	Shalutuo	沙魯脫
Cui furen (fl. 570)		崔夫人
Cui Yingying		崔鶯鶯
Dagong bao	"L'Impartial"	大公報
Dai Jinhua (b. 1959)		戴錦華
Dai Li (f. 1905)		戴禮
Daily Pictorial	*Tuhua ribao*	圖畫日報
Dalu	*The Continent*	大陸
dangfu		蕩婦
Datong shu	*Great Unity*	大通書
Datong tiyu xuetang	Great Unity School of Physical Education	大同體育學堂
Datong xuetang	School of Great Unity	大同學堂
Datong xuexiao	School of Great Unity	大同學校
Daxue	*The Great Learning*	大學
de		德
Dianshizhai huabao	*Stones-into-gold Studio Pictorial*	點石齋畫報
Ding Shi (fl. 100)		丁氏
Diyi mengyang yuan	Number One Kindergarten	第一蒙養院
"Domestic Regulations"	"Nei ze"	內則
Domestic Science	*Kaseigaku*	家政學
dongfang		東方
Donghun Hou (ca. 500)		東昏候
Dong'Ou nü haojie	*Heroine of Eastern Europe*	東歐女豪傑

"Dou E yuan"	"The Injustice Done to Dou E"	竇娥冤
Draft History of the Qing Dynasty	*Qingshi gao*	清史稿
Duanfang (1861–1911)		端方
"Duanji qisheng"		斷機啟聖
duben		讀本
"Duiyu nübao zhi ganyan"		對于女報之感言
Duli shidai		獨立時代
"The Eastern Miscellany"	*Dongfang zazhi*	東方雜誌
"The Eastern Times"	*Shibao*	時報
Education Board	Xue bu	學部
Educational Review	*Jiaoyu zazhi*	教育雜誌
Elementary Learning for Girls and Women	*Nü xiaoxue*	女小學
Eliot, George (1819–80)	Qiyuqi Ailiatuo	奇欲奇愛里阿脫
Elizabeth, Queen of England (1558–1603)	Keluqimeisu Nüwang	克路崎美蘇女王
Enming (1846–1907)		恩銘
enuo		婀娜
Ethics for Female Normal School Students	*Nüzi shifan xiushenxue*	女子師範修身學
Exhortation to Women's Learning	*Nüxue pian*	女學篇
"Famous Women" [Biographies of successful European and American women]	*Ō-Bei joshi risshin den*	欧米女子立身伝
Fan Yuanlian [Jingsheng] (1876–1927)		范源廉 [靜生]
Fang Junying (1884–1923)		方君瑛
Fang Shengdong (1886–1911)		方聲洞
Fang Yuanling (Tang dynasty)		房元齡

Fawcett, [Millicent G.] (1847–1929)	Fueshade furen	傅萼紗德夫人
fei li zhi zheng		非禮之正
feixinghua		非性化
Feiyingge huabao	*Pavilion of Flying Shadows Pictorial*	飛影閣畫報
Feng Bao (fl. 535)		馮寶
Feng furen (fl. 1650)		馮夫人
Feng Liao (Former Han dynasty)		馮嫽
Feng Menglong (1574–1646)		馮夢龍
First Collection of New Songs For Girls	*Nüzi xin changge chuji*	女子新唱歌初集
Forest of Laughter	*Xiaolin bao*	笑林報
fu		賦
fu neng shengzhi buneng yangzhi, mu neng yang- zhi, buneng huaizhi		父能生之不能養之母能養 之不能誨之
Fu Sheng (b. 260 BCE)		伏勝
fuke		婦科
"Fulu"		附錄
Funü shibao	*The Women's Eastern Times*	婦女時報
funü wenti		婦女問題
"Funü yi sheng jiaotache zhi minjie"		婦女亦乘腳踏車之敏捷
Funü zazhi	*Ladies' Journal*	婦女雜誌
"Furen"		婦人
"Furen lun"		婦人論
Fushe		復社
"Fuxing"		婦行
"Fuxue"		婦學
Gailiang zaiban nüxue changge	*Improved and Reprinted Girls' School Songs*	改良再版女學唱歌
Gakusei		學制

"Gan fen"		感憤
"Gan shi"		感時
Gao		高
Gao Qizhuo (1676–1738)		高其倬
Gaoliang		高涼
Garibaldi, Anita (1821–49)	Manita Jialipoerdi furen	馬尼他加鼇波兒地夫人
ge		歌
gegu		割股
gekietsu na minken ronsha		激越な民權論者
"General Discussion of Reform"	"Bianfa tongyi"	變法通議
gong		工
Gongai hui	Humanitarian Association	共愛會
gongdeng		公等
Gongke (fl. 1900)		公恪
gongmin		公民
Gu		顧
Gu Qing		谷清
Guan Panpan (fl. 800)		關盼盼
Guang lienü zhuan	"Biographies of Exemplary Women"	廣列女傳
Guangfu hui	Restoration Society	光復會
Guangren tang	Hall of Great Benevolence	廣仁堂
Guanyin		觀音
Guhuanshi shici ji	*Collected Poems from the Guhuan Studio*	古歡室詩詞集
Gui		閨
Gui fan	*Exemplars of the Inner Quarters*	閨範
Gui Youguang (1506–71)		歸有光
Guide to Great Women Writers of Our Country	*Zuguo nüjie wenhao pu*	祖國女界文豪譜
guixiu		閨秀

Gujin lienü zhuan	*Arrayed Traditions of Ancient and Recent Women's Lives*	古今列女傳
Guo yu	*Discourses of the States*	國語
Guochao guixiu zhengshi ji	*Correct Beginnings: Women's Poetry of Our August Dynasty*	國朝閨秀正始集
guocui		國粹
guojia		國家
guojia zhuyi		國家主義
guomin jiaoyu zhi diyi jizhi		國民教育之第一基址
guomin yi fenzi		國民一分子
guomin zhi mu		國民之母
guoqing		過情
"*Guoshang–Guang lienü zhuan*"	"*National Shame: Guang Lienü Zhuan [Biographies of Exemplary Women]*"	国殇。广列女传
guxi		姑息
Han History	*Han shu*	漢書
Han Ximeng (fl. 1120)		韓希孟
Handan		邯鄲
Hanyu da cidian		漢語大詞典
haojie		豪傑
Hattori Unokichi (1867–1939)		服部宇之吉
He disi		和娣姒
He Qixun		何其洵
Hele shidai		和樂時代
Hengcui nüzi zhiye xuexiao	Hengcui Girls' Vocational School	衡粹女子職業學校
hengsao liuhe you yu		橫掃六合有餘
Heshang	*River Elegy*	河殤
Hong Liangji (1746–1809)		洪亮吉

Hong Xiuquan (1814–64)		洪秀全
Hong Xuanjiao (fl. 1860)		洪宣嬌
Honglou meng	Dream of the Red Chamber	紅樓夢
Hōsei daigaku	University for the Study of Law and Politics	法政大学
Hou Han shu	Later Han History	後漢書
hu		胡
Hu Fanglan (d. 1907)		胡仿蘭
Hua Gui (fl. 1903)		華桂
Hua Mulan (ca. 500)		花木蘭
huabao		畫報
Huadijiaozi		畫荻教子
Huan Shi (Han dynasty)		桓氏
Huang Chonggu (fl. 910)		黃崇嘏
Huang Guohou (b. 1881)		黃國厚
Huang lienü yishi	Surviving Poems of Heroic Woman Huang	黃烈女遺詩
Huang Shuhua (ca. 1850–67)		黃淑華
Huanghuagang		黃花崗
"Huangtiandang"		黃天蕩
Huayang		華陽
Huitu daban gujin xiannü zhuan	Illustrated Large Edition of Biographies of Resourceful Women, Past and Present	繪圖大版古今賢女傳
Huitu lienü zhuan	Illustrated Arrayed Traditions of Women's Lives	繪圖列女傳
huixie		穢褻
Huixiu nü xuetang	Gracious and Refined Girls' School	惠秀女學堂
Humanitarian Association	Gongai hui	共愛會

Hunan diyi nüzi shifan xuexiao	Hunan Number One Girls' Normal School	湖南第一女子師範學校
[Hutchinson], Lucy (1620–80)	Lüzhi	縷志
Illustrated Arrayed Traditions of Women's Lives	*Huitu lienü zhuan*	繪圖列女傳
Illustrated Biographies of Resourceful Women, Past and Present	*Xiuxiang gujin xiannü zhuan*	繡像古今賢女傳
"L'Impartial"	*Dagong bao*	大公報
Improved and Reprinted Girls' School Songs	*Gailiang zaiban nüxue changge*	改良再版女學唱歌
Inukai Tsuyoshi (1885–1932)		犬養毅
Isabella, Queen of Spain (1451–1504)	Yishabaier Nüwang	伊沙百兒女王
Ji Yihui (fl. 1900)		戢翼翬
Jia Baoyu		賈寶玉
Jia fan	*Family Model*	家範
Jiang Kanghu (1883–1954)		江亢虎
Jiang liefu (Ming dynasty)		蔣烈婦
Jiang Shijin (Ming dynasty)		姜士進
Jiang Yunhua (fl. 1905)		蔣韞華
Jiangsu jiaoyu zonghui	Jiangsu General Educational Society	江蘇教育總會
Jiangsu Journal	*Jiangsu*	江蘇
The Jiangsu Journal	*Subao*	蘇報
Jiao Zhongqing (Han dynasty)		焦仲卿
jiaokeshu		教科書
Jiaonü yigui	*Sourcebook on Women's Education*	教女遺規
Jiaoyu zazhi	*Educational Review*	教育雜誌
Jiaozi		教子
jiating jiaoyu		家庭教育

jiaxue		家學
Jicheng tushu gongsi	Compendium Book Company	集成圖書公司
jie		節
Jie Jin (1369–1415)		解縉
jiecao		節操
jiefang		解放
jiefu		節婦
jiegu foujin		借古否今
jielie		節烈
Jiexiao si	Shrine for the Chaste and Filial	節孝祠
jigong haoshan		急公好善
Jin Guliang		金古良
Jin History	*Jin shu*	晉書
Jin shi (Qing dynasty)		金氏
Jin shu	*Jin History*	晉書
jing'ai yingxiong		敬愛英雄
jingbao		京報
jingbiao		旌表
jingjie tang		敬節堂
Jingjie xuetang	School for Revering Chastity	敬節學堂
Jinglou furen		經樓夫人
Jingqun		競群
Jingshan nü xuetang	Jingshan Girls' School	景山女學堂
jinguo neng bing		巾幗能兵
jinguo zhi jie		巾幗之傑
Jingxiong		競雄
Jingzhong ribao	*Daily Alarm*	警鍾日報
Jingzhou		荊州
Jinling shuju	Nanjing Publishing House	金陵書局
jinshi		進士

jinwen		今文
Jishan		吉山
Jissen jogakkō	Jissen Women's School	實踐女學校
jiuji shanhui		救濟善會
"Jiyu shi jian"		季玉詩諫
Jizhi		吉止
Joan [of Arc] (1412–31)	Ru'an, Ruoan, Ruoan Dake, Ru'an Dake niang	如安, 若安, 若安達克, 如安打克孃
Journal of Women's Learning	*Nüxue bao* (Chen Xiefen)	女學報
Ju-E yiyong dui	Volunteer Corps to Resist Russia	拒俄義勇隊
Jun Buyi (Han dynasty)		雋不疑
jun yi silai shu yi gongbu		君以私來淑以公布
junguomin zige		軍國民資格
juren		舉人
kaitong fude		開通婦德
"Kan women nüzi bei renjia chixiao"		看我們女子被人家恥笑
Kang Youwei (1858–1927)		康有為
Kangaku		漢學
Kanhuxue jiaocheng	*A Course in Nursing*	看護學教程
Kanō Jigorō (1860–1938)		嘉納治五郎
Kaseigaku	*Domestic Science*	家政學
Katei zasshi	*Family Journal*	家庭雜誌
Kawahara Misako (1875–1945)		河原操子
keben		課本
kefeng		可風
Kewang	*Aspirations (Yearnings, Expectations)*	渴望
Know the New News	*Zhixin bao*	知新報
Kōbun shoin	Kōbun Academy	宏文書院

Kong Luhua [Jinglou] (fl. 1800)		孔璐華 [經樓]
Konoe Atsumaro (1863–1904)		近衛篤麿
Kou Laigong (961–1023)		寇萊公
Kuai Shoushu [Ruomu] (fl. 1903)		蒯壽樞 [若木]
Kuang Junyi (fl. 1906)		匡君一
kyōkasho		教科書
Ladies' Journal	*Funü zazhi*	婦女雜誌
lanben		籃本
Later Han History	*Hou Han shu*	後漢書
Lei Jian (fl. 1916)		雷瑊
Lei Jin (fl. 1916)		雷瑨
Li Changxia (fl. 1860)		李長霞
Li Faqun (1873–1913)		李發群
Li ji	*Record of Rites*	禮記
Li jing	*Ritual Classic*	禮經
Li Jingrang (Tang dynasty)		李景讓
Li Peng (b. 1928)		李鵬
Li Qiaosong (1872–1933)		李樵松
Li Qingzhao (1084–ca. 1151)		李清照
Li Run (1866–1925)		李閏
Li Shenchuan (fl. 1850)		李慎傳
"Li Taifuren zhi taijiao"		李太夫人之胎教
Li Xiu (fl. ca. 350)		李秀
Li Yi (fl. ca. 300)		李毅
Li Yu (937–78, r. 961–74)		李煜
Li Yuan (566–635)		李淵
Li Yuan (fl. 1906)		李元
Li Zehou (b. 1930)		李泽厚
Li Zhongyi (Yuan dynasty)		李中義
Liang Duan (1757–1825)		梁端

Liang Hongyu (ca. 1100–35)		梁紅玉
Liang liefu		梁烈婦
Liang Tingzuo (fl. 1700)		梁廷佐
Liang Yizhen (fl. 1932)		梁乙真
Liangjiang nüzi shifan xuexiao	Liangjiang Girls' Normal School	兩江女子師範學校
liangqi xianmu		良妻賢母
Lianjun		聯軍
Liao		廖
Liao Yongyun (fl. 1905)		廖詠筠
Liao Zhongkai (1877–1925)		廖仲愷
Liaowang	*Observation*	瞭望
Lichao lienü zhuan	*Arrayed Traditions of Women's Lives Through the Ages*	歷朝列女傳
Lidai lienü lun	*Female Exemplars Through the Ages*	歷代列女論
liefu		烈婦
lienü	exemplary girl/woman	列女
lienü	heroically chaste girl, heroine	烈女
Lienü zhuan buzhu	*Supplementary Notes to the Arrayed Traditions of Women's Lives*	列女傳補注
Lienü zhuan jiao duben	*Arrayed Traditions of Women's Lives: A Collated Reader*	列女傳校讀本
Lienü zhuan jizhu	*Collected Annotations to the Arrayed Traditions of Women's Lives*	列女傳集注
Lienü zhuan zengguang	*Enlarged Arrayed Traditions of Women's Lives*	列女傳增廣
Lieven, [Mrs. Dorothea] (1785–1857)	Luoweikefu furen	絡維恪扶夫人
liezhuan		列傳

lijiao		禮教
Liling		醴陵
Liling nüzi xuetang	Liliing Girls' School	醴陵女子學堂
Lin Daiyu		林黛玉
Lin Shiying (fl. 1911)		林士英
Linchuan Liang shi		臨川梁氏
Ling Rongzhong (1874–1929)		凌容眾
lingqi xianmu		令妻賢母
Liu		劉
Liu Huifang		刘慧芳
Liu Kai (1781–1821)		劉開
Liu-Ri nü xuehui	Study Society of Female Students in Japan	留日女學會
Liu-Ri nü xuehui zazhi	*Magazine of the Study Society of Female Students in Japan*	留日女學會雜誌
Liu-Ri nü xuesheng hui	Association of Female Students in Japan	留日女學生會
Liu Rushi (1618–64)		柳如是
Liu Shi (Yuan dynasty)		劉氏
Liu Tingshi		劉廷式
Liu Xiang (79–8 BCE)		劉向
Liu Zhangqing (Han dynasty)		劉長卿
lixue		理學
Longjiang nüxue wenfan	*Longjiang Women's School Model Essays*	龍江女學文範
Louise (queen of Prussia) (1776–1810)	Liuyishe	流易設
Lower-Level Elementary Female Ethics Textbook	*Chudeng xiaoxue nüzi xiushen jiaokeshu*	初等小學女子修身教科書
Lü		旅
Lü Bicheng (1883–1943)		呂碧城
Lü Kun (1536–1618)		呂坤

Lu Lihua (1900–97)		陸禮華
Lu Qishi nü (pre–Han dynasty)		魯漆室女
Lü Xizhe (1039–1116)		呂希哲
Lu Yin (1895–1934)		盧隱
"Lu'e"		蓼莪
"Lun nüzi dang ju duli zhi xingzhi"		論女子當具獨立之性質
Lun yu	*Analects*	論語
"Lun yuebao zhi yi"		論閱報之益
Luo Pu (d. 1939?)		羅普
Luo Rufang (1515–88)		羅汝芳
Luo Ying (fl. 1905)		羅瑛
Luo Zhenyu (1866–1940)		羅振玉
Lyon, [Mary] (1797–1849)	Lihen	黎痕
Ma Engui [Yinzhi] (fl. 1890)		馬恩桂 [蔭之]
Ma Qiancheng (d. 1615)		馬千乘
Ma Rong (79–166)		馬融
Ma Zhide (fl. 1600)		馬之德
Magazine of the New Chinese Woman	*Zhongguo xin nüjie zazhi*	中國新女界雜誌
Magazine of the Study Society of Female Students in Japan	*Liu-Ri nü xuehui zazhi*	留日女學會雜誌
Mao Qiling (1623–1716)		毛奇齡
Master Han's Illustrations of The Didactic Applications of the "Classic of Songs"	*Han shi waizhuan*	韓詩外傳
meiren		美人
Meiroku zasshi	*Meiji Six Journal*	明六雜誌
Meng Zi (372–289 BCE)		孟子
Michel, Louise (1830–1905)	Luyi Meishier	路易美世兒
Ming History	*Ming shi*	明史

Mingdao nüxue	Enlightened Way Girls' School	明道女學
Ministry of Education	Jiaoyu bu (Republican)	教育部
Ministry of Rites	Li bu	禮部
minzu zhuyi		民族主義
Mo Yan (b. 1956)		莫言
Mou shi		某氏
mousha tuan		謀殺團
mu		模
"Mujiao"		母教
"Mulan shi"	"Ballad of Mulan"	木蘭詩
"Muxing"		母型
"Muyi"		母儀
Nakamura Masanao (1832–91)		中村正直
nanman		南蠻
nannü yiti		男女一體
nannü zheng tiandi zhi dayi ye		男女正天地之大義也
nanquan		男權
nanzi you de bian shi cai, nüzi wu cai bian shi de		男子有德便是才，女子無才便是德
"The National Women's Journal"	*Nübao*	女報
Natural Justice	*Tianyi*	天義
nei		內
Nei xun	*Inner Instruction*	內訓
"Nei ze"	"Domestic Regulations"	內則
Neicheng nüxue chuanxi suo	Inner City Institute for Women's Education	內成女學傳習所
neiyan buchu		內言不出
"New Chinese and Foreign Arrayed Traditions of Women's Lives"	"Zhong-wai xin lienü zhuan"	中外新列女傳

New People's Miscellany	*Xinmin congbao*	新民叢報
New Reader for Girls and Women	*Nüzi xin duben*	女子新讀本
Newest Chinese Reader for Women	*Zuixin funü guowen duben*	最新婦女國文讀本
Newest Ethics Textbook for Girls and Women	*Zuixin nüzi xiushen jiaokeshu*	最新女子修身教科書
niai		溺愛
Niangzi jun	Woman's Army	娘子軍
Nie Jie (fl. 395)		聶姊
Nightingale, [Florence] (1820–1910)	Niejike'er, Nandingge'er	涅幾柯兒, 南丁格爾
Nihon Sekijūjisha kangogaku kyōtei	*The Japanese Red Cross Course on Nursing*	日本赤十字社看護學教程
nü guomin		女國民
Nü guomin hui	Female Citizens' Association	女國民會
Nü guomin juan	Female Citizens' Fund	女國民捐
nü haojie		女豪杰
Nü jie	*Precepts for Women*	女誡
Nü lunyu	*Analects for Women*	女論語
Nü shishuo	*Women's Shishuo*	女世說
Nü sishu	*Four Books for Women*	女四書
Nü xiaojing	*Classic of Filial Piety for Women*	女孝經
Nü xiaoxue	*Elementary Learning for Girls and Women*	女小學
nü xuesheng		女學生
Nü xun	*Women's Instructions*	女訓
nü yingci		女英雌
nü yingxiong		女英雄
nü yingxiong nü haojie		女英雄女豪杰
nü yongshi		女勇士
Nü ze	*Female Regulations*	女則
nü zhangfu		女丈夫

"Nü zhuzuo"		女著作
Nübao	*"The National Women's Journal"*	女報
Nüjiao jingzhuan tongzuan	*Compilation of Classics and Histories for the Instruction of Girls and Women*	女教經傳通纂
nüjie		女傑
Nüjie baolu hui	Women's Railway Protection Association	女界保路會
"Nüjie fengshang zhi bianqian"		女界風尚之變遷
"Nüjie xinwen"		女界新聞
Nuli shidai		奴隸時代
nüquan		女權
nüquan zhuyi		女权主义
nüshi		女士
Nüwa		女媧
Nüwa shi	*Nüwa's Stone*	女媧石
Nüxing canzheng tongmeng hui	Female Suffrage Alliance	女性參政同盟會
nüxing zhuyi		女性主义
Nüxue bao	*"Chinese Girls' Progress" (Xue Shaohui); Journal of Women's Learning* (Chen Xiefen)	女學報
"Nüxue lunwen"		女學論文
Nüxue pian	*Exhortation to Women's Learning*	女學篇
"Nüxue wencong"		女學文叢
nüzhe zhi guang		女哲之光
nüzhong haojie		女中豪傑
nüzhong zhi jie		女中之傑
Nüzi beifa gansi dui	Women Commandos	女子北伐敢死隊

Nüzi beifajun jiuji dui	Women's Auxilary of the Northern Expedition Army	女子北伐軍救急隊
Nüzi canzheng tongmeng hui	Female Suffrage Alliance	女子參政同盟會
Nüzi canzheng tongzhi hui	Association of Female Comrades for Women's Political Participation	女子參政同志會
Nüzi fuquan hui	Association to Recover Women's Rights	女子復權會
nüzi guomin		女子國民
Nüzi hongshizi jun	Women's Red Cross Army	女子紅十字軍
Nüzi houyuan hui	Women's Rearguard Association	女子後援會
Nüzi shangwu hui	Women's Militant Association	女子尚武會
Nüzi shifan jiangyi	*Lectures for Women's Normal Education*	女子師範講義
Nüzi shijie	*Women's World*	女子世界
Nüzi ticao fanben	*Physical Education Reader for Girls*	女子體操範本
Nüzi ticao xuexiao	School of Physical Education for Girls and Women	女子體操學校
Nüzi tongmeng hui	Women's Alliance	女子同盟會
nüzi wenti		女子問題
nüzi yu xiaoren nanyang ye		女子與小人難養也
Observation of the Battles in Northern China	*Hoku Shin kansen ki*	北清觀戰記
Okada Asatarō (1868–1936)		岡田朝太郎
Old Tang History	*Jiu Tang shu*	舊唐書
"On Female Education"	"Lun nüxue"	論女學
"One Hundred Beauties, Past and Present"	"Gujin baimei tu"	古今百美圖

Ōsaka hakurankai		大阪博覧会
Ossoli, [Margaret Fuller] (1810–50)	Asuoli	阿索里
Ou Ning (b. 1969)		欧宁
Oufeng		歐風
Ouyang Xiu (1007–72)		歐陽修
Pan Shu (ca. 500)		潘淑
Pan Ying (fl. 1911)		潘英
Pang E (Later Han dynasty)		龐娥
Patriotic Girls' School	Aiguo nü xuexiao	愛國女學校
penggou		蓬垢
[Perovskaia], Sofia (1853–81)	Sufeiya	蘇菲亞
pifu pifu		匹夫匹婦
Pingjiang		平江
pingquan		平權
Pingxiang Wuben nüxiao	Pingxiang School of Fundamental Women's Learning	萍鄉務本女校
Pingyang gongzhu (d. 623)		平陽公主
pinmin xuexiao		貧民學校
Precepts for Women	*Nü jie*	女戒
Progressive Press	Wenming shuju	文明書局
pujiu zhu		普救主
pujiu zhongsheng		普救眾生
Qi		齊
Qi Liang		杞粱
Qi liefu		戚烈婦
Qi Wanzhen (d. ca. 1911)		戚琬珍
Qian Fengbao (fl. 1903)		錢豐保
Qiaoguo furen		譙國夫人
"Qice si"		齊策四
qili		奇麗

Qin Liangyu (d. 1648)		秦良玉
Qin Xuemei		秦雪梅
qing		情
Qinghua [buxi] xuexiao	Chinese Preparatory School	清華〔補習〕學校
Qingjie tang	Hall of Purity	清潔堂
Qinjian		勤儉
Qiu Jing		秋競
Qiu Tingliang (fl. 1885)		裘廷梁
Qiu Yufang (fl. 1895)		裘毓芳
Qu Jiang [Bogang] (fl. 1907)		屈疆 [伯剛]
"Quan yuebao"		勸閱報
quanzhen		全貞
ranshin zokushi		亂臣賊子
Record of Rites	*Li ji*	禮記
Records of the Grand Historian	*Shi ji*	史記
Ren Qiyun		任啟運
"Ren Zhi"		仁智
rencai		人才
renjie		人傑
renqing		人情
Revolutionary Alliance	Tongmeng hui	同盟會
"Riben Lingmu wenxueshi baodao ge"		日本鈴木文學士寶刀歌
Ribenyu jiangxi suo	Institute for Japanese Language Study	日本語講習所
Rites of Zhou	*Zhou li*	周禮
Roland, Madame (1754–93)	Luolan furen	羅蘭夫人
rong		容
Rousseau, [Jean-Jacques] (1712–78)	Lusuo	盧梭
Ruan furen		阮夫人

"Ruan furen zhanshen jingshi"		阮夫人湛深經史
Ruan Yuan (1764–1849)		阮元
Ruixing		瑞興
"Rulin zhuan"		儒林傳
ryōsai kenbo		良妻賢母
"Same-Sex Love among Women"	"Funü tongxing zhi aiqing"	婦女同性之愛情
sancong		三從
sangang		三綱
Sanzi jing	*Trimetrical Classic*	三字經
School of Fundamental Women's Learning	Wuben nüxiao, Wuben nüshu	務本女校，務本女塾
School of Great Unity	Datong xuexiao	大同學校
Seijo gakkō	Women's School	成女學校
Seiyōrō		青陽楼
Sekai jûni joketshu	*Twelve World Heroines*	世界十二女傑
shan shan e e		善善惡惡
Shan Shili (1858–1943)		單士釐
Shang shu	*Book of Documents*	尚書
shangfeng baisu		傷風敗俗
Shanghai News	*Shenbao*	申報
Shanghai nü xuexiao	Shanghai School for Girls and Women	上海女學校
Shanghai sucheng nügong shifan chuanxi suo	Shanghai Accelerated Normal Handicraft Teacher-Training Institute for Girls	上海速成女工師範傳習所
"Shangwu"		尚武
shangwu jingshen		尚武精神
Shangwu yinshu guan	Commercial Press	商務印書館
Shangyuan		上元
"Shei zhi zui xiqu"		誰之罪戲曲
shelun		社論
Shen Peizhen (fl. 1911)		沈配貞

Shen Yunying (1624–61)		沈雲英
Shen Zhixu (d. 1643)		沈至緒
Shenbao	*Shanghai News*	申報
shendao (*shintō*)		神道
shengxian		聖賢
shenjia zhuyi		身家主義
shi		詩
shi er baili		詩而敗禮
Shi ji	*Records of the Grand Historian*	史記
Shi jing	*Book of Odes*	詩經
Shi jiugu		事舅姑
shi wei manyi jiuzhang		世為蠻夷酋長
shi wei manzhang		世為蠻長
shi wei nanyue shouling		世為南越首領
Shibao	*"The Eastern Times"*	時報
"Shibiao you kui"		師表有虧
shijian		史鑑
Shijie shier nüjie	*Twelve World Heroines*	世界十二女傑
shijie zhuyi		世界主義
Shikan gakkō	Cadet School	士官學校
shimin		市民
Shina jogakusei bu	Chinese Female Student Department	支那女學生部
Shina ryūgakusei bu	Department of Chinese Overseas Students	支那留學生部
Shina ryūgakusei no tame no shūshin kōwa	*Lectures on Ethics for Chinese Overseas Students*	支那留學生のための修身講話
Shinkoku joshibu	Chinese Female Division	清國女子部
Shixing gongai hui	Humanitarian Association for Practical Action	實行共愛會
shiyuan bu jiaren		矢願不嫁人
shizi zhi binü		識字之婢女

shou dushen zhuyi		守獨身主義
shoujie		守節
shuchang		書場
shuncong		順從
Shuntian shibao	*Beijing-Tianjin Times*	順天時報
Shunzhi (r. 1644–62)		順治
"Shuo jie"		說節
"Shuoyong"		說勇
Shuqi		叔齊
Si shu		四書
Sichuan Girls' School	Sichuan nü xuetang	四川女學堂
Sichuan nü xuetang	Sichuan Girls' School	四川女學堂
side		四德
Sili qiming nü xuetang	Private Enlightenment Girls' School	私立啟明女學堂
Sima Guang (1019–86)		司馬光
Sima Qian (145–ca. 86 BCE)		司馬遷
siyi		死義
Society for Renewal	Zuoxin she	作新社
Song History	*Song shi*	宋史
Song Lian (1310–81)		宋濂
Song Ruohua (fl. 830)		宋若華
Song shi (fl. 360)		宋氏
Song Shu (1862–1910)		宋恕
Songling		松陵
de Staël, Madame (1766–1817)	Sutailiu furen	蘇泰流夫人
Stowe, [Harriet] Beecher (1811–96)	Picha, Siduo Biqi	批茶, 斯多婢棲
Students of Hubei	*Hubei xuesheng jie*	湖北學生界
Study Society of Female Students in Japan	Liu-Ri nü xuehui	留日女學會
Su Dongpo ji	Works of Su Dongpo	蘇東坡集

Su Shi [Dongpo] (1037–1101)		蘇軾 [東坡]
Su Xiaokang (b. 1949)		苏晓康
Su Xun [Mingjiu] (1009–66)		蘇洵 [明久]
Su Ziqing [Su Wu] (d. 60 BCE)		蘇子卿 [蘇武]
Subao	*The Jiangsu Journal*	蘇報
Subao guan	*The Jiangsu Journal Office*	蘇報館
Sui History	*Sui shu*	隋書
suibi		隨筆
Suidōbashi	Suidō Bridge	水道橋
Sun Ce (174–200)		孫策
Sun Duokun (fl. 1904)		孫多琨
Sun furen (fl. 320)		孫夫人
Sun Zhongshan (Sun Yat-sen) (1866–1925)		孫中山
suohuan		所歡
Suqian		宿遷
Suzuki Shintarō (fl. 1904)		鈴木信太郎
Tai Jiang (fl. 1122 BCE)		太姜
Tai Ren (fl. 1160 BCE)		太妊
Tai Si (fl. 1140 BCE)		太姒
taijiao		胎教
Taiping guangji	*Expanded Record of Great Peace*	太平廣記
taisō		體操
Tan Sitong (1866–98)		譚嗣同
Tan Zhengbi (fl. 1930)		譚正璧
tanci		彈詞
Tang Linren (fl. 1908)		湯琳任
Tang Qunying (1871–1937)		唐群英
Tang Song jiujing loushi [gao]	*[Drafts] of Poems from the Jiujing Pavilion of the Tang and Song Eras*	唐宋舊經樓詩[稿]

Tao Chengzhang (1878–1912)		陶成章
Tao Ying		陶嬰
Teachings for Girls	*Nü xue*	女學
Teishitsu hakubutsukan	Imperial Palace Museum	帝室博物館
Ten World Heroines	*Shijie shi nüjie*	世界十女傑
Ti Ying (ca. 167 BCE)		緹縈
Tian Jizi (Han dynasty)		田稷子
tianxia		天下
tianxia zhi zheng		天下之正
tiyong		體用
"Tiyu"		體育
"To Sing of Women Officers through the Ages"	"Yong lidai nüjiang"	詠歷代女將
Tō-A jogakkō	East Asian Women's School	東亞女學校
A Tocsin for Women	*Nüjie zhong*	女界鍾
Tokushi kangofu kai	Association of Dedicated Nurses	篤志看護婦會
Tōkyō jogaku kan	Tokyo Women's Academy	東京女學館
Tōkyō joshi kōtō shihan gakkō	Tokyo Senior Women's Normal School	東京女子高等師範學校
Tokyo Senior Women's Normal School	Tōkyō joshi kōtō shihan gakkō	東京女子高等師範學校
tong		銅
Tongbao	*News*	通報
Tongli		同里
Tongmeng hui	Revolutionary Alliance	同盟會
Torishimari kisoku	Control Laws	取り締まり規則
toushen yu minzu zhanzheng zhi panwo		投身於民族戰爭之盤渦
Trimetrical Classic	*Sanzi jing*	三字經
Tuhua ribao	*Daily Pictorial*	圖畫日報

Twelve World Heroines	*Sekai jûni joketshu, Shijie shier nüjie*	世界十二女傑
Vernacular [Journal]	*Baihua*	白話
wai		外
Waicheng nüxue chuanxi suo	Outer City Institute for Women's Education	外成女學傳習所
Wan Chengcang (fl. 1830)		萬承蒼
Wang		王
Wang Anshi (1021–86)		王安石
Wang Anyi (b. 1954)		王安忆
Wang Caipin (d. 1893)		王采蘋
Wang Changguo (1880–1949)		王昌國
Wang Duanshu (1621–after 1701)		王端淑
Wang Geng (fl. 1600)		王庚
"Wang haichao"		望海潮
Wang Jiemu (fl. 1870)		汪節母
Wang Jingwei (1883–1944)		汪精衞
Wang Ling (Former Han dynasty)		王陵
Wang Qi (Spring and Autumn period)		汪踦
Wang shi (name of wives of both Wei Jingyu and Zhao Zhiyi)		王氏
Wang Tingzhen (1757–1827)		汪廷珍
Wang Wan (fl. 1700)		汪琬
Wang Xizhi (ca. 303–61)		王羲之
Wang Yangming (1472–1528)		王陽明
Wang Yifang (615–69)		王義方
Wang Zhaoyuan (1763–1851)		王照圓

Wang zhenfu [liefu]　　　　　　　　　王貞婦 [烈婦]
　　(fl. ca. 1260)

Wang Zhong (1744–94)　　　　　　　　汪中

Wang Zhu (fl. 1900)　　　　　　　　　王朱

wanliannuoli　　　　　　　　　　　頑廉懦立

"Wansheng gongchang　　　　　　　　晚省公娼妨礙女學之交涉
　　fang'ai nüxue zhi
　　jiaoshe"

wanxin　　　　　　　　　　　　　剜心

Wanyan Yun Zhu　　　　　　　　　　完顏惲珠

Wei Cheng　　　　　　　　　　　　韋逞

Wei Chengbo [style name,　　　　　　魏程搏 [息園; 蓮裳]
　　Xiyuan; courtesy name,
　　Lianshang] (fl. 1908)

Wei furen (272–349)　　　　　　　　衛夫人

Wei Jingqing　　　　　　　　　　　魏鏡情 [泉生]
　　[Quansheng] (fl. 1860)

Wei Jingyu (Tang　　　　　　　　　衛敬瑜
　　dynasty)

Wei Pei (1879–1900)　　　　　　　　魏裴

Wei Tingyu (fl. 1890)　　　　　　　魏廷玉

Wei Zhaoting　　　　　　　　　　　魏召亭

"Weimu zhi quanxian"　　　　　　　為母之權限

"Weishi jia"　　　　　　　　　　　魏世家

Wen (fl. 1140 BCE)　　　　　　　　文

Wen Huang　　　　　　　　　　　溫璜

Wen shi muxun　　　　　*Recorded Teachings*　溫氏母訓
　　　　　　　　　　　　of the Mother of
　　　　　　　　　　　　Mr. Wen Huang

wenji　　　　　　　　　　　　　文集

wenming　　　　　　　　　　　文明

wenming jiehun　　　　　　　　　文明結婚

wenming jinbu zhi shi　　　　　　文明進步之時

wenming nü xuesheng　　　　　　文明女學生

Wenming shuju　　　　　Progressive Press　文明書局

wenren		聞人
Wentong shuju	Wentong Press	文通書局
"Wenyi"		文藝
"Wenyuan"		文苑
Willard, Frances (1839–98)	Fulanzhisi, Weinade	扶蘭志斯, 維納德
Women's Eastern Times	*Funü shibao*	婦女時報
Women's Instructions	*Nü xun*	女訓
"Women's Learning"	"Fuxue"	婦學
Women's School	Seijo gakkō	成女学校
Women's School of Purity and Progress	Zhenwen nü xuexiao	貞文女學校
Women's World	*Nüzi shijie*	女子世界
[Wordsworth,] Dorothy (1771–1855)	Duluose	獨羅瑟
Wu (fl. 1122 BCE)		武
Wu furen (fl. 180)		吳夫人
Wu Jin		吳晉
Wu Mengban (d. 1901)		吳孟班
Wu Mulan (fl. 1912)		吳木蘭
Wu Qide (fl. 1905)		吳其德
Wu Sangui (1612–78)		吳三桂
Wu shuang pu	*A Record of Famous Personages*	無雙譜
Wu Weihe (b. 1970)		吳玮禾
Wu Zhihui (1865–1953)		吳稚暉
Wuben nüshu, Wuben nüxiao	School of Fundamental Women's Learning	務本女塾，務本女校
Wujiang		吳江
Wuling		武陵
wulun		五倫
Wuxi baihua bao	*Wuxi Vernacular Journal*	無錫白話報
Wuyue hua		五月花
Xi furen (fl. 535)		洗夫人

Xiahou shi (Han dynasty)		夏候氏
Xiang		湘
Xiangfu		相夫
Xiangshan nü xuexiao	Xiangshan Girls' School	香山女學校
"Xiangyin jiuyi"		鄉飲酒義
xianmu		賢母
Xiao Chaogui (1820–52)		蕭朝貴
Xiao fumu		孝父母
Xiao jing	*Classic of Filiality*	孝經
Xiao Sanniang [Su Sanniang] (ca. 1830–ca. 1854)		蕭三娘 [蘇三娘]
Xiao xue	*Elementary Learning*	小學
Xiao Yin (fl. 1904)		篠驪
xiaobao		小報
Xiaofang		小芳
Xie Daoyun (fl. 350)		謝道韞
Xie Wuliang (fl. 1916)		謝無量
xin		新
Xin shi		辛氏
Xin shitou ji	*The New Story of the Stone*	新石頭記
Xingshi huabao	*Awakening Pictorial*	醒世畫報
xingyi		行誼
Xinmin congbao	*New People's Miscellany*	新民叢報
Xiong Xiling (1870–1937)		熊希齡
xiucai		秀才
Xixiang ji	*The Story of the Western Wing*	西廂記
Xixue Zhongyuan		西學中源
Xu Chuanlin (fl. 1908)		徐傳霖
Xu lienü zhuan	*Continued Arrayed Traditions of Women's Lives*	續列女傳

Xu Wei (1521–93)		徐渭
Xu Xilin (d. 1907)		徐錫麟
Xu Yunhua (fl. 1907)		徐蘊華
Xuan bao	*Digest Magazine*	選報
Xuan of Wei's wife	Xuan Wei furen	衛宣夫人
Xuantong		宣統
xue		學
Xue Baochai		薛寶釵
Xue bu	Education Board	學部
Xue bu tushuju shoushuchu	Book Sales Division of the Education Board	學部圖書局售書處
Xuli hui	Widow Relief Association	恤嫠會
xuli tang		恤嫠堂
Xun Guan (fl. ca. 350)		荀灌
xungen		寻根
xunguo		殉國
xunli shouyi		循禮守義
Xunxi nüxue	Xunxi Girls' School	潯溪女學
xuyan jia		虛言家
Ya		雅
yagasuri		矢絣
yan		言
Yan Shigu (581–645)		顏師古
Yan Zhongcheng (fl. 1750)		顏中承
Yang Feng (Han dynasty)		楊豐
Yang Gonglan (fl. 1903)		楊紉蘭
Yang Jisheng [Zhongming] (1516–55)		楊繼盛 [忠愍]
Yang shi (fl. 1280)		楊氏
Yang Xiang (Han dynasty)		楊香
Yang Xiuqing (d. 1856)		楊秀清
yang xuetang		洋學堂
Yanzi		晏子

Yaoniang (ca. 930)		窅娘
Ye Xiaoluan (1616–32)		葉小鸞
yecha		夜叉
yeman		野蠻
yi		義
Yi jing	*Book of Changes*	易經
Yi li	*Decorum Ritual*	儀禮
yifang		義方
Yifang nüxiao	Yifang Girls' School	藝芳女校
"Yili"		譯例
"Yilie"		義烈
yilie kefeng		義烈可風
yimei zhi lijiao		懿嫩之禮教
Ying Erzi (ca. 300 BCE)		嬰兒子
Ying Liangzhi (1867–1926)		英斂之
yingci		英雌
yingxiong		英雄
Yingxiong zhuan	*Biographies of Heroes* [Plutarch's *Parallel Lives*]	英雄傳
Yixue guan	Translation Study Bureau	譯學館
yongjiang		勇將
you qiuquan zhi hui		有求全之毀
Youai		友愛
youxia		遊俠
Yu Ji (1272–1348)		虞集
Yu Kaifu [Xin] (513–81)		庾開府 [信]
yu Ying		育英
Yu Ze (fl. 341)		虞澤
"Yuan dan"		元旦
Yuan Ji [Suwen] (fl. 1730)		袁機 [素文]
Yuan Mei (1716–98)		袁枚
Yuan Yishan (1190–1257)		元遺山
Yuan Youan (fl. 1900)		袁幼安

Yue Fei (1103–41)		岳飛
Yue Wang gou jian (pre–Han dynasty)		越王勾踐)
yueshi		閱世
Yuhuan		玉環
"Yundong"		運動
yuying		育嬰
yuyingtang		育嬰堂
Zeng Chuangang (d. ca. 1903)		曾傳綱
Zeng Guofan (1811–72)		曾國藩
Zeng nüshi yixue quanshu	*Complete Medical Works of Madame Zeng*	曾女士醫學全書
Zeng Shufan		曾樹蕃
Zeng Yi (1857–1917)		曾懿
"Zengzi Asked"	"Zengzi wen"	曾子問
"Zengzi wen"	"Zengzi Asked"	曾子問
Zhan Kai [Shiqi zhai] (fl. 1907)		詹墍 [思綺齋]
Zhang furen (fl. 1550)		張夫人
Zhang Hanying [Huifen] (1872–1915)		張漢英 [慧芬]
Zhang Qieying (1792–after 1841)		張緙英
Zhang Wenbao (Qing dynasty)		章文寶
Zhang Wenhu (1808–85)		張文虎
Zhang Xiangguo (fl. 1909)		張相國
Zhang Xuecheng (1738–1801)		章學誠
Zhang Zhongshan (fl. 1905)		張仲山
Zhang Zongxiang [Zhonghe] (1877–ca. 1940)		章宗祥 [仲和]
zhanggu		掌故

Zhanguo ce	*Intrigues of the Warring States*	戰國策
Zhao Biniang (d. ca. 1860)		趙碧娘
Zhao shi (d. 1861)		趙氏
Zhao Ziyi		趙子乙
"Zhaoce"		趙策
Zhejiang tongzhi	*Zhejiang Gazetteer*	浙江通志
Zhen Beizi (fl. 1908)		振貝子
Zheng Guanying (1842–1922)		鄭觀應
Zheng Shanguo (572–629)		鄭善果
Zheng shi (fl. 750)		鄭氏
Zheng shi (fl. 1010)		鄭氏
Zheng Yizong (Tang dynasty)		鄭義宗
zhenjie		貞潔
"Zhenjie"		貞節
Zhenjie tang	Hall of Virtue	貞節堂
zhennü		貞女
Zhenwen nü xuexiao	Women's School of Purity and Progress	貞文女學校
zhenxiao		貞孝
zhenxin yili		貞心毅力
Zhenze		震澤
zhi		質
zhicheng zhi dao keyi ganshen		至誠之道可以感神
Zhili diyi nüzi shifan xuetang	Zhili Number One Women's Normal School	直隸第一女子師範學堂
zhisheng		至聖
zhishu		知書
Zhixin bao	*Know the New News*	知新報
zhongda de nüzi wenti		重大的女子問題

Zhongguo furen hui	Chinese Women's Association	中國婦人會
Zhongguo liu xuesheng huiguan	Chinese Overseas Student Hall	中國留學生會館
Zhongguo liu-Ri nü xuesheng hui	Association of Chinese Female Students in Japan	中國留日女學生會
Zhongguo nübao	*Chinese Women's Journal*	中國女報
"Zhongguo nüjie xiao yuefu"		中國女傑小樂府
"Zhongguo nüjie yiyongjia Ti Ying zhuan"		中國女界義勇家緹縈傳
Zhongguo nü xuetang	Chinese Women's School	中國女學堂
Zhongguo xin nühao	*China's New Heroines*	中國新女豪
Zhongguo xin nüjie zazhi	*Magazine of the New Chinese Woman*	中國新女界雜誌
Zhonghua quanguo funü lianhe hui	All China Women's Federation	中华全国妇女联合会
"Zhong-wai xin lienü zhuan"	"New Chinese and Foreign Arrayed Traditions of Women's Lives"	中外新列女傳
Zhongxing ribao	*Zhongxing Daily Newspaper*	中興日報
Zhongzhen hou		忠貞候
zhongzu zhuyi		種族主義
zhongzu zhuyi ciji zhe		種族主義刺激者
Zhou li	*The Rites of Zhou*	周禮
"Zhou shi san mu"		周室三母
Zhu		朱
Zhu Jingyi (b. 1888)		朱敬儀
zhu wo sha yizhong bao tongzhong		助我殺異種保同種
Zhu Xi (1130–1200)		朱熹
Zhu Yongzhen (fl. 1904)		朱永珍
Zhu Yizun (1629–1709)		朱彝尊

Zhuang Yu (fl. 1907)		莊俞
zhuzao		鑄造
zishi		子師
"Ziti xiaozhao nanzhuang"		自題小照男裝
ziyou jiehun		自由結婚
ziyou zhi shuo		自由之說
zuguo zhi nü jun guomin		祖國之女軍國民
zuixin		最新
Zuo Fen (255–300)		左芬
Zuo Xixuan (fl. 1850)		左錫璇
Zuoxin she	Society for Renewal	作新社
Zuo zhuan	*Commentary of Mr. Zuo*	左傳

Bibliography

Abe Hiroshi 阿部洋. *Chūgoku no kindai kyōiku to Meiji Nihon*中国の近代教育と明治日本 (Modern Chinese education and Meiji Japan). Tokyo: Fukumura shuppan kabushiki gaisha, 1990.

———. ed. *Nit-Chū kyōiku bunka kōryū to masatsu: Senzen Nihon no zai-Ka kyōiku jigyō* 日中教育文化交流と摩擦：戦前日本の在華教育事業 (Sino-Japanese educational and cultural exchange and conflict: Japanese educational activities in prewar China). Tokyo: Daiichi shobō, 1983.

"Aiguo nüzi Ruoan Dake de gushi" 愛國女子若安達克的故事 (The story of the patriotic girl, Joan of Arc). *BJNB* (July 21, 1906).

Allen, Joseph R. "Dressing and Undressing the Chinese Woman Warrior." *positions: east asia cultures critique* 4:2 (Fall 1996), 343–79.

Anderson, Benedict. *Imagined Communities: Reflections on the Origin and Spread of Nationalism*. New York: Verso, 1983.

Asakura Kaseki 朝倉禾積, ed. *Fukkoku joketsu Joan jitsuden: Jiyū no shinka* 仏国女傑如安実伝一自由の新花 (A true biography of the French heroine Joan: A new flower of freedom). Tokyo: Chōbōdō, 1886.

Bailey, Paul. *Reform the People: Changing Attitudes towards Popular Education in Early 20th Century China*. Vancouver: University of British Columbia Press, 1990.

———. "'Unharnessed Fillies': Discourse on the 'Modern' Female Student in Early Twentieth Century China." In Lo Jiu-jiung and Lu Miaw-fen, 327–57.

Baosu 保素. "Yongshi shi" 詠史詩 (An ode to history). *XNJZZ* 3 (Apr. 5, 1907), 131–32.

Barlow, Tani E. "International Feminism of the Future." *Signs* 25:4 (Summer 2000), 1099–1105.

———. *The Question of Women in Chinese Feminism*. Durham, NC: Duke University Press, 2004.

Barmé, Geremie R. *In the Red: On Contemporary Chinese Culture*. New York: Columbia University Press, 1999.

Beahan, Charlotte L. "Feminism and Nationalism in the Chinese Women's Press, 1902–1911." *Modern China* 1:4 (Oct. 1975), 379–416.

Beijing baike quanshu zongbianji weiyuan hui 北京百科全书总编辑委员会 (Editorial Compliation Committee of the Beijing Encyclopedia). *Beijing baike quanshu: Tongzhou juan* 北京百科全书：通州卷 (Beijing encyclopedia: Volume on Tongzhou). Beijing: Aolin pike chubanshe, 2001.

Bender, John, and David E. Wellbery. "Introduction." In *Chronotypes: The Construction of Time*, ed. John Bender and David E. Wellbery, 1–15. Stanford, CA: Stanford University Press, 1991.

Benjamin, Walter. "On the Concept of History." In *Walter Benjamin: Selected Writings, Volume 4, 1938–1940*, trans. Edmund Jephcott et al., ed. Howard Eiland and Michael W. Jennings, 389–400. Cambridge, MA: Belknap Press of Harvard University Press, 2003.

———. "Paris, Capital of the Nineteenth Century." In *Reflections: Essays, Aphorisms, Autobiographical Writings*, ed. Peter Demetz, 146–62. New York: Schocken Books, 1986.

Benveniste, Emile. *Problems in General Linguistics*. Trans. Mary Elizabeth Meek. Coral Gables, FL: University of Miami Press, 1971.

"Bi Ruan er gong diyin Kongshi" 畢阮二公締姻孔氏 (The Gentlemen Bi and Ruan are united in wedlock via Lady Kong). In Chen Kangqi, *Langqian jiwen chubi*, 1:1, 138–39.

Biaomeng bianyisuo 彪蒙編譯所 (Enlightenment Bureau for Compilation and Translation). *Nüzi fenlei chidu fanben* 女子分類尺牘範本 (Copybook of classified letters for girls and women). Beijing: Biaomeng shushe, 1908.

Birrel, Anne, trans. "A Peacock Southeast Flew." In *The Columbia Anthology of Traditional Chinese Literature*, ed. Victor Mair, 462–72. New York: Columbia University Press, 1994.

"Bolan huibao" 博覽彙報 (Exhibition report). *ZJC* 2 (Mar. 18, 1903), 133–35.

Boorman, Howard L. ed. *Biographical Dictionary of Republican China*. 4 vols. New York: Columbia University Press, 1967–70.

Booth, Marilyn. "The Egyptian Lives of Jeanne d'Arc." In *Remaking Women: Feminism and Modernity in the Middle East*, ed. Lila Abu-Lughod, 171–211. Princeton, NJ: Princeton University Press, 1998.

———. *May Her Likes Be Multiplied: Biography and Gender Politics in Egypt*. Berkeley: University of California Press, 2001.

———. "'May Her Likes Be Multiplied': 'Famous Women' Biography and Gendered Prescription in Egypt, 1892–1935." *Signs* 22:4 (1997), 827–90.

Bossler, Beverly. "*Final Instructions* by Yang Jisheng." In *Under Confucian Eyes: Writings on Gender in Chinese History*, ed. Susan Mann and Yu-yin Cheng, 119–32. Berkeley: University of California Press, 2001.

Bourdieu, Pierre. *Language and Symbolic Power*. Trans. Gino Raymond and Matthew Adamson, ed. John B. Thompson. Cambridge, MA: Harvard University Press, 1994.

———. *Masculine Domination*. Trans. Richard Nice. Stanford, CA: Stanford University Press, 2001.

———. *Outline of a Theory of Practice.* Trans. Richard Nice. Cambridge, Eng.: Cambridge University Press, 1993.

Bray, Francesca. *Technology and Gender: Fabrics of Power in Late Imperial China.* Berkeley: University of California Press, 1997.

Buck, David D. "Educational Modernization in Tsinan, 1899–1937." In *The City Between Two Worlds*, ed. Mark Elvin and G. W. Skinner, 171–212. Stanford, CA: Stanford University Press, 1974.

Buck-Morss, Susan. *The Dialectics of Seeing: Walter Benjamin and the Arcades Project.* Cambridge, MA: MIT Press, 1999.

"Buji Hangzhou Zhenwen nü xuexiao xiaozhang Huixing nüjie lishi" 補記杭州貞文女學校校長惠興女傑歷史 (Supplement to the history of the heroine Huixing, principal of the Women's School of Purity and Progress in Hangzhou). *STSB* (Feb. 8, 1906). Rpt. in *NQYDSL* 2, 1449–51.

Burton, Antoinette. *Burdens of History: British Feminists, Indian Women, and Imperial Culture, 1865–1915.* Chapel Hill: University of North Carolina Press, 1994.

Butler, Judith. *Gender Trouble: Feminism and Subversion of Identity.* New York: Routledge, 1990.

Bynum, Carolyn. "Women's Stories, Women's Symbols: A Critique of Victor Turner's Theory of Liminality." In *Fragmentation and Redemption: Essays on Gender and the Human Body in Medieval Religion*, 27–51. New York: Zone Books, 1992.

Cahill, James. "Passages of Felt Life: A Genre Shift in Ming-Qing Figure Painting." Unpublished paper.

Cai Dongsu 蔡东苏. "Qingmo Minchu de yibai qishi yu zhong baihua baokan" 清末民初的一百七十余种白话报刊 (Over 170 vernacular journals from the late Qing and early Republican periods). In *QKJS* 5, 493–546.

Cai Shangsi 蔡尚思. *Zhongguo lijiao sixiang shi* 中國禮教思想史 (An intellectual history of Chinese ritual teachings). Hong Kong: Zhonghua shuju, 1991.

Cai Yuanpei 蔡元培. "Wen Fang Junying zijin zhigan (yijiuersan nian qi yue ershiwu ri)" 聞方君英自盡志感一九二三年七月二十五日 (My feelings upon hearing about Fang Junying's suicide, July 25, 1923). In *Cai Yuanpei quanji* 蔡元培全集 (Collected works of Cai Yuanpei), ed. Gao Pingshu 高平叔, 4: 336–37. Beijing: Zhonghua shuju, 1984.

Cai Yun 蔡允. "Xuyan" 緒言 (Preface). In Alice R. James, 1a–b.

Calhoun, Craig. *Nationalism.* Buckingham, Eng.: Open University Press, 1997.

"Canguan Neicheng nüxue chuanxisuo ji" 參觀內城女學傳習所記 (Record of a visit to the Inner City Institute of Women's Education). *STSB* (May 17, 1907).

Cao Rujin 曹汝錦. "Aiguo ji ziai" 愛國及自愛 (Patriotism and self-love). *JS* 3 (June 25, 1903), 158 [0588].

Carlitz, Katherine. "The Daughter, the Singing-Girl, and the Seduction of Suicide." In Ropp, Zamperini, and Zurndorfer, 22–46.

———. "Desire and Writing in the Late Ming Play 'Parrot Island.'" In *Writing Women in Late Imperial China*, ed. Ellen Widmer and Kang-i Sun Chang, 100–130. Stanford, CA: Stanford University Press, 1997.

————. "Mixed Messages in Late Ming Biographies of Exemplary Women." Paper presented at the seminar on "Exemplary Women in Texts and Contexts: The Lienü Tradition from Yuan to Late Qing," Southern California China Colloquium, Center for Chinese Studies, UCLA, Feb. 2001.

————. "Shrines, Governing-Class Identity and the Cult of Widow Fidelity in Mid-Ming Jiangnan." *Journal of Asian Studies* 56:3 (Aug. 1997), 612–40.

————. "The Social Uses of Female Virtue in Late Ming Editions of the *Lienü zhuan*." *Late Imperial China* 12:2 (Dec. 1991), 117–52.

"Chai Shao/Pingyang gongzhu" 柴紹/平陽公主. *Jiu Tang shu* 舊唐書 (Old History of the Tang Dynasty), comp. Liu Xu 劉昫, 58: "Liezhuan" 8: 2314–15. Taipei: Hongshi chubanshe, 1977.

Chakrabarty, Dipesh. *Habitations of Modernity: Essays in the Wake of Subaltern Studies*. Chicago: University of Chicago Press, 2002.

Chang, Kang-i Sun. "A Guide to Ming-Ch'ing Anthologies of Female Poetry and Their Selection Strategies." *Gest Library Journal* 5:2 (1992), 119–60.

————. "Ming-Qing Women Poets and the Notions of 'Talent' and 'Morality.'" In *Culture and State in Chinese History: Conventions, Accommodations, Critiques*, ed. Theodore Huters, R. Bin Wong, and Pauline Yu, 236–58. Stanford, CA: Stanford University Press, 1997.

————. "Women's Poetic Witnessing: Examples from the Late Ming and Late Qing." Unpublished paper.

Chang, Kang-i Sun, and Haun Saussy, eds. *Women Writers of Traditional China: An Anthology of Poetry and Criticism*. Stanford, CA: Stanford University Press, 1999.

"Chang li nüxue" 倡立女學 (Initiative for the establishment of women's education). *STSB* (Sept. 10, 1905).

Chang So-an. "Murder, Suicide, and Ritual Orthodoxy: Evidential Studies in the 19th Century." Paper presented at the Association for Asian Studies annual meeting, Washington D.C., Apr. 2002.

———— [張壽安]. "Shiba shijiu shiji Zhongguo chuantong hunyin guannian de xiandai zhuanhua" 十八, 十九世紀中國傳統婚姻觀念的現代轉化 ("The Rectification of the Orthodox Concept of Marriage in Late Imperial China"). *Jindai Zhongguo funü shi yanjiu* 近代中國婦女史研究 8 (June 2000), 43–87.

Chartier, Roger. *Cultural History: Between Practices and Representations*. Trans. Lydia G. Cochran. Ithaca, NY: Cornell University Press, 1988.

Chatterjee, Partha. *The Nation and Its Fragments: Colonial and Postcolonial Histories*. Princeton, NJ: Princeton University Press, 1993.

Chen Baoquan 陳寶泉, and Gao Buying 高步瀛. *Guomin bidu* 國民必讀 (Citizens' reader). 2 vols. Shanghai: Nanyang guanshuju, 1905.

Chen Chi-yun. "Immanental Human Beings in Transcendent Time: Epistemological Basis of Pristine Chinese Historical Consciousness." In Huang Chun-chieh and Henderson, 45–73.

Chen Dongyuan 陳東原. *Zhongguo funü shenghuo shi* 中國婦女生活史 (A history of the lives of Chinese women). Shanghai: Shangwu yinshuguan, 1928. Rpt. 1937.

"Chen gainü shouzhen" 陳丐女守貞 (Beggar girl Chen preserves her virtue). *QBLC*, 33–34.

"Chen Huizhen buyuan wei chang er si" 陳惠貞不願為娼而死 (Chen Huizhen died because she was not willing to become a singing girl). *QBLC*, 85.

Ch'en, Jerome. "The Chinese Communist Movement to 1927." In *The Cambridge History of China*. Vol. 12, *Republican China, 1912–1949, Part 1*, ed. John King Fairbank, 505–26. Cambridge, Eng.: Cambridge University Press, 1983.

Chen Kangqi 陳康祺. *Langqian jiwen chubi, erbi, sanbi* 郎潛紀聞初筆二筆三筆 (Chronicles of an unpromoted official, parts 1, 2, 3), comp. Jin Shi 晉石. Beijing: Zhonghua shuju, 1984.

———. *Langqian jiwen sibi* 郎潛紀聞四筆 (Chronicles of an unpromoted official, part 4), comp. Zhang Wenling 張文玲. Beijing: Zhonghua shuju, 1990.

———. "Wang shi jiemu lou" 汪氏節母樓 (Lady Wang's building for chaste mothers). In Chen Kangqi, *Langqian jiwen chubi*, 2:2, 345.

Chen Pingyuan 陳平原, and Xia Xiaohong 夏曉虹, eds. *Tuxiang wan-Qing* 图像晚清 (Images of the late Qing). Tianjin: Baihua wenyi chubanshe, 2001.

Chen Shi-hsiang. "An Innovation in Chinese Biographical Writing." *Far Eastern Quarterly* 13 (Nov. 1953), 49–62.

Chen Xiefen 陳擷芬. "Ji Wuben nüxuetang" 記務本女學堂 (Record of School of Fundamental Women's Learning). *Nübao* 女報 4 (1902). Rpt. in *XZSL* 2:2, 598–99.

———. [Chunan nüzi 楚南女子]. "Shijie shi nüjie yanyi" 世界十女傑演義 (Tales from *Ten world heroines*). *Nüxue bao* 女學報 4 (Nov. 1903), 55–58.

Chen Yan 陳衍. "Lienü zhuan jizhu fanli" 列女傳集注凡例 (Introduction to collected annotations to the *Arrayed Traditions of Women's Lives*). In Xiao Daoguan 蕭道管, *Lienü zhuan jizhu* 列女傳集注 (Collected annotations to the *Arrayed Traditions of Women's Lives*), 1a–2a. n.p. Preface dated 1892, published after 1907.

Chen Yan'an 陳彥安. "Chū-Nichi Shina shō kōshi fujin yori no raijō" 駐日支那章公使婦人よりの来状 (Letter from the wife of Chinese minister Zhang, resident in Japan). Jissen joshi daigaku toshokan, Shimoda Utako kankei shiryō, file no. 743 (1918).

———. "Quan nüzi liuxue shuo" 勸女子留學說 (Exhortation for female overseas study). *JS* 3 (June 1903), 155–56 [0585–86].

Chen Yiyi 陳以益. "Nanzun nübei yu xianmu liangqi" 男尊女卑與賢母良妻 (The view that males are superior to females and "wise mothers and good wives"). *Nübao* 女報 1:2 (1909). Rpt. in *XZSL* 2:2, 681–83.

———. "Nülun" 女論 (On women). *Nübao* 女報, supplement (August 1909), 1–29.

Cheng, Eileen J. "Gendered Spectacles: Lu Xun on Gazing at Women and Other Pleasures." *Modern Chinese Literature and Culture* 16:1 (June 2004), 1–35.

———. "The Menacing Public Body: Qiu Jin's Troubling Gender." Paper delivered at the annual meeting of the Association for Asian Studies, New York, Mar. 2003.

"Cheng taifuren zhi naipin" 程太夫人之耐貧 (Mother Cheng endures poverty). *THRB* 20 (Sept. 4, 1909), 3 [1:231].

Cheng, Weikun. "The Challenge of the Actresses: Female Performers and the Cultural Alternatives in Early Twentieth Century Beijing and Tianjin." *Modern China* 22:2 (Apr. 1996), 197–233.

———. "Going Public through Education: Female Reformers and Girls' Schools in Late Qing Beijing." *Late Imperial China* 21:1 (June 2000), 107–44.

Cheng, Yu-yin, trans. "Selected Writings by Luo Rufang (1515–1588)." In *Under Confucian Eyes: Writings on Gender in Chinese History*, ed. Susan Mann and Yu-yin Cheng, 102–16. Berkeley: University of California Press, 2001.

Chow, Esther Ngan-ling. "Making Waves, Moving Mountains: Reflections on Beijing '95 and Beyond." *Signs* 22:1 (Autumn 1996), 185–92.

Chow Kai-wing. *The Rise of Confucian Ritualism in Late Imperial China: Ethics, Classics, and Lineage Discourse*. Stanford, CA: Stanford University Press, 1994.

Chow, Rey. *Women and Chinese Modernity: The Politics of Reading Between West and East*. Minneapolis: University of Minnesota Press, 1991.

"Chuangshe liuxue nüzi sucheng shifan yu Dongjing" 創設留學女子速成師範於東京 (The establishment of an overseas female student accelerated teacher-training course in Tokyo). *SB* (Feb. 26, 1905).

"Chuangshe wanguo Hongshizi kanhufuduizhe Natinggeer furen zhuan" 創設萬國紅十字看護婦隊者奈挺格爾夫人傳 (A biography of the founder of the International Red Cross Nurses' Team, Ms. Nightingale). *XNJZZ* 1, 2 (Feb. 5, Mar. 5, 1907), 59–64, 71–74.

Chubei yingci 楚北英雌. "Zhina nüquan fenyan" 支那女權憤言 (Indignation over the issue of Chinese women's rights). *HB* 2 (Feb. 27, 1903), 95–96 [268 (*sic.*)–70].

Cohen, Paul A. *History in Three Keys: The Boxers as Event, Experience, and Myth*. New York: Columbia University Press, 1997.

Cong Xiaoping. *Teachers' Schools and the Making of the Modern Chinese Nation-State, 1897–1937*. Vancouver: University of British Columbia Press, 2007.

Crossley, Pamela Kyle. *Orphan Warriors: Three Manchu Generations and the End of the Qing World*. Princeton, NJ: Princeton University Press, 1990.

Dai Jinhua. "Rewriting Chinese Women: Gender Production and Cultural Space in the Eighties and Nineties." In *Spaces of Their Own: Women's Public Sphere in Transnational China*, ed. Mayfair Mei-hui Yang, 191–206. Minneapolis: University of Minnesota Press, 1999.

Dai Li 戴禮. *Nü xiaoxue* 女小學 (Elementary learning for girls and women). Beijing: Beijing Hufanqiao jinghua yinshuju, 1908.

"Daoting yushuo" 道聽途說 (Rumors). *Xinmin congbao* 新民叢報 (Mar. 10, 1902).

"Datong shijie zhi nannü" 大同世界之男女 (Males and females in a world of great unity). *THRB* 66 (Oct. 20, 1909).

Despeux, Catherine. "Bien débuter dans la vie: De l'éducation prénatale en Chine." In *Éducation et Instruction en Chine*, ed. Catherine Despeux and Christine Nguyen-Tri, vol. 1, 61–98. Paris: Peters, 2003.

Dikötter, Frank. *Imperfect Conceptions: Medical Knowledge, Birth Defects and Eugenics in China*. New York: Columbia University Press, 1998.

Dillon, E. J. "The Chinese Wolf and the European Lamb." *Contemporary Review* 79 (Jan.–June 1901), 1–31.

[Ding] Chuwo 丁初我. "Nüzi shijie songci" 女子世界頌詞 (Praise for the *Women's World*). *NZSJ* 1 (Jan. 1904).

Ding Yizhuang 定宜庄. "Qingdai funü yu liangxing guanxi" 清代妇女与两性关系 (Qing women and gender relations). In *Zhongguo lishi zhong de funü yu xingbie* 中国历史中的妇女与性别 (Women and gender in Chinese history), ed. Du Fangqin 杜芳琴, 350–416. Tianjin: Tianjin renmin chubanshe, 2004.

———. "Zhenjie, gexing, yu caigan: Qingchao ruguan hou Manzu funü de bianhua he tedian" 贞节，个性，与才干：清朝入关后满族妇女的变化和特点 ("Virginity, Personality, and Ability: Changes and Characteristics of Man Women After the Qing Dynasty Entering Shanhaiguan"). In *Shehui xingbie minzu shequ fazhan yanjiu wenji* 社会性别民族社区发展研究文集 ("Researches on Gender, Ethnicity, and Community Development"), ed. Zhang Xiao 张晓 et al., 467–79. Guiyang: Guizhou renmin chubanshe, 2003.

Dong Jiazun 董家遵. "Lidai jiefu lienü de tongji" 历代节妇烈女的统计 (Statistics on chaste women and heroic girls through the ages, [1937]). Rpt. in *Shoujie, zaijia, chanzu ji qita: Zhongguo gudai funü shenghuomian mianguan* 守节在家缠足及其他－中国古代妇女生活面面观 (Chastity, remarriage, footbinding, etc.: A view of women's lives in ancient China), ed. Shaanxi renmin chubanshe, 110–16. Xi'an: Shaanxi renmin chubanshe, 1990.

Dong Shou 董壽. "Xing nüxue yi" 興女學議 (Argument to promote women's education). *Nübao* 女報 5 (Sept. 2, 1902), 4–7. Rpt. in *XZSL* 2:2, 570–72.

"Dongyang nüquan kuozhang" 東洋女權擴張 (The expansion of women's rights in Japan). *HB* 2 (May 27, 1903), 99 [273].

Dooling, Amy D., and Kristina Torgeson, eds. *Writing Women in Modern China: An Anthology of Women's Literature from the Early Twentieth Century*. New York: Columbia University Press, 1998.

Drucker, Alison R. "The Influence of Western Women on the Anti-Footbinding Movement, 1840–1911." In *Women in China: Current Directions in Historical Scholarship*, ed. Richard W. Guisso and Stanley Johannesen, 179–99. Youngstown, NY: Philo Press, 1981.

Du Chengshu 杜成淑成淑. "Cibei, cibei" 慈悲慈悲 (Mercy, mercy). *NZSJ* n.d. (after January 1906), 119–20.

Du, Fangqin, and Susan Mann. "Competing Claims on Womanly Virtue in Late Imperial China." In *Women and Confucian Cultures in Premodern China, Korea, and Japan*, ed. Dorothy Ko, Jahyun Kim Haboush, and Joan R. Piggot, 219–47. Berkeley: University of California Press, 2003.

Duara, Prasenjit. "De-constructing the Chinese Nation." In Unger, 31–55.

———. "The Discourse of Civilization and Pan-Asianism." *Journal of World History* 12 (2001), 99–130.

———. "The Regime of Authenticity: Timelessness, Gender, and National History in Modern China." *History and Theory: Studies in the Philosophy of History* 37:3 (1998), 287–308.

———. *Rescuing History from the Nation: Questioning Narratives of Modern China.* Chicago: University of Chicago Press, 1995.

———. *Sovereignty and Authenticity: Manchukuo and the East Asian Modern.* Lanham, MD: Rowman and Littlefield, 2003.

Durrant, Stephen W. *The Cloudy Mirror: Tension and Conflict in the Writings of Sima Qian.* Albany: State University of New York Press, 1995.

"E Fu Duan Wushuai quan funü wu zai chanzu shuo" 鄂撫端午帥勸婦女勿再纏足說 (Governor Duanfang of Hubei exhorts women to stop binding their feet). *STSB* (May 27, 1902).

Ebrey, Patricia Buckley, trans. "The *Book of Filial Piety for Women* Attributed to a Woman Née Zheng (ca. 730)." In *Under Confucian Eyes: Writings on Gender in Chinese History*, ed. Susan Mann and Yu-yin Cheng, 47–69. Berkeley: University of California Press, 2001.

———. *The Inner Quarters: Marriage and the Lives of Chinese Women in the Sung Period.* Berkeley: University of California Press, 1993.

Edgren, Sören. "The *Ching-ying hsiao-sheng* and Traditional Illustrated Biographies of Women." *Gest Library Journal: Special Issue, East Asian Women: Materials and Library Research* 5:2 (Winter 1992), 161–74.

Edwards, Louise P. *Men and Women in Qing China: Gender in* The Red Chamber Dream. Honolulu: University of Hawai'i Press, 2001.

———. "Women in the People's Republic of China: New Challenges to the Gender Narrative." In *Women in Asia: Tradition, Modernity, and Globalisation*, ed. Louise Edwards and Mina Roces, 59–84, Ann Arbor: University of Michigan Press, 2000.

Elliott, Mark C. "Manchu Widows and Ethnicity in Qing China." *Comparative Studies in Society and History* 41:1 (Jan. 1999), 33–71.

Elman, Benjamin A. *A Cultural History of Civil Examinations in Late Imperial China.* Berkeley: University of California Press, 2000.

———. *From Philosophy to Philology: Intellectual and Social Aspects of Change in Late Imperial China.* Cambridge, MA: Harvard University Asia Center, 1990.

Elman, Benjamin A., and Alexander Woodside. "Introduction." In *Education and Society in Late Imperial China 1600–1900*, ed. Benjamin A. Elman and Alexander Woodside, 1–15. Berkeley: University of California Press, 1994.

Elvin, Mark. "Female Virtue and the State in China." In Mark Elvin, *Another History: Essays on China from a European Perspective*, 302–51. Canberra: Wild Peony, 1996.

"Er qinü shou yi quanzhen" 二奇女守一全貞 (Two exceptional women maintain their virtue). *QBLC*, 6.

"An Evening with Ou Ning." www.moma.org/exhibitions/film_media/2006/MediaScope_2006.html.

Fang Cheng 方城. "Xiangji Waicheng nüxue chuanxisuo ba da tese" 詳記外城女學傳習所八大特色 (A detailed record of eight important particularities of the Beijing Outer City Institute for Women's Education). *STSB* (Dec. 25, 26, 1906). Rpt. in *NQYDSL* 2, 1127–30.

Fang Hanqi 方汉奇. "Jindai Zhongguo de nü xinwen gongzuozhe" 近代中国的女新闻工作者 (Modern Chinese female workers in the field of journalism). *Zhongguo jizhe* 中国记者 6 (1987), 19–21.

Fang Junji 方君笄. "Xing nüxue yi fu nüquan shuo" 興女學以復女權說 (Promote women's education in order to recover women's rights). *JS* 3 (June 25, 1903), 157 [587].

Fang Liusheng 方瀏生. *Nüzi guowen duben* 女子國文讀本 (Chinese reader for girls). Shanghai: Shangwu yinshuguan, 1905.

"Fang Taigongren shuai san nü toujiang" 方太恭人率三女投江 ([The honorable Lady] Fang leads her three daughters to jump in the river). *QBLC*, 68.

Fang Zhaoying 房兆楹, ed. *Qingmo Minchu yangxue xuesheng timing lu chuji* 清末民初 洋學學生題名錄初輯 (First edition of a roster of late Qing and early Republican overseas students). Taipei: Zhongyang yanjiuyuan, Jindai shi yanjiusuo, 1962.

Felski, Rita. *The Gender of Modernity*. Cambridge, MA: Harvard University Press, 1995.

Feng Erkang 冯尔康. *Qingdai renwu zhuanji shiliao yanjiu* 清代人物传记史料研究 (A study of historical biographical materials for the Qing dynasty). Beijing: Shangwu yinshuguan, 2001.

Feng Ziyou 馮自由. "Nü yishi Zhang Zhujun" 女醫士張竹君 (The female doctor Zhang Zhujun). In *Geming yishi* 革命逸史 (Anecdotal history of the revolution) 2. Rpt. in *NQYDSL* 2, 1375–79.

Fogel, Joshua A. *Nakae Ushikichi in China: The Mourning of Spirit*. Cambridge, MA: Council on East Asian Studies, Harvard University, 1989.

———, ed. *The Role of Japan in Liang Qichao's Introduction of Modern Western Civilization to China*. Berkeley: Institute of East Asian Studies, University of California, Berkeley, 2004.

Fogel, Joshua A., and Peter Zarrow, eds. *Imagining the People: Chinese Intellectuals and the Concept of Citizenship, 1890–1920*. Armonk, NY: M. E. Sharpe, 1997.

Fong, Grace S. "Alternative Modernities, or a Classical Woman of Modern China: The Challenging Trajectory of Lü Bicheng's (1883–1943) Life and Song Lyrics." In Fong, Qian, and Zurndorfer, 12–59.

———. "Female Hands: Embroidery as a Knowledge Field in Women's Everyday Life in Late Imperial and Early Republican China." *Late Imperial China* 25:1 (June 2004), 1–58.

———. "Signifying Bodies: The Cultural Significance of Suicide Writings by Women in Ming-Qing China." In Ropp, Zamperini, and Zurndorfer, 105–42.

Fong, Grace S., Nanxiu Qian, and Harriet Zurndorfer, eds. *Beyond Tradition and Modernity: Gender, Genre, and Cosmopolitanism in Late Qing China*. Leiden: Brill, 2004.

Foqun 佛群. "Nü xuexiao" 女學校 (Girls' schools). *XNJZZ* 3 (Apr. 5, 1907), 137–40.

————. "Xing nüxue shuo" 興女學說 (On promoting women's education). *XN-JZZ* 3 (Apr. 5, 1907), 11–14.

Foucault, Michel. *Discipline and Punish: The Birth of the Prison.* Trans. Alan Sheridan. New York: Vintage, 1979.

————. *Madness and Civilization: A History of Insanity in the Age of Reason.* Trans. Richard Howard. New York: Vintage, 1988.

————. *Technologies of the Self: A Seminar with Michel Foucault.* Ed. Luther H. Martin, Huck Gutman, and Patrick H. Hutton. Amherst: University of Massachusetts Press, 1988.

Fu Xiongxiang 傅熊湘, ed. *Liling xiang tuzhi* 醴陵鄉土志 (Liling township gazetteer). Rpt., Taipei: Zhengwen chubanshe, 1975.

"Funü touhe" 婦女投河 (A woman throws herself into the river). *Xiaolin bao* 笑林報 (July 2, 1907).

"Funü yi sheng jiaotache zhi minjie" 婦女亦乘腳踏車之敏捷 (Women are also adept at riding bicycles). *THRB* 104, 7 [3:43].

"*Funü zazhi* yanjiu zhuanhao" 《婦女雜誌》研究專號 (Special issue on the *Ladies' Journal*). *Jindai Zhongguo funü shi yanjiu* 近代中國婦女史研究 12 (2004).

Furth, Charlotte. "Concepts of Pregnancy, Childbirth and Infancy in Ch'ing Dynasty China." *Journal of Asian Studies* 46:1 (1987), 7–35.

————. *A Flourishing Yin: Gender in China's Medical History, 960–1665.* Berkeley: University of California Press, 1999.

————. "The Patriarch's Legacy: Household Instructions and the Transmission of Orthodox Values." In *Orthodoxy in Late Imperial China*, ed. Kwang-Ching Liu, 187–211. Berkeley: University of California Press, 1990.

————. "Rethinking van Gulik: Sexuality and Reproduction in Traditional Chinese Medicine." In *Engendering China: Women, Culture, and the State*, ed. Christina K. Gilmartin et al., 125–46. Cambridge, MA: Harvard University Press, 1994.

Gao Fengqian 高鳳謙, Cai Yuanpei 蔡元培, and Zhang Yuanji 張元濟. *Zuixin xiushen jiaokeshu* 最新修身教科書 ("Commercial Press's New Primary School Text Books: Elementary Ethics"). 10 vols. Shanghai: Shangwu yinshuguan, 1906.

————. *Zuixin xiushen jiaokeshu, jiaoshou fa* 最新修身教科書教授法 ("Commercial Press's New Primary School Textbooks: Methods for Teaching Elementary Ethics"), vol. 4, 2nd ed. Shanghai: Shangwu yinshuguan, 1906.

Gao Yutong 高毓彤. "Houji" 後記 (Postface). In Dai Li, 1a.

————. "Xu" 序 (Preface). In Dai Li, 1a–3a.

Genette, Gérard. *Palimpsests: Literature in the Second Degree.* Trans. Channa Newman and Claude Doubinsky. Lincoln: University of Nebraska Press, 1997.

————. *Paratexts: Thresholds of Interpretation.* Trans. Jane E. Lewin. Cambridge, Eng.: Cambridge University Press, 1997.

"Gerou yifu" 割肉醫夫 ([A woman] cuts off her own flesh to treat her husband). *BJNB* (Aug. 25, 1906).

Gilmartin, Christina. "Gender, Political Culture, and Women's Mobilization in the Chinese Nationalist Revolution, 1924–27." In *Engendering China: Women,*

Culture, and the State, ed. Christina K. Gilmartin et al., 195–225. Cambridge, MA: Harvard University Press, 1994.

Gong Yuanchang 龔圓常. "Nannü pingquan shuo" 男女平權說 (Equal rights for men and women). *JS* 4 (July 25, 1903), 145 [763].

"Gongai hui tongren quan liuxue qi" 共愛會同人勸留學啟 (Members of the Humanitarian Association exhort overseas study). *JS* 6 (Sept. 21, 1903), 159–61 [1147–49].

"Gongbu zhushi Liu Xun xuewu yaoduan zhe" 工部主事劉撝學物要端折 (Manager of Affairs of the Ministry of Public Works, Liu Xun, on important educational matters). *Nanyang guanbao* 南洋官報 54 (1906). Rpt. in *XZSL* 2:2, 587–88.

Goodman, Bryna, and Wendy Larson. "Introduction, Axes of Gender: Divisions of Labor and Spatial Separation." In *Gender in Motion: Divisions of Labor and Cultural Change in Late Imperial and Modern China*, ed. Bryna Goodman and Wendy Larson, 1–25. Lanham, MD: Rowman and Littlefield, 2005.

Goodrich, L. Carrington, ed., *Dictionary of Ming Biography, 1368–1644*. 2 vols. New York: Columbia University Press, 1976.

Goossaert, Vincent. "1898: The Beginning or the End for Chinese Religion?" *Journal of Asian Studies* 65:2 (May 2006), 307–35.

Gray, J. "Historical Writing in Twentieth-Century China: Notes on Its Background and Development." In *Historians of China and Japan*, ed. W. G. Beasley and E. G. Pulleyblank, 186–212. London: Oxford University Press, 1961.

Gross, David. *The Past in Ruins: Tradition and the Critique of Modernity*. Amherst: University of Massachusetts Press, 1992.

Guang Zhanyun 廣展雲, Guang Yiyun 廣翼雲, and Chen Yuxin 陳與新, comp. *Zuixin funü guowen duben* 最新婦女國文讀本 (Newest Chinese reader for women). 10 vols. (8 extant, 1, 4–10). Fuzhou: Jiaoyu pujishe, 1908.

"Guangxu sanshisan nianfen Xuebu diyici jiaoyu tongji tubiao" 光緒三十三年分學部第一次教育統計圖表 (The Education Board's first statistical table on education, 1907). Rpt. in *XZSL* 2:2, 649–50.

Gui Zhuang 歸莊. "Shu *Gu zhennü zhuan* hou" 書顧貞女傳後 (Written after reading *On Biographies of Faithful Maidens*). In *Gui Zhuang ji* 歸莊集 (Collected writings of Gui Zhuang), 1: 301. Shanghai: Shanghai guji chubanshe, 1984.

"Guifan kefeng" 閨範可風 (A paragon of female virtue worthy to be followed). *STSB* (Aug. 15, 1904). Rpt. in *NQYDSL* 1, 150–51.

Guiji Jinguo 會稽金國書稿 (Jinguo of Guiji). "Jie chanzu shi" 戒纏足詩 (Poem admonishing against footbinding). *Nüxue bao* 女學報 2:4 (Nov. 1903), 52–53.

Guo Yanli 郭廷礼, ed. *Qiu Jin shi wen xuan* 秋瑾诗文选 (Selected poems and essays by Qiu Jin). Beijing: Renmin wenxue chubanshe, 1982.

———, ed. *Qiu Jin yanjiu ziliao* 秋瑾研究资料 (Research materials related to Qiu Jin). Ji'nan: Shandong jiaoyu chubanshe, 1987.

Guo Zhanghai 郭长海, and Li Yabin 李亚彬, eds. *Qiu Jin shiji yanjiu* 秋瑾事迹研究 (Research on Qiu Jin's achievements). Changchun: Dongbei shifan daxue chubanshe, 1987.

Hall, Catherine, Jane Lewis, Keith McClelland, and Jane Rendall, eds. Special Issue on Gender, Nationalisms and National Identities. *Gender and History* 5:2 (Summer 1993).

Han Minghua 韩明华, and Xu Yuzhen 徐玉珍. "Nüzi baihua bao" 女子白话报 ("*Women's Vernacular Journal*"). In *QKJS* 4, 333–40.

"Han Shizhong" 韓世忠. *Xinjiaoben Song shi, bing fubian sanzhong* 新校本宋史并 附編三種 (New edition of the *History of the Song Dynasty* with three supplements), comp. Tuotuo 脫脫, 364: "Liezhuan" 123. Rpt. in *Zhongguo xueshu leibian* 中國學術類編, 11355–73. Taipei: Dingwen shuju, 1990.

Han Xifeng 韩锡锋, ed. "Zhijian cunben mengxue shumu" 知见存本蒙学书目 (List of extant primary-level texts either seen by or known to the author). In *Zhonghua mengxue jicheng* 中华蒙学集成 (Compendium of Chinese primary-level texts), 2083–98. Shenyang: Liaoning jiaoyu chubanshe, 1993.

Hanan, Patrick. "The Missionary Novels of Nineteenth-Century China." *Harvard Journal of Asiatic Studies* 60:2 (Dec. 2000), 413–43.

Handlin, Joanna. "Lü Kun's New Audience: The Influence of Women's Literacy on Sixteenth-Century Thought." In *Women in Chinese Society*, ed. Margery Wolf and Roxane Witke, 13–38. Stanford, CA: Stanford University Press, 1975.

"Hangzhou Zhenwen nü xuexiao xiaozhang Huixing nüshi wei xing nüxue xun-shen jielüe" 杭州貞文女學校校長惠興女士為興女學殉身節略 (A brief record of Huixing, principal of the Hangzhou Women's School of Purity and Progress, who martyred herself for women's education). *SB* (Jan. 13, 1905).

Harrell, Paula. *Sowing the Seeds of Change: Chinese Students, Japanese Teachers, 1895–1905*. Stanford, CA: Stanford University Press, 1992.

———. "The Meiji 'New Woman' and China." In *Late Qing China and Meiji Japan: Political and Cultural Aspects*, ed. Joshua A. Fogel, 109–50. Norwalk, CT: EastBridge, 2004.

Hattori Shigeko 服部繁子. "Huiyi Qiu Jin nüshi" 回忆秋瑾女士 (Reminiscences of Qiu Jin). Trans. Gao Yan 高岩. In Guo Yanli, *Qiu Jin yanjiu ziliao*, 166–92.

———. "Shū Kin joshi no omoide" 秋瑾女子の思い出 (Reminiscences of Qiu Jin). *Tōzai kōshō* 東西交涉 1:1 (1982), 38–51.

Hazama Naoki 狭间直树, ed. *Liang Qichao, Mingzhi Riben, Xifang* 梁启超，明治 日本，西方 (Liang Qichao, Meiji Japan, and the West). Beijing: Shehui kexue wenxian chubanshe, 2001.

He Xiangning 何香凝. "Jinggao wo tongbao jiemei" 敬告我同胞姊妹 (A warning for my sister compatriots). *JS* 4 (June 25, 1903), 144 [762].

———. "When I Learned How to Cook." In *Chinese Women Through Chinese Eyes*, ed. Li Yu-ning, 133–43. Armonk, NY: M. E. Sharpe, 1992.

———. "Wo de huiyi" 我的回憶 (My reminiscences). In *Xinhai geming huiyi lu* 辛亥革命回憶錄 (Memoirs of the 1911 Revolution), ed. Zhongguo renmin zhengzhi xieshang huiyi quanguo weiyuan hui, Wenshi ziliao yanjiu weiyuan hui 中國人民政治協商會議全國委員會文史資料研究委員會, 1: 12–59. Beijing: Wenshi ziliao chubanshe, 1981.

He Zhen 何震 [Zhen Shu 震述]. "Nüzi fuchou lun" 女子復仇論 (Female's revenge). *TY* 3 (July 10, 1907), 7–23.

———. "'Qiu Jin shici' houxu" 《秋瑾诗词》后序 (Postface to *Qiu Jin's Shi and Ci Poetry*). In Wang Zhifu 王芷馥, *Qiu Jin shici* 秋瑾诗词. Tokyo: n.p., 1907. Rpt. in Guo Yanli, *Qiu Jin yanjiu ziliao*, 342–43.

Henderson, John B. *The Development and Decline of Chinese Cosmology*. New York: Columbia University Press, 1984.

Hesse, Carla. *The Other Enlightenment: How French Women Became Modern*. Princeton, NJ: Princeton University Press, 2001.

Hightower, James Robert. *Han Shih Wai Chuan: Han Ying's Illustrations of the Didactic Applications of the "Classic of Songs."* Cambridge, MA: Harvard University Press, 1952.

Hirano Hideo 平野日出雄. *Matsumoto Kamejirō den: Nit-Chū kyōiku no kakehashi* 松本亀二郎伝：日中教育のかけ橋 (A biography of Matsumoto Kamejirō, a bridge between Japanese and Chinese education). Tokyo: Nagata bunkadō, 1982.

Ho, Clara Wing-Chung [Liu Yongcong 劉詠聰]. "The Cultivation of Female Talent: Views on Women's Education in China during the Early and High Qing Periods." *Journal of the Economic and Social History of the Orient* 38:2 (May 1995), 191–223.

"Hong taifuren jiaozi chengming" 洪太夫人教子成名 (Mother Hong teaches her son who becomes famous). *THRB* 8 (Aug. 23, 1909), 3 [1:87].

Howland, Douglas R. *Translating the West: Language and Political Reason in Nineteenth-Century Japan*. Honolulu: University of Hawai'i Press, 2002.

Hsiung Ping-chen. *Children and Childhood in Late Imperial China*. Stanford, CA: Stanford University Press, 2005.

———. "Constructed Emotions: The Bond between Mothers and Sons in Late Imperial China." *Late Imperial China* 15:1 (1994), 87–117.

Hu Binxia 湖彬夏. "Fu Yangjun Baimin lun Meiguo nüzi zhiye shu" 復楊君白民論美國女子職業書 (A response to Mr. Yang Baimin's discussion of women's vocational education in the United States). *JYZZ* 1:6 (July 12, 1909), 19–34 [487–502].

———. "Hu nüshi Binxia yanci (yuzuo)" 胡女士彬夏演詞於左 (Ms. Hu Binxia's speech, [recorded to the left]). *JS* 2 (May 27, 1903), 148–49 [0380–81].

———. [Hu Bin 胡彬]. "Lun Zhongguo zhi shuairuo nüzi bude ci qi zui" 論中國之衰弱女子不得辭其罪 (Women should not abnegate their responsibility for China's weakness). *JS* 3 (June 25, 1903), 156–57 [0586–87].

Hu Fagui 胡發貴. "Qingdai zhenjie guannian shulun" 清代貞節觀念述論 (Discussion of Qing views of chastity). In *Qingshi yanjiu ji* 清史研究集 (Collection of studies on Qing history), 7: 153–70. Beijing: Zhongguo renmin daxue Qingshi yanjiusuo, 1990.

Hu Hsiao-chen 胡曉真. "Wenyuan, duoluo yu Huaman—Wang Yunzhang zhubian shiqi (1915–1920) *Funü zazhi* zhong "nüxing wenxue" de guannian yu shijian" 文苑，多羅與華鬘—王蘊章主編時期 (1915–1920) 《婦女雜誌》中

「女性文學」的觀念與實踐 (The writers' garden, the Toilette case, and the *Kasumam*: Theory and practice of women's literature in the *Ladies' Journal* under the editorship of Wang Yunzhang [1915–20]). *Jindai Zhongguo funü shi yanjiu* 近代中國婦女史研究 12 (Dec. 2004), 169–93.

Hu Shi 胡適. "Zhencao wenti" 貞操問題 (The problem of chastity). *Xin qingnian* 新青年 5:1 (July 15, 1918), 5–14.

Hu Wenkai 胡文楷. *Lidai funü zhuzuo kao* 歷代婦女著作考 (A survey of women writers through the ages). Shanghai: Shangwu yinshuguan, 1957.

Hu Ying. "Naming the First 'New Woman.'" In *Rethinking the 1898 Reform Period: Political and Cultural Change in Late Qing China*, ed. Rebecca E. Karl and Peter Zarrow, 180–211. Cambridge, MA: Harvard University Asia Center, 2002.

———. *Tales of Translation: Composing the New Woman in China, 1898–1918.* Stanford, CA: Stanford University Press, 2000.

———. "Writing Qiu Jin's Life: Wu Zhiying and Her Family Learning." *Late Imperial China* 25:2 (Dec. 2004), 119–60.

Hu Yujin 胡玉縉. *Jiachen Dongyou riji* 甲辰東游日記 (Diary of a trip to Japan in 1904). Sanetō bunko 実藤文庫 (Sanetō Collection) no. 74. Tokyo Hibaya Library Archives.

"Hua Mulan dier" 花木蘭第二 (The second Hua Mulan). *SB* (Jan. 4, 1910).

Huai Xin 懷馨. "Yishen xunzu" 以身殉足 (To die for one's feet). *XNJZZ* 5 (June 5, 1907), 125–29.

"Huaixuhai liu Hu xuejie gongtui diaochayuan Li Xun baogao shu" 淮徐海留滬學界公推調查員李壎報告書 (Report by investigator Li Xun, elected by members of educational circles from Huaixuhai residing in Shanghai). *ShB* (July 22, 1907).

Huang Chun-chieh. "'Time' and 'Supertime' in Chinese Historical Thinking." In Huang Chun-chieh and Henderson, 19–41.

Huang Chun-chieh and John B. Henderson, eds. *Notions of Time in Chinese Historical Thinking.* Hong Kong: Chinese University Press, 2006.

Huang Di 黃第. "Yong lidai nüjiang" 詠歷代女將 (To sing of women officers through the ages). *STSB* (May 5, 1911).

Huang Fu-ch'ing 黃福慶. *Qingmo liu-Ri xuesheng* 清末留日學生 (Chinese students in Japan in the late Qing period). Taipei: Zhongyang yanjiuyuan, jindaishi yanjiusuo, 1975.

———. *Chinese Students in Japan in the Late Qing Period.* Trans. Katherine P. K. Whitaker. Tokyo: Center for East Asian Cultural Studies, 1982.

Huang Lingfang 黃菱舫. "Huang Lingfang nüshi Nüjiezhong xu" 黃菱舫女士女界鐘敘 (Huang Lingfang's discussion of *A Tocsin for Women*). *JS* 5 (Aug. 23, 1903), 132–33 [942–43].

Huang Mo 黃沫. "*Dalu*" 大陆 (*The Continent*). In *QKJS* 2, 115–44.

Huang, Philip C. C. *Code, Custom, and Legal Practice in China: The Qing and the Republic Compared.* Stanford, CA: Stanford University Press, 2001.

"Huashuo *Kewang*" 话说《渴望》(Speaking of *Yearnings*). *Shanghai wenlun* 上海文论 26 (1991: 2), 2–15.

"Huazu nü xuexiao xuejian Xiatian Gezi lun xing Zhongguo nüxue shi" 華族女
學校學監下田歌子論興中國女學事 (The dean of the school for female nobles,
Shimoda Utako, discusses promoting female education in China). Orally
transc. Zhang Yingxu 張 鍈 緒, transc. Yang Du 楊度 *Hunan youxue yibian*
湖南遊學譯編 1 (Nov. 12, 1901), 9–13. Rpt., Taipei: Zhongguo Guomindang,
Zhongyang weiyuan hui, Dangshi shiliao bianzuan weiyuan hui, 1968. [37–41].

"Hubei bu chanzu hui fushe Diyi younü xuetang zhangcheng" 湖北不纏足會附
設第一幼女學堂章程 (Regulations for the Number One Young Girls' School
attached to the Hubei Anti-Footbinding Society). *Jiaoyu congshu* 教育叢書 4:2
(1904), 1.

Huitu Lienü zhuan 繪圖列女傳 (Illustrated biographies of exemplary women).
Zhibuzu zhai edition 知不足齊藏版, 1779. Rpt., Taipei: Zhengzhong shuju,
1971.

"Huixing nüshi wei nüxue xisheng" 惠興女士為女學犧牲 (Ms. Huixing sacrifices
herself for female education). *ShB* (Dec. 30, 1905).

"Huixing nüshi xunxue ji" 惠興女士殉學記 (Record of Huixing, who died for
education). *DFZZ* 3:5 (June 16, 1906), 103–4.

Hummel, Arthur W., ed. *Eminent Chinese of the Ch'ing Period (1644–1912)*. Rpt.,
Taipei: Ch'eng Wen Publishing Company, 1975.

"Hunan nüxue feibi zhi yuanyin" 湖南女學廢閉之原因 (The reason for the closure
of a Hunan girls' school). *Jingzhong ribao* 警鍾日報 (Oct. 26, 1904). Rpt. in
XZSL 2, 652–53.

Hunt, Lynn. *The Family Romance of the French Revolution*. Berkeley: University of
California Press, 1992.

Huters, Theodore. *Bringing the World Home: Appropriating the West in Late Qing
and Early Republican China*. Honolulu: University of Hawai'i Press, 2005.

Idema, Wilt, and Beata Grant, eds. *The Red Brush: Writing Women of Imperial
China*. Cambridge, MA: Harvard University Asia Center, 2004.

Iigura Shōhei 飯倉照平. "Pekin shūhō to Junten jihō" 北京週報と順天時報
(*Peking Weekly* and *Shuntian shibao*). In *Kindai Nihon to Chūgoku* 近代日本と
中国 (Modern Japan and China), ed. Takeuchi Yoshimi 竹内好 and Hashikawa
Bunzō 橋川文治, 1: 341–58. Tokyo: Asahi shinbunsha, 1974.

Ishii Yōko 石井洋子. "Shingai kakumei ki no ryū-Nichi joshi gakusei" 辛亥革命期
の留日女子学生 (Female overseas students in Japan in the era of the 1911 Revolution). *Shiron* 史論 36 (1983), 31–54.

Iwasaki Sodō 岩崎徂堂, and Mikami Kifū 三上寄風. *Sekai jūni joketsu* 世界十二女
傑 (Twelve world heroines). Tokyo: Kōbundō shoten, 1902.

———. *Shijie shier nüjie* 世界十二女傑 (Twelve world heroines). Trans. Zhao
Bizhen 趙必振. Shanghai: Guangzhi shuju, 1903.

James, Alice R. [Ganmu Ailanxi 乾姆愛蘭西]. *Nüzi ticao jiaokeshu* 女子體操教科
書 (Textbook for girls' physical training). Japanese trans. Shirai Kikurō 白井規
矩郎, Chinese trans. Cai Yun 蔡允. Shanghai: Kexue shuju, Wenming shuju,
Qunxue she, 1906.

James, Edward T., ed. *Notable American Women 1607–1950: A Biographical Dictionary*. 3 vols. Cambridge, MA: Belknap Press of Harvard University Press, 1971.

"Ji Dongjing Shijian nü xuexiao Zhongguo nü xuesheng zuye shi" 記東京實踐女學校中國女學生卒業式 (Record of the graduation ceremony for Chinese female students at the Jissen Women's School in Tokyo). *SB* (Aug. 5, 1906).

"Ji jingshi Diyi mengyang yuan" 記京師第一蒙養院 (Record of the Number One Kindergarten in the capital), 1–4. *STSB* (Jan. 13–16, 1908).

"Ji liuxue nüshi zhi tanhua" 紀留學女士之談話 (Record of a conversation with overseas female students). *STSB* (Oct. 6, 1906). Rpt. in *NQYDSL* 2, 1269.

"Ji Shanghai nü zhongxuetang kai diyici nüjie baoluhui" 記上海女中學堂開第一次女界保路會 (Record of the first meeting of the Women's Railway Protection Association at the Shanghai Girls' Middle School). *SB* (Nov. 12, 1907).

"Ji Shanyin Qiu Jin nüshi" 記山陰秋瑾女士 (A record of Ms. Qiu Jin of Shanyin). *STSB* (Mar. 24, 1907).

Jiang Dong 江東. "Ji Hangzhou fangzuhui" 記杭州放足會 (Record of the Hangzhou Foot Liberation Society). *ZJC* 2 (Mar. 18, 1903), 173–78.

Jiang Weiqiao 蔣維喬. "Bianji xiaoxue jiaokeshu zhi huiyi, 1897–1904" 編輯小學教科書之回憶, 1897–1904 (Recollections of editing elementary textbooks, 1897–1904). In Zhang Jinglu, ed., 6: 138–45.

Jiang Weitang 姜纬堂, and Liu Ningyuan 刘宁元, eds. *Beijing funü baokan kao, 1905–1949* 北京妇女报刊考, 1905–1949 (An examination of women's journals and newspapers in Beijing, 1905–49). Beijing: Guangming ribao chubanshe, 1990.

Jiang Zhiyou 蔣智由. "Aiguo nü xuexiao kaixiao yanshuo" 愛國女學校開校演說 (Speech at the opening of the Patriotic Girls' School). *Nübao* 女報 9 (Dec. 1902), 1a–4b.

[———.] "Wuyue hua" 五月花 (The flower of May ["The Mayflower"]). *Xinmin congbao* 新民叢報 12 (July 1902), 8–10.

"Jiangsu jiaoyu zonghui zhi Jiangdu Duan Wushuai shu" 江蘇教育總會致江督端午帥書 (Jiangsu General Educational Association's letter to Liang-Jiang Governor-General Duanfang). *ShB* (July 22, 1907).

"Jiaoyu bu gongbu zhongxuexiao ling shixing guize" 教育部公布中學校令施行規則 (Education Board directives for implementing middle school regulations) (Dec. 2, 1912). Rpt. in *XZYB*, 669–76.

"Jie chanzu shuo" 戒纏足說 (Admonition against footbinding). *Xiangbao leizuan* 湘報類纂, n.d., ca. 1896–98. Rpt. in *NQYDSL* 1, 500–501.

"Jiefu fa" 節婦髮 (Hair of a chaste woman). *THRB* 261:6 (Mar. 28, 1910) [5:190].

"Jiefu yin bijiao zisha" 節婦因逼醮自殺 (A chaste woman kills herself when forced to remarry). *SB* (Feb. 2, 1910).

"Jiehun xinfa" 結婚新法 (A new marriage practice). *STSB* (July 8, 1905).

Jin Jungwon 陳正爰. "Jianjie jindai Yazhou de 'xianqi liangmu' sixiang yicong huigu Riben, Hanguo, Zhongguo de yanjiu chengguo tanqi" 簡介近代亞洲的「賢妻良母」思想一從回顧日本，韓國，中國的研究成果談起 (A brief introduction to modern Asian conceptions of "wise mother and good wife" from the perspective of Japanese, Korean, and Chinese research). *Jindai Zhongguo funü shi yanjiu* 近代中國婦女史研究 10 (Dec. 2002), 200–219.

Jin Shi 晉石. "Chuban shuoming" 出版說明 (Publication explanation). In Chen Kangqi, *Langqian jiwen chubi*, 1–3.

Jin Shuxi 金綏熙 et al. "Yong lidai nüjiang" 詠歷代女將 (To sing of women officers through the ages). *STSB* (May 4–17, 1911).

Jin Tiange 金天翮. *Nüjie zhong* 女界鍾 (A tocsin for women). Ed. Chen Yan 陈雁. Shanghai: Shanghai guji chubanshe, 2003.

———. [Jin Yi 金一]. "Nüzi shijie fakanci" 女子世界發刊詞 (Inaugural essay for the *Women's World*). *NZSJ* 1 (Jan. 1904), 6–8.

Jin Xia 巾俠. "Nüde lun" 女德論 (On women's virtue). *XNJZZ* 1 (Feb. 5, 1907), 7–17.

Jing Han 競厂. *Yong Shijie shier nüjie* 詠世界十二女傑 (To sing of *Twelve World Heroines*). *NZSJ* 3 (Mar. 1904), 2–4 [62–64].

Jing Yuanshan 經元善. "Quan nüzi dushu shuo" 勸女子讀書說 (An exhortation for women to study). In *Juyi chuji* 居易初集 (1899), 1: 39–40. Rpt. in *XZSL* 1:2, 882.

———. "Zhi Zheng Yang Dong sanjun lun ban nügongxue shu" 致鄭楊董三君論辦女公學書 (To Messieurs Zheng, Yang, and Dong concerning the establishment of public schools for girls and women). In *Juyi chuji* 居易初集 (1899), 1: 19–20. Rpt. in *XZSL* 1:2, 881–82.

"Jingbiao lienü" 旌表烈女 (The conferring of imperial honors on a heroic woman). *STSB* (Feb. 27, 1906).

"Jinggao nüjie yijian shu" 敬告女界意見書 (A warning to women). *SB* (Nov. 16, 1907).

Jingqun 競群. "Yifen sanshou" 遺憤三首 (Three poems of indignation). *XNJZZ* 2 (Mar. 5, 1907), 107–8.

Jinguo xumei zhuan 巾蟈鬚眉傳 (Biographies of manly women). 4 vols. Shanghai: Huiwentang shuju, 1900. Rpt., Taipei: Xinwenfeng chuban gongsi, 1978.

"Jinguo zhi jie" 巾幗之傑 (A heroine). *STSB* (Dec. 16, 1904).

Jissen joshi daigaku toshokan 実践女子大学図書館 (Jissen Women's University Library). Shimoda Utako kankei shiryō 下田歌子関係資料 (Materials related to Shimoda Utako). Filed by number.

———. *Shimoda Utako kankei shiryō sōmokuroku* 下田歌子関係資料総目録 (Catalog of materials related to Shimoda Utako). Tokyo: Jissen joshi daigaku toshokan, 1980.

Jissen joshi gakuen hachijū nenshi hensan iinkai 實踐女子學園八十年史編纂委員會 (Editorial committee on [documents related to] the eighty-year history of the Jissen Women's School), ed. *Jissen joshi gakuen hachi jū nen shi* 實踐女子學園八十年史 (The eighty-year history of the Jissen Women's School). Tokyo: Jissen joshi gakuen, 1981.

Jones, Susan Mann. "Hung-Liang-chi (1746–1809): The Perception and Articulation of Political Problems in Late Eighteenth Century China." Ph.D. diss., Stanford University, 1972.

Judge, Joan. "Between *Nei* and *Wai*: Chinese Female Students in Japan in the Early Twentieth Century." In *Gender in Motion: Divisions of Labor and Cultural Change in Late Imperial and Modern China*, ed. Bryna Goodman and Wendy Larson, 121–43. Lanham, MD: Rowman and Littlefield, 2005.

———. "Beyond Nationalism: Gender and the Chinese Student Experience in Japan in the Early 20th Century." In Lo Chui-jung and Lu Miaw-fen, 359–93.

———. "Blended Wish Images: Chinese and Western Exemplary Women at the Turn of the Twentieth Century." Special Issue of *Nan Nü: Men, Women and Gender in Early and Imperial China*, ed. Susan Mann, 6:1 (2004), 102–35. Rpt. in Fong, Qian, and Zurndorfer, 102–35.

———. "Citizens or Mothers of Citizens? Gender and the Meaning of Modern Chinese Citizenship." In *Citizenship in Modern China*, ed. Elizabeth Perry and Merle Goldman, 23–43. Cambridge, MA: Harvard Contemporary China Series, Harvard University Press, 2002.

———. "Exemplary Time and Secular Times: Wei Xiyuan's *Illustrated Biographies* and the Late Qing Moment." Unpublished paper.

———. "The Ideology of 'Good Wives and Wise Mothers': Meiji Japan and Feminine Modernity in Late-Qing China." In *Sagacious Monks and Bloodthirsty Warriors: Chinese Views of Japan in the Ming-Qing Period*, ed. Joshua A. Fogel, 218–48. Armonk, NY: EastBridge, 2001.

———. "The Power of Print? Print Capitalism and News Media in Late Qing and Republican China." *Harvard Journal of Asiatic Studies* 66:1 (June 2006), 233–54.

———. *Print and Politics: 'Shibao' and the Culture of Reform in Late Qing China*. Stanford, CA: Stanford University Press, 1996.

———. "Re-forming the Feminine: Female Literacy and the Legacy of 1898." In *The Historical Legacies of the 1898 Reforms in China*, ed. Rebecca Karl and Peter Zarrow, 158–79. Cambridge, MA: Harvard University Asia Center, 2002.

———. "Talent, Virtue, and the Nation: Chinese Nationalisms and Female Subjectivities in the Early Twentieth Century." *American Historical Review* 106:3 (June 2001), 765–803.

"Jun Buyi mu" 雋不疑母 (The mother of Jun Buyi). *BJNB* (June 20, 1908).

"Jūsan nen buri ni Nihon e kite" 十三年振りに日本へ来て (Return to Japan after thirteen years). Jissen joshi daigaku toshokan, Shimoda Utako kankei shiryō, file no. 752 (1943).

Kandiyoti, Deniz. "Afterword: Some Awkward Questions on Women and Modernity in Turkey." In *Remaking Women: Feminism and Modernity in the Middle East*, ed. Lila Abu-Lughod, 270–87. Princeton, NJ: Princeton University Press, 1998.

———. "Bargaining with Patriarchy." *Gender and Society* 2 (1988), 274–90.

———. "Identity and Its Discontents: Women and the Nation." In *Colonial Discourses and Post-colonial Theory: A Reader*, ed. Patrick Williams and Laura Chrisman, 363–91. New York: Columbia University Press, 1994.

Kang Tongwei 康同薇. "Nüxue libi shuo" 女學利弊說 (The advantages and disadvantages of education for girls and women). *Zhixin bao* 知新報 52 (May 11, 1898). Rpt. in *XZSL* 1:2, 876–80.

"Kanhufu" 看護婦 (Nurses). *BJNB* (Feb. 21, 22, 1906).

Karlgren, Bernhard, trans. *The Book of Odes*. Stockholm: Museum of Far Eastern Antiquities, 1950.

Katayama Seiichi 片山清一. "Meiji shoki no joshi kyōiku ron" 明治初期の女子教育論 (On female education in the early Meiji period). *Mejiro gakuen joshi tanki daigaku kenkyū kiyō* 目白学園女子短期大学研究紀要 4 (Dec. 1967), 79–94.

———. "Meiji yonjū nendai no joshi kyōiku ron 1" 明治40年代の女子教育論 1 (On female education in the Meiji 40s, part 1). *Mejiro gakuen joshi tanki daigaku kenkyū kiyō* 目白学園女子短期大学研究紀要 12 (Dec. 1975), 1–12.

———. "Meiji zenki no shōgakkō shūshinsho ni miru joshi dōtoku no hensen" 明治前期の小学校修身書にみる女子道徳の変遷 (Changes in female ethics as seen through early Meiji elementary ethics texts). *Mejiro gakuen joshi tanki daigaku kenkyū kiyō* 目白学園女子短期大学研究紀要 2 (Nov. 1965), 33–46.

Katō Minryū 加藤眠柳. *Joshi risshi hen* 女子立志編 (Compilation of [biographies of] accomplished women). Tokyo: Naigai shuppan kyōkai, 1903.

Kelleher, Theresa. "Women's Education." In *Sources of Chinese Tradition*, rev. ed., ed. Wm. T. de Bary and Irene Bloom, 1: 819–40. New York: Columbia University Press, 1999.

Kerber, Linda. "The Paradox of Women's Citizenship in the Early Republic: The Case of Martin vs. Massachusetts, 1805." In *Toward an Intellectual History of Women: Essays by Linda Kerber*, 261–302. Chapel Hill: University of North Carolina Press, 1997.

———. "The Republican Mother: Women and the Enlightenment—An American Perspective." In *Toward an Intellectual History of Women: Essays by Linda Kerber*, 41–62. Chapel Hill: University of North Carolina Press, 1997.

Ko, Dorothy. "The Body as Attire: The Shifting Meanings of Footbinding in Seventeenth-Century China." *Journal of Women's History* 8:4 (Winter 1997): 8–27.

———. *Cinderella's Sisters: A Revisionist History of Footbinding*. Berkeley: University of California Press, 2005.

———. "Pursuing Talent and Virtue: Education and Women's Culture in Seventeenth- and Eighteenth-Century China." *Late Imperial China* 13:1 (June 1992), 9–39.

———. *Teachers of the Inner Chambers: Women and Culture in Seventeenth-Century China*. Stanford, CA: Stanford University Press, 1994.

———. "The Written Word and the Bound Foot: A History of the Courtesan's Aura." In *Writing Women in Late Imperial China*, ed. Ellen Widmer and Kang-i Sun Chang, 74–100. Stanford, CA: Stanford University Press, 1997.

Ko Shimoda kōchō sensei denki hensanjo 故下田校長先生傳記編纂所 (Biographical Editorial Office on school principal Shimoda Utako), ed. *Shimoda Utako sensei den* 下田歌子先生傳 (Biography of Shimoda Utako). Tokyo: Ko Shimoda kōchō sensei denki hensanjo, 1943.

Kokuritsu kokkai toshokan 国立国会図書館 (National Diet Library). *Fujin mondai bunken mokuroku. Tosho no bu* 婦人問題文献目録、図書の部 (Catalog of materials related to the women's question, books). 3 vols. Tokyo: Kokuritsu kokkai toshokan, 1980–96.

Kong Jinghui 孔菁慧. *Fengyu ziyou hun: Qiu Jin* 風雨自由魂。秋瑾 (A free spirit of the wind and rain: Qiu Jin). Trans. into Japanese by Fang Zheng 方正, *Jiyū e no tatakai Shū Kin* 自由への闘い秋瑾 (Qiu Jin: Fighting for freedom). Ji'nan: Shandong huabao chubanshe, 2001.

"Kongque dongnan fei" 孔雀東南飛 (A peacock southeast flew). In *Zhongguo lidai wenxue zuopin xuan* 中国历代文学作品选 (A selection of Chinese literary works through the ages), ed. Zhu Dongrun 朱東潤, 1:1, 877–887. Shanghai: Shanghai guji chubanshe, 1982.

Kōtoku Shūsui 幸得秋水. "Furen yu zhengzhi" 婦人與政治 (Women and politics). *TY* 3 (July 10, 1907), 47–50.

———. "Xingde Qiushui laihan" 幸得秋水來函 (Letter from Kōtoku Shūsui). *TY* 3 (July 10, 1907): 51–2.

Kristeva, Julia. "Women's Time." In Julia Kristeva, *The Kristeva Reader*, ed. Toril Moi, 187–213. New York: Columbia University Press, 1986.

Kuang Shanji 匡珊吉. "Nüxue bao" 女学报 (*Journal of Women's Learning*). In *QKJS* 3, 75–78.

Lan Dingyuan 藍鼎元. *Nüxue* 女學 (Teachings for girls), ca. 1712. Rpt., Taipei: Wenhai chubanshe, 1977.

Larson, Wendy. *Women and Writing in Modern China*. Stanford, CA: Stanford University Press, 1998.

Lefebvre, Henri. *Critique of Everyday Life*. Vol. 2, *Foundations for a Sociology of the Everyday*. Trans. John Moore. London: Verso, 1991.

Legge, James, trans. *Confucius: Confucian Analects, The Great Learning and the Doctrine of the Mean*. Rpt., New York: Dover, 1971.

———, trans. *Li Chi Book of Rites: An Encyclopedia of Ancient Ceremonial Usages, Religious Creeds, and Social Institutions*, ed. Ch'u Chai and Winberg Chai. 2 vols. Rpt., New York: University Books, 1967.

———, trans. "The Nei Tse: The Pattern of the Family." In *Li Chi Book of Rites*, trans. Legge, vol. 2, 449–79.

———, trans. *The Works of Mencius*. Rpt., New York: Dover, 1970.

Lei Liangpo 雷良波, Chen Yangfeng 陳陽風, and Xiong Xianjun 熊賢軍. *Zhongguo nüzi jiaoyu shi* 中國女子教育史 (History of Chinese women's education). Wuhan: Wuhan chubanshe, 1993.

Leung, Angela Ki Che. "To Chasten Society: The Development of Widow Homes in the Qing, 1773–1911." *Late Imperial China* 14:2 (Dec. 1993), 1–32.

Levenson, Joseph R. *Confucian China and Its Modern Fate: A Trilogy*. Berkeley: University of California Press, 1972.

Li Dezheng 李德征, Su Weizhi 苏位智, and Liu Tianlu 刘天路. *Baguo lianjun qin-Hua shi* 八国联军侵华史 (A history of the Eight-Power Joint Expeditionary Forces' aggression against China). Ji'nan: Shandong daxue chubanshe, 1990.

Li Junling 李俊岭. "Liu-Ri nü xuehui zazhi" 留日女学会杂志 (*Magazine of the Study Society of Female Students in Japan*). In *QKJS* 3, 682–88.

Li Junzhi 李濬之. *Qing huajia shishi* 清畫家詩史 (Painters and poets of the Qing), Qingdai zhuanji congkan, yilin lei 清代傳記叢刊 · 藝麟類 (Collection of Qing dynasty biographies, the artistic world), 075–077: 12. 3 vols. Taipei: Mingwen shuju, 1985.

"Li Run zijing xunfu" 李閨自剄殉夫 (Li Run martyrs herself for her husband by cutting her throat). In *QBLC*, 80.

"Li taifuren zhi taijiao" 李太夫人之胎教 (Mother Li's fetal education). *THRB* 22 (Sept. 6, 1909), 3 [1:255].

Li Xiaojiang 李小江. "Creating a Public Sphere: A Self-Portrait in the Women's Studies Movement in China." *Asian Journal of Women's Studies* 2 (1996), 70–112.

———. "The Development of Women's Studies in China: A Comparison of Perspectives on the Women's Movement in China and the West." *Copenhagen Discussion Papers* 20 (Apr. 1993).

———. "From 'Modernization' to 'Globalization': Where Are Chinese Women?" *Signs* 26:4 (Summer 2001), 1274–78.

———. "My Path to Womanhood." In *Changing Lives: Life Stories of Asian Pioneers in Women's Studies*, ed. Committee on Women's Studies in Asia, 108–22. New York: Feminist Press at the City University of New York.

———. "Shijimo kan 'Dierxing'" 世纪末看 "第二性" (A fin-de-siecle look at *The Second Sex*). *Dushu* 读书 12 (1999), 98–103.

———. "With What Discourses Do We Reflect on Chinese Women? Thoughts on Transnational Feminism in China." In *Spaces of Their Own: Women's Public Sphere in Transnational China*, ed. Mayfair Mei-hui Yang, 261–77. Minneapolis: University of Minnesota Press, 1999.

Li Xiaojiang, and Zhang Xiaodan. "Creating a Space for Women: Women's Studies in China in the 1980s." *Signs* 20:1 (Autumn, 1994), 137–51.

Li Yu-ning 李又寧. *The Introduction of Socialism into China*. New York: Columbia University Press, 1971.

———. "Xinhai geming xianjin Fang Junying nüshi" 辛亥革命先進 方君瑛女士 (Fang Junying, a progressive woman in the 1911 Revolution). *Zhuanji wenxue* 傳記文學 38:5 (May 1981), 16–19.

———. "Zhongguo xin nüjie zazhi de chuangkan ji neihan: Zhongguo xin nüjie zazhi chongkan xu" 中國新女界雜誌 的創刊及內涵：中國新女界雜誌重刊 序 (The founding and content of *Zhongguo xin nüjie zazhi*, preface to the reprinted edition of *Zhongguo xin nüjie zazhi*). In *Zhongguo funü shilun wenji* 中國婦女史論文集 (Historical essays on Chinese women's history), ed. Li Yuning, 1: 179–241. Taipei: Commercial Publishing, 1992.

"Li Zicheng, Zhang Xianzhong" 李自成 張獻忠. *Xinjiaoben Ming shi, bing fubian liuzhong* 新校本明史并附編六種 (New edition of the *History of the Ming Dynasty* with six supplements), comp. Zhang Tingyu 張廷玉, 359: "Liezhuan" 197 ("Liuzei" 流賊). Rpt. in *Zhongguo xueshu leibian* 中國學術類編, 7948–77. Taipei: Dingwen shuju, 1990.

Liang Qichao 梁啟超. "Bianfa tongyi" 變法通議 (General discussion of reform). In Liang Qichao, *Yinbingshi heji, wenji*, 1:1, 1–92.

———. "Ji Jiangxi Kang nüshi" 記江西康女士 (A record of Ms. Kang [Aide] of Jiangxi). In Liang Qichao, *Yinbingshi heji, wenji*, 1:1, 119–20.

———. "Jinshi diyi nüjie Luolan furen zhuan" 近世第一女傑羅蘭夫人 (Biography of Madame Roland, the foremost heroine of modern times). In Liang Qichao, *Yinbingshi heji, zhuanji*, 6:12, 1–14..

———. "Lun baoguan youyi yu guoshi" 論報館有益於國事 (The beneficial effect of newspapers on national affairs). In Liang Qichao, *Yinbingshi heji, wenji*, 1:1, 100–103.

———. "Lun nüxue" 論女學 (On female education). In Liang Qichao, *Yinbingshi heji, wenji*, 1:1, 37–44. Rpt. in *XZSL*, 869–75.

———. "Xinmin shuo" 新民說 (Renovation of the people). In Liang Qichao, *Yinbingshi heji, zhuanji*, 6:4, 91–162.

———. *Yinbingshi heji, wenji* 飲冰室合集，文集 (Collected works from the ice drinker's studio, essays). Beijing: Zhonghua shuju, 1989.

———. *Yinbingshi heji, zhuanji* 飲冰室合集，專集 (Collected works from the ice drinker's studio, works). Beijing: Zhonghua shuju, 1989.

"Lianjun jielüe jiwen" 聯軍劫掠紀聞 (Record of the plundering by the Joint Expeditionary Forces). *Qingyi bao* 清議報 62 (Nov. 2, 1900), 7–8. Rpt., Taipei: Chengwen chubanshe, 1967, [3952–53].

Liao Xiuzhen 廖秀真. "Qingmo nüxue zai xuezhi shang de yanjin ji nüzi xiaoxue jiaoyu de fazhan, 1897–1911" 清末女學在學制上的演進及女子小學教育的發展, 1897–1911 (Late Qing women's education in the context of the evolution of the educational system and the development of women's elementary education, 1897–1911). In *Zhongguo funü shilun wenji* 中國婦女史論文集 (Historical essays on Chinese women's history), ed. Li Yu-ning 李又寧, 2: 203–55. Taipei: Commercial Publishing, 1992.

"Liefu hanbei xunfu zhongqi" 烈婦含悲殉夫終七 (A heroic woman restrains her grief and dies following the mourning period of forty-nine days). THRB 297, 7 [6:563].

"Liefu xunjie" 烈婦殉節 (A female martyr dies to preserve her chastity). *SB* (May 9, 1910).

Lin Bingzhang 林炳章. *Guimao dongyou riji* 癸卯東游日記 (Diary of a journey to Japan in 1903) (1903). Sanetō bunko 実藤文庫 (Sanetō Collection) no. 67. Tokyo Hibiya Library Archives.

Lin Shuming 林树明. "Xiandai xuezhe de sanwei nüxing wenxueshi kaocha" 现代学者的三位女性文学史考察 (A modern scholar's investigation of three women's literary histories). *Zhongguo xiandai wenxue yanjiu congkan* 中国现代文学研究丛刊 1 (2003), 257–65.

Lin Yinxiang 林蔭湘. "Xu" 序 (Preface). In Xu Dingyi 許定一 (Juxue zi 咀雪子), *Zuguo nüjie wenhao pu* 祖國女界文豪譜 (A guide to great women writers of our country), 2a–2b. Beijing: Jinghua yinshu guan, 1909.

Lin Zongsu 林宗素. "Lin nüshi Zongsu Nüjiezhong xu" 林女士宗素女界鐘敘 (Ms. Lin Zongsu's discussion of *A Tocsin for Women*). *JS* 5 (Aug. 23, 1903), 131–32 [941–42].

Ling Ti'an 凌惕安, comp. "Chen Kangqi" 陳康祺. In *Qingdai Guizhou mingxian xiangzhuan* 清代貴州明賢像傳 (Portraits of famous Qing dynasty worthies of Guizhou), ed. Zhou Junfu 周駿富, vols. 12–13. Taipei: Minwen shuju, 1985.

Lingxi 靈希. "Meiguo da jiaoyujia Lihen nüshi zhuan" 美國大教育家黎痕女士傳 (Biography of the great American educator Ms. [Mary] Lyon). *XNJZZ* 2 (Mar. 5, 1907), 65–70.

———. "Meiguo da xinwenjia Asuoli nüshi zhuan" 美國大新聞家阿索里女士傳 (Biography of the great American journalist Ms. Ossoli). *XNJZZ* 1 (Feb. 5, 1907), 65–72.

Link, Perry. *Mandarin Ducks and Butterflies: Popular Fiction in Early Twentieth Century Chinese Cities*. Berkeley: University of California Press, 1981.

"Liu gaifu shouzhen fuzi" 劉丐婦守貞撫子 (Beggar woman Liu preserves her virtue and cares for her son). *QBLC*, 31–33.

Liu Gengzao 劉賡藻, trans. "Wuguan nüdi Weinade" 無冠女帝維納德 (The uncrowned queen [Frances] Willard). *Xinyi jie* 新譯界 2 (Dec. 16, 1906). Rpt. in *NQYDSL* 1, 341–46.

Liu Huating 刘华庭. "Ji Qingmo daxing huabao: *Tuhua ribao* 记清末大型画报「图画日报」(The major late Qing pictorial: *Daily Pictorial*). *Chuban shiliao* 出版史料 1 (1988), 95–96.

Liu Huiying 刘慧英. "20 shiji chu Zhongguo nüquan qimeng zhong de jiuguo nüzi xingxiang" 20 世纪初中国女权启蒙中的救国女子形象 (The image of female national salvationists in the context of China's early-twentieth-century awakening to women's rights). *Zhongguo xiandai wenxue yanjiu congkan* 中国现代文学研究丛刊 2 (2002), 156–79.

Liu Jihua 劉紀華. "Zhongguo zhenjie guannian de lishi yanbian" 中國貞節觀念的歷史演變 (The historical development of the concept of chastity in China) (1937). Rpt. in *ZGFNS* 4, 101–30.

Liu Jucai 刘巨才. "*Nübao*" 女報 ("*The National Womens Journal*"). In *QKJS* 3, 501–10.

Liu Jung-en, trans. "The Injustice Done to Tou Ngo." In *Six Yüan Plays*, 117–58. Middlesex, Eng.: Penguin, 1972.

Liu, Lydia H. *Translingual Practice: Literature, National Culture, and Translated Modernity, China, 1900–1937*. Stanford, CA: Stanford University Press, 1995.

Liu Mei Ching. "Forerunners of Chinese Feminism in Japan: Students Fighting for Freedom in Japan." Ph.D. diss., University of Leiden, 1988.

Liu Shaotang 劉紹唐. *Minguo renwu xiaozhuan* 民國人物小傳 (Short biographies of Republican-era figures). 19 vols. Taipei: Zhuanji wenxue zazhi she, 1975.

Liu Yazi 柳亞子 [Yalu 亞盧]. "Ai nüjie" 哀女界 (A lament for women). *NZSJ* 9 (Sept. 1904), 1–9. Rpt. in *XZSL* 2:2, 577–81.

———. [Yate 亞特]. "Lun zhuzao guomin mu" 論鑄造國民母 (Educating mothers of citizens). *NZSJ* 7 (July 1904), 1–7. Rpt. in *XZSL* 2:2, 573–77.

———. [Yalu 亞盧]. "Zhongguo diyi nü haojie nü junrenjia Hua Mulan zhuan" 中國第一女豪傑女軍人家花木蘭傳 (Biography of China's premiere female hero and female soldier, Hua Mulan). *NZSJ* 3 (Mar. 1904), 25–32 [199–206].

———. [Pan Xiaohuang 潘小璜]. "Zhongguo minzu zhuyi nü junren Liang Hongyu zhuan" 中國民族主義女軍人梁紅玉傳 (Biography of Liang Hongyu: A female soldier for Chinese nationalism). *NZSJ* 7 (July 1904), 19–24.

Liu Yongcong 劉詠聰 [Clara Wing-Chung Ho]. "Qingchu sichao nüxing cai ming guan guankui" 清初四朝女性才命觀管窺 (A humble examination of views on women's talent and fate during the first four Qing dynastic reign periods). In *ZGFNS* 3, 121–162.

"Liuxue jilu" 留學記錄 (Record of overseas students activities). *HB* 4 (Apr. 27, 1903), 125 [0575].

Lo Jiu-jiung 羅久蓉, and Lu Miaw-fen 呂妙芬, eds. *Wusheng zhi sheng: Jindai Zhongguo de funü yu guojia* 無聲之聲 (III): 近代中國的婦女與國家 ("Voices amid silence [III]: Women and the culture in modern China [1600–1950]"). Taipei: Institute of Modern History, Academia Sinica, 2003.

Lü Meiyi 呂美頤. "Ping Zhongguo jindai guanyu xianqiliangmu zhuyi de lunzheng" 评中国近代关于贤妻良母主义的论争 (A review of the debate on wise wives and good mothers in modern China). *Zhongguo jindai shi* 中国近代史 12 (1995), 15–21.

Lu, Weijing. "True to Their Word: The Faithful Maiden Cult in China, 1650–1850." Ph.D. diss., University of California, Davis, 2001.

———. *True to Their Word: The Faithful Maiden Cult in China, 1650–1850.* Stanford, CA: Stanford University Press, 2008.

Lu Xun 魯迅. *Lu Xun zawen quanji* 魯迅雜文全集 (Complete essays of Lu Xun). Beijing: Jiuzhou tushu, 1995.

———. "My Views on Chastity." In *Women in Republican China: A Sourcebook*, ed. Hua R. Lan and Vanessa L. Fong. Armonk, NY: M. E. Sharpe, 1999.

———. "Wo zhi jielie guan" 我之節烈觀 (My views on chastity). *Xin qingnian* 新青年 5:2 (Aug. 15, 1918), 92–101.

Lufei Bohong 陸費伯鴻. "Lun Zhongguo jiaokeshu shishu" 論中國教科書史書 (A history of Chinese textbooks). In Zhang Jinglu, ed., 1: 212–14.

"Lun jiating jiaoyu" 論家庭教育 (Education in the family). *HS* 6 (July 24, 1903), 43–47 [797–801].

"Lun Liu Yan liang jiefu" 論劉閻兩節婦 (Chaste widows Liu and Yan). *BJNB* (May 13, 1908).

"Lun nüxue yi xianding jiaoke zongzhi" 論女學宜先定教科宗旨 (Female education must first set its curricular objectives). *DFZZ* 4:7 (July 1907), 131–32.

"Lun nüxue yi zhuzhong deyu" 論女學宜注重德育 (Women's education should emphasize ethical education). *DFZZ* 3:6 (July 1906), 118–24.

"Lun Shanghai nü xuesheng zhi zhuangshu" 論上海女學生之裝束 (The dress of female students in Shanghai). *FNSB* 11 (Oct. 20, 1913), 12–13.

Luo Suwen 罗苏文. *Nüxing yu jindai Zhongguo shehui* 女性与近代中国社会 (Women and modern Chinese society). Shanghai: Renmin chubanshe, 1996.

"Luolan furen" 羅蘭夫人 (Madame Roland). *THRB* 115 (Dec. 8, 1909), 3 [3:171].

Ma Junwu 马君武. "Nüshi Zhang Zhujun zhuan" 女士张竹君传 (Biography of

Ms. Zhang Zhujun). In *Ma Junwu ji* 馬君武集 (Writings of Ma Junwu), 1–3. Wuchang: Huazhong shifan daxue chubanshe, 1991.

Maeyama Kanako 前山加奈子. "Chūgoku no josei muke teiki kankōbutsu ni tsuite—sono naiyō to tokuchō" 中国の女性向け定期刊行物について—その内容と特徴 ("Chinese Periodicals for Women from 1898 to 1949—Their Contents and Characteristics"). Rpt. from *Surugadai daigaku ronsō* 駿河台大学論叢 10 (1995), 115–45.

———. "Fu 3, Chūgoku ni okeru josei muke shinbun zasshi ichiran, 1898–1937" 附 3 中国における女性向け新聞、雑誌一覧 1898 年—1937 年 (Appendix 3, A look at Chinese women's newspapers and magazines, 1898–1937), supplement to "Fujo enchi to sono 'entei' tachi: 1930 nendai Chūgoku no feminizumu ron" 「婦女園地」とその「園丁」たちーー 1930 年代中国のフェミニズム論 (The women's garden and its gardeners: Chinese feminism in the 1930s). *Surugadai daigaku ronsō* 駿河台大学論叢 7 (1993), 149–61.

Mann, Susan. "The Education of Daughters in the Mid-Ch'ing Period." In *Education and Society in Late Imperial China, 1600–1900*, ed. Benjamin A. Elman and Alexander Woodside, 19–49. Berkeley: University of California Press, 1994.

———. "'Fuxue' (Women's Learning) by Zhang Xuechang (1738–1801): China's First History of Women's Culture." *Late Imperial China* 13:1 (June 1992), 40–56.

———. "Learned Women in the Eighteenth Century." In *Engendering China: Women, Culture, and the State*, ed. Christina K. Gilmartin et al., 27–46. Cambridge, MA: Harvard University Press, 1994.

———. *Precious Records: Women in China's Long Eighteenth Century*. Stanford, CA: Stanford University Press, 1997.

———. "Presidential Address: Myths of Asian Womanhood." *Journal of Asian Studies* 59:4 (Nov. 2000), 835–62.

———. "Widows in the Kinship, Class, and Community Structures of Qing Dynasty China." *Journal of Asian Studies* 46:1 (Feb. 1987), 37–51.

———. "Womanly Sentiments and Political Crises: Zhang Qieying's Poetic Voice in the Mid-Nineteenth Century." In *Wusheng zhi sheng: Jindai Zhongguo de funü yu guojia* 無聲之聲 (I): 近代中國的婦女與國家 ("Voices Amid Silence [I]: Women and the Culture in Modern China [1600–1950]"), ed. Lu Fangshang 呂芳上, 199–222. Taipei: Institute of Modern History, Academia Sinica, 2003.

———. "Women's Biographies as Family Romance." Keynote address presented at the *Journal of the History of Ideas* Second International Conference on Intellectual History: Chinese Intellectual History. Nanjing, May 2001.

———. "Women's Poems as Inscriptions on the Body Politic." Unpublished paper.

"Maochong nüxuesheng zhi huangdan" 冒充女學生之荒誕 (The ridiculous practice of pretending to be female students). *THRB* 27 (Sept. 11, 1909) [1:319].

Martin-Liao, Tianchi. "Traditional Handbooks of Women's Education." In *Women and Literature in China*, ed. Anna Gerstlachere et al., 165–89. Bochum: Brockmeyer, 1985.

Masini, Federico. *The Formation of Modern Chinese Lexicon and Its Evolution toward a National Language: The Period from 1840–1898.* Journal of Chinese Linguistics Monograph Series 6. Berkeley: University of California Press, 1993.

Matsuo Yōji 松尾洋二. "Liang Qichao yu shizhuan: Dongya jindai jingshen shi de benliu" 梁启超与史传—东亚近代精神史的奔流 (Liang Qichao and historical biography: The flow of the modern East Asian historical spirit). In Hazama Naoki, 244–85.

McClintock, Anne. "'No Longer in Future Heaven': Gender, Race and Nationalism." In *Dangerous Liaisons: Gender, Nation and Postcolonial Perspectives,* ed. Anne McClintock et al., 89–112. Minneapolis: University of Minnesota Press, 1997.

McElroy, Sarah Coles. "Forging a New Role for Women: Zhili First Women's Normal School and the Growth of Women's Education in China, 1901–1921." In *Education, Culture, and Identity in Twentieth-Century China,* ed. Glen Peterson et al., 348–74. Ann Arbor: University of Michigan Press, 2001.

Mei Zhu 梅鑄. "Faguo jiuwang nüjie Ruoan zhuan" 法國救亡女傑若安傳 (Biography of Joan, the heroic French savior). *XNJZZ* 3 (Apr. 5, 1907), 53–82.

Meisner, Maurice. *Li Ta-chao and the Origins of Chinese Marxism.* Cambridge, MA: Harvard University Press, 1967.

Miao Quansun 繆荃孫. *Xu bei zhuanji* 續碑傳記 (Inscriptional biographies, continued). *Jindai Zhongguo shiliao congkan* 近代中國史料叢刊, ed. Shen Yunlong 沈雲龍, vol. 919. Taipei: Wenhai chubanshe, 1973.

Min Erchang 閔爾昌. *Bei zhuanji bu* 碑傳記補 (Inscriptional biographies, supplement). *Jindai Zhongguo shiliao congkan* 近代中國史料叢刊, ed. Shen Yunlong 沈雲龍, vol. 1000. Taipei: Wenhai chubanshe, 1973.

Ming shi 明史 (Ming dynastic history). Beijing: Zhonghua shuju, 1974.

Mingyi nüshi 明夷女史 [Frustrated female worthy]. "Jinggao nüjie tongbao" 敬告女界同胞 (A warning for my female compatriots). *SB* (Aug. 10, 1907).

Mittler, Barbara. *A Newspaper for China? Power, Identity, and Change in Shanghai's News Media, 1872–1912.* Cambridge, MA: Harvard University Asia Center, 2004.

Mou, Sherry J. *Gentlemen's Prescriptions for Women's Lives: A Thousand Years of Biographies of Chinese Women.* Armonk, NY: M. E. Sharpe, 2004.

Mulan tongxiang 木蘭同鄉 [A fellow townswoman of Mulan]. "Gonghe xinnian" 恭賀新年 (Best wishes for the new year). *XNJZZ* 2 (Mar. 5, 1907), 27–33.

Murata Yūjirō 村田雄二郎, ed. *"Fujo zasshi" kara miru kindai Chūgoku josei* 「婦女雜誌」からみる近代中国女性 (Modern Chinese women from the perspective of the *Ladies' Journal*). Tokyo: Kanbun shuppan, 2005.

Murray, Julia K. "Didactic Art for Women: The *Ladies' Classic of Filial Piety.*" In *Flowering in the Shadows: Women in the History of Chinese and Japanese Painting,* ed. Marsha Weidner, 27–53. Honolulu: University of Hawai'i Press, 1990.

Nagayama Moriyoshi 永山盛良. *Taisei meifu den* 泰西名婦伝 (Famous Western women). Tokyo: Seiyōdō shobō, 1901.

Nakamura Takayuki 中村忠行. "Qiu Jin zazu" 秋瑾杂俎 (Miscellaneous reflections on Qiu Jin). Trans. Gao Yan 高岩. In Guo Yanli, *Qiu Jin yanjiu ziliao,* 243–49.

Naruse Jinzō 成瀬仁蔵. *Joshi kyōiku* 女子教育 (On women's education). In *Naruse*

Jinzō chosakushū 成瀬仁蔵著作集 (Naruse Jinzō's works), 2: 33–155. Tokyo: Nihon joshi daigaku, 1974.

———. *Nüzi jiaoyu lun* 女子教育論 (On women's education). Trans. Yang Tingdong 楊廷棟 and Zhou Zupei 周祖培. Shanghai: Zuoxin yishuju, 1901.

Nemoto Shō [Tadashi] 根本正, trans. *Ō-Bei joshi risshin den* 欧米女子立身伝 ("Famous Women" [Biographies of successful European and American women]). Tokyo: Yoshikawa kōbunkan, 1906.

Nivard, Jacqueline. "Bibliographie de la presse féminine chinoise, 1898–1949." *Études Chinoises* 5:1–2 (Spring–Autumn 1986), 185–236.

———. "Women and the Women's Press." *Republican China* 10:1 (Nov. 1984), 37–55.

Nivison, David S. "Aspects of Traditional Chinese Biography." *Journal of Asian Studies* 21:4 (Aug. 1962), 457–63.

Nolte, Sharon H., and Sally Ann Hastings. "The Meiji State's Policy toward Women." In *Recreating Japanese Women, 1600–1945*, ed. Gail Lee Bernstein, 151–74. Berkeley: University of California Press, 1991.

"Nü xuejie zhi guai xianzhuang" 女學界之怪現狀 (A strange phenomenon involving female students). *SB* (Nov. 21, 1910).

"Nü xuesheng shang Zhen beizi shu" 女學生上振貝子書 (Female students offer a petition to the Manchu noble [Zai] Zhen). *HB* 5 (May 27, 1903), 136–38 [728–30].

"Nü xuesheng touhuan" 女學生投繯 (A female student hangs herself). *QBLC*, 85–86.

"Nü xuesheng ying you jun fuzhi" 女學生應有準服制 (Female students' clothing must be regulated). *SB* (Aug. 18, 1906).

"Nü xueshi" 女學士 (Female students). *SB* (Aug. 18, 1910).

"Nü zhenzi zhuan" 女貞子傳 (Biography of a chaste woman). *Caifeng bao* 採風報 (July 13, 1898).

"Nüjie baolu hui chuandan" 女界保路會傳單 (Handbill for the Women's Railway Protection Association). *SB* (Nov. 3, 1907).

"Nüjie jinbu zhi qiandao" 女界進步之前導 (The Chinese women's future progress). *Nüxue bao* 女學報 2:2 (Apr. 12, 1903). Rpt. in *NQYDSL* 1, 521–23 (misdated 1907 in the reprint).

"Nüjie xinwen" 女界新聞 (Women's news). *BJNB* (July 9, 1906).

"Nüshi Du Qingchi disici yanshuo gao" 女士杜清池第四次演說稿 (Transcript of Ms. Du Qingchi's fourth lecture). *STSB* (Nov. 25, 1902).

"Nüshi fangzu bei bi biming haiwen" 女士放足被逼斃命骇聞 (Startling news of a woman being forced to meet a violent death for unbinding her feet). *ShB* (June 14, 1907).

"Nüxue jianxing" 女學漸興 (The gradual development of women's education). *SB* (July 11, 1904).

"Nüzhong zhi jie" 女中之傑 (A heroine among women). *STSB* (Oct. 22, 1904).

"Nüzi chuyang: Xin banben" 女子出洋：新班本 (Females go overseas: A new theater script). *STSB* (Feb. 26, 1907). Rpt. in *NQYDSL* 2, 1271–72.

"Nüzi wei guomin zhi mu" 女子為國民之母 (Women are mothers of citizens). *STSB* (July 19, 1905). Rpt. in *NQYDSL* 1, 606–08.

O'Hara, Albert Richard. *The Position of Woman in Early China According to the Lieh Nü Chuan, "The Biographies of Chinese Women."* Taipei: Meiya Publications, 1971.

Ono Kazuko. *Chinese Women in a Century of Revolution.* Trans. and ed. Joshua A. Fogel. Stanford, CA: Stanford University Press, 1989.

Ōsato Hiroaki 大里浩秋. "Nihonjin no mita Shū Kin: Shū Kin shijitsu no jakkan no saikentō" 日本人の見た秋瑾—秋瑾史実の若干の再検討 (Japanese views of Qiu Jin: A reexamination of a number of historical facts concerning Qiu Jin). *Chūgoku kenkyū geppō* 中国研究月報 453 (Nov. 1985), 1–20.

Osborne, Peter. *The Politics of Time: Modernity and Avant-Garde.* London: Verso, 1995.

Ou Ning 欧宁. "Da zha lan jihua: chuanyue chengshi fudi" 大栅栏计划：穿越城市腹地 (The Da zha lan project: Crossing into the heart of the city). www.dazhalan-project.org/press-cn/press010.htm.

Ozouf, Mona. *Women's Words: Essay on French Singularity.* Chicago: University of Chicago Press, 1997.

Pao Chia-lin 鮑家麟. "Qiu Jin yu Qingmo funü yundong" 秋瑾與清末婦女運動 (Qiu Jin and the late Qing women's movement). In *ZGFNS* 1, 346–82.

———. "Song Shu de funü sixiang" 宋恕的婦女思想 (Song Shu's views on women). In *ZGFNS* 3, 163–82.

Pao Tao Chia-lin. "The Anti-Footbinding Movement in Late Ch'ing China: Indigenous Development and Western Influence." *Jindai Zhongguo funü shi yanjiu* 近代中國婦女史研究 2 (1994), 141–78.

Parker, Andrew, Mary Russo, Doris Sommer, and Patricia Yaeger. "Introduction." In *Nationalisms and Sexualities*, ed. Andrew Parker, et al., 1–18. New York: Routledge, 1992.

Pei Gong 佩公. "Nannü pingdeng de biyao" 男女平等的必要 (The need for equality between men and women). *XNJZZ* 2, 35–44.

———. "Nannü pingdeng de zhenli" 男女平等的真理 (The true principle of equality between men and women). *XNJZZ* 1 (Feb. 5, 1907), 29–40.

Peng Yulian 彭玉麟, and Yin Jiajun 殷家儁, comp. *Hunan sheng Hengyang xian zhi san* 湖南省衡陽縣志三 (Hunan province, Hengyang county gazetteer, vol. 3) (1872). Rpt. in *Zhongguo fangzhi congshu, Huadong difang, diyiyisan hao* 中國方志叢書華東地方第一一三號 (Compendium of Chinese gazetteers, South China, no. 113). Taipei: Chengwen chubanshe, 1970.

Pernoud, Regine. *Joan of Arc by Herself and Her Witnesses.* Trans. Edward Hyams. Lanham, MD: Scarborough House, 1994.

Peterson, Barbara Bennett, ed. *Notable Women of China: Shang Dynasty to the Early Twentieth Century.* Armonk, NY: M. E. Sharpe, 2000.

Pocock, J. G. A. "Modes of Political and Historical Time in Early Eighteenth-Century England." In *Virtue, Commerce, and History: Essays on Political*

Thought and History, Chiefly in the Eighteenth Century, 91–102. Cambridge, Eng: Cambridge University Press, 1985.

Pong, David. *Shen Pao-chen and China's Modernization in the Nineteenth Century*. Cambridge, Eng.: Cambridge University Press, 1994.

Poovey, Mary. "Curing the 'Social Body' in 1832: James Phillips Kay and the Irish in Manchester." In Special Issue on Gender, Nationalisms and National Identities, *Gender and History* 5:2 (Summer 1993), 196–211.

Qian Daxin 錢大昕. "Da wenwu" 答問五 (Response to question five), "Fangjie fuzhuan" 方節婦傳 (Biography of chaste widow Fang), "Xia lienü zhuan" 夏烈女傳 (Biography of the female martyr Xia). In *Qianyan tang wenji* 錢研堂文集 (Essays from the Hall of Subtle Research), 8: 93–106; 40: 633–34, 634–35. Taipei: Commercial Press, 1968.

Qian, Nanxiu 钱南秀. "'Borrowing Foreign Mirrors and Candles to Illuminate Chinese Civilization': Xue Shaohui's Moral Vision in the *Biographies of Foreign Women*." In Fong, Qian, and Zurndorfer, 60–101.

———. "Milk and Scent: Works about Women in the *Shishuo xinyu* Genre." *Nan Nü: Men, Women and Gender in Early and Imperial China* 1:2 (Oct. 1999), 187–236.

———. "The Mother *Nü Xuebao* versus the Daughter *Nü Xuebao*: Generational Differences between 1898 and 1902 Women Reformers." In Nanxiu Qian, Fong, and Smith.

———. "Qingji nüzuojia Xue Shaohui ji qi *Waiguo lienü zhuan*" 清季女作家薛绍徽及其《外国列女传》(The late Qing woman writer Xue Shaohui and her *Arrayed Traditions of Foreign Women*). *Wenxue pinglun congkan* 文学评论丛刊 4:1 (2001), 102–26.

———. "Revitalizing the Xianyuan (*Worthy Ladies*) Tradition: Women in the 1898 Reforms." *Modern China* 29:4 (Oct. 2003), 399–454.

Qian, Nanxiu, Grace S. Fong, and Richard J. Smith, eds. *Different Worlds of Discourse: Transformations of Gender and Genre in Late Qing and Early Republican China*. Leiden: Brill, forthcoming.

Qian Wenbin 錢文彬. "Yong lidai nüjiang" 詠歷代女將 (To sing of women officers through the ages). *STSB* (May 11, 1911).

Qiantang zhuren 錢塘主人 [Jiantang 鑑塘, Yan Xiyuan 顏希源], ed. *Baimei xin yongtu zhuan* 百美新詠圖傳 (New verses and illustrations of one hundred beauties). Prefaces dated 1787, 1790. Rpt., Taipei: Guangwen shuju, 1970.

Qianzhu 潛諸. "Du Shijie shi nüjie" 讀 世界十女傑 (On reading *Ten World Heroines*). *NZSJ* 10 (n.d.), 77–78 [933–34].

"Qiaoguo furen" 譙國夫人 (Woman of the state of Qiao). In *Xinjiaoben Sui shu, fu suoyin* 新校本隋書附索引 (New edition of the *History of the Sui Dynasty*, with index), comp. Wei Zheng 魏徵, 80: "Liezhuan" 45. Rpt. in *Zhongguo xueshu leibian* 中國學術類編, 1800–3. Taipei: Dingwen shuju, 1990.

"Qing ding nü xuesheng fuzhi" 請定女學生服制 (Petition to regulate female students' clothing). "Nü jie xinwen" 女界新聞. *BJNB* (Aug. 9, 1906).

"Qing jin nüxue" 請禁女學 (A plea to ban women's schools). *Xiaolin bao* 笑林報 (Sept. 8, 1907).

Qingjiang Xuce 清江徐珊. "Mulan ci" 木蘭辭 (The ballad of Mulan). *FNSB* 2 (July 10, 1911), 74.

Qiu Jin 秋瑾. "Jinggao jiemeimen" 敬告姐妹們 (Advice for my sisters). *Zhongguo nübao* 中國女報 1. Rpt. in Qiu Jin, *Qiu Jin xianlie*, 142–45.

———. "Jinggao Zhongguo erwanwan nü tongbao" 敬告中國二萬萬女同胞 (Advice for the 200 million female compatriots of China). Rpt. in Qiu Jin, *Qiu Jin xianlie*, 133–35.

———. [Jianhu nüxia Qiu Jin 鑑湖女俠 秋瑾]. "Kanhuxue jiaocheng" 看護學教程 (A course in nursing). *Zhongguo nübao* 中國女報 1 (Jan. 14, 1907), 23–31; 2 (Mar. 4, 1907), 17–26.

———. *Jingwei shi* 精衛石 (Jingwei bird). In Qiu Jin, *Qiu Jin ji*, 117–60.

———. [Jianhu nüxia 鑑湖女俠]. "Mian nüquan" 勉女權 (Urging women's rights). *Zhongguo nübao* 中國女報 2 (Mar. 4, 1907), 47.

———. *Qiu Jin ji* 秋瑾集 (Writings of Qiu Jin). Hong Kong: Changfeng tushu gongsi, 1974.

———. *Qiu Jin xianlie wenji* 秋瑾先烈文集 (Writings of the national martyr Qiu Jin). Taipei: Zhongguo Guomindang, Zhongyang weiyuanhui, Dangshi wei-yuanhui, 1982.

———. "Shijian nü xuexiao fushu Qingguo nüzi shifan gongyi suchengke lüe-zhang qishi" 實踐女學校附屬清國女子師範工藝速成科略章啟事 (Brief regula-tions for the short-term normal and handicraft programs for Chinese women affiliated with the Jissen Women's School). Rpt. in Qiu Jin, *Qiu Jin ji*, 9–10.

———. "Yanshuo de haochu" 演說的好處 (The advantages of public speaking). In Qiu Jin, *Qiu Jin xianlie*, 141–42.

Qiu Liu 秋柳. "Mofan zhi nü xuesheng" 模範之女學生 (The model female stu-dent). *SB* (Dec. 13, 1910).

Qizhan 棨旃. "Yingguo xiaoshuo jia Ailiatuo nüshi zhuan" 英國小說家 愛里阿脫 女士傳 (Biography of the English novelist Lady Eliot). *XNJZZ* 4 (May 5, 1907), 51–55.

Quan Hansheng 全漢昇. "Qingmo de 'Xixue yuanchu Zhongguo' shuo" 清末的 「西學源出中國」說 (The late Qing discourse on "Western learning originat-ing in China"). *Lingnan xuebao* 嶺南學報 4:2 (1935), 57–102.

Rancière, Jacques. "The Archaeomodern Turn." In *Walter Benjamin and the De-mands of History*, ed. Michael P. Steinberg, 24–40. Ithaca, NY: Cornell Univer-sity Press, 1996.

Rankin, Mary Backus. *Early Chinese Revolutionaries: Radical Intellectuals in Shang-hai and Chekiang, 1902–1911*. Cambridge, MA: Harvard University Press, 1971.

———. "The Emergence of Women at the End of the Ch'ing: The Case of Ch'iu Chin." In *Women in Chinese Society*, ed. Margery Wolf and Roxane Witke, 39–66. Stanford, CA: Stanford University Press, 1975.

Raphals, Lisa. "Arguments by Women in Early Chinese Texts." *Nan Nü: Men, Women and Gender in Early and Imperial China* 3:2 (2001), 157–95.

———. *Sharing the Light: Representations of Women and Virtue in Early China.* Albany: State University of New York Press, 1998.

Rawski, Evelyn. *Education and Popular Literacy in Ch'ing China.* Ann Arbor: University of Michigan Press, 1979.

Reed, Christopher R. *Gutenberg in Shanghai: Chinese Print Capitalism, 1867–1937.* Vancouver: University of British Columbia Press, 2004.

Reynolds, Douglas R. *China, 1898–1912: The Xinzheng Revolution and Japan.* Cambridge, MA: Council on East Asian Studies, Harvard University, 1993.

Rhoads, Edward J. M. *Manchus & Han: Ethnic Relations and Political Power in Late Qing and Early Republican China, 1861–1928.* Seattle: University of Washington Press, 2000.

"Riben Daban Bolanhui Zhongguo Fujian chupin yichu Taiwan guan shimo ji" 日本大坂博覽會中國福建出品移出臺灣館始末記 (A complete account of the transfer of Fujianese products from China to the Taiwan Pavilion at the Japanese Osaka Exhibition). *JS* 1 (Apr. 27, 1903), 146–47 [164–65].

"Riben Dongya nü xuexiao fushu Zhongguo nüzi liuxuesheng sucheng shifan xuetang zhangcheng" 日本東亞女學校附屬中國女子留學生速成師範學堂章程 (Regulations for the Chinese female overseas students accelerated normal school affiliated with the Japanese East Asian Women's School). *DFZZ* 2:6 (July 27, 1905), 145–48.

"Riben liuxue nüxuesheng Gongai hui zhangcheng" 日本留學女學生共愛會章程 (Regulations for the female overseas student Humanitarian Association in Japan). *ZJC* 3 (Apr. 17, 1903), 166–69. Rpt. in *JS* 2 (May 27, 1903), 155–57 [0387–89].

"Riben nü shehuidang ji" 日本女社會黨記 (A record of the Japanese female socialist party). *Minli bao* 民立報 (Nov. 20, 1910). Rpt. in *NQYDSL* 1, 305–6.

"Rifu ren jiaoxi" 日婦任教習 (Japanese women become teachers). *Jingzhong ribao* 警鍾日報 (May 22, 1904). Rpt. in *NQYDSL* 1, 293–94.

Riley, Denise. "Does a Sex Have a History?" In *Feminism and History*, ed. Joan Wallach Scott, 17–33. Oxford: Oxford University Press, 1996.

Rofel, Lisa B. "'Yearnings': Televisual Love and Melodramatic Politics in Contemporary China." *American Ethnologist* 21:4 (Nov. 1994), 700–22.

Rongqing 榮慶, Zhang Boxi 張百熙, and Zhang Zhidong 張之洞. "Zouding mengyangyuan zhangcheng ji jiating jiaoyu fa zhangcheng" 奏定蒙養院章程及家庭教育法章程 (Memorial on regulations for kindergartens and for methods of household education), Jan. 13, 1904. Rpt. in *XZYB*, 393–96.

Ropp, Paul S., Paola Zamperini, and Harriet Zurndorfer, eds. Special Theme Issue "Passionate Women: Female Suicide in Late Imperial China." *Nan Nü: Men, Women and Gender in Early and Imperial China* 3:1 (2001).

Rowe, William T. *Saving the World: Chen Hongmou and Elite Consciousness in Eighteenth-Century China.* Stanford, CA: Stanford University Press, 2001.

———. "Women and the Family in Mid-Qing Social Thought: The Case of Chen Hongmou." *Late Imperial China* 13 (Dec. 1992), 1–41.

"Ruan furen zhanshen jingshi" 阮夫人湛深經史 (Lady Ruan's profound knowledge of the classics and histories). *THRB* 2 (Aug. 17, 1909) [1:15].

Rüsen, Jörn. "Making Sense of Time: Towards a Universal Typology of Conceptual Foundations of Historical Consciousness." In Huang Chun-chieh and Henderson, 3–18.

Ryckmans, Pierre. "The Chinese Attitude towards the Past." *The Forty-seventh George Ernest Morrison Lecture in Ethnology*. Canberra: The Australian National University, 1986.

Saeki Megumi 佐伯恵. "Meiji ki no Chūgokujin joshi ryūgakusei—Jissen jogakkō o chūshin ni" 明治期の中国人女子留学生—実践女学校を中心に (Chinese overseas students in the Meiji period: The Jissen Women's School). M.A. thesis, Kyoritsu Women's University, 1994.

Sakaki Mitsuko 坂寄美都子. "Sakaki Mitsuko shi dan" 坂寄美都子氏談 (A conversation with Ms. Sakaki Mitsuko). In Jissen joshi daigaku toshokan, Shimoda Utako kankei shiryō, file no. 3001-1 (Aug. 26, 1968).

———. "Shimoda Utako sanjūshichi nen kaiki kinen kōen" 下田歌子三十七年回忌記念講演 (Memorial lecture thirty-seven years after Shimoda Utako's death). Jissen joshi daigaku toshokan, Shimoda Utako kankei shiryō, file no. 3001-4 (Nov. 8, 1972).

"Sancheng nüxue chuanxisuo kaixue" 三城女學傳習所開學 (Opening of the three city institutes for women's education). *STSB* (Sept. 3, 4, 5, 7, 1909). Rpt. in *NQYDSL* 1, 1190–94.

Sanduo 三多. "Ji Huixing nüjie wei xue xunshen shi" 記惠興女傑為學殉身事 (Record of the heroine Huixing's martyrdom for education). *DGB* (Mar. 14 1906).

Sanetō Keishū 實藤專秀. *Chūgokujin Nihon ryūgaku shi zōho* 中国人日本留学史増補 (A history of Chinese students in Japan, enlarged edition). Tokyo: Kuroshio shuppan, 1970.

Sanetō Keishū 實藤專秀, Tam Yue-him 譚汝謙, and Ogawa Hiroshi 小川博, eds. *Zhongguo yi Ribenshu zonghe mulu* 中國譯日本書綜合目錄 (A synthetic catalog of Chinese translations of Japanese books). Hong Kong: Zhongwen daxue chubanshe, 1981.

Sang Bing 桑兵. "Jindai Zhongguo nüxing shi yanjiu sanlun" 近代中国女性史研究散论 (Random notes on the study of modern Chinese women's history). *Jindai shi yanjiu* 近代史研究 3 (1996), 259–75.

Sang, Tze-lan. *The Emerging Lesbian: Female Same-Sex Desire in Modern China*. Chicago: University of Chicago Press, 2003.

Sangari, Kumkum, and Sudesh Vaid. "Recasting Women: An Introduction." In *Recasting Women: Essays in Indian Colonial History*, ed. Kumkum Sangari and Sudesh Vaid, 2–26. New Brunswick, NJ: Rutgers University Press, 1990.

Savage-Landor, A. Henry. *China and the Allies*. 2 vols. New York: Charles Scribner's Sons, 1901.

Schaberg, David. *A Patterned Past: Form and Thought in Early Chinese Historiography*. Cambridge, MA: Harvard University Asia Center, 2001.

Schama, Simon. *Citizens: A Chronicle of the French Revolution.* New York: Vintage Books, 1989.

Schulz Zinda, Yvonne. "Propagating New 'Virtues': 'Patriotism' in Late Qing Textbooks for the Moral Education of Primary Students." In *Mapping Meanings: The Field of New Learning in Late Qing China*, ed. Michael Lackner and Natascha Vittinghoff, 677–702. Leiden: Brill, 2004.

Schwartz, Benjamin I. *Chinese Communism and the Rise of Mao.* Cambridge, MA: Harvard University Press, 1951.

———. "The Limits of 'Tradition Versus Modernity' as Categories of Explanation: The Case of Chinese Intellectuals." *Daedalus* 101 (Spring 1972), 71–88.

Scott, Joan Wallach, ed. *Feminism and History.* Oxford: Oxford University Press, 1996.

———. *Only Paradoxes to Offer: French Feminists and the Rights of Man.* Cambridge, MA: Harvard University Press, 1998.

Sechiyama Kaku 瀬地山角, and Kihara Yōko 木原葉子. "Higashi Ajia ni okeru ryōsai kenbo shugi" 東アジアにおける良妻賢母主義 ("An Ideology of Female Education in Modern East Asia: A Project to Shape a Modern Society"). *Chūgoku shakai to bunka* 中国社会と文化 4 (June 1989), 277–93.

Shan Zai 善哉. "Funü tongxing zhi aiqing" 婦女同性之愛情 (Same-sex love among women). *FNSB* 7 (June 1911), 36–38.

Shang Wei. Rulin waishi *and Cultural Transformation in Late Imperial China.* Cambridge, MA: Harvard University Press, 2003.

"Shanghai funü zhi xin zhuangshu" 上海婦女之新妝束 (New restrictions on the adornment of women of Shanghai). *FNSB* 1 (May 13, 1911), 54.

"Shanghai nü xuexiaozhang zhi Jiangsu zongxuehui han" 上海女學校長至江蘇總學會函 (A letter from the principal of a Shanghai girls' school to the Jiangsu General Educational Association). *SB* (June 9, 1906).

"Shanghai Zhongguo nüzi ticao xuexiao kaixue jilüe" 上海中國女子體操學校開學記略 (A brief record of the opening of Shanghai's Chinese Girls' School For Physical Education). *Zhili jiaoyu zazhi* 直隸教育雜誌 12 (1908), 106. Rpt. in *XZSL* 2:2, 720–21.

"Shaojie piping" 紹介批評 (Introduction and criticism). *JYZZ* 1.2 (Mar. 16, 1909), 7 [175].

"Sheli zhenjietang xuwen" 設立貞節堂續聞 (Sequel to news of the establishment of a hall for revering chastity). *STSB* (Mar. 24, 1905).

"Shen furen zuoshou Guangxin cheng" 沈夫人佐守廣信城 (Lady Shen helps protect the city of Guangxin). *THRB* 4 (Aug. 19, 1909), [1:39].

"Shen Jiangjun yongduo fushi" 沈將軍勇奪父屍 (Officer Shen courageously seizes her father's corpse). *THRB* 14 (Aug. 29, 1909) [1:159].

Shen Zhaoyi 沈兆褘. *Xinxue shumu tiyao* 新學書目提要 (Annotated bibliography of new learning). Shanghai: Tongya shuju, 1904–5.

"Shen Zhongli guancha shang Duanfang bing" 沈仲禮觀察上端午帥稟 (Shen Zhongli examines the petition sent to Duan Wushuai). *ShB* (June 27, 1907).

"Shenlun xuejie baojie kaihui zhuiduo Huixing nüjie wei tiaohe Man-Han jiexian zhudongli" 申論學界報界開會追悼惠興女傑為調和滿漢界限助動力 (Further discussion of how the memorial service for Huixing sponsored by educators and journalists served to harmonize relations between Manchus and Han). *STSB* (Feb. 9 1906). Rpt. in *NQYDSL* 2, 1451–53.

Shi He 史和, Yao Fushen 姚福申, and Ye Huidi 叶翠娣, eds. *Zhongguo jindai baokan minglu* 中国近代报刊名录 (Directory of modern Chinese newspapers). Fuzhou: Fujian renmin chubanshe, 1991.

Shi Shuyi 施淑儀. "Duiyu liefu xunfu zhi ganyan" 對於烈婦殉夫之感言" (Emotional words on women who follow their husbands in death). *Funü zazhi* 1:8 (Aug. 1915), 6.

Shiina Noritaka 椎名仙卓. *Meiji hakubutsukan kotohajime* 明治博物館事始め (Primer on Meiji museums). Kyoto: Shibunkaku shuppan, 1989.

Shijie shi nüjie 世界十女傑 (Ten world heroines). n.p. 1903.

"Shijie shi nüjie" 世界十女傑 (Ten world heroines). *Subao* 蘇報 (June 12, 1903). Rpt. in *NQYDSL* 2, 820.

"Shijin nüxue" 示禁女學 (Notice to ban women's schools). *STSB* (June 11, 1903).

Shimoda Utako 下田歌子. "Ou-Mi zhuguo nüzi zhi tiyu" 歐米諸國女子之體育 (Female physical education in Europe and the United States). *JS* 1 (Apr. 27, 1903), 90–92 [1016–18].

———. *Shina ryūgakusei no tame no shūshin kōwa* 支那留學生のための修身講話 (Lectures on ethics for Chinese overseas students). Jissen joshi daigaku toshokan, Shimoda Utako kankei shiryo, file no. 181.

Shimomi Takao 下見隆雄. "Ryū Kō *Retsujo den* yori miru Jukyō shakai to bosei genri" 劉向「列女伝」より見る儒教社会と母性原理 (Confucian society and maternal principles in Liu Xiang's *Lienü zhuan*). *Hiroshima daigaku bungakubu kiyō* 広島大学文学部紀要 50 (Mar. 1991), 1–21.

Shirai Kikurō 白井規矩郎. "Yuanxu" 原序 (Original preface). In Alice R. James, 1a–2b.

Shoujuan 瘦鵑. "Meiguo nü jiaoyujia Lihen nüshi yihua" 美國女教育家麗痕女士逸話 (An anecdotal account of the American female educator [Mary] Lyon). *FNSB* 3 (May 13, 1911), 47–49.

"Shouzhen shuo" 守貞說 (On preserving chastity). *Xiaolin bao* 笑林報 (Jan. 2, 1903), 1.

Shu Guobi 蜀郭必, ed. "Funü zhuanglie tan" 婦女壯烈談 (Courageous women). *Xingshi* 醒獅 3, n.d. Rpt. in *NQYDSL* 1, 339.

"Shu jiaoyu Zhongguo funü shi" 述教育中國婦女事 (Description of Chinese female education [in Japan]). *STSB* (Jan. 12, 1906). Rpt. in *NQYDSL* 2, 1270.

"Shuchang yu xuetang zhi guanxi" 書場與學堂之關 係 (The relationship between brothels and schools). *THRB* 130 (Dec. 23, 1909) [3:358].

"Shuntian fu Tongzhou shenmin gongyi tianzu she qi" 順天府通州紳民公議天足社啟 (The gentry and people of Tongzhou in Shuntian [district] advocate the establishment of a natural foot society). *STSB*, Dec. 17, 1904.

"Si zhongnü zhuan" 四忠女傳 (Biographies of four loyal women). *DFZZ* 6:8 (1910), 49–51.

"Sichuan nü xuetang xuesheng Zhongguo furen hui shuji Du Chengshu da Yixue-
guan xuesheng Qu Jiang mishu" 四川女學堂學生中國婦人會書記杜成淑答譯
學館學生 屈疆密書 (Du Chengshu, a student at the Sichuan Girls' School and
secretary of the Chinese Women's Association, responds to a secret letter from
Qu Jiang, a student at the Translation Study Bureau). *DGB* (Feb. 27, 1907).

Sievers, Sharon L. *Flowers in Salt: The Beginnings of Feminist Consciousness in Modern Japan*. Stanford, CA: Stanford University Press, 1983.

von Sivers, Gabriele. "Die mythische Figur Nügua in der anarchistischen
Zeitschrift *Naturgemäfe Rechtilichkeit* (*Tian Yi* 天義), 1907–1908." In *Zwischen
Tradition und Revolution: Lebensentwürfe und Levensvollzüge chinesischer Frauen
an de Schwelle zur Moderne*, ed. Monika Übelhör, 105–30. Marborg: Marborg
University Press, 2001.

Sivin, Nathan. "State, Cosmos, and Body in the Last Three Centuries B.C." *Harvard Journal of Asiatic Studies* 55:1 (June 1995), 5–37.

Smith, Anthony D. *Nationalism and Modernism: A Critical Survey of Recent
Theories of Nations and Nationalism*. London: Routledge, 1998.

Sōgō Masaki 惣郷正明. *Meiji no kotoba jiten* 明治のことば辞典 (Dictionary of
Meiji terms). Tokyo: Tōkyōdō shuppan, 1986.

Sommer, Matthew H. *Sex, Law, and Society in Late Imperial China*. Stanford, CA:
Stanford University Press, 2000.

Song Shu 宋恕. "Biantong pian—kaihua zhang disi" 變通篇 · 開化章第四 (Essay
on adaptation: Fourth essay on the civilizing process). *Liuzhai beiyi* 六齋卑議
18–19. Rpt. in *XZSL* 1:2, 865.

Song Yuanfang 宋原放, and Sun Yong 孙 顒. *Shanghai chuban zhi* 上海出版
志 (Encyclopedia of publishing in Shanghai). Shanghai: Shanghai shehui
kexueyuan chubanshe, 2001.

Strand, David. "Citizens in the Audience: Politics at the Podium in Early Twentieth Century China." In *Citizenship in Modern China*, ed. Elizabeth Perry and
Merle Goldman, 44–69. Cambridge, MA: Harvard Contemporary China Series, Harvard University Press, 2002.

Struve, Lynn A. "Introduction." In *Time, Temporality, and Imperial Transition: East
Asia from Ming to Qing*, ed. Lynn A. Struve, 3–27. Honolulu: Association for
Asian Studies and University of Hawai'i Press, 2005.

[Sun] Qingru 孫清如. "Lun nüxue" 論女學 (On women's education). *XNJZZ* 2
(Mar. 5, 1907), 1–10.

Sun Shiyue 孫石月. *Zhongguo jindai nüzi liuxue shi* 中国近代女子留学史 (The history of Chinese female overseas study). Beijing: Zhongguo heping chubanshe,
1995.

Swann, Nancy Lee. *Pan Chao: Foremost Woman Scholar of China*. Russell and Russell, 1968. Rpt., Ann Arbor: Michigan Classics in Chinese Studies, Center for
Chinese Studies, University of Michigan, 2001.

Taga Akigorō 多賀秋伍郎, comp. *Kindai Chūgoku kyōiku shi shiryō, Shinmatsu hen*
近代中国教育史資料、清末編 (Historical materials for modern Chinese education, the late Qing). Tokyo: Nihon gakujutsu shinkō kai, 1972.

Tai Gong 太公. "Dongjing zashi shi" 東京雜事詩 (Poems on various topics concerning Tokyo). *ZJC* 2 (Mar. 18, 1903), 161–65.

Takamure Itsue 高群逸枝. *Josei no rekishi* 女性の歴史 (The history of women). 2 vols. Tokyo: Rironsha, 1966.

Takano Hiromu 高野弘. "Ji jiefu Ma shi shi" 紀節婦馬氏事 (The virtuous Lady Ma). In Takano Hiromu, *Qisu lu* 泣訴錄 (Record of grievances). Tokyo, 1905. Sanetō bunko 実藤文庫 (Sanetō Collection) no. 996. Tokyo Hibiya Library Archives.

Takeda Taijun 武田泰淳. *Shūfū shūu hito o shūsatsu su* 秋風秋雨人を愁殺す (The tragic execution of the [author] of autumn wind and autumn rain). Tokyo: Chikuma shobō, 1968.

Tan, Christine C. Y. "Prints, Seriality, and *Baimeitu* ("Pictures of One Hundred Beauties") in Nineteenth Century China." Unpublished paper.

"Tan liefu zhuan" 譚烈婦傳 (Biography of the heroic woman Tan). *Qingyi bao* 清議報 (reprinted from *Tianjin guowenbao* 天津國聞報) 4 (Apr. 10 1899). Rpt., Taipei: Chengwen chubanshe, 1967, [601–2].

Tan Sheying 談社英. *Zhongguo funü yundong tongshi* 中國婦女運動通史 (A general history of the Chinese women's movement) (1936). Rpt. in *Minguo congshu* 民國叢書 (Compendium of sources from the Republican period), 2: 18. Shanghai: Shanghai shudian, 1990.

Tan Xuncong 譚訓聰. "Tan Sitong furen shilüe: wei xianzumu Li Taigongren xunfu yishi bianzheng" 譚嗣同夫人事略：為先祖母李太恭人殉夫一事辨正 (A brief biography of Tan Sitong's wife: To correct the record concerning my great grandmother, the honorable Lady Li, martyring herself after the death of her husband). *Yiwen zhi* 藝文誌 30 (Mar. 1968), 21–22.

———. "Xian zumu (Tan Sitong furen) jiachuan" 先祖母(譚嗣同夫人) 家傳 (The family history of my great grandmother [the wife of Tan Sitong]). *Hunan wenxian jikan* 湖南文獻季刊 6–7 (Oct. 1972), 122.

Tang, Xiaobing. *Global Space and the Nationalist Discourse of Modernity: The Historical Thinking of Liang Qichao.* Stanford, CA: Stanford University Press, 1996.

Taylor, Charles. *Modern Social Imaginaries.* Durham, NC: Duke University Press, 2004.

Theiss, Janet. *Disgraceful Matters: The Politics of Chastity in Eighteenth-Century China.* Berkeley: University of California Press, 2004.

———. "From Model Subjects to Model Victims: Chastity Awards in the Rise and Fall of the Qing." Paper presented at the Association of Asian Studies annual meeting, Chicago, 2001.

———. "Managing Martyrdom: Female Suicide and Statecraft in Mid-Qing China." In Ropp, Zamperini, and Zurndorfer, 47–76.

"Tianzu hui Shen Zhongli guancha zhi Song Dunfu guancha shu" 天足會 沈仲禮 觀察致宋敦甫觀察書 (Shen Zongli of the Natural Foot Society examines Song Dunfu's investigative report). *ShB* (July 31, 1907).

T'ien Ju-k'ang [Tian Rukang]. *Male Anxiety and Female Chastity: A Comparative Study of Chinese Ethical Values in Ming-Ch'ing Times.* Leiden: E. J. Brill, 1988.

Tongxiang Xu Xuehua 桐鄉徐雪華. "Du Mulan ci shuhou" 讀木蘭辭書後 (Written after reading the Ballad of Mulan). *FNSB* 1 (May 13, 1911), 82.

"Tongyi Yang Nüshi xu" 同邑楊女士序 (Preface by fellow townswoman Ms. Yang). In Jin Tiange, *Nüjie*, 6–7.

Tsuboya Zenshirō 坪谷善四郎. *Hoku Shin kansen ki* 北清観戦記 (Observation of the battles in northern China). Tokyo: Bunbudō, 1901.

Tu Wei-ming 杜維明. *Ruxue disanqi fazhan de qianjing wenti: Dalu jiangxue, wennan he taolun* 儒學第三期發展的前景問題：大陸講學，問難，和討論 (Prospects for the development of third-wave Confucianism: Lectures, questions, and discussion in mainland China). Taipei: Lianjing chuban shiye gongsi, 1989.

Tuckey, Janet. *Kaiten iseki Fukkoku bidan* 回天偉蹟仏国美談 (The French tale of an extraordinary achievement). Trans. Awaya Kan'ichi 粟屋関一. Tokyo: Dōmei shobō, 1886.

Twitchett, Denis. "Problems of Chinese Biography." In *Confucian Personalities*, ed. Arthur F. Wright and Denis Twitchett, 24–39. Stanford, CA: Stanford University Press, 1962.

Uenuma Hachirō 上沼八郎. "Shimoda Utako to Chūgoku joshi ryūgakusei: Jissen jogakkō 'Chūgoku ryūgakuseibu' to chūshin to shite" 下田歌子と中国女子留学生一実践女学校「中国留学生部」を中心として (Shimoda Utako and the Chinese female overseas students, with a focus on the Chinese Overseas Student Department of the Jissen Women's School). *Jissen Joshi daigaku bungakubu kiyō* 実践女子大学文学部紀要 25 (Mar. 1983), 61–89.

Unger, Jonathan, ed. *Chinese Nationalism*. Armonk, NY: M. E. Sharpe, 1996.

Uno, Kathleen S. "The Origins of 'Good Wife, Wise Mother' in Modern Japan." In *Japanische Frauengeschichte(n)*, ed. Erich Pauer and Regine Mathias, 31–46. Marburg: Förderverein Marburger Japan-Reihe, 1995.

Vissière, A. "Biographie de Jouàn Yuân, Homme d'état, lettré et mathématicien (1764–1849)." *T'oung Pao* (1904), 561–96.

Wa Hun 媧魂. "Bu Tianshi juan zhi yi" 補天石卷之一 (Repairing the firmament, part 1). *XNJZZ* 2 (Mar. 5, 1907), 149–56; 3 (Apr. 5, 1907), 161–74.

Waley, Arthur, trans. *Chinese Poems*. London: George Allen and Unwin, 1962.

Waltner, Ann. "On Not Becoming a Heroine: Lin Dai-yu and Cui Ying-ying." *Signs: Journal of Women in Culture and Society* 15:1 (1989), 61–78.

Wang, C. H. "Towards Defining a Chinese Heroism." *Journal of the American Oriental Society* 95:1 (Jan.–Mar., 1974), 25–35.

Wang Canzhi 王燦芝. *Qiu Jin nüxia yiji* 秋瑾女俠遺集 (Traces of the female knight-errant, Qiu Jin). Beijing: Zhonghua shuju chuban, 1929.

Wang, David Der-wei 王德威. *Fictional Realism in Twentieth-Century China: Mao Dun, Lao She, Shen Congwen*. New York: Columbia University Press, 1992.

———. *Fin-de-Siècle Splendor: Repressed Modernities of Late Qing Fiction, 1849–1911*. Stanford, CA: Stanford University Press, 1997.

———. "Jia Baoyu ye shi liuxuesheng-wan Qing de liuxuesheng xiaoshuo" 賈寶玉也是留學生—晚清的 留學生小說 (Jiao Baoyu is also an overseas student: Late Qing overseas student novels). In Wang Dewei, *Xiaoshuo Zhongguo: wan*

Qing dao dangdai de Zhongguo xiaoshuo 小說中國：晚清到當代的中國小說 (Narrating China: Chinese fiction from the late Qing to the contemporary era), 229–36. Taipei: Maitian chuban gongsi, 1993.

Wang Guangyi 王光宜. "Mingdai nü jiaoyushu yanjiu" 明代女教育書研究 (A study of women's instruction books from the Ming dynasty). M.A. thesis, Taiwan Normal University, Institute of History, 1999.

Wang Hui. *China's New World Order: Society, Politics, and Economy in Transition.* Ed. Theodore Huters. Cambridge MA: Harvard University Press, 2003.

Wang Huiji 王惠姬. "Qingmo Minchu de nüzi liuxue jiaoyu" 清末民初的女子留學教育 (Overseas female education in the late Qing and early Republic). M.A. thesis, National Chengchi University, 1980.

Wang Jianjun 王建軍. *Zhongguo jindai jiaokeshu fazhan yanjiu* 中国近代教科书发展研究 (The development of modern Chinese textbooks). Guangzhou: Guangdong jiaoyu chubanshe, 1996.

"Wang jiemu lou ju shouzhen" 汪節母樓居守貞 (Wang protects her virtue in the building for chaste mothers). *THRB* 18 (Sept. 2, 1909), 3 [1:207].

Wang, Jing. *High Culture Fever: Politics, Aesthetics, and Ideology in Deng's China.* Berkeley: University of California Press, 1996.

Wang Lian 王蓮. "Tongxiang hui jishi: Hubei zhi bu" 同鄉會紀事：湖北之部 (Record of same-place associations, section on Hubei). *HB* 2 (Feb. 1903), 113–16 [0287–90].

———. "Zagan qishou" 雜感七首 (Random thoughts, seven verses). *HB* 1 (Jan. 29, 1903), 105–6 [0115–16].

Wang, Lingzhen. *Personal Matters : Women's Autobiographical Practice in Twentieth-Century China.* Stanford, CA: Stanford University Press, 2004.

Wang Qisheng 王奇生. "Cong shengui zouxiang shijie de nüzi liuxuesheng" 從深閨走向世界的女子留學生 (Female overseas students: From the inner chambers to the outside world). *Mingbao yuekan* 明報月刊 9 (Sept. 1993), 31–33.

Wang Shize 王时泽. "Huiyi Qiu Jin" 回忆秋瑾 (Reminiscences of Qiu Jin). In *Xinhai geming huiyi lu* 辛亥革命回憶錄, ed. Zhongguo renmin zhengzhi xieshang huiyi quanguo weiyuanhui, Wenshi ziliao yanjiu weiyuan hui 中國人民政治協商會議全國委員會文史資料研究委員會, 4: 223–32. Beijing: Zhonghua shuju, 1982.

Wang Yi. "Intellectuals and Popular Television in China: Expectations as a Cultural Phenomenon." *International Journal of Cultural Studies* 2:2 (1999), 222–45.

Wang Yingkun 汪應焜. "Yong lidai nüjiang" 詠歷代女將 (To sing of women officers through the ages). *STSB* (May 9, 1911).

Wang Yinglin 王應麟. *Sanzi jing* 三字經 (The trimetrical classic). Annot. Li Miuhua 李牧華. Taipei: Dahua chuban shiyeh gufen youxian gongsi, n.d.

Wang Zhaoyong 汪兆鏞. *Bei zhuanji sanbian* 碑傳集三編 (Inscriptional biographies, part three). In *Jindai Zhongguo shiliao congkan xubian di qishisanji* 近代中國史料叢刊第73輯 (Sequel series on materials on modern Chinese history, vol. 73), ed. Shen Yunlong 沈雲龍, vol. 730. Taipei: Wenhai chubanshe, 1980.

Wang Zhenda 汪振达. "Qianyan" 前言 (Preface). In Wei Xiyuan 魏息園, *Buyong xing shenpan shu gushi xuan* 不用刑審判书故事选 (Selected stories of trials that did not resort to the use of torture), ed. Wang Zhenda, 1–7. Shanxi: Qunzhong chubanshe, 1987.

Wang Zheng. *Women in the Chinese Enlightenment: Oral and Textual Histories*. Berkeley: University of California Press, 1999.

Warner, Marina. *Joan of Arc: The Image of Female Heroism*. Berkeley: University of California Press, 1981.

Watson, Burton. *Ssu-ma Ch'ien: Grand Historian of China*. New York: Columbia University Press, 1958.

Wei Gong 畏公. "Lun nüzi laodong wenti" 論女子勞動問題 (The problem of female labor). *TY* 5 (Aug. 10, 1907), 71–80.

Wei Xiyuan 魏息園. *Buyong xing shenpan shu gushi xuan* 不用刑審判书故事选 (Selected stories of trials that did not resort to the use of torture), ed. Wang Zhenda 汪振荙. Shanxi: Qunzhong chubanshe, 1987.

"Wenming jiehun" 文明結婚 (Enlightened marriage). *STSB* (Aug. 23, Sept. 10, 13, 1905).

Widmer, Ellen. *Beauty and the Book: Women and Fiction in Nineteenth-Century China*. Cambridge, MA: Harvard University Asia Center, 2006.

———. "*Honglou meng ying* and Three 'Women's Novels' of Late Qing." In Lo Jiu-jiung and Lu Miaw-fen, 301–26.

———. "Inflecting Gender: Zhan Kai/Siqi Zhai's 'New Novels' and Courtesan Sketches." In Fong, Qian, and Zurndorfer, 136–68.

———. "The Rhetoric of Retrospection: May Fourth Literary History and the Ming-Qing Woman Writer." In *The Appropriation of Cultural Capital: China's May Fourth Project*, ed. Milena Doleželová-Velingerová et al., 193–225. Cambridge, MA: Harvard University Asia Center, 2001.

———, trans. "Selected Short Works by Wang Duanshu (1621–after 1702)." In *Under Confucian Eyes: Writings on Gender in Chinese History*, ed. Susan Mann and Yu-yin Cheng, 178–95. Berkeley: University of California Press, 2001.

Wright, Arthur F. "Values, Roles, and Personalities." In *Confucian Personalities*, ed. Arthur F. Wright and Denis Twitchett, 3–23. Stanford, CA: Stanford University Press, 1962.

Wright, Mary Clabaugh. "Introduction." In *China in Revolution: The First Phase, 1900–1913*, ed. Mary Clabaugh Wright, 1–63. New Haven, CT: Yale University Press, 1968.

"Wu lienü yi buyuan gaidi ziyi" 武烈女以不願改適自縊 (Heroic woman Wu hangs herself to avoid remarriage). *QBLC*, 86–87.

Wu Pei-yi. "Yang Miaozhen: A Woman Warrior in Thirteenth Century China." *Nan Nü: Men, Women and Gender in Early and Imperial China* 4:2 (2002), 137–69.

Wu Ruoan 吳若安. "Wu Ruoan 'Huiyi Shanghai Wuben nüshu'" 吳若安回忆上海务本女塾 (Wu Ruoan's "Reminiscences of the Shanghai School of Fundamental Women's Learning"). In "Wu Ruoan koushu, Xia Shiduo zhengli" 吳若安

口述，夏世铎整理 (Wu Ruoan's oral narration, arranged by Xia Shiduo), 1986. Rpt. in *XZSL* 2:2, 602–09.

Wu Shijian 吳士鑑 et al. *Qing gongci* 清宮詞 (Qing palace poetry). Beijing: Beijing guji chubanshe, 1986.

Wu Tao 吳濤, ed. *Nüzi shifan xiushenxue* 女子師範修身學 (Ethics for female normal school students). Beijing: Beijing diyi shuju, 1907.

Wu Weihe, and Bai Chongmin. "Casting the Mold of Female Body and Identity: Reinterpreting Guang Lienü Zhuan [Biographies of Exemplary Women]," trans. Sasha S. Welland. In *Cruel/Loving Bodies* (Ku/ai shenti 酷／爱身体), 48–51. Catalog of exhibit held at Shanghai Duolun Museum of Modern Art (多伦现代美术馆), June 2004, n.p. Rpt. in *Yishu: Journal of Contemporary Chinese Art* 2:3 (2003), 15–19.

Wu Yanyin 吳研因. "Qingmo yilai woguo xiaoxue jiaokeshu gaiguan" 清末以來我國小學教科書概觀 (A review of Chinese elementary textbooks from the late Qing). In Zhang Jinglu, ed., 6: 149–60.

Wu Youru 吳友如. "Gujin baimei tu" 古今百美圖 (One hundred beauties, past and present). In *Wu Youru huabao* 吳友如畫寶 (A treasury of Wu Youru's illustrations). 3 vols. 1908. Rpt., Shanghai: Shanghai guji shudian, 1983, 2: 1, 2.

Wu Zhiying 吳芝瑛. "Ji Qiu Jin nüxia yishi" 記秋瑾女俠遺事 (Traces of the female knight-errant Qiu Jin). Rpt. in Qiu Jin, *Qiu Jin ji*, 185–86.

"Wuben nüshu ji youzhishe yundonghui ji" 務本女塾及幼稚舍運動會記 (Record of the athletic meet for the School of Fundamental Women's Learning and its nursery). *SB* (Nov. 13, 1905). Rpt. in *XZSL* 2:2, 600.

"Wuben nüshu zengshe chudeng, gaodeng nüzi xiaoxue guize" 務本女塾增設初等高等女子小學規則 (The School of Fundamental Women's Learning adds regulations for lower- and higher-level elementary education). *Zhili jiaoyu zazhi* 直隸教育雜誌 1:17, 48–49. Rpt. in *XZSL* 2:2, 594–95.

"Wuben nü xuexiao dierci gailiang guize" 務本女學校第二次改良規則 (Second set of reformed regulations for the School of Fundamental Women's Learning). *Zhili jiaoyu zazhi* 直隸教育雜誌 1:17, 35–49. Rpt. in *XZSL* 2, 590–94.

"Xia shi nü juru toushui" 夏氏女懼辱投水 (Lady Xia threw herself in the river out of fear of disgrace). *QBLC*, 37.

Xia Xiaohong 夏晓虹. "Gudian xinyi: Wan-Qing ren dui jingdian de jieshuo—yi Ban Zhao yu *Nü jie* wei zhongxin" 古典新义：晚清人对经典的解说 — 以班昭与《女戒》为中心 (Reinterpreting the classics: Late Qing commentaries on the classics—with a focus on Ban Zhao's *Precepts for Women*). *Zhonggguo xueshu* 中國學術 3 (2000), 82–103.

———. "Ms. Picha and Mrs. Stowe." In *Translation and Creation: Readings of Western Literature in Early Modern China, 1840–1918*, ed. David Pollard, 241–51. Amsterdam: John Benjamins, 1998.

———. "Wan-Qing funü shenghuo zhong de xin yinsu" 晚清妇女生活中的新因素 (New elements in the lives of late Qing women). In Xia Xiaohong, *Wan-Qing shehui yu wenhua* 晚清社会与文化 (Late Qing society and culture), 249–310. Wuhan: Hubei jiaoyu chubanshe, 2000.

———. "Wan-Qing nüxing dianfan de duoyuan jingguan—cong Zhongwai nüjie zhuan dao nübao zhuanji lan" 晚清女性典范的多元景观—从中外女杰传到女报传记栏 (The richly varied landscape of female models in the late Qing: From biographies of Chinese and Western heroines to biography columns in women's journals). Zhongguo xiandai wenxue yanjiu congkan 中国现代文学研究丛刊 110:3 (2006), 17–45.

———. Wan-Qing nüxing yu jindai Zhongguo 晚清女性与近代中国 (Late Qing women and modern China). Beijing: Beijing daxue chubanshe, 2004.

———. "Wan-Qing nüxue zhong de Man Han maodun—Huixing zisha shijian jiedu" 晚清女学中的满汉矛盾—惠兴自杀事件解读 (Manchu-Han tensions in late Qing women's education: An interpretation of Huixing's suicide). In Wan-Qing nüxing yu jindai Zhongguo 晚清女性与近代中国 (Late Qing women and modern China), 223–56. Beijing: Beijing daxue chubanshe, 2004.

———. "Wan-Qing ren yanzhong de Qiu Jin zhi si" 晚清人眼中的秋瑾之死 (Late Qing views of Qiu Jin's death). Xueren 学人 10 (Sept., 1996), 429–69.

———. Wan-Qing wenren funü guan 晚清文人妇女观 (Late Qing literati views of women). Beijing: Zujia chubanshe, 1995.

———. "Zhong-Xi hebi de jiaoyu lixiang: Shanghai 'Zhongguo nüxuetang' kaoshu" 中西合璧的教育理想—上海"中国女学堂"考述 (A harmonious merging of Chinese and Western educational ideals: An examination of Shanghai's "Chinese Girls' School"). In Xia Xiaohong, Wan-Qing nüxing yu jindai, 3–37.

"Xiangguo zhuzhong nüxue jiaokeshu" 相國 注重女學教科書 ([Zhang] Xiangguo [of the Education Board] stresses the importance of textbooks for women's education). JYZZ 1.4 (July 12, 1909), 37 [477].

"Xiangshan nü xuexiao shiban jianzhang" 香山女學校試辦簡章 (Provisional regulations for the Xiangshan Girls' School). NZSJ 7 (July 1904), 74.

Xiao Daoguan 蕭道管. Lienü zhuan jizhu 列女傳集注 (Collected annotations to the Arrayed Traditions of Women's Lives). n.p. Preface dated 1892, published after 1907.

Xiao Yin 筱驥. "Lun nüjie yixue zhi guanxi" 論女界醫學之關係 (The relationship between women and medicine). XNJZZ 1 (Feb. 5, 1907), 19–27.

"Xiaonü xunmu" 孝女殉母 (A filial daughter martyrs herself for her mother). STSB (June 9, 1906).

Xie Chongxie 謝允燮. Chudeng xiaoxue nüzi xiushen jiaokeshu 初等小學女子修身教科書 (Lower-level elementary female ethics textbook). Shanghai: Zhongguo jiaoyu gailiang hui, 1906.

Xie Zhangfa 谢长法. "Qingmo de liu-Ri nüxuesheng" 清末的留日女学生 (Overseas female students in Japan in the late Qing). Jindai shi yanjiu 近代史研究 2:86 (1995), 272–79.

"Xinshu jieshao" 新書介紹 (Introduction to new books). DFZZ 1:2 (Apr. 10, 1904), 3 [223].

Xiong Yuezhi 熊月之. "Dazhong wenhua yunzhengxiawei 大眾文化雲蒸霞蔚 (A rich and vibrant mass culture). In Shanghai tongshi, diliu juan, Wan-Qing wenhua 上海通史，第六卷，晚清文化 (Comprehensive history of Shanghai.

Vol. 6, Late Qing culture), ed. Xiong Yuezhi, 479–525. Shanghai: Shanghai renmin chubanshe, 1999.

———. "Degrees of Familiarity with the West in Late Qing Society." In *Translation and Creation: Readings of Western Literature in Early Modern China, 1840–1918*, ed. David Pollard, 25–35. Amsterdam: John Benjamins, 1998.

———. *Xixue dongjian yu wan-Qing shehui* 西学东渐与晚清社会 ("The Dissemination of Western Learning and the Late Qing Society"). Shanghai: Shanghai renmin chubanshe, 1994.

———. "*Zhongguo xin nüjie*" 中国新女界 (*New Chinese Women*). In *QKJS* 1, 565–77.

Xu Bai 徐白 et al. *Hebei sheng, Tong xian zhiyao* 河北省通縣志要 (Hebei province, Tong county gazetteer), 1941. Zhongguo fangzhi congshu, Huabei difang 136. Rpt., Taipei: Chengwen chubanshe, 1968.

Xu Chuying 徐楚影. "*Funü shibao*" 妇女时报 (*Women's Eastern Times*). In *QKJS* 5, 150–58.

Xu Chuying, and Chen Xinduan 陈新段. "*Funü zazhi*" 妇女杂志 (*Ladies' Journal*). In *QKJS* 5, 351–61.

Xu Dingyi 許定一 [Juxue luzhu ren 咀雪廬主人]. *Zuguo nüjie weiren zhuan* 祖國女界偉人傳 (Biographies of great women of our country). Yokohama: Xinminshe, 1906.

———. [Juxue zi 咀雪子]. *Zuguo nüjie wenhao pu* 祖國女界文豪譜 (A guide to great women writers of our country). Beijing: Jinghua yinshuguan, 1909.

Xu Huiqi 許慧琦 [Rachel Xu]. "Nala zai Zhongguo: xin nüxing xingxiang de suzao ji qi yanbian, 1920s–1930s" 「娜拉」在中國：新女性形像的塑造及其演變，1920s–1930s (Nora in China: The construction and evolution of the image of the new woman, 1920s–1930s). Ph.D. diss., National Chengchi University, History Research Institute, 2001.

Xu Huiqi 徐輝琪, Liu Jucai 刘巨才, and Xu Yuzhen 徐玉珍, eds. *Zhongguo jindai funü yundong lishi ziliao, 1840–1918* 中国近代妇女运动历史资料 1840–1918 (Historical materials on the modern Chinese women's movement, 1840–1918). Beijing: Zhongguo funü chubanshe, 1991.

Xu Jiaxing 許家惺. *Zuixin nüzi xiushen jiaokeshu* 最新女子修身教科書 (Newest ethics textbook for girls and women). Shanghai: Qunxueshe, 1906.

Xu Shuangyun 徐双韵. "Ji Qiu Jin" 记秋瑾 (Remembering Qiu Jin). In Guo Yanli, *Qiu Jin yanjiu ziliao*, 205–22.

Xu Xingwu 徐興無. "Qingdai Wang Zhaoyuan *Lienü zhuan buzhu* yu Liang Duan *Lienü zhuan jiaoduben*" 清代王照圓《列女傳補注》與梁端《列女傳校讀本》 (Wang Zhaoyuan's *Annotated Lienü zhuan* and Liang Duan's *Lienü zhuan: An Annotated Reader* in the Qing period). In *Ming Qing wenxue yu xingbie yanjiu* 明清文學與性別研究 (Studies of literature and gender in the Ming-Qing period), ed. Zhang Hongsheng 張宏生, 916–31. Nanjing: Jiangsu guji chubanshe, 2002.

Xu Yuzhen 徐玉珍. "*Nüzi shijie*" 女子世界 (*Women's World*). In *QKJS* 1, 461–73.

Xu Zihua 徐自華. *Xu Zihua shiwen ji* 徐自華詩文集 (Collected poems and essays by Xu Zihua). Ed. Guo Yanli 郭廷礼. Beijing: Zhonghua shuju, 1990.

Xue Shaohui 薛紹徽, and Chen Shoupeng 陳壽彭. *Waiguo lienü zhuan* 外國列
女傳 (Arrayed traditions of foreign women's lives). Nanjing: Jingling Jiangchu
bianyi zongju, 1906.

"Xuebu shending Sun nüshi chengshu" 學部審定孫女士呈書 (The Education
Board approves Ms. Sun's petition). *JYZZ* 1:10 (Nov. 7, 1909), 72–73 [852–53].

"Xuebu shenzhong nüsheng youxue" 學部慎重女生游學 (The Education Board is
cautious about female overseas study). *JYZZ* 2.8 (Sept. 13, 1910), 64.

"Xuebu zou zunni nüxue fuse zhangcheng zhai" 學部奏遵擬女學服色章程摺
(Education Board memorial proposes regulations for female school dress). *SB*
(Jan. 26, 1910).

"Xuebu zouding nüzi shifan xuetang zhangcheng zhe" 學部奏定女子師範學堂
章程折 (The Education Board's memorial on the enactment of regulations
for women's normal schools). In *Da Qing Guangxu xinfaling* 大清光緒新法
令 (New laws under Emperor Guangxu of the Great Qing Dynasty), 13: 35–40
(Mar. 8, 1907). Rpt. in *XZSL* 2:2, 666–74.

"Xuebu zouding nüzi xiaoxuetang zhangcheng" 學部奏定女子小學堂章程 (The
Education Board's memorial on the enactment of regulations for women's
elementary schools). In *Da Qing Guangxu xinfaling* 大清光緒新法令 (New
laws under Emperor Guangxu of the Great Qing Dynasty), 13: 40–47 (Mar. 8,
1907). Rpt. in *XZSL* 2:2, 657–66.

"Xuesheng qingbo beige" 學生輕薄被革 (A student who acted disrespectfully is
expelled [from his job]). *STSB* (Feb. 26, 1907).

"Xun Song xiaonü Guan" 荀崧 小女灌 (Xun Song's daughter, Guan). In *Xinjiaoben Jin shu, bingfu bian liu zhong* 新校本晉書並附編六種 (New edition of the
History of the Jin Dynasty with six supplements), comp. Fang Xuanling 房玄
齡. 96: "Liezhuan" 616. Rpt. in *Zhongguo xueshu leibian* 中國學術類編, 2515.
Taipei: Dingwen shuju, 1990.

Yamazaki Jun'ichi 山崎純一. *Kyōiku kara mita Chūgoku joseishi shiryō no kenkyū:
"Onna shisho" to "Shin fufu" sanbu sho* 教育から見た中国女性史資料の研究：
「女四書」と「新婦譜」三部書 (A documentary study of Chinese women's
history as seen from the perspective of education: The *Four Books for Women* and
three editions of the *Standard Guide for the New Wife*). Tokyo: Meiji shoin, 1966.

Yamazumi Masami 山住正己. "Kyōkasho" 教科書 (Textbooks). In *Nihon shi
daijiten* 日本史大事典 (Encyclopedia of Japanese history), 3: 780–83. Tokyo:
Heibonsha, 1993.

Yan Ansheng 嚴安生. *Nihon ryūgaku seishin shi: kindai Chūgoku chishikijin no
kiseki* 日本留学精神史：近代中国知識人の軌跡 (A history of the spirit of overseas study in Japan: Traces of modern Chinese intellectuals). Tokyo: Iwanami
shoten, 1994.

Yan Bin 燕斌 [Lianshi 煉石]. "Benbao duiyu Nüzi guomin juan zhi yanshuo" 本報
對於女子國民捐之演說 (A lecture by this journal on the female citizens' fund).
XNJZZ 1 (Feb. 5, 1907), 41–50.

———. "Benbao wuda zhuyi yanshuo" 本報五大主義演說 (Lecture on the five principle concerns of this journal). *XNJZZ* 2 (Mar. 5, 1907), 11–20; 3 (Apr. 5, 1907), 15–20.

———."Fakanci" 發刊詞 (Inaugural statement). *XNJZZ* 1 (Feb. 5, 1907), 1–3.

———. "Liu-Ri nüxue xuejie jinshi ji" 留日女學學界近事記 (Record of recent developments in the female overseas student community). *XNJZZ* 2 (Mar. 5, 1907), 83–86; 3 (Apr. 5, 1907), 83–99.

———. "Luo Ying nüshi zhuan" 羅瑛女士傳 (Biography of Ms. Luo Ying). *XNJZZ* 5 (June 5, 1907), 51–54.

———. "Riben furen zhi zhengzhi yundong" 日本婦人之政治運動 (Japanese women's political movements). *XNJZZ* 2 (Mar. 5, 1907), 105–6.

Yan Fu 嚴復. "Lun Hushang chuangxing nüxuetang" 論滬上創興女學堂 (The establishment of schools for girls and women in Shanghai). In *Wan-Qing wenxuan* 晚清文選 (A selection of literary works from the late Qing) (1898), 695–97. Rpt. in *XZSL* 1:2, 880–81.

———. *Yan Fu ji* 嚴復集 (Yan Fu's works). 5 vols. Beijing: Zhonghua shuju, 1986.

"Yan taifuren fa cangpiao zhenji" 顏太夫人發倉票賑饑 (Yan's mother issues granary tickets to aid the starving). *THRB* 6 (Aug. 21, 1909), 3 [1:63].

Yan Xiyuan 顏希源 (Jiantang zhuren 鑑塘主人), comp., Wang Hui 王翽, illust. *Baimei xin yongtu zhuan*百美新詠圖傳 (New poems and pictures for one hundred beauties). Prefaces dated 1787, 1790. Rpt., Beijing: Zhongguo shudian, 1998.

"Yang ling kuxing lienü zhi candu" 楊令酷刑烈女之慘毒 (The grievous poison of Magistrate Yang's cruel punishment of an heroic woman). *SB* (Apr. 3, 1910).

Yang Qianli 楊千里. *Nüzi xin duben* 女子新讀本 (New reader for girls and women), 2 vols. Shanghai: Wenming shuju, 1905.

———. "Nüzi xin duben daoyan" 女子新讀本導言 (Introduction to the *New Reader for Girls and Women*). *NZSJ* 8 (Aug. 1904), 81–83 [759–61].

"Yanshuo Fulanzhisi" 演說扶蘭志斯 (Frances). *BJNB* (May 2, 3, Dec. 12, 13 1908).

"Yanshuo Wang Licai tongxin dinghun fa" 演說王立才通信訂婚法 (Wang Licai's method of epistolary betrothal). *STSB* (Feb. 21, 1906).

Ye Haowu 葉浩吾. "Aiguo nü xuexiao lunli jiaoxi Ye Haowu jun jiangyi" 愛國女學校倫理教習葉浩吾君講議 (Lecture delivered by Patriotic Girls' School ethics teacher Ye Haowu). *Jingzhong ribao* 警鐘日報 (Apr. 21, 1904). Rpt. in *XZSL* 2:2, 624–26.

Ye, Weili. *Seeking Modernity in China's Name: Chinese Students in the United States, 1900–27*. Stanford, CA: Stanford University Press, 2001.

Ye Zhongling 葉中泠, ed., Jiang Weiqiao 蔣維喬, coll. *Nüzi xin changge chuji* 女子新唱歌初集 (First collection of new songs for girls). Shanghai: Shangwu yin-shuguan, 1907.

Yeh, Catherine Vance. "Creating the Urban Beauty: The Shanghai Courtesan in Late Qing Illustrations." In *Writing and Materiality in China: Essays in Honor of Patrick Hanan*, ed. Judith T. Zeitlin and Lydia H. Liu with Ellen Widmer, 397–447. Cambridge, MA: Harvard University Asia Center, 2003.

———. *Shanghai Love: Courtesans, Intellectuals, and Entertainment Culture, 1850–1910*. Seattle, WA: University of Washington Press, 2006.

Yeh, Michelle. "Revolutionizing Chinese Poetry: The Transition from Traditional to Modern Poetry in the Early Twentieth Century." Unpublished manuscript.

Yi Qin 憶琴. "Lun Zhongguo nüzi zhi qiantu" 論中國女子之前途 (The future of Chinese women). *JS* 4 (July 25, 1903), 141–43 [759–61].

———. "Lun Zhongguo nüzi zhi qiantu, xu" 論中國女子之前與續 (The future of Chinese women, continued). *JS* 5 (Aug. 23, 1903), 129–31 [939–41].

Yi Zongkui 易宗夔. *Xinshi shuo* 新世說 (Tales of the new world). 1918. Rpt., Shanghai: Shanghai guji shudian, 1982.

"Yingguo nüjie Niejikeer zhuan" 英國女傑 涅幾柯兒傳 (Biography of Florence Nightingale). Freely translated by Gan Hui 乾慧, recorded by Zhi Du 智度. *Nüxue bao* 女學報 2:4 (Nov. 1903), 37–41.

Yongli 勇立. "Xing nüxue yi" 興女學議 (Argument for female education). *DFZZ* 3:13 (Feb. 7, 1907), 241–44

Yosano Akiko 類謝野晶子. "Zhencao lun" 貞操論 (On chastity). Trans. Zhou Zuoren 周作人. *Xin qingnian* 新青年 (May 18, 1918), 386–94.

Yoshimura Toratarō 吉村寅太郎. *Nihon genji kyōiku* 日本現時教育 (Contemporary Japanese education). Tokyo: Kinkōdō, 1898.

———. "Riben xianshi jiaoyu" 日本現時教育 (Contemporary Japanese education). Trans. Luo Zhenchang 羅振常. *Jiaoyu congshu* 教育叢書 3 (1903), 1–22.

"Yu xiannü gongyi xuetang gaiming qiandi" 育賢女工藝學堂改名遷地 (The handicrafts school for cultivating talented girls changes its name and location) *SB* (Jan. 2, 1905).

Yu Zhengxie 俞正燮. "Jiefu shuo" 節婦說 (On chaste widows) and "Zhennü shuo" 貞女說 (On faithful maids). In *Guisi leigao* 癸巳類稿 (Miscellaneous writings of 1833), 13: 493–94, 494–95. Taipei: Shijie shuju, 1966.

"Yuan hu lienü da laoye weimian henxin" 冤乎烈女大老爺未免很心 (The cruelty of an old man who wronged a heroic woman). *THRB* 216 (Mar. 31, 1910) [5:227].

Yuan Jisun 袁驥孫. "Yong lidai nüjiang" 詠歷代女將 (To sing of women officers through the ages). *STSB* (May 6, 1911).

"Zaiji" 載記 (Chronicles) 10. In *Xinjiaoben Jin shu, bingfu bian liu zhong* 新校本晉 書並附編六種 (New edition of the *History of the Jin Dynasty* with six supplements), comp. Fang Xuanling 房玄齡, 110. Rpt. in *Zhongguo xueshu leibian* 中國學術類編, 2846. Taipei: Dingwen shuju, 1990.

"Zai-Ri Zhongguo liuxue sheng, qi yi" 在日中國留學生其一 (Overseas Chinese students in Japan, 1). *STSB* (July 21, 22, 23, 1905). Rpt. in *NQYDSL* 2, 1254–57.

Zarrow, Peter. "He Zhen [Ho Chen] and Anarcho-Feminism in China." *Journal of Asian Studies* 47:4 (1988), 796–813.

———. "Introduction: Citizenship in China and the West." In *Imagining the People: Chinese Intellectuals and the Concept of Citizenship, 1890–920*, ed. Joshua A. Fogel and Peter G. Zarrow, 3–38. Armonk, NY: M. E. Sharpe, 1997.

Zeng Fuqian 曾福謙. "Yong lidai nüjiang" 詠歷代女將 (To sing of women officers through the ages). *STSB* (May 13, 1911).

Zeng Qiqiu 曾启球. "Xianqu Tang Qunying de wannian shenghuo" 先驱唐群英的

晚年生活 (The vanguard Tang Qunying's later years). *Zongheng* 纵横 8 (1998), 27–28.

Zeng Yi 曾懿. *Nüxue pian* 女學篇 (Exhortation to women's learning). Changsha: n.p., 1907.

Zhang Boxi 張百熙. "Xu" 序 (Preface). In Zeng Yi, 2a–3a.

Zhang Hanying 張漢英 [Hanying 漢英]. "Tizeng Hunan liuxuesheng jiandu Chen Gong xiaozhao sishou" 題贈湖南留學生監督陳公小照四首 (Four poems inscribed on a portrait of the supervisor of the Hunan overseas students, Mr. Chen). *XNJZZ* 1, 90.

Zhang Jing 張敬, annot. and trans. *Lienü zhuan jinzhu jinyi* 列女傳今註今譯 (Newly annotated and translated [edition of the] *Arrayed Traditions of Women's Lives* [by Liu Xiang 劉向]), ed. Zhonghua wenhua fuxing yundong zonghui 中華文化復興運動總會, Guoli bianyiguan Zhonghua congshu bianshen weiyuanhui 國立編譯館中華叢書編審委員會. Taipei: Taiwan shangwu yinshuguan, 1994.

Zhang Jinglu 張靜廬. "Jiaokeshu zhi fakan gaikuang" 教科書之發刊概況 (The general situation of textbook publication). In Zhang Jinglu, ed., 1: 219–53.

———, ed. *Zhongguo jinxiandai chuban shiliao* 中國近現代出版史料 (Historical sources on modern and contemporary Chinese publishing). 8 vols. Rpt. Shanghai: Shanghai shudian chubanshe, 2003.

Zhang Qin 章梫. "Hanlin yuan jianfeng Zhang Qin jincheng wei daijin *Nü xiaoxue* sijuan gongqing" 翰林院檢封 章梫謹呈為代進女小學四卷恭請 (Zhang Qin of the Hanlin Academy respectfully requests approval for the four-juan *Elementary Learning for Girls and Women*). In Dai Li, 1a–2a.

Zhang Wenling 張文玲. "Qianyan" 前言 (Introductory remarks). In Chen Kangqi, *Langqian jiwen sibi*, 1–2.

Zhang Xuecheng. "Fuxue" 婦學 (Women's learning). In *Zhaodai congshu* 昭代叢書 (Compendium of materials from an illustrious age), ed. Zhang Chao 張潮, 63: 1–10. n.p. Shikaitang kan ben, 1876.

———. "Fuxue." Trans. Susan Mann. In Kang-i Sun Chang and Saussy, 784–99.

Zhang Yihe 章义和 and Chen Chunlei 陈春雷. *Zhenjie shi* 贞节史 (A history of chastity). Shanghai: Shanghai wenyi chubanshe, 1999.

Zhang Zhidong 張之洞. "Zha xuewuchu ban jingjie yuying xuetang" 札學務處辦敬節育嬰學堂 (Document concerning the establishment of schools in halls for revering chastity and orphanages by Committees of Educational Affairs). In *Zhang Wenxiang gong quanji* 張文襄公全集 (Collected words of Zhang Zhidong), Gongdu 公牘, juan 25. Beijing: Chuxue jinglu, 1937.

Zhang Zhujun 張竹君. "Zhang Zhujun zai Aiguo nü xuexiao yanshuo" 張竹君在愛國女學校演說 (Lecture delivered by Zhang Zhujun at the Patriotic Girls' School). *Jingzhong ribao* 警鍾日報 (May 2–3, 1904). Rpt. in *XZSL* 2:2, 620–22.

Zhao Erxuan 趙爾巽 et al. *Qingshi gao* 清史稿 (Draft history of the Qing dynasty). 48 vols. Beijing: Zhonghua shuju, 1977.

Zhao Fengjie 趙鳳喈. *Zhongguo funü zai falü shang zhi diwei* 中國婦女在法律上之地位 (The legal position of Chinese women). Taipei: Daoxiang chubanshe, 1993.

"Zhenfu shou" 貞婦手 (A chaste woman's hand). *THRB* 216 (Mar. 28, 1910) [5:191].

Zheng Yunshan 郑云山, Gong Yanming 龚延明, and Lin Zhengchiu 林正秋. *Hangzhou yu Xihu shihua* 杭州与西湖史话 (Historical anecdotes about Hangzhou and West Lake). Shanghai: Shanghai renmin chubanshe, 1980.

"Zhenjie kefeng" 貞節可風 (A model of virtue). *STSB* (Mar. 5, 1903, reprinted Mar. 6, 1903), 4.

Zhi Da 志達. "Nandao nüchang zhi Shanghai" 男盜女娼之上海 (The Shanghai of male bandits and female prostitutes). *TY* 5 (Aug. 10, 1907), 95–97.

"Zhi Nanyang quanyehui yanjiuhui shu" 致南洋勸業會研究會書 (Letter to the Research Association of the Nanyang Society for the Promotion of Industry). *SB* (Aug. 5, 1910).

"Zhili chuangban tianzuhui yanshuo" 直隸創辦天足會演說 (Lecture on the establishment of a natural foot society in Zhili). *XNJZZ* 4 (May 5, 1907), 29–40.

"Zhili nü xuetang baxue shimo ji" 直隸女學堂罷學始末記 (Full record of the strike at the Zhili Girls' School). *Nübao* 女報 3 (1909): 127. Rpt. in *XZZL* 2:2, 717–18.

"Zhina nüzi zhi aiguo xin" 支那女子之愛國心 (The patriotic spirit of Chinese women). *HB* 3 (Mar. 29, 1903), 65–67 [0383–85].

Zhongguo jindai qikan pianmu huilu 中国近代期刊篇目汇录 (A catalog of the titles [of articles] in modern Chinese periodicals). Shanghai: Shanghai renmin chubanshe, 1979–84.

"Zhongguo liudong nüxuesheng" 中國留東女學生 (Chinese overseas students in Japan). *STSB* (Aug. 4, 1905). Rpt. in *NQYDSL* 2, 1266–68

"Zhongguo liuxue nüsheng biye" 中國留學女生畢業 (Chinese overseas students graduate). *STSB* (Apr. 11, 1907). Rpt. in *NQYDSL* 2, 1272–73.

"Zhongguo nü liuxuesheng zhi diaocha" 中國女留學生之調查 (Investigation of Chinese female overseas students). *SB* (July 31, 1905).

"Zhongguo nüjie dayiyongjia Chunyu Ti Ying xiaozhuan" 中國女傑大義勇家淳于緹縈小傳 (A short biography of the righteous and courageous Chinese heroine Chunyu Ti Ying). *STSB* (Apr. 18, 1907).

Zhonghua Minguo kaiguo wushi nian wenxian bianzuan weiyuanhui 中華民國開國五十年文獻編纂委員會 [Compilation Committee of Documents on the Fifty Years of the Republic of China]. *Lieqiang qinlüe* 列強侵略 (Invasion of the great powers). Taipei: Zhonghua Minguo kaiguo wushi nian wenxian bianzuan weiyuanhui, 1965.

Zhonghua shuju Shanghai bianjisuo 中華書局. 上海編輯所 (Shanghai Editorial Office of Zhonghua shuju). *Qiu Jin shiji* 秋瑾史跡 (Historical traces of Qiu Jin). Beijing: Zhonghua shuju, 1958.

"Zhong-wai xin lienü zhuan" 中外新列女傳 (New Chinese and foreign arrayed traditions of women's lives). *THRB* 2, 4, 6, 8, 12, 14, 16, 18, 20, 22, 25 (Aug. 17, 19, 21, 23, 27, 29, 31, Sept. 2, 4, 6, 9, 1909).

Zhou Bangdao 周邦道. *Jindai jiaoyu xianjin zhuanlüe chuji* 近代教育先進傳略初

集 (Biographical sketches of the forebears of modern education, first collection). Taipei: Zhonghua wenhua daxue chubanbu, 1982.

Zhou Chunying周春英. "Qishi nü you Lu shuo" 漆室女憂魯說 (On the woman of Qishi's lament for the state of Lu). *Nübao* 女報 2 (1909).

Zhou [Qin?] 周[勤?]. "Gan Mulan congjun" 感木蘭從軍 (Moved by [the story of] Mulan joining the army). *FNSB* 21 (Mar. 1917), 99.

Zhou Hanguang 周漢光. "Qingmo de nüzi jiaoyu" 清末的女子教育 (Women's education in the late Qing). *Zhongguo lishi xuehui shixue jikan* 中國歷史學會史學集刊 18 (1986), 241–69.

Zhou Wanyao 周捥窈. "Qingdai Tongcheng xuezhe yu funü de jiduan daode xingwei" 清代桐城學者與婦女的極端道德行為 (Tongcheng scholars and extreme female virtuous behavior in the Qing dynasty). In *ZGFNS* 4, 185–251.

Zhou Yichuan 周一川. *Chūgokujin josei Nihon ryūgaku shi kenkyū* 中国人女性日本留学史研究 (Research on Chinese female overseas students in Japan). Tokyo: Kokusho kankōkai, 2001.

———. "Qingmo liu-Ri xuesheng zhong de nüxing" 清末留日學生中的女性 (Female overseas students in Japan in the late Qing). *Lishi yanjiu* 歷史研究 202 (1989, 6), 49–64.

———. "Shinmatsu-Minkoku shonen ni okeru Nihon ryūgaku Chūgokujin joshi gakusei zō no hensen" 清末民国初年における日本留学中国人女子学生像の変遷 (Changes in the image of Chinese female overseas study in Japan in the late Qing and early Republic). *Ochanomizu joshi daigaku ningen bunka kenkyū nenpō* お茶の水女子大学人間文化研究年報 19 (1995), 65–71.

Zhou Yiqun. "Virtue and Talent: Women and *Fushi* in Early China." *Nan Nü: Men, Women and Gender in Early and Imperial China* 5:1 (2003), 1–42.

Zhu Dianyi 朱點衣. "Yong lidai nüjiang" 詠歷代女將 (To sing of women officers through the ages). *STSB* (May 7, 1911).

"Zhu Gongai hui zhi qiantu" 祝共愛會之前途 (In celebration of the Humanitarian Association's future). *JS* 6 (Sept. 21, 1903), 162–63 [1150–51].

Zhu Huizhen 朱惠貞. "Qishi nü" 漆室女 (The woman of Qishi). *FNSB* 2 (July 10, 1911).

"Zhu liefu shakou er si" 朱烈婦殺寇而死 (The heroic woman Zhu kills a bandit and dies). *QBLC*, 68.

Zhu Shou 朱綬. *Dongyou jicheng* 東游紀程 (Record of travels to Japan), 1899. Sanetō bunko 実藤文庫 (Sanetō Collection) no. 35. Tokyo Hibiya Library Archives.

"Zhu Xiugu yi si bao weihunfu" 朱秀姑以死報未婚夫 (Zhu Xiugu dies to preserve her [fidelity to] her fiancée). *QBLC*, 67–68.

Zhuan Kun 轉坤. "Shijie gujin furen daiyu lun (xu dier qi)" 世界古今婦人待遇論「續第二期」 (The treatment of women, past and present, throughout the world [continued from issue 2]). *XNJZZ* 3 (Apr. 5, 1907), 31–38.

Zi Gu 子穀. "Nüjie Guoerman" 女傑郭耳縵 (The heroine [Emma] Goldman). *Guomin riribao huibian* 國民日日報彙編 3. Rpt. in *NQYDSL* 1, 337–38.

"Zicha Nüxue changge" 咨查女學唱歌 (Investigation of *School Songs for Girls*). *STSB* (Apr. 28, 1907).

"Zifa zhi mu" 子發之母 (The mother of Zifa). *BJNB* (May 2, 1907).

"Zouqing jingbiao Huixing nüshi" 奏情旌表惠興女士 (Petition for a testimonial of merit for Ms. Huixing). *DGB* (July 13, 1906).

"Zouwei Wansheng jielie funü ruci zhe" 奏為晚省節烈婦女入祠摺 (Memorial petitioning for the entrance of virtuous and heroic women of Anhui into the shrine for virtuous women). *STSB* (Feb. 21, 1907).

Zurndorfer, Harriet. "The 'Constant World' of Wang Chao-yüan: Women, Education, and Orthodoxy in 18th Century China—A Preliminary Investigation." In *Family Process and Political Process in Modern Chinese History* 1, 581–619. Taipei: Academia Sinica, Institute of Modern History, 1992.

Index

The authorized representative in the EU for product safety and compliance is:
Mare Nostrum Group
B.V Doelen 72
4831 GR Breda
The Netherlands

www.ingramcontent.com/pod-product-compliance
Lightning Source LLC
Chambersburg PA
CBHW022346280326
41935CB00007B/89

9 780804 773263